BOUNDARIES

readings in
DEVIANCE, CRIME AND CRIMINAL JUSTICE

A Customized Reader

General Editors

Bradley R.E. Wright
University of Connecticut

Ralph B. McNeal, Jr.
University of Connecticut

Compiled by

Clinton Sanders
University of Connecticut
Sociology 217
Deviant Behavior
Vol. 1

PEARSON

Custom
Publishing

Director of Database Publishing: Michael Payne
Sponsoring Editor: Robin J. Lazrus
Development Editor: Catherine O'Keefe
Editorial Assistant: Ana Díaz-Caneja
Marketing Manager: Kathleen Kourian
Operations Manager: Eric M. Kenney
Production Project Manager: Marianne C. Groth
Database Project Specialist: Elizabeth MacKenzie-Lamb
Rights Editor: Francesca Marcantonio
Cover Designer: Renée Sartell and Kristen Kiley

Cover Art: "Chain with Broken Link," courtesy of Emanuele Taroni/PhotoDisc. "Fence," courtesy of PhotoDisc. "Cubed Face," courtesy of Getty Images.

PEARSON CUSTOM PUBLISHING
75 Arlington St., Suite 300
Boston, MA 02116

SOCIOLOGY READERS FROM PEARSON CUSTOM PUBLISHING

Create the reader that matches **your** syllabus!

Effective pedagogical apparatus - headnotes, end-of-selection questions, and optional introductions included with all selections!

Intersections: Readings in Sociology
www.intersectionsreader.com

An archive of 380 of the best classic and contemporary readings in sociology. Readings not only elucidate the discipline, but also help spark student interest in the entire area through the richness, diversity, and breadth of its readings. Select only the content you wish to use in your course to reflect your teaching methods and course perspective.

Inequalities: Readings in Diversity and Social Life
www.inequalitiesreader.com

The most comprehensive collection of high-quality readings on multiple forms of inequality and how they intersect. More than 175 classic and contemporary articles reflect theoretical, conceptual, and global perspectives to match the goals and objectives of your sociology or interdisciplinary —oriented course.

Crossroads: Readings in Social Problems
www.crossroadsreader.com

An essential source of over 300 essays and readings that illuminate and help explain central ideas and issues in the study of social problems. Choose from a rich and diverse archive of high quality articles that cover topics and present perspectives germane to your course.

Boundaries: Readings in Deviance, Crime and Criminal Justice
www.boundariesreader.com

More than 350 classic and contemporary readings that cover all the topics addressed in deviance, criminology and criminal justice courses. The richness of this repository of readings provides unlimited flexibility and timely solutions to create a reader that fits your course and teaching style.

Reading Women's Lives: The Customizable Reader for Women's Studies
www.readingwomenslives.com

Nearly 500 selections are available including literature, pieces that reflect multicultural and cross-cultural diversity, readings drawn from the social sciences and third-wave feminism readings. Nineteen optional thematic introductions to key topics in Women's Studies — themes such as The Body, Difference and Inequality, Feminism and the Women's Movement, Sexualities, and Socialization.

www.pearsoncustom.com/sociology

Contents

V

Theory

Media

Organization/Subculture

Self and Deviant Beliefs

Crime

Work

VIII

The Discovery of Hyperkinesis: Notes on the Medicalization of Deviant Behavior*

PETER CONRAD

Drake University, Des Moines, Iowa

Today, many human behaviors that used to be considered deviant or delin-quent are now treated as medical problems that require drug treatment. For example, what was once thought of as unruly or disruptive behavior from overly energetic children is now classified as Attention Deficit Disorder (ADD) or Attention Deficit Hyperactivity Disorder (ADHD). Physicians treat these disorders with drugs, and many school districts officially classify ADD sufferers as special-education students. Using hyperkinesis (a precur-sor to ADD and ADHD diagnoses) as an example, Peter Conrad examines how a behavior becomes "medicalized." He also describes the consequences of medicalization for social control of deviant behavior.

☺ Introduction

The increasing medicalization of deviant behavior and the medical institu-tion's role as an agent of social control has gained considerable notice (Freidson, 1970; Pitts, 1971; Kitterie, 1971; Zola, 1972). By medicalization we mean defining behavior as a medical problem or illness and mandating or licensing the medical profession to provide some type of treatment for it. Examples include alcoholism, drug addiction and treating violence as a genetic or brain disorder. This redefinition is not a new function of the medical institution: psychiatry and public health have always been

"The Discovery of Hyperkinesis: Notes on the Medicalization of Deviant Behavior," by Peter Conrad, reprinted from *Social Problems*, vol. 23, no. 1, 1975, pp. 12–21.

concerned with social behavior and have traditionally functioned as agents of social control (Foucault, 1965; Szasz, 1970; Rosen, 1972). Increasingly sophisticated medical technology has extended the potential of this type of social control, especially in terms of psychotechnology (Chorover, 1973). This approach includes a variety of medical and quasi-medical treatments or procedures: psychosurgery, psychotropic medications, genetic engineering, antibuse, and methadone.

This paper describes how certain forms of behavior in children have become defined as a medical problem and how medicine has become a major agent for their social control since the discovery of hyperkinesis. By discovery we mean both origin of the diagnosis and treatment for this disorder; and discovery of children who exhibit this behavior. The first section analyzes the discovery of hyperkinesis and why it suddenly became popular in the 1960's. The second section will discuss the medicalization of deviant behavior and its ramifications.

❧ The Medical Diagnosis of Hyperkinesis

Hyperkinesis is a relatively recent phenomenon as a medical diagnostic category. Only in the past two decades has it been available as a recognized diagnostic category and only in the last decade has it received widespread notice and medical popularity. However, the roots of the diagnosis and treatment of this clinical entity are found earlier.

Hyperkinesis is also known as Minimal Brain Dysfunction, Hyperactive Syndrome, Hyperkinetic Disorder of Childhood, and by several other diagnostic categories. Although the symptoms and the presumed etiology vary, in general the behaviors are quite similar and greatly overlap.[1] Typical symptom patterns for diagnosing the disorder include: extreme excess of motor activity (hyperactivity); very short attention span (the child flits from activity to activity); restlessness; fidgetiness; often wildly oscillating mood swings (he's fine one day, a terror the next); clumsiness; aggressive-like behavior; impulsivity; in school he cannot sit still, cannot comply with rules, has low frustration level; frequently there may be sleeping problems and acquisition of speech may be delayed (Stewart, 1966; 1970; blender, 1971). Most of the symptoms for the disorder are deviant behaviors.[2] It is six times as prevalent among boys as among girls. We use the term hyperkinesis to represent all the diagnostic categories of this disorder.

❂ The Discovery of Hyperkinesis

It is useful to divide the analysis into what might be considered *clinical factors* directly related to the diagnosis and treatment of hyperkinesis and *social factors* that set the context for the emergence of the new diagnostic category.

Clinical Factors

Bradley (1937) observed that amphetamine drugs had a spectacular effect in altering the behavior of school children who exhibited behavior disorders or learning disabilities. Fifteen of the thirty children he treated actually became more subdued in their behavior. Bradley termed the effect of this medication paradoxical, since he expected that amphetamines would stimulate children as they stimulated adults. After the medication was discontinued the children's behavior returned to premedication level.

A scattering of reports in the medical literature on the utility of stimulant medications for "childhood behavior disorders" appeared in the next two decades. The next significant contribution was the work of Strauss and his associates (Strauss and Lehtinen, 1947) who found certain behavior (including hyperkinesis behaviors) in postencephaletic children suffering from what they called minimal brain injury (damage). This was the first time these behaviors were attributed to the new organic distinction of minimal brain damage.

This disorder still remained unnamed or else it was called a variety of names (usually just "childhood behavior disorder"). It did not appear as a specific diagnostic category until Laufer, et al. (1957) described it as the "hyperkinetic impulse disorder" in 1957. Upon finding "the salient characteristics of the behavior pattern . . . are strikingly similar to those with clear cut organic causation" these researchers described a disorder with no clear-cut history or evidence for organicity (Laufer, et al., 1957).

In 1966 a task force sponsored by the U.S. Public Health Service and the National Association for Crippled Children and Adults attempted to clarify the ambiguity and confusion in terminology and symptomology in diagnosing children's behavior and learning disorders. From over three dozen diagnoses, they agreed on the term "minimal brain dysfunction" as an overriding diagnosis that would include hyperkinesis and other disorders (Clements, 1966). Since this time M.B.D. has been the primary formal diagnosis or label.

In the middle 1950's a new drug, Ritalin, was synthesized, that has many qualities of amphetamines without some of their more undesirable side effects. In 1961 this drug was approved by the F.D.A. for use with children. Since this time there has been much research published on the use of Ritalin in the treatment of childhood behavior disorders. This medication became the "treatment of choice" for treating children with hyperkinesis.

Since the early sixties, more research appeared on the etiology, diagnosis and treatment of hyperkinesis (cf. DeLong, 1972; Grinspoon and Singer, 1973; Cole, 1975)—as much as three-quarters concerned with drug treatment of the disorder. There had been increasing publicity of the disorder in the mass media as well. The *Reader's Guide to Periodical Literature* had no articles on hyperkinesis before 1967, one each in 1968 and 1969 and a total of forty for 1970 through 1974 (a mean of eight per year).

Now hyperkinesis has become the most common child psychiatric problem (Gross and Wilson, 1974: 142); special pediatric clinics have been established to treat hyperkinetic children and substantial federal funds have been invested in etiological and treatment research. Outside the medical profession, teachers have developed a working clinical knowledge of hyperkinesis' symptoms and treatment (cf. Robin and Bosco, 1973); articles appear regularly in mass circulation magazines and newspapers so that parents often come to clinics with knowledge of this diagnosis. Hyperkinesis is no longer the relatively esoteric diagnostic category it may have been twenty years ago, it is now a well-known clinical disorder.

Social Factors

The social factors affecting the discovery of hyperkinesis can be divided into two areas: (1) The Pharmaceutical Revolution; (2) Government Action.

(1) *The Pharmaceutical Revolution.* Since the 1930's the pharmaceutical industry has been synthesizing and manufacturing a large number of psychoactive drugs, contributing to a virtual revolution in drug making and drug taking in America (Silverman and Lee, 1974).

Psychoactive drugs are agents that effect the central nervous system. Benzedrine; Ritalin, and Dexedrine are all synthesized psychoactive stimulants which were indicated for narcolepsy, appetite control (as "diet pills"), mild depression, fatigue, and more recently hyperkinetic children.

Until the early sixties there was little or no promotion and advertisement of any of these medications for use with childhood disorders.[3] Then two major pharmaceutical firms (Smith, Kline and French, manufacturer of Dexedrine and CIBA, manufacturer of Ritalin) began to advertise in medical journals and through direct mailing and efforts of the "detail men." Most of this advertising of the pharmaceutical treatment of hyperkinesis was directed to the medical sphere; but some of the promotion was targeted for the educational sector also (Hentoff, 1972). This promotion was probably significant in disseminating information concerning the diagnosis and treatment of this newly discovered disorder.[4] Since 1955 the use of psychoactive medications (especially phenothiazines) for the treatment of persons who are mentally ill, along with the concurrent dramatic decline in inpatient populations, has made psychopharmacology an integral part of treatment for mental disorders. It has also undoubtedly increased the confidence in the medical profession for the pharmaceutical approach to mental and behavioral problems.

(2) *Government Action.* Since the publication of the U.S.P.H.S. report on M.B.D. there have been at least two significant governmental reports on treating school children with stimulant medications for behavior disorders. Both of these came as a response to the national publicity created by the *Washington Post* report (1970) that five to ten percent of the 62,000 grammar school children in Omaha, Nebraska were being treated with "behavior modification drugs to improve deportment and increase learning potential" (quoted in Grinspoon and Singer, 1973). Although the figures were later found to be a little exaggerated, it nevertheless spurred a Congressional investigation (U.S. Government Printing Office, 1970) and a conference sponsored by the Office of Child Development (1971) on the use of stimulant drugs in the treatment of behaviorally disturbed school children.

The Congressional Subcommittee on Privacy chaired by Congressman Cornelius E. Gallagher held hearings on the issue of prescribing drugs for hyperactive school children. In general, the committee showed great concern over the facility in which the medication was prescribed; more specifically that some children at least were receiving drugs from general practitioners whose primary diagnosis was based on teachers' and parents' reports that the child was doing poorly in school. There was also a concern with the absence of follow-up studies on the long-term effects of treatment.

The H.E.W. committee was a rather hastily convened group of professionals (a majority were M.D.'s) many of whom already had commitments to drug treatment for children's behavior problems. They recommended that only M.D.'s make the diagnosis and prescribe treatment, that the pharmaceutical companies promote the treatment of the disorder only through medical channels, that parents should not be coerced to accept any particular treatment and that long-term follow-up research should be done. This report served as blue ribbon approval for treating hyperkinesis with psychoactive medications.

❧ Discussion

We will focus discussion on three issues: How children's deviant behavior became conceptualized as a medical problem; why this occurred when it did; and what are some of the implications of the medicalization of deviant behavior.

How does deviant behavior become conceptualized as a medical problem? We assume that before the discovery of hyperkinesis this type of deviance was seen as disruptive, disobedient, rebellious, anti-social or deviant behavior. Perhaps the label "emotionally disturbed" was sometimes used, when it was in vogue in the early sixties, and the child was usually managed in the context of the family or the school or in extreme cases, the child guidance clinic. How then did this constellation of deviant behaviors become a medical disorder?

The treatment was available long before the disorder treated was clearly conceptualized. It was twenty years after Bradley's discovery of the "paradoxical effect" of stimulants on certain deviant children that Laufer named the disorder and described its characteristic symptoms. Only in the late fifties were both the diagnostic label and the pharmaceutical treatment available. The pharmaceutical revolution in mental health and the increased interest in child psychiatry provided a favorable background for the dissemination of knowledge about this new disorder. The latter probably made the medical profession more likely to consider behavior problems in children as within their clinical jurisdiction.

There were agents outside the medical profession itself that were significant in "promoting" hyperkinesis as a disorder within the medical framework. These agents might be conceptualized in Becker's terms as "moral entrepreneurs," those who crusade for creation and enforcement of the rules (Becker, 1963).[5] In this case the moral entrepreneurs were the pharmaceutical companies and the Association for Children with Learning Disabilities.

The pharmaceutical companies spent considerable time and money promoting stimulant medications for this new disorder. From the middle 1960's on, medical journals and the free "throwaway" magazines contained elaborate advertising for Ritalin and Dexedrine. These ads explained the utility of treating hyperkinesis and urged the physician to diagnose and treat hyperkinetic children. The ads run from one to six pages. For example, a two-page ad in 1971 stated:

> MBD . . . MEDICAL MYTH OR DIAGNOSABLE DISEASE ENTITY What medical practitioner has not, at one time or another, been called upon to examine an impulsive, excitable hyperkinetic child? A child with difficulty in concentrating. Easily frustrated. Unusually aggressive. A classroom rebel. In the absence of any organic pathology, the conduct of such children was, until a few short years ago, usually dismissed as . . . spunkiness, or evidence of youthful vitality. But it is now evident that in many of these children the hyperkinetic syndrome exists as a distinct medical entity. This syndrome is readily diagnosed through patient histories, neurologic signs, and psychometric testing—has been classified by an expert panel convened by the United States Department of Health, Education and Welfare as Minimal Brain Dysfunction, MBD.

The pharmaceutical firms also supplied sophisticated packets of "diagnostic and treatment" information on hyperkinesis to physicians, paid for professional conferences on the subject, and supported research in the identification and treatment of the disorder. Clearly these corporations had a vested interest in the labeling and treatment of hyperkinesis; CIBA had $13 million profit from Ritalin alone in 1971, which was 15 percent of the total gross profits (Charles, 1971; Hentoff, 1972).

The other moral entrepreneur, less powerful than the pharmaceutical companies, but nevertheless influential, is the Association for Children with Learning Disabilities. Although their focus is not specifically on hyperkinetic children, they do include it in their conception of Learning Disabilities along with aphasia, reading problems like dyslexia and perceptual motor problems. Founded in the early 1950's by parents and professionals, it has functioned much as the National Association for Mental Health does for mental illness: promoting conferences, sponsoring legislation, providing social support. One of the main functions has been to disseminate information concerning this relatively new area in education, Learning Disabilities. While the organization does have a more educational than medical perspective, most of the literature indicates that for hyperkinesis members have adopted the medical model and the medical approach to the problem. They have sensitized teachers and schools to the conception of hyperkinesis as a medical problem.

The medical model of hyperactive behavior has become very well accepted in our society. Physicians find treatment relatively simple and the results sometimes spectacular. Hyperkinesis minimizes parents' guilt by emphasizing "its not their fault, its an organic problem" and allows for nonpunitive management or control of deviance. Medication often makes a child less disruptive in the classroom and sometimes aids a child in learning. Children often like their "magic pills" which make their behavior more socially acceptable and they probably benefit from a reduced stigma also. There are, however, some other, perhaps more subtle ramifications of the medicalization of deviant behavior.

❧ The Medicalization of Deviant Behavior

Pitts has commented that "medicalization is one of the most effective means of social control and that it is destined to become the main mode of *formal* social control" (1971: 391). Kitterie (1971) has termed it "the coming of the therapeutic state."

Medicalization of mental illness dates at least from the seventeenth century (Foucault, 1965; Szasz, 1970). Even slaves who ran away were once considered to be suffering from the disease *drapedomania* (Chorover, 1973). In recent years alcoholism, violence, and drug addiction as well as hyperactive behavior in children have all become defined as medical problems, both in etiology or explanation of the behavior and the means of social control or treatment.

There are many reasons why this medicalization has occurred. Much scientific research, especially in pharmacology and genetics, has become technologically more sophisticated, and found more subtle correlates with human behavior. Sometimes these findings (as in the case of XYY chromosomes and violence) become etiological explanations for deviance. Pharmacological technology that makes new discoveries affecting behavior (e.g., antibuse, methadone and stimulants) are used as treatment for deviance. In part this application is encouraged by the prestige of the medical profession and its attachment to science. As Freidson notes, the medical profession has first claim to jurisdiction over anything that deals with the functioning of the body and especially anything that can be labeled illness (1970:251). Advances in genetics, pharmacology and "psychosurgery" also may advance medicine's jurisdiction over deviant behavior.

Second, the application of pharmacological technology is related to the humanitarian trend in the conception and control of deviant behavior. Alcoholism is no longer sin or even moral weakness, it is now a disease. Alcoholics are no longer arrested in many places for "public drunkenness," they are now somehow "treated," even if it is only to be dried out. Hyperactive children are now considered to have an illness rather than to be disruptive, disobedient, overactive problem children. They are not as likely to be the "bad boy" of the classroom; they are children with a medical disorder. Clearly there are some real humanitarian benefits to be gained by such a medical conceptualization of deviant behavior. There is less condemnation of the deviants (they have an illness, it is not their fault) and perhaps less social stigma. In some cases, even the medical treatment itself is more humanitarian social control than the criminal justice system.

There is, however, another side to the medicalization of deviant behavior. The four aspects of this side of the issue include (1) the problem of expert control; (2) medical social control; (3) the individualization of social problems; and (4) the "depoliticization" of deviant behavior.

1. *The problem of expert control.* The medical profession is a profession of experts; they have a monopoly on anything that can be conceptualized as illness. Because of the way the medical profession is organized and the mandate it has from society, decisions related to medical diagnoses and treatment are virtually controlled by medical professionals.

Some conditions that enter the medical domain are not *ipso facto* medical problems, especially deviant behavior, whether alcoholism, hyperactivity or drug addiction. By defining a problem as medical it is removed from the public realm where there can be discussion by ordinary people and put on a plane where only medical people can discuss it. As Reynolds states,

> The increasing acceptance, especially among the more educated segments of our populace, of technical solutions—solutions administered by disinterested politically and morally neutral experts—results in the withdrawal of more and more areas of human experience from the realm of public discussion. For when drunkenness, juvenile delinquency, sub par performance and extreme political beliefs are seen as symptoms of an underlying illness or biological defect the merits and drawbacks of such behavior or beliefs need not be evaluated (1973:220–221).

The public may have their own conceptions of deviant behavior but that of the experts is usually dominant.

2. *Medical social control.* Defining deviant behavior as a medical problem allows certain things to be done that could not otherwise be considered; for example, the body may be cut open or psychoactive medications may be given. This treatment can be a form of social control.

In regard to drug treatment Lennard points out: "Psychoactive drugs, especially those legally prescribed, tend to restrain individuals from behavior and experience that are not complementary to the requirements of the dominant value system" (1971:57). These forms of medical social control presume a prior definition of deviance as a medical problem. Psychosurgery on an individual prone to violent outbursts requires a diagnosis that there was something wrong with his brain or nervous system. Similarly, prescribing drugs to restless, overactive and disruptive school children requires a diagnosis of hyperkinesis. These forms of social control, what Chorover (1973) has called "psychotechnology," are very powerful and often very efficient means of controlling deviance. These relatively new and increasingly popular forms of social control could not be utilized without the medicalization of deviant behavior. As is suggested from the discovery of hyperkinesis, if a mechanism of medical social control seems useful, then the deviant behavior it modifies will develop a medical label or diagnosis. No overt malevolence on the part of the medical profession is implied: rather it is part of a complex process, of which the medical profession is only a part. The larger process might be called the individualization of social problems.

3. *The individualization of social problems.* The medicalization of deviant behavior is part of a larger phenomenon that is prevalent in our society, the

individualization of social problems. We tend to look for causes and solutions to complex social problems in the individual rather than in the social system. This view resembles Ryan's (1971) notion of "blaming the victim;" seeing the causes of the problem in individuals rather than in the society where they live. We then seek to change the "victim" rather than the society. The medical perspective of diagnosing an illness in an individual lends itself to the individualization of social problems. Rather than seeing certain deviant behaviors as symptomatic of problems in the social system, the medical perspective focuses on the individual diagnosing and treating the illness, generally ignoring the social situation.

Hyperkinesis serves as a good example. Both the school and the parents are concerned with the child's behavior; the child is very difficult at home and disruptive in school. No punishments or rewards seem consistently to work in modifying the behavior; and both parents and school are at their wits' end. A medical evaluation is suggested. The diagnoses of hyperkinetic behavior leads to prescribing stimulant medications. The child's behavior seems to become more socially acceptable, reducing problems in school and at home.

But there is an alternate perspective. By focusing on the symptoms and defining them as hyperkinesis we ignore the possibility that behavior is not an illness but an adaptation to a social situation. It diverts our attention from the family or school and from seriously entertaining the idea that the "problem" could be in the structure of the social system. And by giving medications we are essentially supporting the existing systems and do not allow this behavior to be a factor of change in the system.

4. *The depoliticization of deviant behavior.* Depoliticization of deviant behavior is a result of both the process of medicalization and individualization of social problems. To our western world, probably one of the clearest examples of such a depoliticization of deviant behavior occurred when political dissenters in the Soviet Union were declared mentally ill and confined in mental hospitals (cf. Conrad, 1972). This strategy served to neutralize the meaning of political protest and dissent, rendering it the ravings of mad persons.

The medicalization of deviant behavior depoliticizes deviance in the same manner. By defining the overactive, restless and disruptive child as hyperkinetic we ignore the meaning of behavior in the context of the social system. If we focused our analysis on the school system we might see the child's behavior as symptomatic of some "disorder" in the school or classroom situation, rather than symptomatic of an individual neurological disorder.

❧ Conclusion

I have discussed the social ramifications of the medicalization of deviant behavior, using hyperkinesis as the example. A number of consequences of this medicalization have been outlined, including the depoliticization of deviant behavior, decision-making power of experts, and the role of medicine as an agent of social control. In the last analysis medical social control may be the central issue, as in this role medicine becomes a *de facto* agent of the *status quo*. The medical profession may not have entirely sought this role, but its members have been, in general, disturbingly unconcerned and unquestioning in their acceptance of it. With the increasing medical knowledge and technology it is likely that more deviant behavior will be medicalized and medicine's social control function will expand.

Endnotes

* This paper is a revised version of a paper presented at the meetings of the Society for the Study of Social Problems in San Francisco, August 1975. It was partially supported by a National Science Foundation dissertation grant (SOC 74–22043). I would like to thank Drs. Martin Kozloff, James E. Teele, John McKinlay and the anonymous referees for comments on earlier drafts of this paper.

[1] The U.S.P.H.S. report (Clements, 1966) included 38 terms that were used to describe or distinguish the conditions that it labeled Minimal Brain Dysfunction. Although the literature attempts to differentiate M.B.D., hyperkinesis, hyperactive syndrome, and several other diagnostic labels, it is our belief that in practice they are almost interchangeable.

[2] For a fuller discussion of the construction of the diagnosis of hyperkinesis, see Conrad (forthcoming), especially Chapter 6.

[3] The American Medical Association's change in policy in accepting more pharmaceutical advertising in the late fifties may have been important. Probably the F.D.A. approval of the use of Ritalin for children in 1961 was more significant. Until 1970, Ritalin was advertised for treatment of "functional behavior problems in children." Since then, because of an F.D.A. order, it has only been promoted for treatment of M.B.D.

[4]The drug industry spends fully 25 percent of its budget on promotion and advertising. See Coleman et al. (1966) for the role of the detail men and how physicians rely upon them for information.

[5]Freidson also notes the medical professional role as moral entrepreneur in this process also:

The profession does treat the illnesses laymen take to it, but it also seeks to discover illness of which the laymen may not even be aware. One of the greatest ambitions of the physician is to discover and describe a "new" disease or syndrome . . . (1970:252)

References

Becker, Howard S. 1963. The Outsiders. New York: Free Press.

Bradley, Charles. 1937. "The behavior of children receiving Benzedrine." American Journal of Psychiatry 94(March): 577–585.

Charles, Alan. 1971. "The case of Ritalin." New Republic 23 (October): 17–19.

Chorover, Stephen L. 1973. "Big brother and psychotechnology." Psychology Today (October): 43–54.

Clements, Samuel D. 1966. "Task force 1: Minimal brain dysfunction in children." National Institute of Neurological Diseases and Blindness, Monograph no. 3. Washington, D.C.: U.S. Department of Health, Education, and Welfare.

Cole, Sherwood. 1975. "Hyperactive children: The use of stimulant drugs evaluated." American Journal of Orthopsychiatry 45(January): 28-37.

Coleman, James, Elihu Katz, and Herbert Menzel. 1966. Medical Innovation. Indianapolis: Bob Merrill.

Conrad, Peter. 1972. "Ideological deviance: An analysis of the Soviet use of mental hospitals for political dissenters." Unpublished manuscript.

_____. Forthcoming "Identifying hyperactive children: A study in the medicalization of deviant behavior." Unpublished Ph.D. dissertation, Boston University.

DeLong, Arthur R. 1972. "What have we learned from psychoactive drugs research with hyperactives?" American Journal of Diseases in Children 123(February): 177–180.

Foucault, Michael. 1965. Madness and Civilization. New York: Pantheon.

Grinspoon, Lester and Susan Singer. 1973. "Amphetamines in the treatment of hyperactive children." Harvard Educational Review 43 (November): 515–555.

Gross, Mortimer B. and William E. Wilson. 1974. Minimal Brain Dysfunction. New York: Brunner Mazel.

Hentoff, Nat. 1972. "Drug pushing in the schools: The professionals." The Village Voice 22(May): 21–23.

Kitterie, Nicholas. 1971. The Right to Be Different. Baltimore: Johns Hopkins Press.

Laufer, M. W., Denhoff, E., and Solomons, G. 1975. "Hyperkinetic impulse disorder in children's behavior problems." Psychosomatic Medicine 19(January): 38–49.

Leonard, Henry L. and Associates. 1971. Mystification and Drug Misuse. New York: Harper and Row.

Office of Child Development. 1971. "Report of the conference on the use of stimulant drugs in treatment of behaviorally disturbed children." Washington, D.C.: Office of Child Development, Department of Health, Education and Welfare, January 11–12.

Pitts, Jesse. 1968. "Social control: The concept." In David Sills (ed.), International Encyclopedia of the Social Sciences, Volume 14. New York: Macmillan.

Reynolds, Janice M. 1973. "The medical institution." Pp. 198–324 in Larry T. Reynolds and James M. Henslin, American Society: A Critical Analysis. New York: David McKay.

Robin, Stanley S. and James J. Bosco. 1973. "Ritalin for school children: The teachers perspective." Journal of School Health 47(December): 624–628.

Rosen, George. 1972. "The evolution of social medicine." Pp. 30–60 in Howard E. Freeman, Sol Levine, and Leo Reeder, Handbook of Medical Sociology. Englewood Cliffs, N.J.: Prentice-Hall.

Ryan, William. 1970. Blaming the Victim. New York: Vintage.

Silverman, Milton and Philip R. Lee. 1974. Pills, Profits and Politics. Berkeley: University of California Press.

Sroufe, L. Alan and Mark Stewart. 1973. "Treating problem children with stimulant drugs." New England Journal of Medicine 289(August 23): 407–421.

Stewart, Mark A. 1970. "Hyperactive Children." Scientific American 222(April): 794–798.

Stewart, Mark A., A. Ferris, N. P. Pitts and A. G. Craig. 1966. "The hyperactive child syndrome." American Journal of Orthopsychiatry 36(October): 861–867.

Strauss, A. A. and L. E. Lehtinen. 1947. Psychopathology and Education of the Brain-Injured Child. Vol. 1. New York: Grune and Strattan.

U.S. Government Printing Office. 1970. "Federal involvement in the use of behavior modification drugs on grammar school children of the right to privacy inquiry: Hearing before a subcommittee of the committee on government operations." Washington, D.C.: 91st Congress, 2nd session (September 29).

Wender, Paul. 1971. Minimal Brain Dysfunction in Children. New York: John Wiley and Sons.

Zola, Irving. 1972. "Medicine as an institution of social control. Sociological Review 20 (November): 487–504.

◉ ◉ ◉

Questions

1. What role did clinical and social factors play in the discovery of hyperkinesis? Which of the two roles do you think contributed more to the definition of hyperkinesis as an official medical disorder?

2. What role did pharmaceutical companies and the Association for Children with Learning Disabilities play in defining hyperkinesis as a medical disorder?

3. What are the four problems with medicalizing social control? Of these four, which represents the worst outcome of medicalizing social control? Why?

4. Several other deviant behaviors have been redefined as medical disorders, including alcoholism and drug addiction. Are there any similarities between how those disorders are treated or controlled compared to the treatment and control of hyperkinesis? If so, what are they?

Deviance as Fun

JEFFREY W. RIEMER

> *Often, we engage in behavior because it brings us a thrill or enjoyment. Some of the thrill lies in knowing that the behavior goes against the norms of society and risking the stigma that would result if someone discovered us. But sometimes, the fun is attributed to the behavior itself. In this article, Jeffrey Riemer claims that, for many adolescents, deviance is simply fun. As you read this selection, ask yourself why there are so many theories to explain deviant behavior and so little attention paid to what may be quite obvious: Young people engage in deviant behavior for the fun of it.*

*D*eviant behavior as a fun activity has been consistently ignored in the work of social scientists. Rarely has deviance been considered a spontaneous, "just for the hell of it" activity, in which the participants engage simply for the pleasure it provides. Rather than incorporating this simple, yet potentially useful dimension into our understanding of deviance phenomena, sociologists have continued to be preoccupied with elaborating the more sober social, psychological and sociological explanations for this activity.

Deviance is seldom treated as a frivolous, flippant activity. Yet, this hedonistic "pleasure of the moment" explanation squares well with a common sense interpretation for some of the behavior usually recognized as deviant. In an era of multi-causal explanations we may be inadvertently ignoring an important dimension for better understanding deviant behavior.

Vandalism could be partially explained this way, as could some instances of pre-marital and extra-marital sex, homosexuality (or bisexuality), drug use (or experimentation), drunkenness, shoplifting, auto theft, gambling, fist fights, reckless driving, profanity and prostitution, at least from the client's point of view—to mention a few.

Gustav Ichheiser (1970) has suggested that we are often "blind" to the obvious. We overlook or ignore what we believe everyone already knows. He suggests that what is "taken for granted" is usually neglected or treated as unimportant. This seems to be what has happened with the fun dimen-

"Deviance as Fun," by Jeffrey Riemer, reprinted from *Adolescence*, vol. 16, 1981, pp. 39–43.

sion of deviance. When something squares well with common sense knowledge it does not nullify its theoretical importance.

❦ The Literature

Some social scientists have treated this dimension of deviance in an ancillary way in their writings, while most have totally ignored it. In fact, at least one has been literally forced to recognize this alternative by a respondent who was unwilling to accept a more sophisticated interpretation of her behavior constructed by serious-minded social scientists. Simmons relates the following:

> Several years ago a lesbian interrupted my interview with her and said, "We've kept talking about emotional turmoil and male avoidance. But the truth is I go to bed with her because it's fun." (Simmons, 1969:63)

Garfinkel (1964) has actually created deviant behavior by purposely having his students violate "taken for granted" background expectancies in routine social situations in an attempt to understand the common sense world and how social order emerges. Many of his quasi-experimental researches are quite humorous and, in addition, demonstrate subject reactions to folkway violations as well as experimenter discomfort and pleasure at being "deviant." But Garfinkel fails to interpret any of his research designs as exercises in "fun" or "deviance."

Deviant behavior texts through the years have routinely ignored this dimension with no mention of "fun," "pleasure," "hedonism," or the like, in reference to the causal or contributory factors that influence deviant behavior. Most theorists have continued to delve into the more serious publicly recognized forms of objectionable behavior, often including what is usually recognized as criminal behavior (Thio, 1978; Goode, 1978; Akers, 1977; Sagarin and Montanino, 1977). Certainly, all crime is deviance but not all deviance is crime (Glaser, 1971).

Mundane deviance has been typically neglected. Denzin has argued that sociologists should pay more attention to the "mundane, routine, ephemeral, or normal" forms of deviance that surround all of our everyday life experiences (Denzin, 1970: 121). However, his suggestion has fallen on deaf ears or met objection. Most current students of deviant behavior continue to agree with Gibbons and Jones (1971) who argue that "omnibus" definitions of deviance are unfruitful and loaded with triviality. Mundane deviance is seen as inconsequential and not worth consideration.

The major exception is Lofland (1969) who, is passing, recognized the "deviance as fun" alternative.

> At least some kinds of prohibited activities are claimed by some parts of the population to be in themselves fun, exciting and adventurous. More than simply deriving pleasant fearfulness from violating the prohibition per se, there can exist claims that the prohibited activity itself produces a pleasant level of excitation. (Lofland, 1971: 109)

Even so, after eight years we find little incorporation of this argument.

Research studies have also consistently ignored the deviance as fun dimension. Research into deviant behavior regularly employs the more accepted sophisticated conceptual frameworks for describing and explaining the behavior in question. Again, a somber and serious approach is taken.

One exception, Riemer (1978), has looked at deviance in the work place as a fun activity. Four activities that building construction workers routinely engage in while being paid to work are discussed. These include: drinking alcoholic beverages, "girl watching" and other sexually related activities, stealing, and loafing. Each of these activities are engaged in periodically by some workers as a pleasant change of pace from the routine and boredom of work when the opportunities arise. These activities typically arise spontaneously (given the opportunity) with the workers giving a "just for the hell of it" rationale for their participation. This fun explanation is not meant to be the sole reason for this worker behavior but it cannot be ignored as contributory.

Unfortunately, it is the juvenile delinquency theorists who have taken a more assimilating view of deviance as a fun activity. Ferdinand (1966) in developing a typology of delinquency, included the "mischievous-indulgent" and the "disorganized acting-out" types which are both motivated in their actions by some degree of hedonism and spontaneity. Along this same line, Gibbons (1965) developed a series of delinquent categories in which he included the "casual gang delinquent" (who regards himself as a non-delinquent but likes to have fun) and the "auto-thief joyrider."

Similarly, Briar and Pilirvin have argued for the influence of situationally induced motives to deviate. They suggest that some delinquency may be

> prompted by short-term situationally induced desires experienced by all boys to obtain valued goods, to portray courage in the presence of, or be

loyal to peers, to strike out at someone who is disliked, or simply to "get kicks." (Briar and Piliavin, 1965: 36)

Matza (1961) and Cohen (1955) have also built an "adventure," "play" and "fun" dimension into their explanations of delinquent behavior.

To offer a twist on the Matza and Sykes (1961) thesis that much juvenile behavior could be analyzed as an extension of adult behavior, it is argued here that some adult deviance could be analyzed as an extension of juvenile delinquency. Some deviant behavior may arise as a simple pleasure-seeking activity.

◉ Implications

The argument presented here is not meant to dispute any particular theoretical orientation for deviant behavior. Rather, it calls attention to them all for neglecting a seemingly fruitful area of pursuit for helping to explain this behavior. Certainly, the fun dimension should not be construed as a unidimensional explanation for deviance phenomena. It is simply another perspective that should be incorporated into our existing approaches.

A deviance as fun argument suggests that all persons are deviant at least some of the time. Each of us departs from prevailing normative standards on occasion, weighing the possibility of being publicly designated as deviant and sanctioned accordingly, and choosing a seemingly pleasant diversion from our normative routines. Accordingly, this fun dimension implies a "normal" deviance that exists in society (Durkheim, 1964; Goffman, 1963).

For most of us, most of the time, these pleasant diversions remain nonproblematic. But occasionally an act that begins innocently evolves into a serious legal infraction, e.g., the party-goer who drinks to excess as "the life of the party" and as a result of the intoxication becomes involved in a serious traffic accident on the journey home. What began as fun turned into tragedy.

What is pleasurable, enjoyable, or fun lies in the eyes of the beholder. The current labeling and political theorists might well address what is considered acceptable fun. "One man's pleasure is another man's pain."

The choice to violate normative standards is a choice we all have. For some, this choice represents an enjoyable and exciting alternative. It is within this context that we may learn more about deviant behavior and social control.

References

Akers, Ronald L. *Deviant Behavior*. Belmont, California: Wadsworth, 1977.

Becker, Howard S. *Outsiders*. New York: Free Press, 1963.

Birenbaum, Arnold and Edward Sagarin. *Norms and Human Behavior*. New York: Praeger, 1976.

Briar, Scott and Irving Piliavin. "Delinquency, Situational Inducements, and Commitment to Conformity," *Social Problems*, 1965, 13 (Summer): 35–45.

Cohen, Albert K. *Delinquent Boys: The Culture of the Gang*. Glencoe, Ill.: Free Press, 1955.

Davis, Nanette J. *Sociological Constructions of Deviance*. Dubuque, Iowa: Wm. C. Brown Company, 1975.

Denzin, Norman K. "Rules of Conduct and the Study of Deviant Behavior: Some Notes on the Social Relationship," in *Deviance and Respectability,* Jack D. Douglas (Ed.). New York: Basic Books, 1970, pp. 120–159.

Durkheim, Emile. *The Rules of Sociological Method*. New York: The Free Press, 1964.

Feldman, Saul D. *Deciphering Deviance*. Boston: Little, Brown, 1978.

Ferdinand, Theodore N. *Typologies of Delinquency: A Critical Analysis*. New York: Random House, 1966.

Finestone, Harold. "Cats, Kicks and Color," *Social Problems*, 1957, 5 (July): 3–13.

Garfinkel, Harold. "Studies of the Routine Grounds of Everyday Activities," *Social Problems,* 1964, 11 (Winter): 225–250.

Gibbons, Don C. *Changing the Lawbreaker: The Treatment of Delinquents and Criminals*. Englewood Cliffs, N.J.: Prentice-Hall, 1965.

Gibbons, Don C. and Joseph F. Jones. "Some Critical Notes on Current Definitions of Deviance," *Pacific Sociological Review,* 1971, 14 (January): 20–37.

Glaser, Daniel. *Social Deviance*. Chicago: Markham, 1971.

Goffman, Erving. *Stigma*. Englewood Cliffs, N.J.: Prentice-Hall, 1963.

Goode, Erich. *Deviant Behavior*. Englewood Cliffs, N.J.: Prentice-Hall, 1978.

Ichheiser, Gustav. *Appearances and Realities*. San Francisco: Jossey-Bass, 1970.

Lofland, John. *Deviance and Identity*. Englewood Cliffs, N.J.: Prentice-Hall, 1969.

Matza, David. "Subterranean Traditions of Youth," *Annals of the American Academy of Political and Social Science,* 1961, 338 (November).

Matza, David and Gresham M. Sykes. "Juvenile Delinquency and Subterranean Values," *American Sociological Review,* 1961, 26: 712–719.

Riemer, Jeffrey W. "'Deviance' as Fun—A Case of Building Construction Workers at Work," in *Social Problems—Institutional and Interpersonal Perspectives,* K. Henry (Ed.), Glenview, Ill.: Scott, Foresman, 1978, pp. 322–332.

Sagarin, Edward and Fred Montanino (Eds.). *Deviants: Voluntary Actors in a Hostile World.* Morristown, N.J.: General Learning Press, 1977.

Simmons, J.L. *Deviants.* Berkeley: Glendessary Press, 1969.

Thio, Alex. *Deviant Behavior.* Boston: Houghton Mifflin, 1978.

◉ ◉ ◉

Questions

1. What kinds of behavior might fit the "fun" explanation?

2. How applicable to crime is the "deviance-as-fun" explanation? Can it be possible that "crime is fun"?

3. To what degree do theories of deviance, delinquency, and crime recognize and incorporate the deviance-as-fun concept?

4. How much of the deviance-as-fun concept is attributed to the thrill of breaking social norms? How much of it is attributed to the behavior itself?

Studying Deviance in Four Settings: Research Experiences with Cabbies, Suicides, Drug Users, and Abortionees

JAMES M. HENSLIN

Participant observation is now a commonly used method of sociological inquiry, but this was not always the case. Though many researchers recognize the strengths of this method, others have maintained that it has various weaknesses. In this selection, James Henslin examines the obstacles that researchers encounter when using participant observation to study deviant behavior. He cites examples from his own research to highlight the potential limitations of the method. He also discusses how he overcame these limitations.

We would say then that the sociologist (that is, the one we would really like to invite to our game) is a person intensively, endlessly, shamelessly interested in the doings of men. His natural habitat is all the human gathering places of the world, wherever men come together. . . . And since he is interested in men, nothing that men do can be altogether tedious for him. . . . The sociologist, in his quest for understanding, moves through the world of men without respect for the usual lines of demarcation. Nobility and degradation, power and obscurity, intelligence and folly—these are equally *interesting* to him, however unequal they may be in his personal values or tastes. Thus his questions may lead him to all possible levels of society, the best and the least known places, the most respected and the most despised. . . . We could say that the sociologist, but for the

"Studying Deviance in Four Settings: Research Experiences with Cabbies, Suicides, Drug Users, and Abortionees," by James M. Henslin, reprinted from *Research on Deviance*, Jack Douglas (Ed.), 1972, pp. 35–70. Copyright ©1972 by Random House, Inc.

grace of his academic title, is the man who must listen to gossip despite himself, who is tempted to look through keyholes, to read other people's mail, to open closed cabinets. . . . Perhaps some little boys consumed with curiosity to watch their maiden aunts in the bathroom later become inveterate sociologists. . . . What interests us is the curiosity that grips any sociologist in front of a closed door behind which there are human voices. If he is a good sociologist, he will want to open that door, to understand these voices. Behind each closed door he will anticipate some new facet of human life not yet perceived and understood. The sociologist will occupy himself with matters that others regard as too sacred or as too distasteful for dispassionate investigation. He will find rewarding the company of priests or of prostitutes. . . . Peter L. Berger (1963: 18–19)

I don't ever remember watching any maiden aunts in the bathroom when I was a child! Before some psychiatrist says that I have probably repressed this guilty aspect of my past, let me quickly add that I did not even have a maiden aunt. But Berger does pose an interesting question, that of motivation for sociological research. As a sociologist, he of course denies a psychological or psychiatric basis for sociological research. I would also join his defense of "sociological keyhole watching," agreeing that a sociologist has license to be a Professional Peeping Tom without having to launch into a defense against accusations of sublimated voyeurism. Fortunately, the sociologist does not have to "psychologize" underlying motivations for his research activities and interests, and he is permitted to give a more straightforward (read "superficial," if you are inclined that way) account for his involvement. However, the question can still legitimately be asked why some of us are more interested in prostitutes than in priests.

The first research setting I entered was that of cab-driving. At the time I was (1) a very broke first-year graduate student without an assistantship but with a family, and (2) in need of gathering original data for a term paper for a class in "Social Interaction." I had no special interest in cab drivers; I did not know any cab drivers personally; I did not have any theories that I wanted to prove or disprove, nor did I have any "drums that I wanted to beat" regarding either the working class in general or cab drivers in particular. My total experience with cab drivers at that time had consisted of riding in a cab as passenger about three times. However, since I had already planned on working during the Christmas vacation in order to supplement our meager family income and I was too late to apply for a post office job, I thought that cab-driving might be suitable for fulfilling both needs: money and data. Consequently, I chose for the topic of my term paper the simple subject: "An Analysis of Greetings That Passengers Give Cab Drivers as They Enter Cabs," and I took a job as cabbie for Metro Cab Company of St. Louis (a pseudonym).

This turned out to be a fortuitous choice that greatly affected both my professional and personal lives. I found myself "in the midst of data," suddenly immersed in a world that I really hadn't known existed, and so overwhelmed by data that I began taking extensive field notes of my experiences with passengers, dispatchers, and cab drivers. I became so involved in this "world of data" that I never did write the simple paper that had been the partial purpose for my entering this setting. This initial entrance into the world of cabbies established a frame for both my general interests in deviance as a major subject of sociological analysis and for my general methodological orientation in sociology, that of participant-observation. And I am happy to share with readers . . . the experiences and methodological insights that I have gained through my studies of deviance.[1]

It might be asked what is deviant about doing research on cab drivers. In the first place, the methodology that I happened onto because of the job that I took—that is, participant-observation—does not fit in with the "hard," "scientific," mathematical, hypotheses-testing research that is so prevalent in current sociology and that seems to have been elevated to a sacred or even semidivine status. The methodology of participant-observation, although traditional and still popular in sociology, is, at best, considered second-rate and, at worst, thought to be an irrelevant, archaic, obsolete, and even obstructionist nonscientific approach to the study of human behavior. Given the current orientation of sociology, the approach of participant-observation is in itself a deviant approach to the study of man. In many areas of sociology participant-observers are not accepted but are merely "tolerated" as sort of curious reminders of prescientific sociology. They are treated as sort of aged relatives who overstay their visit, remnants of the musty past-that-was and that somehow should no longer be; they are sometimes venerable because of their previous position, but ordinarily it is embarrassing that they are still present because they are so out-of-step with the way things are, mere relics of a former world that no longer seems to apply.

Being relegated to this definitely secondary, sometimes questionable, and perhaps deviant position forces participant-observers themselves into doing something they frequently observe among the deviants they study doing—defending their deviant orientation in sociology, using "deviance disavowal" (Davis 1964). This results in the peculiar situation of specialists in the study of deviance having to take up the cudgel of rhetoric in defense of the deviant position in which they find themselves (e.g., Lofland 1969, Matza 1969, and Polsky 1967). Although this defense is usually made without the motivation behind it being spelled out, it seems to me that the lowly status of participant-observation in sociology can account for much of the "deviance disavowal" on the part of participant-observers. I am quite happy to join this "chorus of defense" in behalf of the method that I also find so amenable to sociological research.

In the second place, my cabbie research was deviant because of the particular type of participant-observation I chose—covert participant-observation. Because of its seeming threat to a privacy about which we seem to be more and more concerned in our society, covert participant-observation is the deviant form of a deviant method. Perhaps simply listening to and observing persons who did not know that I was gathering data on what they were doing would have been sufficient to call my approach deviant, but I chose to go one step further and do what some consider to be indefensible— use a hidden tape recorder in order to investigate the comments and actions of passengers and fellow cab drivers, with neither their awareness nor their permission.

• • •

In a third sense, this cabbie research was deviant not, as above, in the choice of methodology, but in the selection of occupation itself. While cab-driving is not a deviant occupation in the same sense that prostitution is, it is "offbeat," and cabbies themselves certainly cannot be described as a conventional group of men in our society. Cab drivers are just "not respectable." While they may not be as "disreputable" as are criminals or even pool hustlers (Polsky 1967), they are certainly not as "respectable" as teachers, ministers, businessmen, or *today's* medical men.

Although cab drivers are not deviant in and of themselves, they do have certain things in common with some types of deviants, for example, the hours they keep. Many of them drive from 3:00 P.M. to 3:00 A.M. They also frequently engage in off-duty activities with fellow cabbies until 6:00 or 7:00 A.M. before going home to sleep for a few hours, after which they get up for another shift, and so on, in an ever-recurring cycle.

Furthermore, the occupation of cab-driving itself leads to an inevitable association of cab drivers and deviance. Apart from any particular predilections that the cab driver might have, he is inevitably exposed to deviance because of his occupation. Because of his job, he is often called on to take drunks home, deliver and pick up call girls, and deliver lovers to their meeting places, as well as on rarer occasions being called on to search out a trysting husband for an enraged wife or to drop off and pick up burglars at their "places of work."[2]

But there is an additional reason why I put the deviant label on cab drivers, and that is because of the deviant activities that cab drivers themselves engage in. I am here referring not to cab drivers serving as middlemen for deviance, as above, where they provide the vehicular transportation for call girls, but rather to such common activities of cab drivers as shooting craps, rolling drunks, overcharging in various forms, and, in some cases, extortion and pimping, as well as to the ways in which they communicate the techniques of such practices to the novice cab driver.

⚉ The Benefits of a Subjective Perspective: Studying Cabbies

The major advantage of using participant-observation to study a group such as cab drivers is that the sociological researcher is able to gain the *subjective perspective*. Participant-observation allows the researcher to understand deviance from the viewpoint of the deviant himself. By experiencing the life style of the cab driver, sharing his occupational problems and compensations, and coming into direct contact with the social forces that impinge upon him, the researcher is able to understand forces that cause deviance to be a "normal" or logical outcome of the cab driver's experience. Participant-observation gives the researcher the insight that *not to be deviant in such a situation would be deviant.*

Because of the *pressures* to which the cab driver is subjected (e.g., the goals of economic success that he has been socialized into believing he must reach, the pressures that his family correspondingly places on him to achieve these goals, the everyday occupational tensions and pressures he is subject to, and the unfavorable economic situation in which he finds himself), the *opportunities* for deviance to which he is continually exposed, and the *sharing with fellow occupational members of a common outlook* that is accepting toward certain deviances, deviance becomes normal. It is this subjective perspective that the researcher engaged in participant-observation can grasp, a perspective that I am firmly convinced would be impossible to achieve outside this particular method (cf. Matza 1969).

Participant-observation also allows one to understand such things as why craps is such a common game among cab drivers. Through this method the researcher is able to understand the relationship between the *structure* of the occupation and craps, to see that cab-driving provides the opportunity for crapshooting, that it produces both financial and personal needs on the part of cab drivers to shoot craps, and that it also recruits workers who find craps to be need-satisfying. By experiencing the game himself and seeing that it makes financial goals appear accessible, provides feelings of both control over and escape from their life situation, and also provides much needed primary relations, the participant-observer is able to understand why craps can become so meaningful to cab drivers. As a sociologist, he is also able to see that cab drivers have a propensity to shoot craps because of craps' simplicity, its speed, the mobility and availability of its equipment, its opportunity for expressivity, and its similarity to the world of cab-driving (Henslin 1967, 1970a). Without actually experiencing the occupational problems of cab drivers and the situation in which they shoot craps, it is extremely unlikely that a sociological researcher would gain much insight into or understanding of the reasons why crapshooting is so attractive to cab drivers.

In sociological research the participant-observation method is more advantageous for gaining meaningful information about the subjects than official statistics or someone's omniscient ideas about what those persons are like. If one were to use either official statistics or the sociological omniscience approach to the study of cab drivers, for example, how much could be learned about cab drivers? Official statistics might yield certain information concerning their arrest rate, if it were available, and one would be able to obtain certain economic information about cab drivers across the nation. But given this information, how much would one actually know about the world of the cab driver? Official statistics simply do not talk about his world, and economic and demographic data appear to me to be typically devoid of meaning unless they are related to the realities of everyday life. Although sociological omniscience, like official statistics, can provide some insight into situations that cab drivers face, it, too, is unable to reproduce the meaning of those events for the cab driver himself, does not allow us to accurately picture the cab driver's world as he sees it, and does not allow us to grasp the cab driver's motivations as he interacts within the world that is so peculiarly his. Only by actually getting out with cabbies themselves, preferably by driving a cab and experiencing cab-driving life, with its attendant problems and satisfactions, or by hanging around cab drivers, or at least by interviewing cabbies in depth, can such information and a view of his world ever be gained.

. . .

The Benefits of a Subjective Perspective: Studying Suicides, Drug Users, and Abortionees

The need for dealing firsthand with subjects being studied is also borne out by my experiences with a second form of deviance, that of suicide. While there is much official information on the subject of suicide, and while sociological omniscience can perhaps provide some insight into this area (although I find very little of it in sociological writings on suicide), it is only through contact with persons who are suicidal, with those who have attempted suicide, or with those who knew a suicide victim intimately that we are able to reconstruct the meanings of experiences of life for the suicide himself—that is, only by somehow getting into the suicide's world can we picture it and see on what basis the suicide defined certain events in his life and on the basis of those definitions made certain significant decisions, literally life-and-death decisions.

What can official statistics or a sociological approach that does not include speaking to relevant respondents tell us about the world of the suicide or about his family? From the statistics we might learn some data that are interesting or that are "hard" (and ipso facto desirable and desired by some), but beyond such superficial characteristics, what would we know about his world? Would we, for example, understand the reasons why someone committed suicide if our statistics indicate that a certain proportion of suicide victims had lost their jobs, had been demoted, or had separated from their spouses within three months of their committing suicide? But by interviewing or "talking with" persons who express suicidal desires, or with persons who have attempted suicide, or with the families and friends of suicides, we can become familiar in depth with how suicides have reacted to their lives' problems, to their biographical facts, and we can get at or close to their definitions and interpretations of the significant events in their lives. This insight enables us to piece together *motives* for the act of suicide.

The advantage of a sociological method that includes participation of some sort by the researcher, or one that at least includes detailed observation, is that the researcher can understand an actor's own conception of reality—how he sees himself in the context of some life situation—and thereby gain insight into *his* motivation for a particular act. Understanding of this kind is, or should be, a goal for the social sciences. It seems that observation that involves participation of some sort holds the key for the development of a science of human behavior, and such a method is very different from gathering economic and/or biographical statistics.

The benefit of the subjective perspective has also been driven home to me by my research in another area of deviance, that of drug use. In this area official statistics could provide us with some general biographical information and could tell us something about general drug patterns, at least as far as arrest rates reflect differences in geographical, sex, age, residential, occupational, and ethnic distributions. Perhaps something could even be told us by the great sociological "as if," that is, by the sociologist who imagines how it *might* be *if* he were "one of those." But in either case, what would we actually learn about drug users? If one is interested in the *process* by which someone becomes a drug user, one must at least talk to drug users. It is only through some form of association with people who have personally experienced drugs that one is able to understand the significance of such things as different styles of drug use, different patterns of reaction to life's stresses, and the meaning of drugs for the individual in the context of his particular biography. A "talking approach"—that is, interviewing respondents, as I am currently doing with drug users—has the potential, at least, of yielding such information; however, much more "data in depth" and relevant definitions could be gained if I were to participate directly in their life situation and experience the varying problematic situations that confront them.

What, for example, could we possibly determine about such specifics of drug use as the effects of drugs on sexual experience (how perceptions of sexual experiences change while one is under the influence of drugs) unless we at least speak to persons who have had sexual experiences while under the influence of drugs—or unless we take the option of becoming participant-observers in the full sense of the word, and engage in sexual activities while under such influence? Official information is entirely lacking in this area, and sociological omniscience would really have to be omniscient if it were to come up with anything worthwhile on this subject. Even pharmacological characteristics of drugs cannot tell us how the *perceptions* of the user change (Henslin 1970c, 1970d).

A similar situation exists in the study of abortion that I am currently conducting. Statistics on abortion are so inadequate that it is extremely difficult to even approximate with any accuracy the extent of abortion in the United States. And that mythical omniscient sociologist could not be of any help either if he were to try his "as if" approach, if he were to try to imagine what it would be like if he were to undergo an abortion. What experiences could he possibly have that would qualify him for such suppositioning? One must, then, attempt to somehow enter the world of women seeking and undergoing abortions in order to know what is happening within that world. Once one talks to women who are about to have or who have just had an abortion (and, preferably, also watches abortions being performed), one is able to understand something about the dilemma that the woman faces as she unexpectedly finds herself with an unwanted pregnancy. The researcher can gain insight into her attempts to neutralize society's dictates as she begins her lonesome search for the abortionist and can understand something about her feelings as she undergoes the actual abortion and as she relates to her friends and relatives in the postabortion phase of her experience (Henslin 1971).

Through no Martian situation would one be able to reconstruct such social meanings. It takes participation of some sort in the lives of one's subjects in order to understand or to reconstruct the social meanings of their activities. It is only through such participation that we can relate the perceptions of people, their internal states of mind and feelings, with their external actions. The importance of these perceptions and states of mind is that they provide the actor with the meanings by which he interprets his own external behaviors. Such participation requires, at a minimum, that one talk to relevant subjects, but some sort of immersion in the lives of the subjects is required if one is to reconstruct their relevant social meanings. It is sometimes the case that such immersion can take place through detailed or depth interviews, but it is ordinarily more easily obtained through participation in and sharing of life styles with the subjects.

• • •

❧ Covert Versus Overt Participant-Observation

To get at the meaning of deviance for the members of some group and the relationship of that deviance to other aspects of their lives may require not simply participant-observation but *covert* participant-observation. It is sometimes the case that information can be best obtained by working secretly from the inside. In fact, I would say that this is frequently the case because members of a group share a certain amount of information with one another on the basis of their membership in the same group. They feel that they can confidently share this information not only because they have a "common culture" and therefore share the same perspective on this information, but also because, frequently, revelation of this information outside the group will harm all the members of the group, including the one who revealed it. It is with fellow members of the group that the "front is down." If a researcher who is known to be a researcher steps into such a setting, he will be suspect because he could impart this shared information to others without bringing harm to himself. Now it is at least theoretically possible that this same information could be obtained by other methods; for example, by overt participant-observation. Granted that the members of the group being studied have as much confidence and rapport with the researcher as they do with a fellow member of their group and granted further that they have complete confidence in the trustworthiness of the researcher to hold the anonymity of their information intact, it might be possible to gain access to this same information—that is, it *might* be. But with covert participant-observation, the uncertainty is removed, and once one is fully accepted as a member of the group, one has access to this information.

Persons who belong to a group that is significant to them have a *shared world*, a common culture that tends to cause them to see the world and to interpret their experiences in very similar ways. This common culture provides a frame that surrounds their everyday experiences, yielding a similar interpretation of events that impinge upon that "world-held-in-common." Since this shared world frequently is the very thing that participant-observers are trying to study, it seems that whenever possible those things that can serve as a barrier to information about it should be avoided. It would appear that if one is identified as a researcher, no matter how great the rapport, a gap remains between the identity of known researcher and that of group member, a gap that leads to differential access to information. It is always possible that the overt participant-observer will gain access to this information, and in some cases he will feel confident that he has done so, but he can never know for certain whether this is true or not unless he has actually been a full member of the group. There will always be, at the minimum, an "insider's view" that the overt participant-observer can only *speak about* rather than *speak from*, which he would have been able to do had he actually been a member himself. This qualitative distinction differentiates the data obtained by the research approaches of covert and overt participant-observation.

It is possible, then, to argue that there is both a quantitative and a qualitative difference between the data gathered through covert and overt participant-observation. However, one could attempt to reverse this argument and take the position that there is certain information that can be obtained through overt participant-observation that cannot be obtained through covert participant-observation. And this is true. For example, one problem inherent in covert participant-observation is that there are certain questions that the researcher dare not ask because they do not belong to the member role that he is playing. Asking questions that the researcher role allows but the member role precludes would disrupt the flow of interaction, drawing attention to one's self and possibly causing the researcher to "blow his cover." (Many times, for example, I wanted to ask passengers direct questions, but, as with the question "What is a passenger?" discussed earlier, these questions would have been inappropriate for a cab driver to ask and had to be reluctantly foregone.) This problem can often be overcome by supplementing covert participant-observation with other information-gathering techniques following the cessation of the covert participant-observer role; frequently, however, the stimulus to ask the question is based on some particular interaction situation that will not recur in the same way, and the opportunity is lost for good. Being able to follow such leads is the advantage of the overt participant-observer role, but, as discussed earlier, the information losses inherent in a "less-than-full-member" status make the covert participant-observer role the superior research technique.

◉ Covert Participant-Observation and Ethics

Even if covert participant-observation has the research potential that I have outlined above, what about its ethicality? Kai T. Erikson (1967) has levied a charge against covert participant-observation, arguing that "using masks" in research is unethical because it "compromises both the people who wear them and the people for whom they are worn." Erikson takes the position that it is unethical for a sociologist to deliberately misrepresent his identity for the purpose of entering a private domain to which he could not otherwise gain access or to deliberately misrepresent the character of the research in which he is engaged. (For a similar position, see Barnes 1963.) My particular research on cab drivers would escape Erikson's ethical castigation because my identity was never misrepresented. I represented myself for what I was, a student, and I also gave accurate biographical data to the management of the cab company. Erikson (1967: 372) does specify that social settings to which the sociologist can gain legitimate access, access without misrepresentation, are settings in which he can use his "trained eye" to observe without having to reveal himself as an investigator. However, certain sociological research is censured by this ethical stance; for example, that by Caudill (1952); Festinger et al. (1956); Sullivan et al. (1958); Lofland and Lejeune (1960); and Humphreys (1970).

There is, however, more to the ethical question in sociological research than misrepresentation of identity or purpose. A person who desires to take a strong ethical stance could say, for example, that whenever anyone enters a social setting, he does so as a normal member of that setting, unless he announces a different identity. In other words, he is by his *very act of entering that setting* declaring to other persons there that he has no ulterior research or observational purposes, that he is merely a member like any other. Such an ethical stance means, however, that sociologists would have to constantly reveal their identities *as sociologists* to others in whatever settings they entered or else they would be forbidden from ever utilizing information that they had fortuitously gained from such settings. Additionally, whatever the research design—whether it is experimental, survey, or some other—some form of deceit of purposes appears to always be involved, since revealing exactly what one is looking for would so bias the outcome that the social scientist might as well pack up his research instruments and go home (Roth 1962).

The problem with ethics is that they are not absolute but, rather, are only a matter of definition. And, having undergone differing socialization experiences, different people apply quite different definitions of ethicality to the same situation. This, I assume, is the major reason why the American Sociological Association has been having a difficult time for several years in gaining agreement on a code of professional research ethics for its membership. It would appear that, whatever ethical stance one takes or whatever code of ethics one develops or adopts, exceptions would invariably develop and such a code would face the probability that in a short time definitions of ethicality and unethicality would undergo change. (For a contrary position, see Seeley 1967.) Sometimes this change is even antipodal, as in the case of dissecting cadavers by the medical profession. It appears to me that each researcher must act according to his own system of morality. For example, I would consider any research on my part to be immoral, no matter what method was used, if harm came to my respondents through my findings. However, this stance is based on my own system of morality, and I do not feel that I can impose my system on others, nor do I consider it appropriate for others to force theirs on me. I should emphasize at this point that this position refocuses the ethical question, shifting the emphasis from the ethics inherent in a particular methodology to the ethics of the results of the methodology.

❧ Validity Checks

I want to now turn to other problems connected with research into deviance in general and research done through participant-observation in particular. The first such problem is that of *validity*. Douglas, in his article "Observing Deviance," writes of the need of comparing findings gained through the *role of researcher* with understandings gained from involvement in the activity *as a member* and suggests that such comparisons can serve as a validity check. This appears to me to be an excellent principle to follow, and it was one that was inadvertently applied to my cab-driving research. I had utilized various sorts of checks on my research, for example, the use of a tape recorder to insure the accuracy of quotations, but I had not run any check of validity regarding my interpretations of the world of the cab driver with someone else who knew that world. This validity check, however, was applied to my research in an unanticipated fashion. Dr. Irving Louis Horowitz, one of the senior professors at Washington University at that time, unexpectedly asked to read my dissertation. As a prospective Ph.D. I was filled with trepidation regarding the outcome of this examination by Horowitz, who possessed an intimate knowledge both of the cab-driving world (at one time in his ascent from the New York ghetto, he had driven a cab) and of sociology. Horowitz's reaction to what I had written validated my findings, however—that is, he agreed that the world of the cab driver had been accurately presented.

This brings me to a related problem in sociological research—that of determining whether the researcher's experiences as a member of a group are representative of experiences of members of that group or whether they are representative of the particular background that the researcher brings with him when he enters it. Since the sociological researcher ordinarily has educational and socialization experiences that are atypical of the members of the group he is studying, it is likely that he will react in atypical fashion to what he experiences within that world. In other words, although he is acting as an insider, he might still be perceiving interaction from an outsider's point of view—without even knowing it.

How, then, can the sociological researcher know that his perspective matches that of the members of the group that he is studying? Their life situation, after all, dictates that they shall be members of the group, while the researcher has voluntarily decided to join the group in order to study it; this means that *membership in the group does not have the same meaning for the researcher as it does for the regular members.* Since there is this built-in differential perspective due to differences in the educational, socialization, social-class frame as well as dissimilar motivation for joining the group, some validation of interpretations appears desirable. It is precisely at this point that subjecting one's findings and interpretations to persons who are "bona fide members" of the group can serve as a validity check.

To apply this principle to my own research, my interpretations of and experiences with cab drivers should not be examined only by sociologists who are "former cab drivers." Former-cab-drivers-who-are-now-sociologists are not the same as cab-drivers-who-are-still-cab-drivers. The former have been drastically changed through an exacting, rigorous, and sometimes oppressive socialization process as they learned to be sociologists. They no longer see the world from the perspective of the cab driver, although they are familiar with that perspective and can determine whether or not what is being written rings true. To apply such a validity check, I should, rather, submit my findings to those who currently identify themselves as cabbies, who earn their livelihood as cabbies, and who are "nothing but cabbies."

. . .

● Blowing One's Cover

Another problem connected with covert participant-observation that overt participant-observers do not face is the ever-present potential risk of "blowing one's cover"—that is, exposing one's research identity. As Douglas says in "Observing Deviance," there are certain types of research in which such an eventuality could prove dangerous. In my research with cab drivers there was not much danger to my person if I made a mistake and blew my cover, since I was doing covert participant-observation in an occupation that was open to members of the public. This is drastically different from penetrating the Mafia or, on the other hand, the F.B.I. However, I did get involved in certain aspects of cabbie activities that were deviant, such as crapshooting, which could have possibly led to recriminations for the crapshooters if their activity had become known to the wrong outsiders. My closest brush with blowing my cover occurred one night after shooting craps with the cabbies. I had just finished surreptitiously taping the crap-game, and I was going to give one of the cabbies that had been in the game a ride home. While we were walking to my car, the microphone attached to the patch-cord fell through a hole in the manilla folder in which I had been carrying it. I noticed the microphone dangling in the air at about the level of my knees as we were walking. I quickly glanced at my partner, but he was looking ahead and didn't notice what was happening, and so I shifted the folder to the side opposite him and cautiously worked the dangling microphone back into the folder. I had no cover story for such a contingency, nor do I know how I would have explained my possession at that time of a tape recorder with the sounds of the last hour's game on it.

Blowing my cover would not have had the potentially dangerous consequences that would have resulted had "more criminal" activities been involved. However, it is possible that, having been exposed as a "spy in their midst," I would not have been trusted by the cabbies from that point on. They would have realized that I could utilize this information for their occupational harm, and they certainly would have been suspicious as to whether I might be representing the "fuzz." In the investigation of criminal activities, the potential harm to the subjects is much greater, and the potential retribution for the covert participant-observer who unfortunately blows his cover is, of course, correspondingly greater.

. . .

❦ Problems of "Front" and Role Conflict

As Douglas says in "Observing Deviance," most sociologists are concerned with the straight world, and they remain protected and somewhat isolated in the environment of academia. However, as part of their identification with the academic community, sociologists frequently wear beards. If a bearded sociologist wishes to do research among certain "straights," his beard, which is part of his ordinarily acceptable front for his university position, can become a disrupting force.

The problem that this presented for my suicide research was whether the beard would hinder the rapport between respondents and researcher that is needed in order to gather data in such a sensitive area. In this case I made the decision to try and do the research with the beard, and this turned out to be a sound decision. The beard did not seem to hinder rapport, but, on the contrary, it seemed to lend an air of legitimacy to my role as researcher. In making appointments, I introduced myself as being from the university, to give the research the academic respectability requisite for gaining entrance into these respondents' lives. The beard appeared to further legitimate this academic respectability, defining me as "one of those people from over there," "one of those professors." It furthermore seemed to legitimate the research itself because, although people with good sense might not be interested in such a morbid topic as death, professors, who are looked on by perhaps most of our citizens as not being usual anyway, might be. There was, however, one woman who was put off by the beard. She associated beards with hippies, and hippies with a rather undesirable type of person. I was never able to fully neutralize the hostility that she expressed during the interview. But this was the only negative case of which I was aware.

The problem of front, the legitimation of presentation of one's self and purpose, is one that all of us continually face, even in our everyday lives. Ordinarily, however, front is not problematic to us because we are so socialized into our roles that we take the props that belong to those roles as being part of our persons; we wear our masks naturally, and we give off cues that match very well the various roles that we are called on to play. It is when either something goes wrong with our ordinary role performances or when we are called on to play a role that we are not familiar with that we must start questioning our whole role behavior, including our response repertoire and our whole front, along with its various props (Goffman 1959).

The *presentation of front* is especially problematic when one is engaged in research into deviance because, as outlined above, certain suspicions attach to a researcher who has chosen an offbeat topic in the first place, and because the legitimation of purpose must be successfully presented to potential respondents in order to create and maintain the requisite rapport. Although my front was for the most part very successful in the suicide research, there was one case where it failed almost entirely. The very first evening appointment I made was with a widow who was about thirty years old. She had become suspicious about the legitimacy of someone doing research on the subject of suicide who wanted to speak to her in her home, and she had checked with her next-door neighbor, a policeman. When I arrived for the appointment, I was greeted in a rather unusual way—fortunately the only one of its kind in the research—I was "cordially" invited to take a ride in a patrol car. The policeman's comment, "Anybody visiting widows at night has to be up to no good," very aptly summarizes my reception that evening. In order to avoid the imputation of sexual motives for the research (and this was extremely problematic since more males commit suicide in our society than females, and a good proportion of widows work during the day and are available for interviewing primarily at night), I hired a female research assistant. The two of us, arriving together, put up a front that appeared to be quite acceptable, since there were no similar incidents during the remainder of the research. This solution had the additional benefit of providing two simultaneous interviews whenever two respondents were present and also made certain that no interviews were conducted in the presence of a third party.

An additional problem existed in the suicide research, one of role conflict. I felt a conflict between my role as researcher and as helper-of-fellow-humans-in-distress—that is, some sort of generalized humane role. When, in the course of my interviewing, I encountered individuals in need of professional guidance or therapy, individuals greatly disturbed by the suicide of someone who had been close to them, and in some instances even individuals extremely suicidal themselves, was I simply to play the role of researcher and not look beyond this? Was I simply to ask my questions, then politely leave and forget these people even though I felt that I held, because of a different life situation, certain keys to their well-being? Should the researcher ever step out of his role as researcher? If the answer to this last question is "no," it certainly legitimates noninvolvement for one's self and reduces the problem considerably. How nice it would be simply to say, "That isn't my role" or "They would have been in the same situation if I hadn't appeared on the scene." However, whether it was the role that I desired or not, I *did* appear on the scene.

The solution that I developed to handle this role conflict was the common one of role segregation (Sarbin 1954: 253). I first played the role of researcher and then, where it seemed warranted, that of professional helper. In this way I was able to satisfactorily resolve this conflict. In cases where persons were disturbed about the death, when the interview was finished, I would assure them that the emotions they were experiencing that were so troubling to themselves were normal, that these emotions were ordinarily experienced by others who had had someone close to them commit suicide, and that, therefore, they should not be disturbed about them. Some form of this general statement became almost a part of the standard repertoire of my visits, since most respondents were disturbed in some way and also looked upon me, as a researcher in this area, as someone who knew the answers. In some cases I also stepped beyond this "consoling role" into one in which I directed people to professional help. Others would probably handle this conflict between researcher role and therapist role quite differently, but each person must deal with such moral dilemmas according to the ethics into which he has been socialized.[3]

In drug research, my beard was a natural prop, especially valuable in helping me gain entrance into the drug subculture. The difficulties in gaining rapport with subjects who are engaged in illegal activities, especially activities that carry frightening penalties to anyone apprehended, are well known. One must establish a trust-relationship with potential respondents, and crucial to this establishment is the conviction on the part of the respondent that the researcher does not in some way represent his enemies. In this case respondents had to be convinced that I was not "straight" myself, or that at least my sympathies were with them, or that at a very minimum I definitely did not represent the long arm of any official organization, including the university administration, reaching out for them.

In this case, entree into the drug subculture was gained through a student who had been in one of my classes and who was quite involved in the drug subculture himself. His "okay" then legitimated my presence, but, in addition to this, my "not looking straight," my "personal style," also helped to establish rapport. It was here that my beard and casual clothes became valuable, and as my contacts with the drug subculture continued over time I noticed that I was allowing my hair to grow longer.

Although playing such a role maximizes rapport and contacts with members of the drug subculture, it can also create problems with university administrators. Most university administrators are not exactly known for their radicalism or even their liberality, and the university with which I am affiliated is no exception. Accordingly, when it came time for administrative approval for the research that I had already begun, usually a mere technicality, my front, while positive for purposes of the study, became negative for purposes of securing approval and economic cooperation from the university administration. Thus, another form of role conflict developed because of deviance research—that between the characteristics that facilitate the research and the characteristics that are deemed a mark of university respectability.

The "halo effect" was at work, associating me with the type of research I was doing and creating fear on the part of some members of the committee to which I had submitted my project that the university, by approving research into drug use, was in some way acknowledging or even approving drug use. As a result, my methodology was overtly scrutinized very carefully, and there were questions raised covertly concerning my possible involvement in the drug subculture. Since I was not using drugs, I assume that their suspicions that I might be connected with the drug subculture were based only on my choice of research topic and on my "personal style."

In addition to this "guilt by association," there was the related problem of "doubling deviance."[4] I had chosen not only to do research in an area of deviance involving illegal drug use by students, but also to include gathering data on perceptions of their sexual experiences while under the influence of drugs, most of which involve premarital sex. In my relationship with the committee, I could sense a general feeling, at least on the part of some of the committee members, that such research is better left undone. When it comes to official approval of research into deviance, one of the factors operating is the feeling in regard to some types of deviance that if the deviance is quiet and unnoticeable, it is almost the same as if it did not exist—that is, if it is not brought to anyone's attention, it does not have to be dealt with. By researching such deviance, and by requesting university approval for such research, moreover, the existence of the deviance is brought into the open, where it must be acknowledged. This means that one must officially acknowledge that there is a problem and, if there is a problem, the feeling is that something must be done about it. Thus, if one does not do such research and, thereby, does not raise the deviance to a level where it is visible, administrators and others feel much more secure.

◉ Moral Dilemmas in Deviance Research

In addition to the moral problem already discussed—that of conflict between the researcher role and a helper role—deviance research contains certain moral dilemmas that are ordinarily not discussed in print: the problem of the motivation to experiment with the deviance and the problem of "intimate knowledge." Exposure to deviant activities through secondary contacts such as interviewing can lead the researcher to desire to experience the deviance itself. For example, the researcher may find that he wishes to experiment with drugs, to determine whether drugs will affect him in the same way as they do his respondents or to gain greater insight into the subjective meaning of the respondent's world (cf. Yablonsky 1968). If such motivation for the deviant experience develops, it is also frequently combined with an increased opportunity for such experiences through the contacts the researcher makes in his research and an increased knowledge about the skills that are needed to accomplish the experience. In the case of drugs, for example, not only does he have the opportunity to experiment, but he also learns techniques of administering drugs, information about doses, the right price to pay, and methods of concealment of the purchase. The dilemmas that this poses for the researcher, again, must be solved according to the personal and professional ethics of the particular researcher.

Another moral dilemma facing researchers in the area of deviance is that of "guilty knowledge." Polsky (1967) speaks about the sociologist gaining knowledge of and access to criminal acts, both witnessing them and learning about them secondhand, and his need to make a moral decision regarding his stance concerning these acts and his ability to stand up under police investigation.

There is another form of guilty knowledge, however, that researchers frequently encounter in deviance research, one that we might term "*intimate knowledge*," that is, becoming familiar with the intimate details of a subject's life. Interviews that are conducted in depth, as well as data gathered by participant-observation, can lead to such intimate knowledge. Examples of intimate knowledge that I gained in my suicide research include familiarity with intimate details of familial interaction and conflicts that affect the significant others of a suicide, an awareness of the pressing personal problems that a particular individual is having in his adjustment to the death by suicide of someone who was close to him, the proneness of a respondent to suicide himself and the ways by which he is attempting to handle this potentially lethal desire, as well as knowledge of actions of the respondent toward the deceased that may, in fact, have contributed to his death.

"Intimate knowledge" is perhaps a form of "guilty knowledge," but it does not necessarily involve knowledge about someone's guilt in some matter. It is knowledge that one would ordinarily not possess unless one were a member of the household or a very close friend of the respondent, or unless one were in some official capacity or had been sought out as a counselor. Such intimate knowledge can make the researcher feel rather uncomfortable, but in his research he gains such knowledge. What does he do with it? How is he supposed to react to the respondent? He must react as though this knowledge made no difference, when, in fact, it does. It does make a difference to the researcher because *he knows* that he is aware of intimate aspects of his respondents' lives, and he must find some way of handling or dealing with his awareness.

Frequently the very nature of the research solves the problem of intimate knowledge. Sociologists become familiar with intimate details of their respondents' lives, but usually never see their respondents again. As such, the "uncomfortability" is of short duration, occurring only while they are interviewing a respondent. In some cases such "uncomfortability" does not appear when the respondent is being interviewed, but takes place when some future interaction with the respondent becomes necessary. This delayed reaction can arise particularly if the researcher later interacts with the respondent in a way that is not related to the research.

An example of intimate knowledge that tends to affect interaction in this way, making for a somewhat awkward situation, involves intimate sexual details of a respondent's life, such as those gained from a college girl concerning her perceptions of sexual responses under the influence of drugs. Initially, when the question is asked and the answer given, this can lead to a feeling of "uncomfortability" on the part of both respondent and researcher. If the interaction between the respondent and researcher is limited to the research setting, such "uncomfortability" is of short duration and little consequence. However, if the researcher and researchee are later put into an interactional situation that is outside of the researcher-respondent role, what does the researcher do with his knowledge? It is impossible to dismiss it entirely from his mind, and there is an "overlay" of the researcher-respondent role still left in the ensuing interaction. This is the case if, for example, the same girl now becomes your student, or if she begins to date a friend of yours, or if you have to deal with her in some social capacity.

Another example is that of a woman who becomes a respondent in abortion research, revealing intimate details of her sexual life and aspects of her "situational deviance." This woman fleetingly becomes an unwilling participant in illegal abortion, an interaction that she herself sometimes defines as immoral, after which she then moves back into her regular respectable routines. Some time after the interview, in some unexpected capacity, the researcher meets this individual and is called upon to interact as though he possessed no intimate knowledge. Such interactions become problematic to both the respondent and the researcher, and each researcher must develop his own techniques for handling these difficulties.

◉ Obtaining and Interviewing Respondents

Another major problem in deviance research is that of obtaining respondents. Although this problem is not unique with deviance research, but is common throughout sociology, the methodological problems in sampling techniques are multiplied when the sociologist researches deviance. In a small number of cases standardized sampling techniques can be used, but the population must be clearly defined in advance. Such techniques apply, for example, if one wants to generalize one's sample to a particular inmate population or to some category of arrested and/or convicted felons. However, where the population is not known, standardized sampling techniques cannot be used. And when standardized samples are not used, questions concerning the generalizability of one's findings are always left hanging.

Where there is a developed subculture of deviants and one is able to gain entry into that subculture and establish rapport with potential respondents, the recruitment of respondents is greatly facilitated. This is the case with my drug research. Drug users on a college campus ordinarily know several other users, and there is a communication or exchange network that exists among members of this subculture.

When, however, there is no developed subculture of deviance, the problem of gaining access to respondents is greatly increased. The researcher is then faced with a greater than usual problem of finding out who potential respondents are, as well as facing the usual problems of gaining entry or making contact with these potential respondents and establishing rapport with them. This is the case with abortion. Our whole legal approach to abortion has made it a secretive act that ordinarily isolates the abortionee from persons who could be of help to her in solving her problem (Henslin 1971; Manning 1971; Schur 1965). This isolation almost entirely prevents the development of a subculture of abortion. Abortionees, for the most part, remain individuated, without bonds growing between persons who have experienced the same deviance. This is not to deny that bonds between abortionees exist, but there is no widespread sharing of experiences, no common defining of the situation such as one finds with homosexuality, no public meetings held by and for abortionees, and, for the most part, there are no clubs or organizations centering around this deviance.

The problem that this individuating aspect of abortion presents for the researcher is that it is not possible to make just one major contact with an individual who has experienced abortion and then to be introduced, by that one individual, into a whole network of others who have been involved in the same deviance. This possibility might exist if the researcher were fortunate enough to gain the rapport of an abortionist who would then allow him to study his "patients." However, such contacts are ordinarily serendipitous since abortionists, understandably enough, appear rather hesitant to share information regarding their clients, their *modus operandi,* or other aspects of their work situation.

How then is the problem solved of gaining abortionee respondents? Since one is not able to locate a major contact and work through her to expand one's contacts, one must "send out as many feelers" as possible. I handled this problem by making abortion a possible topic for students doing original research in my courses in deviance and in social psychology, provided that they were able to gain interviews with friends or acquaintances who had undergone abortions and that they would tape these interviews and include them in their research papers. Additionally, I told practically every student with whom I was even slightly acquainted, and many that I didn't even know that well, that if they knew someone who had undergone an abortion, I would like to talk to her. Some of the students actively sought out such respondents for me. In some cases, potential respondents would not talk to me about the experience, but consented to be interviewed by their friends, who taped the interviews for me. Most, however, came into my office to be interviewed. In other cases, I had a sociologist-friend in a distant city administer a depth interview based on an outline that I supplied him to respondents that he was able to contact. He then taped these interviews and sent them to me.

The point that I am making here is that it takes ingenuity to gain interviews with respondents who have engaged in certain forms of deviance and who have something to fear regarding their own egos, their professional lives, or their social lives as a result of this information being leaked to others.[5] In situations in which an interview poses some threat to respondents or in which the absence of a subculture prevents respondents from being easily localized, the researcher must "push" potential contacts if he is to gain interviewees.

. . .

◉ Motivations of Respondents

The problem of motivation of respondents in sociological research has not been adequately analyzed. In my own research I have steadfastly refused to pay my respondents. I am not only tight, but I am also suspicious of such motivation. There is not much question regarding the motivation of respondents who do not know that they are respondents (for example, "respondents" in covert participant-observation studies), since they are not acting as respondents but are playing their ordinary roles. Their motivations, then, are the motivations of people who are in the everyday process of revealing and concealing information about their selves—that is, presenting fronts and validating self-images.

In order to understand and properly evaluate information given by members of a group being studied by covert participant-observation, one must have an adequate understanding of their motivations to conceal and reveal information. The motivations themselves then become part of the data. For example, if it is a part of the common culture of a particular group to show bravado or to present the self in a particular form through jokes, joking, bragging, occupational anecdotes, and so on, the researcher must understand these behaviors as being part of the normative expectations of the group. He should not accept such behaviors at face value, but should interpret them within the framework of the motivations for information disclosure that that group has.

Knowledge of the motivation of respondents is also important for understanding and evaluating information disclosures that are made in depth interviews, since if the respondent is motivated to present a particular front, this will shape the data in a particular way. Unfortunately, we frequently know very little about such motivations for participation in this type of interviewing, and we know even less about the biases that we are incorporating into our results.

As Douglas says in "Observing Deviance," one must know what is being exchanged in the interview or other form of research if one is going to properly evaluate the motivations of respondents and the information that is gained through the research. Too often sociologists think of themselves as being the only ones receiving anything during interviewing. This idea of the interviewee as the giver and the interviewer as the receiver is quite inadequate, since interviewees are receiving as well as giving. Consequently, the researcher should always ask himself the question: "What is the interviewee receiving?"

One particular motivation that I have been able to tap in my research has been that of *altruism*. In the suicide research, for example respondents were specifically told: "Not much is known about suicide and what happens to families following a suicide. We need to know much more about this, and we would appreciate very much being able to talk to you." Furthermore, although it was not directly stated, the impression was implicitly left that their cooperation would somehow help other families in a similar situation. Tapping this altruistic motivation led to a high response rate and the establishment of solid rapport with the respondents in the suicide research. Supposedly what was being exchanged, at least on one level, was my satisfying their need for altruism in return for their giving me their cooperation.

I also frequently tapped altruism in the research on abortion. This was again altruism for the sake of science. Potential respondents and potential contacts with potential respondents were told that, although there are many abortionees around, it is very difficult to find women who are willing to discuss their abortion experiences with a researcher. I emphasized how little we know about the abortion experience, and how much I would appreciate it if they would talk to me or could arrange for someone else to do so.

There are, I am certain, many other motives for cooperating in research on abortion, such as a desire to share an experience with someone whom they feel they can trust, a desire to get things off one's chest through speaking to an anonymous listener, and so on. But, whatever the exchange that I have been able to offer, this approach has been rather effective, even to the point of getting a woman who had put in a full day at work to drive forty miles through rush-hour traffic to a university she had never been to before, to an office of someone she had never met, to speak to someone about intimate details of her life. This particular respondent, moreover, had not shared this experience with anyone other than her boyfriend and one girlfriend.

The motivation of respondents in drug research seems to be of a somewhat different nature. Although altruism for the sake of sharing knowledge for scientific gains is present in some cases, the motivation of drug respondents seems to be more on the level of curiosity itself—that is, respondents wonder what the researcher has in mind in his research and what it will be like to be interviewed or to participate in the research. Curiosity about the research appears to be the major motivation, and it is a good motivation to tap among drug users, at least among college students who are drug users, because college drug users appear to be very curious about experiences in life. Their curiosity, in fact, is perhaps one of the major motivations for initial drug usage.

Another major motivation of respondents in both abortion and drug research is that of responding to personal requests or meeting the expectations that friends and acquaintances have of the individual. In abortion and drug research, it is very seldom that I directly approach an individual to request his cooperation as a respondent. Rather, prospective respondents are approached for me by others who know of the individual's involvement in the particular form of deviance. This motivates the potential respondent to cooperate because of the expectations of the one who is requesting his cooperation—that is, to act on the basis of their friendship. It is, in general, difficult to refuse the request of a friend if the time required to satisfy the request is not unreasonable.

Deviants cooperate and give me research data, and I, on my part, give them such things as friendship, attention, understanding, acceptance, a sympathetic ear, anonymity, insight, satisfaction of curiosity, fulfillment of altruistic needs, self-aggrandizement, the chance to cooperate with that magical thing called "science," fulfillment of obligations incurred within a friendship network, and/or an opportunity to establish obligations that their friend must repay at some future date.

Ordinarily, that which is received by the respondent in exchange for the information that he gives must be inferred from certain aspects of the interaction. Very seldom is such an exchange made explicit by the respondent. However, this sometimes happens, as in the example above of providing a home for cats. Another exchange was most explicitly spelled out to me in a recent telephone call in which a male voice flatly stated: "She will come in and talk to you if you will give her the name of an abortionist." Again, the unanticipated moral decisions that must be made when one does research into deviance!

Endnotes

[1] My apologies to the reader for referring so frequently in this essay to my own research. I ordinarily try not to do this, but because this article is meant to share with others some of the problems and experiences that I encountered, and to do so through a first-person approach, this is inevitable. Nevertheless, I feel somewhat uncomfortable about it.

[2] From my field notes and files.

[3] One of my graduate students, Carol McCart, felt essentially this same role conflict in participant-observer research that she did for my course in deviance. She did research in a half-way house for exconvicts, and she wrote in her paper:

How can you talk to a man who has been confined within two maximum security prisons (Alcatraz and Leavenworth) for 13 years, with no interested human relationships, with no family or friends who give a damn whether he lives or dies, with no job and one disappointing interview after another, who is frantically searching for some shred of hope to which he can cling, and simply "walk away from him"? How can you not be involved? How can you feel his need and ignore it? How can you interview man after man who has been permanently damaged by the penal system and remain objective about that system? How can you objectively study a person as though he were an object only, when he is a human being?

[4]Cf. "putative deviation" in Lemert (1951: 56).

[5]One form of contact that has probably been underused is that of direct advertising. Recently one of my students advertised in the student newspaper for divorcees, stating that she wanted to contact them for research purposes. She received an excellent response, including several faculty members who were willing to reveal intimate details of their lives to a freshman student!

References

Barnes, J. A. 1963 "Some Ethical Problems in Modern Field Work," *British Journal of Sociology,* 14, 118–134.

Becker, Howard S. 1963 *Outsiders: Studies in the Sociology of Deviance.* New York: Free Press.

Berger, Peter L. 1963 *Invitation to Sociology: A Humanistic Perspective.* Garden City, N.Y.: Anchor Books.

Caudill, William C. 1952 "Social Structure and Interaction Processes in a Psychiatric Ward," *American Journal of Orthopsychiatry,* 22, 314–334.

Davis, Fred 1964 "Deviance Disavowal: The Management of Strained Interaction by the Visibly Handicapped," in Howard S. Becker (ed.), *The Other Side: Perspectives on Deviance.* New York: Free Press.

Erikson, Kai T. 1967 "A Comment on Disguised Observation in Sociology," *Social Problems,* 14, 366–373.

Festinger, Leon, Henry W. Riecken, and Stanley Schacter 1956 *When Prophecy Fails.* Minneapolis: University of Minnesota Press.

Goffman, Erving 1959 *The Presentation of Self in Everyday Life.* Garden City, N.Y.: Anchor Books.

Henslin, James M. 1967 "Craps and Magic," *American Journal of Sociology,* 73, 316–330. (See also the attack on and the defense of this article in *American Journal of Sociology,* 74 [November 1968], 304–305.)

_____. 1970a "Why Craps and Cabbies?" (unpublished paper).

_____. 1970c "Changes in Perceptions of Sexual Experiences of College Students While Under the Influence of Drugs," paper delivered at The National Academy of Sciences, Washington, D.C., February 1970.

_____. 1970d "Sex, Drugs, and the American College Scene," in Edward Sagarin (ed.), *Sex and the American Scene.* Chicago: Quadrangle Books.

_____. 1971 "Criminal Abortion: Making the Decision and Neutralizing the Act," in James M. Henslin (ed.), *Studies in the Sociology of Sex*. New York: Appleton-Century-Crofts, 113–135.

Humphreys, Laud 1970 *Tearoom Trade: Impersonal Sex in Public Places*. Chicago: Aldine.

Lemert, Edwin M. 1951 *Social Pathology: A Systematic Approach to the Theory of Sociopathic Behavior*. New York: McGraw-Hill.

Lofland, John 1969 *Deviance and Identity*. Englewood Cliffs, N.J.: Prentice-Hall.

_____. and Robert A. Lejeune 1960 "Initial Interaction of Newcomers in Alcoholics Anonymous: A Field Experiment in Class Symbols and Socialization," *Social Problems*, 8, 102–111.

Manning, Peter K. 1971 "Fixing What you Feared: Notes on the Campus Abortion Search," in James M. Henslin (ed.), *Studies in the Sociology of Sex*. New York: Appleton-Century-Crofts, 137–166.

Matza, David 1969 *Becoming Deviant*. Englewood Cliffs, N.J.: Prentice-Hall.

Polsky, Ned 1967 *Hustlers, Beats, and Others*. Garden City, N.Y.: Anchor Books.

Roth, Julius A. 1962 "Comments on 'Secret Observation,'" *Social Problems*, 9, 283–284.

Sarbin, Theodore R. 1954 "Role Theory," in Gardner Lindzey (ed.), *Handbook of Social Psychology*, Vol. I: *Theory and Method*, Chap. 6. Reading, Mass.: Addison-Wesley.

Schur, Edwin M. 1965 *Crimes Without Victims: Deviant Behavior and Public Policy*. Englewood Cliffs, N.J.: Prentice-Hall.

Seeley, John R. 1967 "The Making and Taking of Problems: Toward an Ethical Stance," *Social Problems*, 14, 382–389.

Sullivan, Mortimer A., Stuart A. Queen, and Ralph C. Patrick, Jr. 1958 "Participant Observation as Employed in the Study of a Military Training Program," *American Sociological Review*, 23, 660–667.

Yablonsky, Lewis 1968 *The Hippie Trip*. New York: Pegasus.

◉ ◉ ◉

Questions

1. What limitations does participant observation have as a research methodology for studying deviant behavior?

2. What strengths does participant observation offer as a research methodology for studying deviant behavior?

3. How can a researcher balance the tension between "overt and covert participation"? What are the shortcomings of each method of participation?

4. How can sociologists conduct "checks" to ensure that the findings from participant observation are valid?

5. Explain the moral dilemmas that might arise when researchers use participant observation.

6. Discuss the tensions associated with a researcher's "role conflict"; that is, being an academic as well as an individual submersed in the deviant subculture he or she is studying.

7. In your opinion, do the benefits of covert participant observation (for example, access and understanding) outweigh the potential costs (that is, possession of "guilty knowledge," or participation in illicit and illegal activity)? In other words, given the benefits and costs, do you think covert participation is justified? Why or why not?

Moral Entrepreneurs: The Creation and Enforcement of Deviant Categories

Howard Becker

Behavioral norms, or unspoken rules, exist at all levels of society. Some of these tell us how we should behave, while others tell us how we should not behave. How do specific rules come into existence? In this selection, Howard Becker addresses this question by examining the impact of "rule creators." He also explores the ways in which norms are enforced ("rule enforcers") and the relationship between rule creators and rule enforcers.

Rules are the products of someone's initiative and we can think of the people who exhibit such enterprise as *moral entrepreneurs*. Two related species—rule creators and rule enforcers—will occupy our attention.

◎ Rule Creators

The prototype of the rule creator, but not the only variety as we shall see, is the crusading reformer. He is interested in the content of rules. The existing rules do not satisfy him because there is some evil which profoundly disturbs him. He feels that nothing can be right in the world until rules are made to correct it. He operates with an absolute ethic; what he sees is truly and totally evil with no qualification. Any means is justified to do away with it. The crusader is fervent and righteous, often self-righteous.

It is appropriate to think of reformers as crusaders because they typically believe that their mission is a holy one. The prohibitionist serves as an excellent example, as does the person who wants to suppress vice and sexual delinquency or the person who wants to do away with gambling.

These examples suggest that the moral crusader is a meddling busy-body, interested in forcing his own morals on others. But this is a one-sided view. Many moral crusades have strong humanitarian overtones. The crusader is not only interested in seeing to it that other people do what he thinks right. He believes that if they do what is right it will be good for them. Or he may feel that his reform will prevent certain kinds of exploitation of one person by another. Prohibitionists felt that they were not simply forcing their morals on others, but attempting to provide the conditions for a better way of life for people prevented by drink from realizing a truly good life. Abolitionists were not simply trying to prevent slave owners from doing the wrong thing; they were trying to help slaves to achieve a better life. Because of the importance of the humanitarian motive, moral crusaders (despite their relatively single-minded devotion to their particular cause) often lend their support to other humanitarian crusades. Joseph Gusfield has pointed out that:

> The American temperance movement during the 19th century was a part of a general effort toward the improvement of the worth of the human being through improved morality as well as economic conditions. The mixture of the religious, the equalitarian, and the humanitarian was an outstanding facet of the moral reformism of many movements. Temperance supporters formed a large segment of movements such as sabbatarianism, abolition, woman's rights, agrarianism, and humanitarian attempts to improve the lot of the poor. . . .

> In its auxiliary interests the WCTU revealed a great concern for the improvement of the welfare of the lower classes. It was active in campaigns to secure penal reform, to shorten working hours and raise wages for workers, and to abolish child labor and in a number of other humanitarian and equalitarian activities. In the 1880's the WCTU worked to bring about legislation for the protection of working girls against the exploitation by men.[1]

As Gusfield says,[2] "Moral reformism of this type suggests the approach of a dominant class toward those less favorably situated in the economic and social structure." Moral crusaders typically want to help those beneath them to achieve a better status. That those beneath them do not always like the means proposed for their salvation is another matter. But this fact—that moral crusades are typically dominated by those in the upper levels of the social structure—means that they add to the power they derive from the legitimacy of their moral position, the power they derive from their superior position in society.

Naturally, many moral crusades draw support from people whose motives are less pure than those of the crusader. Thus, some industrialists supported Prohibition because they felt it would provide them with a more manageable labor force.[3] Similarly, it is sometimes rumored that Nevada gambling interests support the opposition to attempts to legalize gambling in California because it would cut so heavily into their business, which depends in substantial measure on the population of Southern California.[4]

The moral crusader, however, is more concerned with ends than with means. When it comes to drawing up specific rules (typically in the form of legislation to be proposed to a state legislature or the Federal Congress), he frequently relies on the advice of experts. Lawyers, expert in the drawing of acceptable legislation, often play this role. Government bureaus in whose jurisdiction the problem falls may also have the necessary expertise, as did the Federal Bureau of Narcotics in the case of the marijuana problem.

As psychiatric ideology, however, becomes increasingly acceptable, a new expert has appeared—the psychiatrist. Sutherland, in his discussion of the natural history of sexual psychopath laws, pointed to the psychiatrist's influence.[5] He suggests the following as the conditions under which the sexual psychopath law, which provides that a person "who is diagnosed as a sexual psychopath may be confined for an indefinite period in a state hospital for the insane,"[6] will be passed.

> First, these laws are customarily enacted after a state of fear has been aroused in a community by a few serious sex crimes committed in quick succession. This is illustrated in Indiana, where a law was passed following three or four sexual attacks in Indianapolis, with murder in two. Heads of families bought guns and watch dogs, and the supply of locks and chains in the hardware stores of the city was completely exhausted. . . .
>
> A second element in the process of developing sexual psychopath laws is the agitated activity of the community in connection with the fear. The attention of the community is focused on sex crimes, and people in the most varied situations envisage dangers and see the need of and possibility for their control. . . .
>
> The third phase in the development of these sexual psychopath laws has been the appointment of a committee. The committee gathers the many conflicting recommendations of persons and groups of persons, attempts

to determine "facts," studies procedures in other states, and makes recommendations, which generally include bills for the legislature. Although the general fear usually subsides within a few days, a committee has the formal duty of following through until positive action is taken. Terror which does not result in a committee is much less likely to result in a law.[7]

In the case of sexual psychopath laws, there usually is no government agency charged with dealing in a specialized way with sexual deviations. Therefore, when the need for expert advice in drawing up legislation arises, people frequently turn to the professional group most closely associated with such problems:

> In some states, at the committee stage of the development of a sexual psychopath law, psychiatrists have played an important part. The psychiatrists, more than any others, have been the interest group back of the laws. A committee of psychiatrists and neurologists in Chicago wrote the bill which became the sexual psychopath law of Illinois; the bill was sponsored by the Chicago Bar Association and by the state's attorney of Cook County and was enacted with little opposition in the next session of the State Legislature. In Minnesota all the members of the governor's committee except one were psychiatrists. In Wisconsin the Milwaukee Neuropsychiatric Society shared in pressing the Milwaukee Crime Commission for the enactment of a law. In Indiana the attorney-general's committee received from the American Psychiatric Association copies of all of the sexual psychopath laws which had been enacted in other states.[8]

The influence of psychiatrists in other realms of the criminal law has increased in recent years.

In any case, what is important about this example is not that psychiatrists are becoming increasingly influential, but that the moral crusader, at some point in the development of his crusade, often requires the services of a professional who can draw up the appropriate rules in an appropriate form. The crusader himself is often not concerned with such details. Enough for him that the main point has been won; he leaves its implementation to others.

By leaving the drafting of the specific rule in the hands of others, the crusader opens the door for many unforeseen influences. For those who draft legislation for crusaders have their own interests, which may affect the legislation they prepare. It is likely that the sexual psychopath laws drawn by psychiatrists contain many features never intended by the citizens who spearheaded the drives to "do something about sex crimes," features which do however reflect the professional interests of organized psychiatry.

❧ The Fate of Moral Crusades

A crusade may achieve striking success, as did the Prohibition movement with the passage of the Eighteenth Amendment. It may fail completely, as has the drive to do away with the use of tobacco or the anti-vivisection movement. It may achieve great success, only to find its gains whittled away by shifts in public morality and increasing restrictions imposed on it by judicial interpretations; such has been the case with the crusade against obscene literature.

One major consequence of a successful crusade, of course, is the establishment of a new rule or set of rules, usually with the appropriate enforcement machinery being provided at the same time. I want to consider this consequence at some length later. There is another consequence, however, of the success of a crusade which deserves mention.

When a man has been successful in the enterprise of getting a new rule established—when he has found, so to speak, the Grail—he is out of a job. The crusade which has occupied so much of his time, energy, and passion is over. Such a man is likely, when he first began his crusade, to have been an amateur, a man who engaged in a crusade because of his interest in the issue, in the content of the rule he wanted established. Kenneth Burke once noted that a man's occupation may become his preoccupation. The equation is also good the other way around. A man's preoccupation may become his occupation. What started as an amateur interest in a moral issue may become an almost full-time job; indeed, for many reformers it becomes just this. The success of the crusade, therefore, leaves the crusader without a vocation. Such a man, at loose ends, may generalize his interest and discover something new to view with alarm, a new evil about which something ought to be done. He becomes a professional discoverer of wrongs to be righted, of situations requiring new rules.

When the crusade has produced a large organization devoted to its cause, officials of the organization are even more likely than the individual crusader to look for new causes to espouse. This process occurred dramatically in the field of health problems when the National Foundation for Infantile Paralysis put itself out of business by discovering a vaccine that eliminated epidemic poliomyelitis. Taking the less constraining name of The

National Foundation, officials quickly discovered other health problems to which the organization could devote its energies and resources.

The unsuccessful crusade, either the one that finds its mission no longer attracts adherents or the one that achieves its goal only to lose it again, may follow one of two courses. On the one hand, it may simply give up its original mission and concentrate on preserving what remains of the organization that has been built up. Such, according to one study, was the fate of the Townsend Movement.[9] Or the failing movement may adhere rigidly to an increasingly less popular mission, as did the Prohibition Movement. Gusfield has described present-day members of the WCTU as "moralizers-in-retreat."[10] As prevailing opinion in the United States becomes increasingly anti-temperance, these women have not softened their attitude toward drinking. On the contrary, they have become bitter at the formerly "respectable" people who no longer will support a temperance movement. The social class level from which WCTU members are drawn has moved down from the upper-middle class to the lower-middle class. The WCTU now turns to attack the middle class it once drew its support from, seeing this group as the locus of acceptance of moderate drinking. The following quotations from Gusfield's interviews with WCTU leaders give some of the flavor of the "moralizer-in-retreat":

> When this union was first organized, we had many of the most influential ladies of the city. But now they have got the idea that we ladies who are against taking a cocktail are a little queer. We have an undertaker's wife and a minister's wife, but the lawyer's and the doctor's wives shun us. They don't want to be thought queer.

> We fear moderation more than anything. Drinking has become so much a part of everything—even in our church life and our colleges.

> It creeps into the official church boards. They keep it in their iceboxes. . . . The minister here thinks that the church has gone far, that they are doing too much to help the temperance cause. He's afraid that he'll stub some influential toes.[11]

Only some crusaders, then, are successful in their mission and create, by creating a new rule, a new group of outsiders. Of the successful, some find they have a taste for crusades and seek new problems to attack. Other crusaders fail in their attempt and either support the organization they have created by dropping their distinctive mission and focusing on the problem of organizational maintenance itself or become outsiders themselves, continuing to espouse and preach a doctrine which sounds increasingly queer as time goes on.

◉ Rule Enforcers

The most obvious consequence of a successful crusade is the creation of a new set of rules. With the creation of a new set of rules we often find that a new set of enforcement agencies and officials is established. Sometimes, of course, existing agencies take over the administration of the new rule, but more frequently a new set of rule enforcers is created. The passage of the Harrison Act presaged the creation of the Federal Narcotics Bureau, just as the passage of the Eighteenth Amendment led to the creation of police agencies charged with enforcing the Prohibition Laws.

With the establishment of organizations of rule enforcers, the crusade becomes institutionalized. What started out as a drive to convince the world of the moral necessity of a new rule finally becomes an organization devoted to the enforcement of the rule. Just as radical political movements turn into organized political parties and lusty evangelical sects become staid religious denominations, the final outcome of the moral crusade is a police force. To understand, therefore, how the rules creating a new class of outsiders are applied to particular people we must understand the motives and interests of police, the rule enforcers.

Although some policemen undoubtedly have a kind of crusading interest in stamping out evil, it is probably much more typical for the policeman to have a certain detached and objective view of his job. He is not so much concerned with the content of any particular rule as he is with the fact that it is his job to enforce the rule. When the rules are changed, he punishes what was once acceptable behavior just as he ceases to punish behavior that has been made legitimate by a change in the rules. The enforcer, then, may not be interested in the content of the rule as such, but only in the fact that the existence of the rule provides him with a job, a profession, and a *raison d'être*.

Since the enforcement of certain rules provides justification for his way of life, the enforcer has two interests which condition his enforcement activity: first, he must justify the existence of his position and, second, he must win the respect of those he deals with.

These interests are not peculiar to rule enforcers. Members of all occupations feel the need to justify their work and win the respect of others.

Musicians, as we have seen, would like to do this but have difficulty finding ways of successfully impressing their worth on customers. Janitors fail to win their tenants' respect, but develop an ideology which stresses the quasi-professional responsibility they have to keep confidential the intimate knowledge of tenants they acquire in the course of their work.[12] Physicians, lawyers, and other professionals, more successful in winning the respect of clients, develop elaborate mechanisms for maintaining a properly respectful relationship.

In justifying the existence of his position, the rule enforcer faces a double problem. On the one hand, he must demonstrate to others that the problem still exists: the rules he is supposed to enforce have some point, because infractions occur. On the other hand, he must show that his attempts at enforcement are effective and worthwhile, that the evil he is supposed to deal with is in fact being dealt with adequately. Therefore, enforcement organizations, particularly when they are seeking funds, typically oscillate between two kinds of claims. First, they say that by reason of their efforts the problem they deal with is approaching solution. But, in the same breath, they say the problem is perhaps worse than ever (though through no fault of their own) and requires renewed and increased effort to keep it under control. Enforcement officials can be more vehement than anyone else in their insistence that the problem they are supposed to deal with is still with us, in fact is more with us than ever before. In making these claims, enforcement officials provide good reason for continuing the existence of the position they occupy.

We may also note that enforcement officials and agencies are inclined to take a pessimistic view of human nature. If they do not actually believe in original sin, they at least like to dwell on the difficulties in getting people to abide by rules, on the characteristics of human nature that lead people toward evil. They are skeptical of attempts to reform rule-breakers.

The skeptical and pessimistic outlook of the rule enforcer, of course, is reinforced by his daily experience. He sees, as he goes about his work, the evidence that the problem is still with us. He sees the people who continually repeat offenses, thus definitely branding themselves in his eyes as outsiders. Yet it is not too great a stretch of the imagination to suppose that one of the underlying reasons for the enforcer's pessimism about human nature and the possibilities of reform is that fact that if human nature were perfectible and people could be permanently reformed, his job would come to an end.

In the same way, a rule enforcer is likely to believe that it is necessary for the people he deals with to respect him. If they do not, it will be very difficult to do his job; his feeling of security in his work will be lost. Therefore, a good deal of enforcement activity is devoted not to the actual enforcement of rules, but to coercing respect from the people the enforcer deals with. This means that one may be labeled as deviant not because he has actually broken a rule, but because he has shown disrespect to the enforcer of the rule.

Westley's study of policemen in a small industrial city furnishes a good example of this phenomenon. In his interview, he asked policemen, "When do you think a policeman is justified in roughing a man up?" He found that "at least 37% of the men believed that it was legitimate to use violence to coerce respect."[13] He gives some illuminating quotations from his interviews:

> Well, there are cases. For example, when you stop a fellow for a routine questioning, say a wise guy, and he starts talking back to you and telling you you are no good and that sort of thing. You know you can take a man in on a disorderly conduct charge, but you can practically never make it stick. So what you do in a case like that is to egg the guy on until he makes a remark where you can justifiably slap him and, then, if he fights back, you can call it resisting arrest.

> Well, a prisoner deserves to be hit when he goes to the point where he tries to put you below him.

> You've gotta get rough when a man's language becomes very bad, when he is trying to make a fool of you in front of everybody else. I think most policemen try to treat people in a nice way, but usually you have to talk pretty, rough. That's the only way to set a man down, to make him show a little respect.[14]

What Westley describes is the use of an illegal means of coercing respect from others. Clearly, when a rule enforcer has the option of enforcing a rule or not, the difference in what he does may be caused by the attitude of the offender toward him. If the offender is properly respectful, the enforcer may smooth the situation over. If the offender is disrespectful, then sanctions may be visited on him. Westley has shown that this differential tends to operate in the case of traffic offenses, where the policeman's discretion is perhaps at a maximum.[15] But it probably operates in other areas as well.

Ordinarily, the rule enforcer has a great deal of discretion in many areas, if only because his resources are not sufficient to cope with the volume of rule-breaking he is supposed to deal with. This means that he cannot tackle everything at once and to this extent must temporize with evil. He cannot do the whole job and knows it. He takes his time, on the assumption that the problems he deals with will be around for a long while. He establishes priorities, dealing with things in their turn, handling the most pressing problems immediately and leaving others for later. His attitude toward his work, in short, is professional. He lacks the naive moral fervor characteristic of the rule creator.

If the enforcer is not going to tackle every case he knows of at once, he must have a basis for deciding when to enforce the rule, which persons committing which acts to label as deviant. One criterion for selecting people is the "fix." Some people have sufficient political influence or know-how to be able to ward off attempts at enforcement, if not at the time of apprehension then at a later stage in the process. Very often, this function is professionalized; someone performs the job on a full-time basis, available to anyone who wants to hire him. A professional thief described fixers this way:

> There is in every large city a regular fixer for professional thieves. He has no agents and does not solicit and seldom takes any case except that of a professional thief, just as they seldom go to anyone except him. This centralized and monopolistic system of fixing for professional thieves is found in practically all of the large cities and many of the small ones.[16]

Since it is mainly professional thieves who know about the fixer and his operations, the consequence of this criterion for selecting people to apply the rules to is that amateurs tend to be caught, convicted, and labeled deviant much more frequently than professionals. As the professional thief notes:

> You can tell by the way the case is handled in court when the fix is in. When the copper is not very certain he has the right man, or the testimony of the copper and the complainant does not agree, or the prosecutor goes easy on the defendant, or the judge is arrogant in his decisions, you can always be sure that someone has got the work in. This does not happen in many cases of theft, for there is one case of a professional to twenty-five or thirty amateurs who know nothing about the fix. These amateurs get the hard end of the deal every time. The coppers bawl out about the thieves, no one holds up his testimony, the judge delivers an oration, and all of them get credit for stopping a crime wave. When the professional hears the case immediately preceding his own, he will think, "He should have got ninety years. It's the damn amateurs who cause all the heat in the stores."

Or else he thinks, "Isn't it a damn shame for that copper to send that kid away for a pair of hose, and in a few minutes he will agree to a small fine for me for stealing a fur coat?" But if the coppers did not send the amateurs away to strengthen their records of convictions, they could not sandwich in the professionals whom they turn loose.[17]

Enforcers of rules, since they have no stake in the content, of particular rules themselves, often develop their own private evaluation of the importance of various, kinds of rules, and infractions of them. This set of priorities may differ considerably from those held by the general public. For instance, drug users typically believe (and a few policemen have personally confirmed it to me) that police do not consider the use of marijuana to be as important a problem or as dangerous a practice as the use of opiate drugs. Police base this conclusion on the fact that, in their experience, opiate users commit other crimes (such as theft or prostitution) in order to get drugs, while marijuana users do not.

Enforcers, then, responding to the pressures of their own work situation, enforce rules and create outsiders in a selective way. Whether a person who commits a deviant act is in fact labeled a deviant depends on many things extraneous to his actual behavior: whether the enforcement official feels that at this time he must make some show of doing his job in order to justify his position, whether the misbehaver shows proper deference to the enforcer, whether the "fix" has been put in, and where the kind of act he has committed stands on the enforcer's list of priorities.

The professional enforcer's lack of fervor and routine approach to dealing with evil may get him into trouble with the rule creator. The rule creator, as we have said, is concerned with the content of the rules that interest him. He sees them as the means by which evil can be stamped out. He does not understand the enforcer's long-range approach to the same problems and cannot see why all the evil that is apparent cannot be stamped out at once.

When the person interested in the content of a rule realizes or has called to his attention the fact that enforcers are dealing selectively with the evil that concerns him, his righteous wrath may be aroused. The professional is denounced for viewing the evil too lightly, for failing to do his duty. The moral entrepreneur, at whose instance the rule was made, arises again to say that the outcome of the last crusade has not been satisfactory or that the gains once made have been whittled away and lost.

◉ Deviance and Enterprise: A Summary

Deviance—in the sense I have been using it, of publicly labeled wrongdoing—is always the result of enterprise. Before any act can be viewed as deviant, and before any class of people can be labeled and treated as outsiders for committing the act, someone must have made the rule which defines the act as deviant. Rules are not made automatically. Even though a practice may be harmful in an objective sense to the group in which it occurs, the harm needs to be discovered and pointed out. People must be made to feel that something ought to be done about it. Someone must call the public's attention to these matters, supply the push necessary to get things done, and direct such energies as are aroused in the proper direction to get a rule created. Deviance is the product of enterprise in the largest sense; without the enterprise required to get rules made, the deviance which consists of breaking the rule could not exist.

Deviance is the product of enterprise in the smaller and more particular sense as well. Once a rule has come into existence, it must be applied to particular people before the abstract class of outsiders created by the rule can be peopled. Offenders must be discovered, identified, apprehended and convicted (or noted as "different" and stigmatized for their nonconformity, as in the case of legal deviant groups such as dance musicians). This job ordinarily falls to the lot of professional enforcers who, by enforcing already existing rules, create the particular deviants society views as outsiders.

It is an interesting fact that most scientific research and speculation on deviance concerns itself with the people who break rules rather than with those who make and enforce them. If we are to achieve a full understanding of deviant behavior, we must get these two possible foci of inquiry into balance. We must see deviance, and the outsiders who personify the abstract conception, as a consequence of a process of interaction between people, some of whom in the service of their own interests make and enforce rules which catch others who, in the service of their own interests, have committed acts which are labeled deviant.

Endnotes

[1]Joseph R. Gusfield, "Social Structure and Moral Reform: A Study of the Woman's Christian Temperance Union," *American Journal of Sociology,* LXI (November, 1955), 223.

[2]*Ibid.*

[3]See Raymond G. McCarthy, editor, *Drinking and Intoxication* (New Haven and New York: Yale Center of Alcohol Studies and The Free Press of Glencoe, 1959), pp. 395–396.

[4]This is suggested in Oscar Lewis, *Sagebrush Casinos: The Story of Legal Gambling in Nevada* (New York: Doubleday and Co., 1953), pp. 233–234.

[5]S. Edwin H. Sutherland, "The Diffusion of Sexual Psychopath Laws," *American Journal of Sociology,* LVI (September, 1950), 142–148.

[6]*Ibid.,* p. 142.

[7]*Ibid.,* pp. 143–145.

[8]*Ibid.,* pp.145–146.

[9]Sheldon Messinger, "Organizational Transformation: A Case Study of a Declining Social Movement," *American Sociological Review,* XX, (February, 1955), 3–10.

[10]Gusfield, *op, cit.,* pp. 227–228.

[11]*Ibid.,* pp. 227, 229–230.

[12]See Ray Gold, "Janitors Versus Tenants: A Status-Income Dilemma," *American Journal of Sociology,* LVII (March, 1952), 486–493.

[13]William A. Westley, "Violence and the Police," *American Journal of Sociology,* LIX (July, 1953), 39.

[14]*Ibid.*

[15]See William A. Westley, "The Police: A Sociological Study of Law, Custom, and Morality" (unpublished PhD. dissertation, University of Chicago, Department of Sociology, 1951).

[16]Edwin H. Sutherland (editor), *The Professional Thief* (Chicago: University of Chicago Press, 1937), pp. 87–88.

[17]*Ibid.,* pp. 91–92.

◉ ◉ ◉

Questions

1. What role do "moral crusaders" play in the development of rules and laws? Cite some contemporary examples of successful and unsuccessful moral crusades.

2. Becker discusses the role of professionals, in particular psychologists, in creating some rules. Do you think the role of professionals has become more or less prominent in recent times? Provide examples to support your claim.

3. What is the relationship between rule enforcers and rules? How might rule enforcers' differential enforcement of rules lead to problems when people are dealing with deviance and crime?

4. Becker contends that rule creators are concerned with rule content but not enforceability, and that rule enforcers are concerned with enforceability but not content. What kinds of problems may arise from these two groups' having competing interests?

5. What does Becker mean when he claims that rule enforcers must deal with a "double problem"? How might this "double problem" be resolved?

Toward a Marxian Theory of Deviance

STEVEN SPITZER
University of Pennsylvania

In this selection, Stephen Spitzer elaborates the relationship between social class and deviant behavior in a capitalist society. He contends that in order to understand which behavior is classified as deviance, as well as which individuals are labeled as deviant, we must first understand the role of social class and power. In this excerpt, he discusses how "problem populations" are created, why some of these problem populations are classified as deviant, and how they are subsequently classified as either "social junk" or "social dynamite."

*W*ithin the last decade American sociologists have become increasingly reflective in their approach to deviance and social problems. They have come to recognize that interpretations of deviance are often ideological in their assumptions and implications, and that sociologists are frequently guilty of "providing the facts which make oppression more efficient and the theory which makes it legitimate to a larger constituency" (Becker and Horowitz, 1972:48). To combat this tendency students of deviance have invested more and more energy in the search for a critical theory. This search has focused on three major problems: (1) the definition of deviance, (2) the etiology of deviance, and (3) the etiology of control.

◉ Traditional Theories and Their Problems

Traditional theories approached the explanation of deviance with little equivocation about the phenomenon to be explained. Prior to the 1960s the subject matter of deviance theory was taken for granted and few were disturbed by its preoccupation with "dramatic and predatory" forms of

---

"Toward a Marxian Theory of Deviance," by Stephen Spitzer, reprinted from *Social Problems,* vol. 22, June 1975, pp. 638–651.

social behavior (Liazos, 1972). Only in recent years have sociologists started to question the consequences of singling out "nuts," "sluts," "perverts," "lames," "crooks," "junkies," and "juicers" for special attention. Instead of adopting conventional wisdom about *who* and *what* is deviant, investigators have gradually made the definitional problem central to the sociological enterprise. They have begun to appreciate the consequences of studying the powerless (rather than the powerful)—both in terms of the relationship between *knowledge of* and *control over* a group, and the support for the "hierarchy of credibility" (Becker, 1967) that such a focus provides. Sociologists have discovered the significance of the definitional process in their own, as well as society's response to deviance, and this discovery has raised doubts about the direction and purpose of the field.

Even when the definitional issue can be resolved critics are faced with a second and equally troublesome problem. Traditional theories of deviance are essentially *non-structural* and *ahistorical* in their mode of analysis. By restricting investigation to factors which are manipulable within existing structural arrangements these theories embrace a "correctional perspective" (Matza, 1969) and divert attention from the impact of the political economy as a whole. From this point of view deviance is *in* but not *of* our contemporary social order. Theories that locate the source of deviance in factors as diverse as personality structure, family systems, cultural transmission, social disorganization and differential opportunity share a common flaw—they attempt to understand deviance apart from historically specific forms of political and economic organization. Because traditional theories proceed without any sense of historical development, deviance is normally viewed as an episodic and transitory phenomenon rather than an outgrowth of long-term structural change. Sensitive sociologists have come to realize that critical theory must establish, rather than obscure, the relationship between deviance, social structure and social change.

A final problem in the search for a critical theory of deviance is the absence of a coherent theory of control. More than ever before critics have come to argue that deviance cannot be understood apart from the dynamics of control. Earlier theories devoted scant attention to the control process precisely because control was interpreted as a natural response to behavior generally assumed to be problematic. Since theories of deviance viewed control as a desideratum, no theory of control was required. But as sociologists began to question conventional images of deviance they revised their impressions of social control. Rather than assuming that societal reaction was necessarily defensive and benign, skeptics announced that controls could actually cause deviance. The problem was no longer simply to explain the independent sources of deviance and control, but to understand the reciprocal relationship between the two.

In elevating control to the position of an independent variable a more critical orientation has evolved. Yet this orientation has created a number of problems of its own. If deviance is simply a *status,* representing the outcome of a series of control procedures, should our theory of deviance be reduced to a theory of control? In what sense, if any, is deviance an achieved rather than an ascribed status? How do we account for the historical and structural sources of deviance apart from those shaping the development of formal controls?

◉ Toward a Theory of Deviance Production

A critical theory must be able to account for both *deviance* and *deviants.* It must be sensitive to the process through which deviance is subjectively constructed and deviants are objectively handled, as well as the structural bases of the behavior and characteristics which come to official attention. It should neither beg the explanation of deviant behavior and characteristics by depicting the deviant as a helpless victim of oppression, nor fail to realize that his identification as deviant, the dimensions of his threat, and the priorities of the control system are part of a broader social conflict. While acknowledging the fact that deviance is a *status* imputed to groups who share certain structural characteristics (e.g. powerlessness) we must not forget that these groups are defined by more than these characteristics alone.[1] We must not only ask why specific members of the underclass are selected for official processing, but also why they behave as they do. Deviant statuses, no matter how coercively applied, are in some sense achieved and we must understand this achievement in the context of political-economic conflict. We need to understand why capitalism produces both patterns of activity and types of people that are defined and managed as deviant.

In order to construct a general theory of deviance and control it is useful to conceive of a process of deviance production which can be understood in relationship to the development of class society. *Deviance production involves all aspects of the process through which populations are structurally generated, as well as shaped, channeled into, and manipulated within social categories defined as deviant.* This process includes the development of and changes in: (1) deviant definitions, (2) problem populations, and (3) control systems.

Most fundamentally, deviance production involves the development of and changes in deviant categories and images. A critical theory must examine where these images and definitions come from, what they reflect about the structure of and priorities in specific class societies, and how they are related to class conflict. If we are to explain, for example, how mental retardation becomes deviance and the feebleminded deviant we need to examine the structural characteristics, economic and political dimensions of the society in which these definitions and images emerged. In the case of American society we must understand how certain correlates of capitalist development (proletarianization and nuclearization of the family) weakened traditional methods of assimilating these groups, how others (the emergence of scientific and meritocratic ideologies) sanctioned intellectual stratification and differential handling, and how still others (the attraction of unskilled labor and population concentrations) heightened concern over the "threat" that these groups were assumed to represent. In other words, the form and content of deviance definition must be assessed in terms of its relationship to both structural and ideological change.

A second aspect of deviance production is the development of and changes in problem behaviors and problem populations. If we assume that class societies are based on fundamental conflicts between groups, and that harmony is achieved through the dominance of a specific class; it makes sense to argue that deviants are culled from groups who create specific problems for those who rule. Although these groups may victimize or burden those outside of the dominant class, their problematic quality ultimately resides in their challenge to the basis and form of class rule. Because problem populations are not always "handled," they provide candidates for, but are in no sense equivalent to, official deviants. A sophisticated critical theory must investigate where these groups come from, why their behaviors and characteristics are problematic, and how they are transformed in a developing political economy. We must consider, for instance, why Chinese laborers in 19th century California and Chicanos in the Southwest during the 1930s became the object of official concern, and why drug laws evolved to address the "problems" that these groups came to represent (Helmer and Vietorisz, 1973; Musto, 1973).

The changing character of problem populations is related to deviance production in much the same way that variations in material resources affect manufacturing. Changes in the quantity and quality of raw materials influence the scope and priorities of production, but the characteristics of the final product depend as much on the methods of production as the source material. These methods comprise the third element in deviance production—the development and operation of the control system. The theory must explain why a system of control emerges under specific conditions and account for its size, focus and working assumptions. The effectiveness of the system in confronting problem populations and its internal structure must be understood in order to interpret changes in the form and content of control. Thus, in studying the production of the "mentally ill" we must not only consider why deviance has been "therapeutized," but also how this development reflects the subleties of class control. Under capitalism, for example, formal control of the mad and the birth of the asylum may be examined as a response to the growing demands for order, responsibility and restraint (cf. Foucault, 1965).

The Production of Deviance in Capitalist Society

The concept of deviance production offers a starting point for the analysis of both deviance and control. But for such a construct to serve as a critical tool it must be grounded in an historical and structural investigation of society. For Marx, the crucial unit of analysis is the mode of production that dominates a given historical period. If we are to have a Marxian theory of deviance, therefore, deviance production must be understood in relationship to specific forms of socio-economic organization. In our society, productive activity is organized capitalistically and it is ultimately defined by "the process that transforms on the one hand, the social means of subsistence and of production into capital, on the other hand the immediate producers into wage labourers" (Marx, 1967:714).

There are two features of the capitalist mode of production important for purposes of this discussion. First, as a mode of production it forms the foundation or infrastructure of our society. This means that the starting point of our analysis must be an understanding of the economic organization of capitalist societies and the impact of that organization on all aspects of social life. But the capitalist mode of production is an important starting point in another sense. It contains contradictions which reflect the internal tendencies of capitalism. These contradictions are important because they explain the changing character of the capitalist system and the nature of its impact on social, political and intellectual activity. The formulation of a Marxist perspective on deviance requires the interpretation of the process through which the contradictions of capitalism are expressed. In particular, the theory must illustrate the relationship between specific contradictions, the problems of capitalist development and the production of a deviant class.

The superstructure of society emerges from and reflects the ongoing development of economic forces (the infrastructure). In class societies this superstructure preserves the hegemony of the ruling class through a system of class controls. These controls, which are institutionalized in the family, church, private associations, media, schools and the state, provide a mechanism for coping with the contradictions and achieving the aims of capitalist development.

Among the most important functions served by the superstructure in capitalist societies is the regulation and management of problem populations. Because deviance processing is only one of the methods available for social control, these groups supply raw material for deviance production, but are by no means synonymous with deviant populations. Problem populations tend to share a number of social characteristics, but most important among these is the fact that their behavior, personal qualities and/or position threaten the *social relations of production* in capitalist societies. In other words, populations become generally eligible for management as deviant when they disturb, hinder or call into question any of the following:

1) capitalist modes of appropriating the product of human labor (e.g. when the poor "steal" from the rich)

2) the social conditions under which capitalist production takes place (e.g. those who refuse or are unable to perform wage labor)

3) patterns of distribution and consumption in capitalist society (e.g. those who use drugs for escape and transcendence rather than sociability and adjustment)

4) the process of socialization for productive and non-productive roles (e.g. youth who refuse to be schooled or those who deny the validity of "family life")[2]

5) the ideology which supports the functioning of capitalist society (e.g. proponents of alternative forms of social organization)

Although problem populations are defined in terms of the threat and costs that they present to the social relations of production in capitalist societies, these populations are far from isomorphic with a revolutionary class. It is certainly true that some members of the problem population, may under specific circumstances possess revolutionary potential. But this potential can only be realized if the problematic group is located in a position of functional indispensability within the capitalist system. Historically, capitalist societies have been quite successful in transforming those who are problematic and indispensable (the protorevolutionary class) into groups who are either problematic and dispensable (candidates for deviance processing), or indispensable but not problematic (supporters of the capitalist order). On the other hand, simply because a group is manageable does not mean that it ceases to be a problem for the capitalist class. Even though dispensable problem populations cannot overturn the capitalist system, they can represent a significant impediment to its maintenance and growth. It is in this sense that they become eligible for management as deviants.

Problem populations are created in two ways—either directly through the expression of fundamental contradictions in the capitalist mode of production or indirectly through disturbances in the system of class rule. An example of the first process is found in Marx's analysis of the "relative surplus-population."

Writing on the "General Law of Capitalist Accumulation" Marx explains how increased social redundance is inherent in the development of the capitalist mode of production:

> With the extension of the scale of production, and the mass of the labourers set in motion, with the greater breadth and fullness of all sources of wealth, there is also an extension of the scale on which greater attraction of labourers by capital is accompanied by their greater repulsion. . . . The labouring population therefore produces, along with the accumulation of capital produced by it, the means by which itself is made relatively superfluous, . . . and it does this to an always increasing extent (Marx, 1967: 631).

In its most limited sense the production of a relative surplus-population involves the creation of a class which is economically redundant. But insofar as the conditions of economic existence determine social existence, this process helps explain the emergence of groups who become both threatening and vulnerable at the same time. The marginal status of these populations reduces their stake in the maintenance of the system while their powerlessness and dispensability renders them increasingly susceptible to the mechanisms of official control.

The paradox surrounding the production of the relative surplus-population is that this population is both useful and menacing to the accumulation of capital. Marx describes how the relative surplus-population "forms a disposable industrial army, that belongs to capital quite as absolutely as if the latter had bred it at its own cost," and how this army, "creates, for the changing needs of the self-expansion of capital, a mass of human material always ready for exploitation" (Marx, 1967:632).

On the other hand, it is apparent that an excessive increase in what Marx called the "lowest sediment" of the relative surplus-population, might seriously impair the growth of capital. The social expenses and threat to social harmony created by a large and economically stagnant surplus-population could jeopardize the preconditions for accumulation by undermining the ideology of equality so essential to the legitimation of production relations in bourgeois democracies, diverting revenues away from capital investment toward control and support operations, and providing a basis for political organization of the dispossessed.[3] To the extent that the relative surplus population confronts the capitalist class as a threat to the social relations of production it reflects an important contradiction in modern capitalist societies: a surplus-population is a necessary product of and condition for the accumulation of wealth on a capitalist basis, but it also creates a form of social expense which must be neutralized or controlled if production relations and conditions for increased accumulation are to remain unimpaired.

Problem populations are also generated through contradictions which develop in the system of class rule. The institutions which make up the superstructure of capitalist society originate and are maintained to guarantee the interests of the capitalist class. Yet these institutions necessarily reproduce, rather than resolve, the contradictions of the capitalist order. In a dialectical fashion, arrangements which arise in order to buttress capitalism are transformed into their opposite—structures for the cultivation of internal threats. An instructive example of this process is found in the emergence and transformation of educational institutions in the United States.

The introduction of mass education in the United States can be traced to the developing needs of corporate capitalism (cf. Karier, 1973; Cohen and Lazerson, 1972; Bowles and Gintis, 1972; Spring, 1972). Compulsory education provided a means of training, testing and sorting, and as similating wage-laborers, as well as withholding certain populations from the labor market. The system was also intended to preserve the values of bourgeois society and operate as an "inexpensive form of police" (Spring, 1973:31). However, as Gintis (1973) and Bowles (1973) have suggested, the internal contradictions of schooling can lead to effects opposite of those intended. For the poor, early schooling can make explicit the oppressiveness and alienating character of capitalist institutions, while higher education can instill critical abilities which lead students to "bite the hand that feeds them." In both cases educational institutions create troublesome populations (i.e. drop outs and student radicals) and contribute to the very problems they were designed to solve.

After understanding how and why specific groups become generally bothersome in capitalist society, it is necessary to investigate the conditions under which these groups are transformed into proper objects for social control. In other words, we must ask what distinguishes the generally problematic from the specifically deviant. The rate at which problem populations are converted into deviants will reflect the relationship between these populations and the control system. This rate is likely to be influenced by the:

(1) *Extensiveness and Intensity of State Controls.* Deviance processing (as opposed to other control measures) is more likely to occur when problem management is monopolized by the state. As state controls are applied more generally the proportion of official deviants will increase.

(2) *Size and Level of Threat Presented by the Problem Population.* The larger and more threatening the problem population, the greater the likelihood that this population will have to be controlled through deviance processing rather than other methods. As the threat created by these populations exceeds the capacities of informal restraints, their management requires a broadening of the reaction system and an increasing centralization and coordination of control activities.

(3) *Level of Organization of the Problem Population.* When and if problem populations are able to organize and develop limited amounts of political power, deviance processing becomes increasingly less effective as a tool for social control. The attribution of deviant status is most likely to occur when a group is relatively impotent and atomized.

(4) *Effectiveness of Control Structures Organized through Civil Society.* The greater the effectiveness of the organs of civil society (i.e. the family, church, media, schools, sports) in solving the problems of class control, the less the likelihood that deviance processing (a more explicitly political process) will be employed.

(5) *Availability and Effectiveness of Alternative Types of Official Processing.* In some cases the state will be able effectively to incorporate certain segments of the problem population into specially created "pro-social" roles. In the modern era, for example, conscription and public works projects (Piven and Cloward, 1971) helped neutralize the problems posed by troublesome populations without creating new or expanding old deviant categories.

(6) *Availability and Effectiveness of Parallel Control Structures.* In many instances the state can transfer its costs of deviance production by supporting or at least tolerating the activities of independent control networks which operate in its interests. For example, when the state is denied or is reluctant to assert a monopoly over the use of force it is frequently willing to encourage vigilante organizations and private police in the suppression of problem populations. Similarly, the state is often benefited by the policies and practices of organized crime, insofar as these activities help pacify, contain and enforce order among potentially disruptive groups (Schelling, 1967).

(7) *Utility of Problem Populations.* While problem populations are defined in terms of their threat and costs to capitalist relations of production, they are not threatening in every respect. They can be supportive economically (as part of a surplus labor pool or dual labor market), politically (as evidence of the need for state intervention) and ideologically (as scapegoats for rising discontent). In other words, under certain conditions capitalist societies derive benefits from maintaining a number of visible and uncontrolled "troublemakers" in their midst. Such populations are distinguished by the

fact that while they remain generally bothersome, the costs that they inflict are most immediately absorbed by other members of the problem population. Policies evolve, not so much to eliminate or actively suppress these groups, but to deflect their threat away from targets which are sacred to the capitalist class. Victimization is permitted and even encouraged, as long as the victims are members of an expendable class.

Two more or less discrete groupings are established through the operations of official control. These groups are a product of different operating assumptions and administrative orientations toward the deviant population. On the one hand, there is *social junk* which, from the point of view of the dominant class, is a costly yet relatively harmless burden to society. The discreditability of social junk resides in the failure, inability or refusal of this group to participate in the roles supportive of capitalist society. Social junk is most likely to come to official attention when informal resources have been exhausted or when the magnitude of the problem becomes significant enough to create a basis for "public concern." Since the threat presented by social junk is passive, growing out of its inability to compete and its withdrawal from the prevailing social order, controls are usually designed to regulate and contain rather than eliminate and suppress the problem. Clear-cut examples of social junk in modern capitalist societies might include the officially administered aged, handicapped, mentally ill and mentally retarded.

In contrast to social junk, there is a category that can be roughly described as *social dynamite*. The essential quality of deviance managed as social dynamite is its potential actively to call into question established relationships, especially relations of production and domination. Generally, therefore, social dynamite tends to be more youthful, alienated and politically volatile than social junk. The control of social dynamite is usually premised on an assumption that the problem is acute in nature, requiring a rapid, and focused expenditure of control resources. This is in contrast to the handling of social junk frequently based on a belief that the problem is chronic and best controlled through broad reactive, rather than intensive and selective measures. Correspondingly, social dynamite is normally processed through the legal system, with its capacity for active intervention, while social junk is frequently (but not always)[4] administered by the agencies and agents of the therapeutic and welfare state.

Many varieties of deviant populations are alternatively or simultaneously dealt with as either social junk and/or social dynamite. The welfare poor, homosexuals, alcoholics and "problem children" are among the categories reflecting the equivocal nature of the control process and its dependence on the political, economic and ideological priorities of deviance production. The changing nature of these priorities and their implications for the future may be best understood by examining some of the tendencies of modern capitalist systems.

⊛ Monopoly Capital and Deviance Production

Marx viewed capitalism as a system constantly transforming itself. He explained these changes in terms of certain tendencies and contradictions immanent within the capitalist mode of production. One of the most important processes identified by Marx was the tendency for the organic composition of capital to rise. Simply stated, capitalism requires increased productivity to survive, and increased productivity is only made possible by raising the ratio of machines (dead labor) to men (living labor). This tendency is self-reinforcing since, "the further machine production advances, the higher becomes the organic composition of capital needed for an entrepreneur to secure the average profit." (Mandel, 1968:163). This phenomenon helps us explain the course of capitalist development over the last century and the rise of monopoly capital (Baran and Sweezy, 1966).

For the purposes of this analysis there are at least two important consequences of this process. First, the growth of constant capital (machines and raw material) in the production process leads to an expansion in the overall size of the relative surplus-population. The reasons for this are obvious. The increasingly technological character of production removes more and more laborers from productive activity for longer periods of time. Thus, modern capitalist societies have been required progressively to reduce the number of productive years in a worker's life, defining both young and old as economically superfluous. Especially affected are the unskilled who become more and more expendable as capital expands.

In addition to affecting the general size of the relative surplus-population, the rise of the organic composition of capital leads to an increase in the relative stagnancy of that population. In Marx's original analysis he distinguished between forms of superfluous population that were floating and stagnant. The floating population consists of workers who are "sometimes repelled, sometimes attracted again in greater masses, the number of those employed increasing on the whole, although in a constantly decreasing proportion to the scale of production" (1967:641). From the point of view of capitalist accumulation the floating population offers the greatest economic flexibility and the fewest problems of social control because they are most effectively tied to capital by the "natural laws of production." Unfortunately (for the capitalists at least), these groups come to comprise a smaller and smaller proportion of the relative surplus-population. The increasing specialization of productive activity raises the cost of reproducing labor and heightens the demand for highly skilled and "internally controlled" forms of wage labor (Gorz, 1970). The process through which unskilled workers are alternatively absorbed and expelled from the labor force is thereby impaired, and the relative surplus-population comes to be made up of increasing numbers of persons who are more or less permanently redundant. The boundaries between the "useful" and the "useless" are more clearly delineated, while standards for social disqualification are more liberally defined.

With the growth of monopoly capital, therefore, the relative surplus-population begins to take on the character of a population which is more and more absolute. At the same time, the market becomes a less reliable means of disciplining these populations and the "invisible hand" is more frequently replaced by the "visible fist." The implications for deviance production are twofold: (1) problem populations become gradually more problematic—both in terms of their size and their insensitivity to economic controls, and (2) the resources of the state need to be applied in greater proportion to protect capitalist relations of production and insure the accumulation of capital.

❧ State Capitalism and New Forms of Control

The major problems faced by monopoly capitalism are surplus population and surplus production. Attempts to solve these problems have led to the creation of the welfare/warfare state (Baran and Sweezy, 1966; Marcuse, 1964; O'Connor, 1973; Gross, 1970). The warfare state attacks the problem of overconsumption by providing "wasteful" consumption and protection for the expansion of foreign markets. The welfare state helps absorb and deflect social expenses engendered by a redundant domestic population. Accordingly, the economic development of capitalist societies has come to depend increasingly on the support of the state.

The emergence of state capitalism and the growing interpenetration of the political and economic spheres have had a number of implications for the organization and administration of class rule. The most important effect of these trends is that control functions are increasingly transferred from the organs of civil society to the organs of political society (the state). As the maintenance of social harmony becomes more difficult and the contradictions of civil society intensify, the state is forced to take a more direct and extensive role in the management of problem populations. This is especially true to the extent that the primary socializing institutions in capitalist societies (e.g. the family and the church) can no longer be counted on to produce obedient and "productive" citizens.

Growing state intervention, especially intervention in the process of socialization, is likely to produce an emphasis on general-preventive (integrative), rather than selective-reactive (segregative) controls. Instead of waiting for troublemakers to surface and managing them through segregative techniques, the state is likely to focus more and more on generally applied incentives and assimilative controls. This shift is consistent with the growth of state capitalism because, on the one hand, it provides mechanisms and policies to nip disruptive influences "in the bud," and, on the other, it paves the way toward a more rational exploitation of human capital. Regarding the latter point, it is clear that effective social engineering depends more on social investment and anticipatory planning than coercive control, and societies may more profitably manage populations by viewing them as human capital, than as human waste. An investment orientation has long been popular in state socialist societies (Rimlinger, 1961, 1966), and its value, not surprisingly, has been increasingly acknowledged by many capitalist states.[5]

In addition to the advantages of integrative controls, segregative measures are likely to fall into disfavor for a more immediate reason—they are relatively costly to formulate and apply. Because of its fiscal problems the state must search for means of economizing control operations without jeopardizing capitalist expansion. Segregative handling, especially institutionalization, has been useful in manipulating and providing a receptacle for social junk and social dynamite. Nonetheless, the per capita cost of this type of management is typically quite high. Because of its continuing reliance on segregative controls the state is faced with a growing crisis—the overproduction of deviance. The magnitude of the problem and the inherent weaknesses of available approaches tend to limit the alternatives, but among those which are likely to be favored in the future are:

(1) *Normalization.* Perhaps the most expedient response to the overproduction of deviance is the normalization of populations traditionally managed as deviant. Normalization occurs when deviance processing is reduced in scope without supplying specific alternatives, and certain segments of the problem population are "swept under the rug." To be successful this strategy requires the creation of invisible deviants who can be easily absorbed into society and disappear from view.

A current example of this approach is found in the decarceration movement which has reduced the number of inmates in prisons (BOP, 1972) and mental hospitals (NIMH, 1970) over the last fifteen years. By curtailing commitments and increasing turn-over rates the state is able to limit the scale and increase the efficiency of institutionalization. If, however, direct release is likely to focus too much attention on the shortcomings of the state a number of intermediate solutions can be adopted. These include subsidies for private control arrangements (e.g., foster homes, old age homes) and decentralized control facilities (e.g. community treatment centers, halfway houses). In both cases, the fiscal burden of the state is reduced while the dangers of complete normalization are avoided.

(2) *Conversion.* To a certain extent the expenses generated by problem and deviant populations can be offset by encouraging their direct participation in the process of control. Potential troublemakers can be recruited as policemen, social workers and attendants, while confirmed deviants can be "rehabilitated" by becoming counselors, psychiatric aides and parole officers. In other words, if a large number of the controlled can be converted into a first line of defense, threats to the system of class rule can be transformed into resources for its support.[6]

(3) *Containment.* One means of responding to threatening populations without individualized manipulation is through a policy of containment or compartmentalization. This policy involves the geographic segregation of large populations and the use of formal and informal sanctions to circumscribe the challenges that they present. Instead of classifying and handling

problem populations in terms of the specific expenses that they create, these groups are loosely administered as a homogeneous class who can be ignored or managed passively as long as they remain in their place.

Strategies of containment have always flourished where social segregation exists, but they have become especially favored in modern capitalist societies. One reason for this is their compatibility with patterns of residential segregation, ghettoization, and internal colonialism (Blauner, 1969).

(4) *Support of Criminal Enterprise.* Another way the overproduction of deviance may be eased is by granting greater power and influence to organized crime. Although predatory criminal enterprise is assumed to stand in opposition to the goals of the state and the capitalist class, it performs valuable and unique functions in the service of class rule (McIntosh, 1973). By creating a parallel opportunity structure, organized crime provides a means of support for groups who might otherwise become a burden on the state. The activities of organized crime are also important in the pacification of problem populations. Organized crime provides goods and services which ease the hardships and deflect the energies of the underclass. In this role the "crime industry" performs a cooling-out function and offers a control resource which might otherwise not exist. Moreover, insofar as criminal enterprise attempts to reduce uncertainty and risk in its operations, it aids the state in the maintenance of public order. This is particularly true to the extent that the rationalization of criminal activity reduces the collateral costs (i.e. violence) associated with predatory crime (Schelling, 1967).

☻ Conclusion

A Marxian theory of deviance and control must overcome the weaknesses of both conventional interpretations and narrow critical models. It must offer a means of studying deviance which fully exploits the critical potential of Marxist scholarship. Mote than "demystifying" the analysis of deviance, such a theory must suggest directions and offer insights which can be utilized in the direct construction of critical theory. Although the discussion has been informed by concepts and evidence drawn from a range of Marxist studies, it has been more of a sensitizing essay than a substantive analysis. The further development of the theory must await the accumulation of evidence to refine our understanding of the relationships and tendencies explored. When this evidence is developed the contributions of Marxist thought can be more meaningfully applied to an understanding of deviance, class conflict and social control.

Endnotes

[1]For example, Turk (1969) defines deviance primarily in terms of the social position and relative power of various social groups.

[2]To the extent that a group (e.g. homosexuals) blatantly and systematically challenges the validity of the bourgeois family it is likely to become part of the problem population. The family is essential to capitalist society as a unit for consumption, socialization and the reproduction of the socially necessary labor force (cf. Frankford and Snitow, 1972; Secombe, 1973; Zaretsky, 1973).

[3]O'Connor (1973) discusses this problem in terms of the crisis faced by the capitalist state in maintaining conditions for profitable accumulation and social harmony.

[4]It has been estimated, for instance, that 1/3 of all arrests in America are for the offense of public drunkenness. Most of these apparently involve "sick" and destitute "skid row alcoholics" (Morris and Hawkins, 1969).

[5]Despite the general tendencies of state capitalism, its internal ideological contradictions may actually frustrate the adoption of an investment approach. For example, in discussing social welfare policy Rimlinger (1966:571) concludes that "in a country like the United States, which has a strong individualistic heritage, the idea is still alive that any kind of social protection has adverse productivity effects. A country like the Soviet Union, with a centrally planned economy and a collectivist ideology, is likely to make an earlier and more deliberate use of health and welfare programs for purposes of influencing productivity and developing manpower."

[6]In his analysis of the lumpenproletariat Marx (1964) clearly recognized how the underclass could be manipulated as a "bribed tool of reactionary intrigue."

References

Baran, Paul and Paul M. Sweezy. 1966. Monopoly Capital. New York: Monthly Review Press.

Becker, Howard S. 1967. "Whose side are we on?" Social Problems 14(Winter): 239–247.

Becker, Howard S., and Irving Louis Horowitz. 1972. "Radical politics and sociological research: observations on methodology and ideology." American Journal of Sociology 78(July):48–66.

Blauner, Robert. 1969. "Internal colonialism and ghetto revolt." Social Problems 16 (Spring): 393–408.

Bowles, Samuel. 1973. "Contradictions in United States higher education." Pp. 165–199 in James H. Weaver (ed.), Modern Political Economy: Radical Versus Orthodox Approaches. Boston: Allyn and Bacon.

Bowles, Samuel, and Herbert Gintis. 1972. "I.Q. in the U.S. class structure." Social Policy 3(November/December): 65–96.

Bureau of Prisons. 1972. National Prisoner Statistics. Prisoners in State and Federal Institutions for Adult Felons. Washington, D.C.: Bureau of Prisons.

Cohen, David K., and Marvin Lazerson. 1972. "Education and the corporate order." Socialist Revolution (March/April): 48–72.

Foucault, Michel. 1965. Madness and Civilization. New York: Random House.

Frankford, Evelyn, and Ann Snitow. 1972. "The trap of domesticity: notes on the family." Socialist Revolution (July/August): 83–94.

Gintis, Herbert. 1973. "Alienation and power." Pp. 431–465 in James H. Weaver (ed.), Modern Political Economy: Radical Versus Orthodox Approaches. Boston: Allyn and Bacon.

Gorz, Andre. 1970. "Capitalist relations of production and the socially necessary labor force." Pp. 155–171 in Arthur Lothstein (ed.), All We Are Saying. . . New York: G. P. Putnam.

Gross, Bertram M. 1970. "Friendly fascism: a model for America." Social Policy (November/December): 44–52.

Helmer, John, and Thomas Vietorisz. 1973. "Drug use, the labor market and class conflict." Paper presented at Annual Meeting of the American Sociological Association.

Karier, Clarence J. 1973. "Business values and the educational state." Pp. 6–29 in Clarence J. Karier, Paul Violas, and Joel Spring (eds.), Roots of Crisis: American Education in the Twentieth Century. Chicago: Rand McNally.

Liazos, Alexander. 1972. "The poverty of the sociology of deviance: nuts, sluts and preverts." Social Problems 20(Summer): 103–120.

Mandel, Ernest. 1968. Marxist Economic Theory (Volume I) . New York: Monthly Review Press.

Marcuse, Herbert. 1964. One-Dimensional Man. Boston: Beacon Press.

Marx, Karl. 1964 Class Struggles in France 1848–1850. New York: International Publishers.

———. 1967. Capital (Volume I). New York: International Publishers.

Matza, David. 1969. Becoming Deviant. Englewood Cliffs: Prentice Hall.

McIntosh, Mary. 1973. "The growth of racketeering." Economy and Society (February): 35–69.

Morris, Norval, and Gordon Hawkins. 1969. The Honest Politician's Guide to Crime Control. Chicago: University of Chicago Press.

Musto, David F. 1973. The American Disease: Origins of Narcotic Control. New Haven: Yale University Press.

National Institute of Mental Health. 1970. Trends in Resident Patients—State and County Mental Hospitals, 1950–1968. Biometry Branch, Office of Program Planning and Evaluation. Rockville, Maryland: National Institute of Mental Health.

O'Connor, James. 1973. The Fiscal Crisis of the State. New York: St. Martin's Press.

Piven, Frances, and Richard A. Cloward. 1971. Regulating the Poor: The Functions of Public Welfare. New York: Random House.

Rimlinger, Gaston V. 1961. "Social security, incentives, and controls in the U.S. and U.S.S.R." Comparative Studies in Society and History 4 (November): 104–124.

_____. 1966. "Welfare policy and economic development: a comparative historical perspective." Journal of Economic History (December): 556–571.

Schelling, Thomas. 1967. "Economics and criminal enterprise." Public Interest (Spring): 61–78.

Secombe, Wally. 1973. "The housewife and her labour under capitalism." New Left Review (January-February): 3–24.

Spring, Joel. 1972. Education and the Rise of the Corporate State. Boston: Beacon Press.

_____. 1973. "Education as a form of social control." Pp. 30–39 in Clarence J. Karier, Paul Violas, and Joel Spring (eds.), Roots of Crisis: American Education in the Twentieth Century. Chicago: Rand McNally.

Turk, Austin T. 1969. Criminality and Legal Order. Chicago: Rand McNally and Company.

Zaretsky, Eli. 1973. "Capitalism, the family and personal life: parts 1 & 2." Socialist Revolution (January-April/May-June): 69–126, 19–70.

◉ ◉ ◉

Questions

1. Define "problem populations." How would you characterize this group?

2. What two ways are problem populations generated in a capitalist system? Is there any relationship between these two methods? If so, explain.

3. What influences whether a problem population is classified, and subsequently treated, as deviant?

4. What are the similarities and differences between "social junk" and "social dynamite"?

5. What might influence whether a group is classified as social junk as opposed to social dynamite?

Social Structure and Anomie

ROBERT K. MERTON
Harvard University

This classic article by Robert Merton explains the role of social structure in generating anomie, or a sense of lawlessness and alienation, within individuals. Merton also discusses the intersection between one's adoption (or not) of culturally prescribed goals and one's adoption (or not) of accepted means of achieving those goals. Merton's resulting framework identifies particular responses to stress and anomie, including conformity, innovation, ritualism, retreatism, and rebellion.

There persists a notable tendency in sociology theory to attribute the malfunctioning of social structure primarily to those of man's imperious biological drives which are not adequately restrained by social control. In this view, the social order is solely a device for "impulse management" and the "social processing" of tensions. These impulses which break through social control, be it noted, are held to be biologically derived. Nonconformity is assumed to be rooted in original nature.[1] Conformity is by implication the result of an utilitarian calculus or unreasoned conditioning. This point of view, whatever its other deficiencies, clearly begs one question. It provides no basis for determining the nonbiological conditions which induce deviations from prescribed patterns of conduct. In this paper, it will be suggested that certain phases of social structure generate the circumstances in which infringement of social codes constitutes a "normal" response.[2]

The conceptual scheme to be outlined is designed to provide a coherent, systematic approach to the study of socio-cultural sources of deviate behavior. Our primary aim lies in discovering how some social structures *exert a definite pressure* upon certain persons in the society to engage in nonconformist rather than conformist conduct. The many ramifications of

---

"Social Structure and Anomie," by Robert Merton, reprinted from *American Sociological Review*, vol. 3, 1938, pp. 672–682.

the scheme cannot all be discussed; the problems mentioned outnumber those explicitly treated.

Among the elements of social and cultural structure, two are important for our purposes. These are analytically separable although they merge imperceptibly in concrete situations. The first consists of culturally defined goals, purposes, and interests. It comprises a frame of aspirational reference. These goals are more or less integrated and involve varying degrees of prestige and sentiment. They constitute a basic, but not the exclusive, component of what Linton aptly has called "designs for group living." Some of these cultural aspirations are related to the original drives of man, but they are not determined by them. The second phase of the social structure defines, regulates, and controls the acceptable modes of achieving these goals. Every social group invariably couples its scale of desired ends with moral or institutional regulation of permissible and required procedures for attaining these ends. These regulatory norms and moral imperatives do not necessarily coincide with technical or efficiency norms. Many procedures which from the standpoint of *particular individuals* would be most efficient in securing desired values, e.g., illicit oil-stock schemes, theft, fraud, are ruled out of the institutional area of permitted conduct. The choice of expedients is limited by the institutional norms.

To say that these elements, culture goals and institutional norms, operate jointly is not to say that the ranges of alternative behaviors and aims bear some constant relation to one another. The emphasis upon certain goals may vary independently of the degree of emphasis upon institutional means. There may develop a disproportionate, at times, a virtually exclusive, stress upon the value of specific goals, involving relatively slight concern with the institutionally appropriate modes of attaining these goals. The limiting case in this direction is reached when the range of alternative procedures is limited only by technical rather than institutional considerations. Any and all devices which promise attainment of the all important goal would be permitted in this hypothetical polar case.[3] This constitutes one types of cultural malintegration. A second polar type is found in groups where activities originally conceived as instrumental are transmuted into ends in themselves. The original purposes are forgotten and ritualistic adherence to institutionally prescribed conduct becomes virtually obsessive.[4] Stability is largely ensured while change is flouted. The range of alternative behaviors is severely limited. There develops a tradition-bound, sacred society characterized by neophobia. The occupational psychosis of the bureaucrat may be cited as a case in point. Finally, there are the intermediate types of groups where a balance between culture goals and institutional means is maintained. These are the significantly integrated and relatively stable, though changing, groups.

An effective equilibrium between the two phases of the social structure is maintained as long as satisfactions accrue to individuals who conform to both constraints, viz., satisfactions from the achievement of the goals and satisfactions emerging directly from the institutionally canalized modes of striving to attain these ends. Success, in such equilibrated cases, is twofold. Success is reckoned in terms of the product and in terms of the process, in terms of the outcome and in terms of activities. Continuing satisfactions must derive from sheer *participation* in a competitive order as well as from eclipsing one's competitors if the order itself is to be sustained. The occasional sacrifices involved in institutionalized conduct must be compensated by socialized rewards. The distribution of statuses and roles through competition must be so organized that positive incentives for conformity to roles and adherence to status obligations are provided *for every position* within the distributive order. Aberrant conduct, therefore, may be viewed as a symptom of dissociation between culturally defined aspirations and socially structured means.

Of the types of groups which result from the independent variation of the two phases of the social structure, we shall be primarily concerned with the first, namely, that involving a disproportionate accent on goals. This statement must be recast in a proper perspective. In no group is there an absence of regulatory codes governing conduct, yet groups do vary in the degree to which these folkways, mores, and institutional controls are effectively integrated with the more diffuse goals which are part of the culture matrix. Emotional convictions may cluster about the complex of socially acclaimed ends, meanwhile shifting their support from the culturally defined implementation of these ends. As we shall see, certain aspects of the social structure may generate countermores and antisocial behavior precisely because of different emphases on goals and regulations. In the extreme case, the latter may be so vitiated by the goal emphasis that the range of behavior is limited only by considerations of technical expediency. The sole significant question then becomes, which available means is most efficient in netting the socially approved value.[5] The technically most feasible procedure, whether legitimate or not, is preferred to the institutionally prescribed conduct. As this process continues, the integration of the society becomes tenuous and anomie ensues.

Thus, in competitive athletics, when the aim of victory is shorn of its institutional trappings and success in contests becomes construed as "winning the game" rather than "winning through circumscribed modes of activity," a premium is implicitly set upon the use of illegitimate but technically efficient means. The star of the opposing football team is surreptitiously slugged; the wrestler furtively incapacitates his opponent through ingenious but illicit techniques; university alumni covertly subsidize "students" whose talents are largely confined to the athletic field. The emphasis on the goal has so attenuated the satisfactions deriving from sheer participation in the competitive activity that these satisfactions are virtually confined to a successful outcome. Through the same process, tension generated by the desire to win in a poker game is relieved by successfully dealing oneself four aces, or, when the cult of success has become completely dominant, by sagaciously shuffling the cards in a game of solitaire. The faint twinge of uneasiness in the last instance and the surreptious nature of public delicts indicate clearly that the institutional rules of the game *are known* to those who evade them, but that the emotional supports of these rules are largely' vitiated by cultural exaggeration of the success goal.[6] They are microcosmic images of the social macrocosm.

Of course, this process is not restricted to the realm of sport. The process whereby exaltation of the end generates a *literal demoralization,* i.e., a deinstitutionalization, of the means is one which characterizes many[7] groups in which the two phases of the social structure are not highly integrated. The extreme emphasis upon the accumulation of wealth as a symbol of success[8] in our own society militates against the completely effective control of institutionally regulated modes of acquiring a fortune.[9] Fraud, corruption, vice, crime, in short, the entire catalogue of proscribed behavior, becomes increasingly common when the emphasis on the *culturally induced* success goal becomes divorced from a coordinated institutional emphasis. This observation of crucial theoretical importance in examining the doctrine that antisocial behavior most frequently derives from biological drives breaking through the restraints imposed by society. The difference is one between a strictly utilitarian interpretation which conceives man's ends as random and an analysis which finds these ends deriving from the basic values of the culture.[10]

Our analysis can scarcely stop at this juncture. We must turn to other aspects of the social structure if we are to deal with the social genesis of the varying rates and types of deviate behavior characteristic of different societies. Thus far, we have sketched three ideal types of social orders constituted by distinctive patterns of relations between cultural ends and means. Turning from these types of *culture patterning,* we find five logically possible, alternative modes of adjustment or adaptation *by individuals* within the culture-bearing society or groups.[11] These are schematically presented in the following table, where (+) signifies "acceptance," (-) signifies "elimination" and (±) signifies "rejection and substitution of new goals and standards."

		Culture and Goals	Institutionalized Means
I.	Conformity	+	+
II.	Innovation	+	-
III.	Ritualism	-	+
IV.	Retreatism	-	-
V.	Rebellion[12]	±	±

Our discussion of the relation between these alternative responses and other phases of the social structure must be prefaced by the observation that persons may shift from one alternative to another as they engage in different social activities. These categories refer to role adjustments in specific situations, not to personality *in toto.* To treat the development of this process in various spheres of conduct would introduce a complexity unmanageable within the confines of this paper. For this reason, we shall be concerned primarily with economic activity in the broad sense, "the production, exchange, distribution and consumption of goods and services" in our competitive society, wherein wealth has taken on a highly symbolic cast. Our task is to search out some of the factors which exert pressure upon individuals to engage in certain of these logically possible alternative responses. This choice, as we shall see, is far from random.

In every society, Adaptation I (conformity to both culture goals and means) is the most common and widely diffused. Were this not so, the stability and continuity of society could not be maintained. The mesh of expectancies which constitutes every social order is sustained by the modal behavior of its members falling within the first category. Conventional role behavior oriented toward the basic values of the group is the rule rather than the exception. It is this fact alone which permits us to speak of a human aggregate as comprising a group or society.

Conversely, Adaptation IV (rejection of goals and means) is the least common. Persons who "adjust" (or maladjust) in this fashion are, strictly speaking, *in* the society if not *of* it. Sociologically, these constitute the true "aliens." Not sharing the common frame of orientation, they can be included within the societal population merely in a fictional sense. In this category are *some* of the activities of psychotics, psychoneurotics, chronic autists, pariahs, outcasts, vagrants, vagabonds, tramps, chronic drunkards and drug addicts.[13] These have relinquished, in certain spheres of activity, the culturally defined goals, involving complete aim-inhibition in the polar case, and their adjustments are not in accord with institutional norms. This is not to say that in some cases the source of their behavioral adjustments is not in part the very social structure which they have in effect repudiated nor that their very existence within a social area does not constitute a problem for the socialized population.

This mode of "adjustment" occurs, as far as structural sources are concerned, when both the culture goals and institutionalized procedures have been assimilated thoroughly by the individual and imbued with affect and high positive value, but where those institutionalized procedures which promise a measure of successful attainment of the goals are not available to the individual. In such instances, there results a twofold mental conflict insofar as the moral obligation for adopting institutional means conflicts with the pressure to resort to illegitimate means (which may attain the goal) and inasmuch as the individual is shut off from means which are both legitimate *and* effective. The competitive order is maintained, but the frustrated and handicapped individual who cannot cope with this order drops out. Defeatism, quietism and resignation are manifested in escape mechanisms which ultimately lead the individual to "escape" from the requirements of the society. It is an expedient which arises from continued failure to attain the goal by legitimate measures and from an inability to adopt the illegitimate route because of internalized prohibitions and institutionalized compulsives, *during which process the supreme value of the success-goal has as yet not been renounced.* The conflict is resolved by eliminating *both* precipitating elements, the goals and means. The escape is complete, the conflict is eliminated and the individual is a-socialized.

Be it noted that where frustration derives from the inaccessibility of effective institutional means for attaining economic or any other type of highly valued "success," that Adaptations II, III, and V (innovation, ritualism and rebellion) are also possible. The result will be determined by the particular personality, and thus, the *particular* cultural background, involved. Inadequate socialization will result in the innovation response whereby the conflict and frustration are eliminated by relinquishing the institutional means and retaining the success-aspiration; an extreme assimilation of institutional demands will lead to ritualism wherein the goal is dropped as beyond one's reach but conformity to the mores persists; and rebellion occurs when emancipation from the reigning standards, due to frustration or to marginalist perspectives, leads to the attempt to introduce a "new social order."

Our major concern is with the illegitimacy adjustment. This involves the use of conventionally proscribed but frequently effective means of attaining at least the simulacrum of culturally defined success—wealth, power, and the like. As we have seen, this adjustment occurs when the individual has assimilated the cultural emphasis on success without equally internalizing the morally prescribed norms governing means for its attainment. The question arises, While phases of our social structure predispose toward this mode of adjustment? We may examine a concrete instance, effectively analyzed by Lohman,[14] which provides a clue to the answer. Lohman has shown that specialized areas of vice in the near north side of Chicago constitute a "normal" response to a situation where the cultural emphasis upon pecuniary success has been absorbed, but where there is little access to conventional and legitimate means for attaining such success. The conventional occupational opportunities of persons in this area are almost completely limited to manual labor. Given our cultural stigmatization of manual labor, and its correlate, the prestige of white collar work, it is clear that the result is a strain toward innovational practices. The limitation of opportunity to unskilled labor and the resultant low income can not compete *in terms of conventional standards of achievement* with the high income from organized vice.

For our purposes, this situation involves two important features. First, such antisocial behavior is in a sense "called forth" by certain conventional values of the culture *and* by the class structure involving differential access to the approved opportunities for legitimate, prestige-bearing pursuit of the culture goals. The lack of high integration between the means-and-end elements of the cultural pattern and the particular class structure combine to favor a heightened frequency of antisocial conduct in such groups. The second consideration is of equal significance. Recourse to the first of the alternative responses, legitimate effort, is limited by the fact that actual advance toward desired success-symbols through conventional channels is, despite our persisting open-class ideology,[15] relatively rare and difficult for those handicapped by little formal education and few economic resources. The dominant pressure of group standards of success is, therefore, on the gradual attenuation of legitimate, but by and large ineffective, strivings and the increasing use of illegitimate, but more or less effective, expedients of vice and crime. The culture demands made on persons in this situation are incompatible. On the one hand, they are asked to orient their conduct toward the prospect of accumulating wealth and on the other, they are largely denied effective opportunities to do so institutionally. The consequences of such structural inconsistency are psychopathological personality, and/or antisocial conduct, and/or revolutionary activities. The equilibrium between culturally designated means and ends becomes highly unstable with the progressive emphasis on attaining the prestige-laden ends by any means whatsoever. Within this context, Capone represents the triumph of amoral intelligence over morally prescribed "failure," when the channels of vertical mobility are closed or narrowed[16] *in a society which places a high premium on economic affluence and social ascent for all its members.*[17]

This last qualification is of primary importance. It suggests that other phases of the social structure besides the extreme emphasis on pecuniary success, must be considered if we are to understand the social sources of antisocial behavior. A high frequency of deviate behavior is not generated simply by "lack of opportunity" or by this exaggerated pecuniary emphasis. A comparatively rigidified class structure, a feudalistic or caste order, may limit such opportunities far beyond the point which obtains in our society today. It is only when a system of cultural values extols, virtually above all else, certain *common* symbols of success *for the population at large* while its social structure rigorously restricts or completely eliminates access to approved modes of acquiring these symbols *for a considerable part of the same population,* that antisocial behavior ensues on a considerable scale. In other words, our egalitarian ideology denies by implication the existence of noncompeting groups and individuals in the pursuit of pecuniary success. The same body of success-symbols is held to be desirable for all. These goals are held to *transcend class lines,* not to be bounded by them, yet the actual social organization is such that there exist class differentials in the accessibility of these *common* success-symbols. Frustration and thwarted aspiration lead to the search for avenues of escape from a culturally induced intolerable situation; or unrelieved ambition may eventuate in illicit attempts to acquire the dominant values.[18] The American stress on pecuniary success and ambitiousness for all thus invites exaggerated anxieties, hostilities, neuroses and antisocial behavior.

This theoretical analysis may go far toward explaining the varying correlations between crime and poverty.[19] Poverty is not an isolated variable. It is one in a complex of interdependent social and cultural variables. When viewed in such a context, it represents quite different states of affairs. Poverty as such, and consequent limitations of opportunity, are not sufficient to induce a conspicuously high rate of criminal behavior. Even the often mentioned "poverty in the midst of plenty" will not necessarily lead to this result. Only insofar as poverty and associated disadvantages in competition for the culture values approved for *all* members of the society is linked with the assimilation of a cultural emphasis on monetary accumulation as a symbol of success is antisocial conduct a "normal" outcome. Thus, poverty is less highly correlated with crime in southeastern Europe than in the United States. The possibilities of vertical mobility in these European areas would seem to be fewer than in this country, so that neither poverty *per se* nor its association with limited opportunity is sufficient to account for the varying correlations. It is only when the full configuration is considered, poverty, limited opportunity and a commonly shared system of success symbols, that we can explain the higher association between poverty and crime in our society than in others where rigidified class structure is coupled with *differential class symbols of achievement.*

In societies such as our own, then, the pressure of prestige-bearing success tends to eliminate the effective social constraint over means employed to this end. "The-end-justifies-the-means" doctrine becomes a guiding tenet for action when the cultural structure unduly exalts the end and the social organization unduly limits possible recourse to approved means. Otherwise put, this notion and associated behavior reflect a lack of cultural coordination. In international relations, the effects of this lack of integration are notoriously apparent. An emphasis upon national power is not readily coordinated with an inept organization of legitimate, i.e., internationally defined and accepted, means for attaining this goal. The result is a tendency toward the abrogation of international law, treaties become scraps of paper, "undeclared warfare" serves as a technical evasion, the bombing of civilian populations is rationalized,[20] just as the same societal situation induces the same sway of illegitimacy among individuals.

The social order we have described necessarily produces this "strain toward dissolution." The pressure of such an order is upon outdoing one's competitors. The choice of means within the ambit of institutional control will persist as long as the sentiments supporting a competitive system, i.e., deriving from the possibility of outranking competitors and hence enjoying the favorable response of others, are distributed throughout the entire system of activities and are not confined merely to the final result. A stable social structure demands a balanced distribution of affect among its various segments. When there occurs a shift of emphasis from the satisfactions deriving from competition itself to almost exclusive concern with successful competition, the resultant stress leads to the breakdown of the regulatory structure.[21] With the resulting attenuation of the institutional imperatives, there occurs an approximation of the situation erroneously held by utilitarians to be typical of society generally wherein calculations of advantage and fear of punishment are the sole regulating agencies. In such situations, as Hobbes observed, force and fraud come to constitute the sole virtues in view of their relative efficiency in attaining goals,—which were for him, of course, not culturally derived.

It should be apparent that the foregoing discussion is not pitched on a moralistic plane. Whatever the sentiments of the writer or reader concerning the ethical desirability of coordinating the means and goals phases of the social structure, one must agree that lack of such coordination leads to anomie. Insofar as one of the most general functions of social organization is to provide a basis for calculability and regularity of behavior, it is increasingly limited in effectiveness as these elements of the structure become dissociated. At the extreme, predictability virtually disappears and what may be properly termed cultural chaos or anomie intervenes.

The statement, being brief, is also incomplete. It has not included an exhaustive treatment of the various structural elements which predispose toward one rather than another of the alternative responses open to individuals; it has neglected, but not denied the relevance of, the factors determining the specific incidence of these responses; it has not enumerated the various concrete responses which are constituted by combinations of specific values of the analytical variables; it has omitted, or included only by implication, any consideration of the social functions performed by illicit responses; it has not tested the full explanatory power of the analytical scheme by examining a large number of group variations in the frequency of deviate and conformist behavior; it has not adequately dealt with rebellious conduct which seeks to refashion the social framework radically; it has not examined the relevance of cultural conflict for an analysis of culture-goal and institutional-means malintegration. It is suggested that these and related problems may be profitably analyzed by this scheme.

*S*ndnotes

[1] E.g., Ernest Jones, *Social Aspects of Psychoanalysis,* 28, London, 1924. If the Freudian notion is a variety of the "original sin" dogma, then the interpretation advanced in this paper may be called the doctrine of "socially derived sin."

[2] "Normal" in the sense of a culturally oriented, if not approved, response. This statement does not deny the relevance of biological and personality differences which may be significantly involved in the *incidence* of deviate conduct. Our focus of interest is the social and cultural matrix; hence we abstract from other factors. It is in this sense, I take it, that James S. Plant speaks of the "normal reaction of normal people to abnormal conditions." See his *Personality and the Cultural Pattern,* 248, New York, 1937.

[3] Contemporary American culture has been said to tend in this direction. See André Siegfried, *America Comes of Age,* 26–37, New York, 1927. The alleged extreme(?) emphasis on the goals of monetary success and material prosperity leads to dominant concern with technological and social instruments designed to produce the desired result, inasmuch as institutional controls become of secondary importance. In such a situation, innovation flourishes as the *range of means* employed is broadened. In a sense, then, there occurs the paradoxical emergence of "materialists" from an "idealistic" orientation. Cf. Durkheim's analysis of the cultural conditions which predispose toward crime and innovation, both of which are aimed toward efficiency, not moral norms. Durkheim was one of the first to see that "contrairement aux idées courantes le criminel n'apparait plus comme un être radicalement insociable, comme une sorte d'elément parasitaire, de corps étranger et inassimilable, introduit au sein de la société; c'est un agent régulier de la vie sociale." See *Les Régles de la Méthode Sociologique,* 86–89, Paris, 1927.

[4] Such ritualism may be associated with a mythology which rationalizes these actions so that they appear to retain their status as means, but the dominant pressure is in the direction of strict ritualistic conformity, irrespective of such rationalizations. In this sense, ritual has proceeded farthest when such rationalizations are not even called forth.

[5]In this connection, one may see the relevance of Elton Mayo's paraphrase of the title of Tawney's well known book. "Actually the problem is *not that of the sickness of an acquisitive society; it is that of the acquisitiveness of a sick society.*" *Human Problems of an Industrial Civilization*, 153, New York, 1933. Mayo deals with the process through which wealth comes to be a symbol of social achievement. He sees this as arising from a state of anomie. We are considering the unintegrated monetary-success goal as an element in producing anomie. A complete analysis would involve both phases of this system of interdependent variables.

[6]It is unlikely that interiorized norms are completely eliminated. Whatever residuum persists will induce personality tensions and conflict. The process involves a certain degree of ambivalence. A manifest rejection of the institutional norms is coupled with some latent retention of their emotional correlates. "Guilt feelings," "sense of sin," "pangs of conscience" are obvious manifestations of this unrelieved tension; symbolic adherence to the nominally repudiated values or rationalizations constitute a more subtle variety of tensional release.

[7]"Many," and not all, unintegrated groups, for the reason already mentioned. In groups where the primary emphasis shifts to institutional means, i.e., when the range of alternatives is very limited, the outcome is a type of ritualism rather than anomie.

[8]Money has several peculiarities which render it particularly apt to become a symbol of prestige divorced from institutional controls. As Simmel emphasized, money is highly abstract and impersonal. However acquired, through fraud or institutionally, it can be used to purchase the same goods and services. The anonymity of metropolitan culture, in conjunction with this peculiarity of money, permits wealth, the sources of which may be unknown to the community in which the plutocrat lives, to serve as a symbol of status.

[9]The emphasis upon wealth as a success symbol is possibly reflected in the use of the term "fortune" to refer to a stock of accumulated wealth. This meaning becomes common in the late sixteenth century (Spenser and Shakespeare). A similar usage of the Latin *fortuna* comes into prominence during the first century B.C. Both these periods were marked by the rise to prestige and power of the "bourgeosie."

[10]See Kingsley Davis, "Mental Hygiene and the Class Structure," *Psychiatry*, 1928, 1, esp. 62–63; Talcott Parsons, *The Structure of Social Action*, 59–60, New York, 1937.

[11]This is a level intermediate between the two planes distinguished by Edward Sapir, namely, culture patterns and personal habit systems. See his "Contribution of Psychiatry to an Understanding of Behavior in Society," *Amer. J. Sociol.*, 1937 42:862–70.

[12]This fifth alternative is on a plane clearly different from that of the others. It represents a *transitional* response which seeks to *institutionalize* new procedures oriented toward revamped cultural goals shared by the members of the society. It thus involves efforts to *change* the existing structure rather than to perform accomodative actions *within* this structure, and introduces additional problems with which we are not at the moment concerned.

[13]Obviously, this is an elliptical statement. These individuals may maintain some orientation to the values of their particular differentiated groupings within the larger society or, in part, of the conventional society itself. Insofar as they do so, their conduct cannot be classified in the "passive rejection" category (IV). Nels Anderson's description of the behavior and attitudes of the bum, for example, can readily be recast in terms of our analytical scheme. See *The Hobo,* 93–98, *et passim,* Chicago, 1923.

[14]Joseph D. Lohman, "The Participant Observer in Community Studies," *Amer. Sociol. Rev.,* 1937, 2:890–98.

[15]The shifting historical role of this ideology is a profitable subject for exploration. The "office-boy-to-president" stereotype was once in approximate accord with the facts. Such vertical mobility was probably more common then than now, when the class structure is more rigid. (See the following note.) The ideology largely persists, however, possibly because it still performs a useful function for maintaining the *status quo.* For insofar as it is accepted by the "masses," it constitutes a useful sop for those who might rebel against the entire structure, were this consoling hope removed. This ideology now serves to lessen the probability of Adaptation V. In short, the role of this notion has changed from that of an approximately valid empirical theorem to that of an ideology, in Mannheim's sense.

[16]There is a growing body of evidence, though none of it is clearly conclusive, to the effect that our class structure is becoming rigidified and that vertical mobility is declining. Taussig and Joslyn found that American business leaders are being *increasingly* recruited from the upper ranks of our society. The Lynds have also found a "diminished chance to get ahead" for the working classes in Middletown. Manifestly, these objective changes are not alone significant; the individual's subjective evaluation of the situation is a major determinant of the response. The extent to which this change in opportunity for social mobility has been recognized by the least advantaged classes is still conjectural, although the Lynds present some suggestive materials. The writer suggests that a case in point is the increasing frequency of cartoons which observe in a tragi-comic vein that "my old man says everybody can't be President. He says if ya can get three days a week steady on W.P.A. work ya ain't doin' so bad either." See F.

W. Taussig and C. S. Joslyn, *American Business Leaders,* New York, 1932; R. S. and H. M. Lynd, *Middletown in Transition,* 67 ff., chap. 12, New York 1937.

[17]The role of the Negro in this respect is of considerable theoretical interest. Certain elements of the Negro population have assimilated the dominant caste's values of pecuniary success and social advancement, but they also recognize that social ascent is at present restricted to their own caste almost exclusively. The pressures upon the Negro which would otherwise derive from the structural inconsistencies we have noticed are hence not identical with those upon lower-class whites. See Kingsley Davis, *op cit.,* 63; John Dollard, *Caste and Class in a Southern Town,* 66 ff., New Haven, 1936; Donald Young, *American Minority People,* 581, New York, 1932.

[18]The psychical coordinates of these processes have been partly established by the experimental evidence concerning *Aspruchsniveaus* and levels of performance. See Kurt Lewin, Vorsatz, Wille and Bedurfnis, Berlin, 1926; N. F. Hoppe, "Erfolg und Misserfolg," *Psychol. Forschung,* 1930, 14:1–63; Jerome D. Frank, "Individual Differences in Certain Aspects of the Level of Aspiration," *Amer. J. Psychol,* 1935, 47:119–28.

[19]Standard criminology texts summarize the data in this field. Our scheme of analysis may serve to resolve some of the theoretical contradictions which P. A. Sorokin indicates. For example, "not everywhere nor always do the poor show a greater proportion of crime . . . many poorer countries have had less crime than the richer countries. . . . The [economic] improvement in the second half of the nineteenth century, and the beginning of the twentieth, has not been followed by a decrease of crime." See his *Contemporary Sociological Theories* 560–61, New York, 1928. The crucial point is, however, that poverty has varying social significance in different social structures, as we shall see. Hence, one would not expect a linear correlation between crime and poverty.

[20]See M. W. Royce, *Aerial Bombardment and the International Regulation of War,* New York, 1928.

[21]Since our primary concern is with the socio-cultural aspects of this problem, the psychological correlates have been only implicitly considered. See Karen Horney, *The Neurotic Personality of Our Time,* New York, 1937, for a psychological discussion of this process.

◉ ◉ ◉

Questions

1. How is the intersection between goals and means relevant for generating deviant behavior?

2. How might you extend Merton's athletics analogy (that is, winning is the goal and "by all means necessary" is the strategy) to explain deviant behavior? Cite examples from the world of sport that fit each of Merton's five categories.

3. According to Merton, which of the following would have the greatest effect on the generation of deviant behavior: highly placed goals that may be unreasonable or unattainable *or* structurally blocked access to legitimate means of achieving the goals? Explain your reasoning.

4. Which type of deviant behavior does Merton's theoretical framework best describe? Does his theory work better for some subgroups than others? If so, which group's deviant behavior does the theory best explain?

5. To what degree does Merton's framework reflect society's motto of "by whatever means necessary" to achieve specific goals? With what type of behavior or action might you typically associate this statement?

Feminist Theory, Crime, and Justice

SALLY S. SIMPSON
University of Maryland

This article overviews the feminist perspective as applied to the study of criminal behavior. The feminist perspective is not a single theory but rather a collection of viewpoints on gender inequality and oppression, including liberal, socialist, and radical perspectives. The author, Sally Simpson, summarizes these viewpoints and applies them to key issues in criminology, including the study of female offenders, female victims, and females in the criminal justice system.

◉ "Why Can't a Woman be More Like a Man?"

One is tempted to respond to Henry Higgins's familiar lament with a cynical observation: criminological theory assumes a woman is like a man. As many feminist-criminologists have noted (early critics include Heidensohn, 1968; Klein, 1973; and Smart, 1976), most middle-range and macro theories of crime generously assume that what is true for the gander is true for the goose (see also Harris, 1977). As tempting as this simple assertion might be, however, a closer inspection reveals a more complicated picture.

Some feminist critics (Daly and Chesney-Lind, 1988) suggest that criminology, like other social sciences, is androcentric, that is, study of crime and the justice process is shaped by male experiences and understandings of the social world. Such studies/realities form the core of "general" theories of crime/deviance without taking female experience, as crime participant or victim, into account:

"Feminist Theory, Crime, and Justice," by Sally S. Simpson, reprinted from *Criminology*, vol. 27, no. 4, 1989, pp. 605–631.

[Men] create the world from their own point of view, which then becomes the truth to be described . . . Power to create the world from one's point of view is power in its male form (MacKinnon, 1982:23).

Not all criminological research has ignored women, but all too often, pre1970s research on female offenders and victims of crime fell prey to unreflecting sexism and, in its more extreme form, misogyny. Females who deviated from expected roles were viewed as morally corrupt, hysterical, diseased, manipulative, and devious (Glueck and Glueck, 1934). Law-violating and -conforming behaviors were believed to stem from the same etiological source—the female nature (Edwards, 1985; Klein, 1973).[1] A woman, it seemed—whether good or bad—could never be like a man.

These observations are not new, but they reflect a different voice, a feminist voice, that has been added to the criminological discourse. The purpose of this review essay is to introduce feminist criminology and its intellectual parent, feminism, to the uninitiated reader. It would be presumptuous to suggest that all relevant studies and arguments about gender and crime are included here. Such an extensive review is more appropriate for a book, and depending on the topic, it has likely already been done and done well (e.g., Eaton, 1986; Freedman, 1981; Heidensohn, 1985; Mann, 1984; Naffine, 1988; Smart, 1976). Instead, illustrative examples of different types of feminist thinking are presented to show how feminism has reframed our points of reference, underlying assumptions, and understandings about crime, victimization, and the justice process.

To achieve these aims, the paper is organized into three sections. First, the perspectives and methods that constitute feminist analysis are sorted and differentiated. Second, three areas of criminological study (the female offender, female victim, and criminal justice processing) are discussed because they are key areas in which feminist approaches have been incorporated. Third, directions for further integration are suggested.

❧ Feminism: Perspectives and Methods

Feminism is best understood as both a world view and a social movement that encompasses assumptions and beliefs about the origins and conse-quences of gendered social organization as well as strategic directions and actions for social change. As such, feminism is both analytical and empirical. In its incipient form, feminist research almost exclusively focused on women—as a way of placing women at the center of inquiry and building a base of knowledge. As it has matured, feminism has become more encompassing, taking into account the gendered understanding of all aspects of human culture and relationships (Stacey and Thorne, 1985:305).

It would be a mistake, however, to think of feminism as a single theory. Feminism has expanded into a diverse set of perspectives and agendas, each based on different definitions of the "problem," competing conceptions of the origins and mechanisms of gender inequality/oppression, and divergent strategies for its eradication. Collectively, these perspectives share a concern with identifying and representing women's interests, interests judged to be insufficiently represented and accommodated within the mainstream (Oakley, 1981:335).

Liberal Feminism

Liberal feminism was conceived within a liberal-bourgeois tradition that called for women's equality of opportunity and freedom of choice (Eisenstein, 1981). For the most part, liberal feminists see gender inequality[2] emerging from the creation of separate and distinct spheres of influence and traditional attitudes about the appropriate role of men and women in society (Pateman, 1987). Such attitudes are reinforced by discrimination against women in education, the work place, politics, and other public arenas.

Liberals do not believe the system to be inherently unequal; discrimination is not systemic. Rather, men and women can work together to "androgynize" gender roles (i.e., blend male and female traits and characteristics; Bem, 1974) and eliminate outdated policies and practices that discriminate against women. Affirmative action, the equal rights amendment, and other equal opportunity laws/policies are advocated as redistributive measures until a meritocratic gender restructuring of society occurs.

Socialist Feminism

For socialists, gender oppression is an obvious feature of capitalist societies. Depending on whether one is a socialist woman (Marxist-feminist) or a socialist-feminist, however, the weight that one gives to capitalism as a necessary and/or sufficient cause of that oppression will vary (Eisenstein, 1979). If one is the former, gender (and race) oppression is seen as secondary to and reflective of class oppression.

Socialist-feminists attempt a synthesis between two systems of domination, class and patriarchy (male supremacy). Both relations of production and reproduction are structured by capitalist patriarchy (Beauvoir, 1960; Hartmann, 1979; Mitchell, 1971). Gender difference, as a defining characteristic of power and privilege in a capitalist society can only be attacked by constructing a completely different society, one that is free of gender and class stratification (Oakley, 1981).

Radical Feminism

The origins of patriarchy, and the subordination of women therein, are seen by radical feminists to rest in male aggression and control of women's sexuality. Men are inherently more aggressive than women, who, because of their relative size disadvantages and dependency on men during child-bearing years, are easy to dominate and control. The arguments of radical feminists (e.g., Atkinson, 1974; Barry, 1979; Firestone, 1970; Rich, 1980) bring sexuality to the analytical fore. The "personal" is "political" (Millett, 1971). Sex not gender is the crucial analytical category; male domination, not class, is the fundamental origin of female subordination. Radical feminists' political and social agendas encompass lesbian separatism (Atkinson, 1984) and technological control of reproduction (Firestone, 1970).

Women of Color

In her eloquent "Ain't I a woman" speech, Sojourner Truth (1851) informed white suffragists of their myopia about race by highlighting how as a black woman her experience was different from theirs. Joseph and Lewis (1981) remind us that Truth's commentary is no less relevant today. Many women of color see the women's liberation movement as hopelessly white and middle class, immune to their concerns. As Hooks (1987:62) observed,

> Most people in the United States think of feminism . . . as a movement that aims to make women the social equals of men. . . . Since men are not equals in white supremacist, capitalist, patriarchal class structure, which men do women want to be equal to?

The alternative frameworks developed by women of color heighten feminism's sensitivity to the complex interplay of gender, class, and race oppression. Patriarchy permeates the lives of minority women, but it does not take the same form that it does for whites (Brittan and Maynard, 1984). Though these contributions may not have coalesced yet into a coherent theoretical framework (at least according to Jagger and Rothenberg, 1984), radical (Lorde, 1988), socialist (Mullins, 1986), and Marxist (Davis, 1981) women of color have provided possible points of integration with theories of race oppression (e.g., Joseph, 1981a, 1981b; Wellman, 1977).

In sum, feminist theory is not one perspective; it is a cacophony of comment and criticism "concerned with demystifying masculine knowledge as objective knowledge" (Brittan and Maynard, 1984:210) and offering insights from a women's perspective.

𝓕eminist 𝓜ethods

> The male epistemological stance, which corresponds to the world it creates, is objectivity; the ostensibly uninvolved stance, the view from a distance and from no particular perspective, apparently transparent to its reality. It does not comprehend its own perspectivity, does not recognize what it sees as subject like itself, or that the way it apprehends its world is a form of its subjection and presupposes it (MacKinnon (1982:23–24).

Concern over the nonobjective consequences of so-called objective normal science (Kuhn, 1970) has led some feminists to challenge the scientific enterprise. Keller (1982) arranges these challenges on a political spectrum from slightly left of center (liberal feminists) to the more radical left. The liberal critique takes an equal employment opportunity approach by observing the relative absence of women from the scientific community. This view "in no way conflicts either with traditional conceptions of science or with current liberal, egalitarian politics" (p. 114).

From this point, however, the criticisms become increasingly fundamental to the way knowledge is produced; they range from charges of bias in selecting research topics and interpreting results to rejecting rationality and objectivity as purely male products. More radical feminists have adopted a methodological strategy that is in direct opposition to the scientific method. In order to "see" women's existence (which has been invisible to objective scientific methods) "feminist women must deliberately and courageously integrate . . . their own experiences of oppression and discrimination . . . into the research process" (Miles, 1983:121). *Feminist methods* are necessarily subjectivist, transdisciplinary, nonhierarchical, and empowering.

Where one falls along Keller's feminist-political spectrum will determine one's choice of methods (i.e., quantitative versus qualitative) and whether one sees methods and theory as interrelated as opposed to separate and distinct. Thus, methods used by feminists are more diverse than typically credited (for examples, see Jayarate, 1983; Reinhartz, 1983; Stacey and Thorne, 1985).

Together, the above theoretical and methodological points form a feminist perspective. All have been incorporated into criminology, but some have had a greater impact than others. The goal in the next section is to identify the ways in which these approaches and methods have changed the way criminologists address the problems of crime and justice.

◉ Incorporating the Frameworks

The Female Offender

The stirrings of feminist criminology are nearly two decades old. Heidensohn (1968:171), in a "pre-feminist" paper, bemoaned the state of knowledge about female deviance and called for a "crash programme of research which telescopes decades of comparable studies of males." Later, Klein (1973) and Smart (1976) were to bring explicitly feminist perspectives to their critiques of extant theoretical and empirical work on the female offender. Klein, a Marxist-feminist, noted the absence of economic and other social explanations for female crime. Smart, working within more of a radical feminist perspective, stressed the linkages among sexist theory, patriarchy, and sexism in practice—specifically identifying the relationship between stereotypical assumptions about the causes of female crime and how female offenders are controlled and treated.

Both Klein and Smart set an agenda for a new feminist criminology, but their more radical approaches were derailed by the publication of Simon's *Women and Crime* and F. Adler's *Sisters in Crime* (1975). Claiming that a "new" female offender was emerging (white collar and/or male like), Simon and Adler generated tremendous interest in female crime (a clear aim of incipient feminism). But, tying the female offender's emergence to women's liberation brought about a "moral panic" (Smart, 1976), which was viewed by some as a backlash to the women's movement.[3] In Chesney-Lind's (1980:29) words, it represented "another in a century long series of symbolic attempts to keep women subordinate to men by threatening those who aspire for equality with the images of the witch, the bitch, and the whore."[4]

As with many social problems of our day, female crime became interesting only when it transcended the expected boundaries of class, race, and gender. As a "quasi-theory," the liberation-crime relationship had great appeal for nonfeminist criminologists.[5] But tests of the thesis were less than supportive. In fact most discredited it (Austin, 1982; Giordano et al., 1981), and others found evidence of a link between female crime and economic marginalization (Datesman and Scarpitti, 1980; Gora, 1982; Mukherjee and Fitzgerald, 1981; Steffensmeier, 1978, 1981; Steffensmeier and Cobb, 1981). The new female offender identified by Simon and Adler was more myth than reality (Steffensmeier, 1978). These conclusions did not differ substantially from Klein's (1973), yet they came years after her original critique—a fact that dramatically illustrates the marginality of feminist criminology at the time. Yet, subsequent research on the causes of female crime has clearly buttressed the economic/class perspectives of Marxist/socialist feminists as well as the "opportunity" perspectives of the liberal feminists (Ageton, 1983; Box, 1983; Box and Hale, 1984; Elliott and Ageton, 1980; Giordano et al., 1981).

In retrospect, feminist criminology both gained and lost from the narrow focus on liberation and crime. On the plus side, we gained a better insight into the historical (Mukherjee and Fitzgerald, 1981) and cross-cultural (F. Adler, 1981; Plenska, 1980) patterns of female crime. But because the liberation thesis was so limited, it diverted attention from the material and structural forces that shape women's lives and experiences. It is in these areas that women of color and socialist and radical feminist criminologists are more apt to focus etiological attention (Hagan et al., 1985, 1987; Lewis, 1981; Miller, 1985; Rafter and Natalizia, 1981; Wilson, 1985).

Women Victims: The Radical Feminist Critique

Liberal feminism has dominated studies of the female offender, but the same is not true of victimology (Daly and Chesney-Lind, 1988). Shifting away from analyses that blame the victim for her victimization (Amir, 1967),[6] radical feminists have constructed alternative interpretations of offender-victim relationships and victim experiences of criminal justice (Chapman and Gates, 1978; Klein, 1981; Wood, 1981).

Brownmiller's (1975) historical and cross-cultural study of rape brought a radical feminist perspective to the center of public consciousness. Building on the argument that rape is not a crime of sex but rather an act of power and dominance (Greer, 1970), Brownmiller concluded that rape is a tool in the arsenal of all men to control all women.

Radical feminists have reframed the ways in which rape is commonly understood in our society. Rather than a crime of sex, it is more apt to be viewed as one of male power, control, and domination. Brownmiller's work, coupled with that of other radical feminists (e.g., Griffin, 1979; Riger and Gordon, 1981), opened a floodgate of inquiry into rape and other types of victimizations that are "uniquely feminine" (Wilson, 1985:4), such as pornography (Dworkin, 1981), battering (Dobash and Dobash, 1979; Martin, 1976; Straus et al., 1980), incest (Finkelhor, 1979; Moyer, 1985; Stanko, 1985) and sexual harassment (MacKinnon, 1979; Stanko, 1985).

Guiding much of this research is the radical feminist critique of official conceptions and definitions of violence, which are viewed as male centered and incapable of incorporating the full range of female experiences of violence (i.e., from intimidation and coercion to physical violence and death). A woman-centered definition of violence is one that portrays violence as a form of social domination rather than a random and/or noninstrumental form of expression (Hanmer, 1981:32).

Radical feminists have dominated but not monopolized feminist perspectives in this area. Socialist feminists, liberals, and women of color have also participated in the dialogue. Gordon's (1988) research of family violence is implicitly critical of some radical feminists' overly deterministic conception of patriarchy. Such an image, she argues, denies agency to women and cannot incorporate "the chronic conflict, unpredictability, and ambivalent emotions that have characterized relations between the sexes" (xi–xii).

In another historical study, Tomes (1978) links variations in spousal abuse to changes in the economic position of the working class generally and the male's position within the family specifically. As the working class improved its economic position and males cemented greater power within their families, the official incidence of working-class battering decreased.

Based on her findings, Tomes argues that feminists may need to reconceptualize the relationship among male power, female economic dependency, and battering. Dependency is not necessarily tied to greater abuse; in fact, the opposite may be true. A wife's economic independence may exert a greater challenge to male authority within the family, thus creating a climate in which husbands resort to battering as a means to reestablish their control.

Studies that find great variety in the cross-cultural prevalence and incidence of rape and battering (e.g., Pagelow, 1981; Sanday, 1981) have forced feminists to examine patriarchal relations across different societal and situational arrangements (e.g., Wilson, 1985). If female victimization is a function of changing the needs of a capitalist/patriarchal system, then male domination and its relationship to female victimization need not be viewed as inevitable or immutable.

Around the themes of rape and control of sexuality, patriarchy and racism marry and divorce in intricate ways (Davis, 1981). In the United States, white racism and fear gave rise to mythological constructions of black sexuality. Black males are perceived as sexual threats and have been hunted and hanged for their "rape potential." For black victims of rape, the justice process is not simply gendered—it is racially gendered. Data indicate that black-on-black rapes are not taken as seriously by authorities as those that involve white victims (Kleck, 1981; LaFree, 1980). Such findings have led one prominent black scholar (Joseph, 1981b:27) to comment, "It must be considered an impossibility for white men to rape Black women in the eyes of justice and in the minds of many. Black women apparently are considered as something other than 'women.'"

Gender and Justice Processing

A final area to be discussed in this literature review is gendered justice. Comedian Richard Pryor once called attention to discrimination in the U.S. criminal justice system by defining justice as "just us." His concern with differential sentencing practices is one shared by feminists who primarily study the conditions under which criminal justice is gendered and with what consequences. Although liberal approaches typically dominate the gender-and-justice research, other feminist perspectives are gaining ground—especially in research on courts and corrections.

There are many stages in the criminal justice system at which gender may have an impact on decision making. The findings of some of the better-known studies of several strategic points in the decision-making process are summarized below.

Police

Arguments about whether and how justice is gendered must begin with police behavior. That police decisions to arrest can be influenced by extralegal factors such as the demeanor of the offender (Black, 1980), has been established. It is less clear how gender, either alone or in conjunction with other characteristics, may consciously or inadvertently influence police behavior.

In the liberal "equal treatment" tradition, Moyer and White (1981) test police bias in response decisions under "probable" responses to hypothetical situations. Neither gender nor race had an effect on police behavior once crime type, especially as it interacts with demeanor of the offender, was controlled. On the other hand, Freyerhern's (1981) comparison of juvenile male and female probabilities of transition from self-report incident to police contact and arrest, finds males to be more likely to incur police contact and arrest than females. Both of these studies are methodologically problematic, however. Moyer and White cannot generalize their findings to real police encounters and Freyerhern (1981:90) does not calculate transition probabilities across individual offense categories, nor does he include status offenses. Avoiding some of these methodological traps but still working within a liberal tradition, Visher (1983) finds the interaction between race and gender to be a key factor influencing arrest decision. Visher finds police chivalry only toward white females once "legal" factors are controlled. She hypothesizes that black females are treated more harshly than their white counterparts because they are less apt to display expected (i.e., traditional) gender behaviors and characteristics when they encounter a mostly white and male police force.

Race and gender are also found to interact through victim characteristics (Smith et al., 1984). An analysis of 272 police-citizen encounters, in which both a suspected offender and victim were present, revealed that white female victims received more preferential treatment from police than black female victims. Thus, although chivalry may be alive and well for white women, it appears to be dead (if it ever existed) for blacks.

Courts

Police contact is not the only point in justice processing at which discrimination can occur. Women have been found to receive more lenient treatment in the early stages of court processing (i.e., bail, release on own recognizance, and/or cash alternatives to bail; I. Nagel, 1983) and further into the process, e.g., conviction and sentencing (Bernstein et al., 1977; S. Nagel and Weitzman, 1972; Simon, 1975). Other studies find no gender bias when controlling for crime seriousness and prior record (Farrington and Morris, 1983) or little effect from extralegal factors when legal factors and bench bias are controlled (I. Nagel, 1983). Variation in sentencing may be related to so-called counter-type offenses, that is, women are treated more harshly when processed for nontraditional female crimes, like assault (Bernstein et al., 1977; S. Nagel and Weitzman, 1972), or when they violate female sexual norms (Chesney-Lind, 1973; Schlossman and Wallach, 1978). Given variable-specification problems, however, some of these findings are potentially spurious.

Once again, race may confound these effects. Spohn et al. (1982) address the issue of paternalism in sentencing, especially for black women. Controlling for prior record and attorney type, they found that black women are incarcerated significantly less often than black men, but about as often as white men. They conclude that the apparently lenient treatment of black women is not due to paternalism in their favor but rather to the racial discrimination against black vis-à-vis white men.

Studies of court processing are not entirely dominated by liberal perspectives. More critical perspectives emphasize social power and patriarchal control as the primary mechanisms through which justice is gendered (Kruttschnitt, 1982, 1984). Eaton (1986:35) argues that magistrate courts in Great Britain (the lower courts) reinforce the dominant imagery of justice (i.e., courts are ostensibly fair and just) while they maintain the status quo: "It is in these courts that the formal rules of society—the laws—are endorsed; it is here, too, that the informal, unwritten rules regulating social relations [e.g., gender, class, and race] are re-enacted."

When are females apt to be subjected to formal mechanisms of control? When other, more informal, constraints are lacking or disrupted. Kruttschnitt (1982, 1984) suggests that sentencing outcomes are affected by a woman's social status and/or her respectability. Differential sentencing among women is tied to the degree to which women are subjected to formal versus informal social control in their everyday lives.

Daly (1987a, 1989b) and Eaton (1986, 1987) offer convincing evidence that the most important factor determining sentence outcome, once prior record and offense seriousness are controlled, is marital and/or familial status.[7] Marital status has been found to matter for women (married receive more lenient sentences) but not for men (Farrington and Morris, 1983; I. Nagel, 1981) or to be as important for both (Daly, 1987a, 1987b).

Pretrial release and sentencing are seen to be both "familied" and "gendered." They are familied in that court decisions regarding the removal of men and women from families "elicit different concerns from the court" (Daly 1987a:154). They are gendered in that women's care of others and male economic support for families represent "different types of dependencies in family life" (p. 154). Men and women without family responsibilities are treated similarly, but more harshly than familied men and women. Women with families, however, are treated with the greatest degree of leniency due to "the differing social costs arising from separating them from their families" (Daly, 1987b:287). The economic role played by familied men can, more easily, be covered by state entitlement programs, but it is putatively more difficult to replace the functional role of familied women. Judges rationalize such sentencing disparities as necessary for keeping families together (Daly, 1989b).

As these latter studies suggest, much of the observed gender bias in processing may not be a case of overt discrimination for or against women relative to men. Instead, judicial decisions may be influenced by broader societal concerns about protecting nuclear families (Daly, 1989b) and the differing roles and responsibilities contained therein (Eaton, 1986). It is not clear that such forms of justice are overtly paternalistic, nor are they necessarily racist. Rather, in a society that stratifies other rights and privileges by gender, race, and class, "equality" in sentencing may not be just (Daly, 1989a).

Eaton (1986:10–11) takes a somewhat different view of familied justice. In her opinion, the courts reflect the needs and interests of patriarchy and capitalism, in which attendant inequities are reproduced. "Family-based" justice is a visible manifestation of the patriarchal and capitalist need to maintain and protect the nuclear family—within which gender and productive/reproductive relations first emerge.

Corrections

As it became clear that, compared with males, female prisoners were treated differently (in some cases more leniently and in others more harshly), liberal feminist perspectives came to dominate research questions and policy considerations (see, Haft, 1980; Heide, 1974; Simon, 1975).

The linkages between female incarceration and male control of female sexuality are developed by radical feminists (Chesney-Lind, 1973; Smart, 1976). Rasche (1974), for example, describes how prostitutes with venereal disease were prosecuted and institutionalized, with the "cure" as a condition of release. Nondiseased prostitutes were less likely to go to jail or prison. Certain prison practices, such as checking for evidence of a hymen during forced physical examinations and vaginal contraband searches, have been used as techniques to control the sexuality of youthful offenders and to humiliate and degrade female inmates (Burkhart, 1973; Chesney-Lind, 1986).

Socialist feminists emphasize how prison tenure and treatment vary by class and race (Freedman, 1981; French, 1977, 1978; Lewis, 1981; Rafter, 1985). In her historical accounting of the development of women's prisons, Rafter (1985:155) observes how race determined whether and where a woman was sent to prison.

> Comparison of incarceration rates and in-prison treatment of black women and white women demonstrates that partiality was extended mainly to whites. Chivalry filtered them out of the prison system, helping to create the even greater racial imbalances among female than male prisoner populations. And partiality toward whites contributed to the development of a bifurcated system, one track custodial and predominantly black, the other reformatory and reserved mainly for whites.

The bifurcated system of women's corrections emerges in part from two competing images of female nature. In one view, women are seen as fragile and immature creatures, more childlike than adult. Consequently, the female offender is perceived as a "fallen woman," in need of guidance but not a true danger to society (Rasche, 1974). The reformatory is perfectly suited to such an offender. Primarily staffed by reform-minded middle-class women, reformatory training programs emphasized skills that would turn the white, working-class misdemeanants into proper (and class-appropriate) women, that is, good servants or wives (Rafter, 1985:82).

In custodial prisons, however, a different archetype dominated. Women's "dark side," their inherent evil and immorality (Smart, 1976) shaped prison philosophy. Here, the predominantly black felons (who were perceived as more masculine, more self-centered, volatile, and dangerous) were treated like men—only, given the conditions of their incarceration (i.e., fewness of numbers and at the mercy of violent male offenders), their equality was tantamount to brutal treatment and often death (Rafter, 1985:181).

The degree to which prisons function as something other than just places of punishment and/or treatment is a popular theme in neo-Marxist literature. Extending this interpretation to women, Marxist-feminists (e.g., Wilson, 1985; Hartz-Karp, 1981) argue that prisons, like other institutions of social control (e.g., mental health facilities), retool deviant women for gender-appropriate roles in capitalist patriarchal societies:

> If deviant women are more frequently assigned to the mental health system for social control than to the criminal justice system, it is perhaps because of the superior ability of the mental health system to "re-tool" worn-out or rebellious domestic workers. (Wilson, 1985:18)

Societal control of female deviance serves the needs of capital. When those needs change, so too will the mechanisms and directions of social control.[8]

In this vein, Carlen (1983) demonstrates how "down, out and disordered" women in Scotland are disciplined through medical and judicial apparatuses. Most of the imprisoned are poor women; many have histories of alcohol and drug abuse, and a large number come from violent homes. These life experiences combine, setting into motion a cycle of deviance, imprisonment, and patriarchal and class discipline that is tenacious and defeating:

> Being seen as neither wholly mad nor wholly bad, [women] are treated to a disciplinary regime where they are actually infantalised at the same time as attempts are made to make them feel guilty about their double, triple, quadruple, or even quintuple refusal of family, work, gender, health, and reason (Carlen, 1983:209).

❧ Where to Go from Here?

In 1976, Carol Smart suggested a number of topics for feminist research.[9] A decade later, feminist criminology has amassed a considerable body of knowledge in most of these areas—so much so in fact that feminists now are more self-critical—especially in the areas of policy and legislative changes (see Daly and Chesney-Lind, 1988). This is a positive step. It suggests not only that a feminist voice is being heard, but that it is loud enough to produce disagreement and intellectual exchange. Nonetheless, certain areas in criminology either have been underexposed or are resistant to feminist concerns. Thus, some new directions for feminist criminology are discussed below.[10]

Race and Crime

Poorly conceived offender self-report surveys provided criminologists with the empirical justification to ignore the race-crime relationship, and the prevailing political climate reinforced our myopia. There is enormous risk in ignoring that relationship, however. First, based on more sophisticated crime measures (e.g., National Youth Survey, National Crime Survey, cohort studies), it is clear that the race-crime relationship is an essential one. Second, and not unlike the gender-crime relationship, such reticence leaves the interpretive door open to less critical perspectives.

Feminist criminologists have great potential in this area, but the data are sparse and problematic and the analytic contributions few. Too often we rely on quantitative studies that dichotomize race into white and black, or the nonwhite category is broadened to include groups other than blacks (see, e.g., Tracy et al., in press). In the former instance, other ethnic/racial groups are ignored; in the latter, such inclusive categorizations assume etiological and historical/cultural invariance between groups.

Clearly, one of the first places for feminists to start is to target women of color for greater research. Available data indicate that there are significant differences between black and white female crime rates (Ageton, 1983; Chilton and Datesman, 1987; Hindelang, 1981; Laub and McDermott, 1985; Mann, 1987; Young, 1980). Simpson (1988), Miller (1985), and Lewis (1981) argue that the unique structural and cultural positioning of black women produces complex cultural typescripts that exert push-pull pressures for crime, pressures that may not exist for white women.

Miller's (1985:177–178) ethnography of lower-class deviant networks describes how certain types of male and female criminality (e.g., hustling, pimping, and other instrumental crimes) are interdependent in minority communities. Female crime also appears to have a group-directed and - enacted dimension (see Young, 1980). The collective nature of such minority offending may stem from the fact that it emerges, in part, from the integrated and extended domestic networks of underclass blacks (Miller, 1985) and from joint participation in gang activities (Campbell, 1984).

These observations do not imply, however, that patriarchy is absent from these communities. Male dominance and control are reproduced within interpersonal relationships (not necessarily familial) and embodied in informal organizations, like gangs (Campbell, 1984) and state social service agencies. Some female offending can be interpreted as challenging patriarchal control and asserting independence (Campbell, 1984:135); much can be attributed to both economic necessity and the pull and excitement of street life (Campbell, 1984; Miller, 1985). Female participation in violent crime may stem from abusive relationships between men and women (Browne, 1987; Mann, 1987) and/or the frustration, alienation, and anger that are associated with racial and class oppression (Simpson, 1988).

Research by Hill and Suval (1988) suggests that the causes of crime may differ for black and white women, which raises questions about whether current theories of female crime, including feminist perspectives, are white-female centered. Given the paucity of data on how gender structures relationships within minority communities and families, it is impossible to say. More quantitative research is needed on minority groups other than blacks (e.g., Chicanos and other Hispanics, Asians, Native Americans) to establish a better knowledge base, but qualitative studies that probe culture and subjective differences between women of color and whites are also essential (Mullins, 1986). Feminist criminologists are guilty of the "add race and stir" shortsightedness that pervades feminist thinking. We would do well to heed Spelman's (1988:166) reminder of how to understand and approach differences among women:

> If we assume there are differences among women, but at the same time they are all the same as women, and if we assume the woman part is what we know from looking at the case of white middle-class women, then we appear to be talking only about white middle-class women. This is how white middle-class privilege is maintained even as we purport to recognize the importance of women's differences.

Elite Crime

In 1977, Harris admonished criminologists for their failure to use "the sex variable" as the empirical building block for all theories of criminal deviance.

Apparently (though not surprisingly) this was interpreted to apply only to street crime. The entire area of white-collar, corporate, and organizational crime has not been examined from a feminist perspective.

Officially, women are underrepresented in white-collar crime data although recent Bureau of Justice Statistics (1987) data suggest that women have made inroads into this formerly male domain. Similar claims are made regarding female penetration of the upper reaches of organized crime (Simpson, 1987). Yet, Daly (1988) finds neither the crime types nor the offenders themselves to be particularly elite.

Much of our information on female participation in organized crime is anecdotal, derived from the nonsystematic observations of male crime participants. Consequently, there has been little systematic research on women's penetration of and mobility within illicit markets. The official data on corporate and other white-collar offending are equally problematic (see Reiss and Biderman, 1980). Given that both the data and interpretation/theory in these areas are suspect, feminist researchers must first develop an empirical base with which to answer the following types of questions. Is elite crime a male domain (Steffensmeier, 1983)? What are the motivations and characteristics of women who do participate (Daly, 1988; Zietz, 1981)? How are they similar and different from male offenders (P. Adler, 1985; Block, 1977; Simpson, 1987)? What explains the official increase in female participation in white-collar offenses?

At this point, feminists have barely scratched the surface of the elite crime area. Daly (1988) is providing some direction, but much more needs to be done.

Deterrence

Gender confounds the anticipated relationship between objective sanction risks and criminal activity, that is, given that female sanction risks are low, women should have high rates of law breaking. Yet, as virtually all measures of crime document, the exact opposite is true. This empirical relationship has left deterrence theorists scrambling to make sense of the inconsistency.

Richards and Tittle (1981:183–185) argue that there are at least five lines of reasoning that would predict that women perceive higher levels of risk than do men. Using measures derived from these hypotheses, they find two variables, stakes in conformity and perceptions of visibility, to be highly associated with gender differences in perceived chances of arrest:

> Women may think that legal sanction is relatively certain because they are more likely to think of themselves as subject to surveillance and general social sanctions than are men. Their greater relative stakes in conformity may make deviance more threatening for them, and lead to high sanction risk estimates (p. 196).

The social control literature, in general, characterizes female conformity in a stereotypical manner. Conforming females are seen as passive, compliant, and dependent. Instead, Naffine (1988:131) suggests that the conforming women be seen as "involved and engrossed in conventional life. But . . . also actively concerned about the effects of her behavior on her loved ones, particularly emotionally and financially dependent children." (Naffine is especially critical of Hagan et al., 1979, 1985, 1987.)

Naffine's image of conformity is partially influenced by Gilligan's (1982) work in moral development theory. Gilligan's research discovers that men and women use "a different voice" when they talk about moral responsibility. If the moral calculus of reasoning about crime is different between men and women, Gilligan may have identified a new way of conceptualizing gender differences in (1) perceived threat of sanction and (2) male-female crime rates. According to her theory, men often make moral decisions based on an "ethic of justice," while women employ a model of decision making based on an "ethic of care." The former is a more abstract model, expressed as a set of principles defining rights and rules (e.g., Kohlberg, 1981). In the latter, decisions are governed by "a psychological logic of relationships, which contrasts with the formal logic of fairness that informs the justice approach" (Gilligan, 1982:73).

A woman's decision to violate the law will depend on her definition of the moral domain (i.e., how will my act affect those around me, those who count on me). It is not surprising that in some deterrence studies (Finley and Grasmick, 1985) women score significantly higher than men on measures of internalized guilt. Because women are responsible for the care of relationships, any act that may result in their removal from that role is apt to produce a tremendous sense of guilt. Guilt may be negated if the needs of the family (for food or other valued items) outweigh the "immorality" of breaking the law to obtain them or if others are available to take on the responsibilities of care.

Gilligan's theory can be used to explain why most women do not violate the law and why they score higher on most measures of deterrence. It can also explain class and race differences in female crime rates. Lower-class and minority women are more apt to find themselves in situations that require a renegotiation of the moral domain and, given their kinship networks, they have a greater chance of finding care substitutes (Miller, 1985). Not surprisingly, Finley and Grasmick (1985) report that blacks score lower on certainty and severity of guilt than their white counterparts.

Some critics suggest that Gilligan's findings are biased (she interviewed mostly middle-class students) or that they may be a function of subordinate female social position, not real differences in ethical philosophies (Tronto, n.d.). These are important criticisms that must be addressed before we proceed too enthusiastically. Gilligan's conceptualization of differences in gender-based moral reasoning, however, are an important contribution and warrant further research.

❧ Conclusion

Feminist criminology has changed dramatically since Klein (1973) and Smart (1976) first called attention to it. Replicating the same political and analytical development as the broader feminist movement, feminist contributions to the study of crime and justice began with more liberal approaches and have recently been giving way to more radical critiques. Liberal feminist dominance rests, in part, in ideological coherence—these approaches correspond closely with the ideas and beliefs embodied in most capitalist democracies. Thus, liberalism in any form is less threatening and more acceptable than a feminism that questions white, male, and/or capitalist privilege.[11] Additionally, liberal feminists speak in the same voice as a majority of social scientists, that is, they are rational, objective, and (typically) quantitative. Consequently, their data and interpretations carry more weight within the scientific community and among their peers.

Though liberal/quantitative approaches offer important insights into gender as a "variable" problem (Stacey and Thorne, 1985), criminologists need to be more ecumenical in studying gendered society. If we emphasize qualitative (e.g., Campbell, 1984; Carlen, 1986; Eaton, 1986; Miller, 1985), historical (Gordon, 1988; Freedman, 1981; Rafter, 1985), and subjectivist (Stacey and Thorne, 1985) approaches in addition to quantitative, the detail and texture of how crime and justice are gendered will lead to richer theory and better criminology.

There are areas in criminology into which feminists have only marginally ventured or in which their contributions have been of little consequence. In their review of feminist criminology, Daly and Chesney-Lind (1988:512–513) discuss the problems that feminists have had building and developing theories of female crime. It is not coincidental that the areas targeted for further research in this paper (e.g., race and crime, elite crime, and deterrence) all focus on this problematic area. Until we can better deal with the empirical complexities of criminal offending, it will be too easy for our critics to dismiss feminist contributions to the study of crime as facile, rhetorical, and/or atheoretical.

Endnotes

[1]This is not to suggest that biological reductionism is absent in studies/theories of male criminality. Such explanations of male crime abound (e.g., Wilson and Herrnstein, 1985). However, with the demise of phrenology, social factors replaced biology as key etiological forces. These explanations have not been seriously challenged. Conversely, until the feminist critique of the 1970s, biogenic/psychogenic models of female crime went, for the most part, unchallenged.

[2]Phillips (1987) argues that the choice of terms describing gender relations imply particular views of what the problem is. So, inequality (a term favored by liberals and some women of color) suggests that women deserve what men and/or whites are granted. Oppression (socialists and women of color) implies a complex combination of forces (ideological, political, and economic) that keep woman in her place. Subordination is a term favored by radical feminists and some women of color who identify the holder of power as the culprit (men and whites respectively).

[3]The links between women's liberation and changing patterns of female criminality were made before. Bishop (1931) complained that women's liberation during the 1920s had three negative results: (1) more women were turning criminal; (2) a "better" class of women were becoming criminal more often; and (3) women were becoming sexually criminal at a younger age (cited in Rasche, 1974).

[4]To be fair, both Simon and Adler had more to offer than mere speculation about the "dark side" of women's liberation. Simon's research documents the basic inequities between male and female correctional facilities and treatments. By attributing these differences to male chivalry toward women, she takes a liberal feminist approach to the problem of gender and justice, an approach that heavily influenced later works in this area. Adler's work, while more impressionistic than Simon's, attempted to explain differences in crime rates between white and black females. Although her interpretations gave rise to more systematic exam-

inations of intra-gender race differences in crime that are highly critical of her interpretations and methods, the issues she raised are of primary importance to most feminist criminologists today.

[5]A research focus on gender alone does not qualify one as a feminist just as a focus on class does not make one a marxist. Rather, as part of their endeavor, feminist criminologists must seriously consider the nature of gender relations and the peculiar brand of oppression that patriarchal relations bring (Leonard, 1982).

[6]Precipitous behavior has ranged from dressing provocatively, saying no to sex while "meaning" yes, "nagging" a spouse, Lolita-like seductiveness on the part of the victim, and so on.

[7]These effects appear to be strongest for black defendants (Daly, 1989a).

[8]Cloward and Piven (1979) and Box (1983) assert that female deviance is handled by the medical community, in part, because women are more likely to direct their deviance inward (i.e., they privatize it into self-destructive behaviors, like depression and suicide). Such behavior is conceptualized as sickness (like "hysteria" earlier) and is thus subject to the formal control of the psychiatric community.

[9]The relevant topics are the female offender and the attitudes of criminal justice personnel toward her; criminal justice processing; gender and corrections; and the structure and purpose of law.

[10]To suggest that feminists need to identify areas "appropriate" for feminist critique implies that knowledge, as currently constructed, is selectively androcentric. I would argue that criminology as a whole, like other academic disciplines, needs a feminist "overhaul."

[11]Stacey and Thorne (1985:308) argue that more radical feminist thinking has been marginalized—ghettoized within Marxist sociology, which ensures that feminist thinking has less of a chance to influence mainstream sociological paradigms and research.

References

Adler, Freda. 1975. Sisters in Crime: The Rise of the New Female Criminal. New York: McGraw-Hill.

_____. 1981. The Incidence of Female Criminality in the Contemporary World. New York: New York University Press.

Adler, Patricia. 1985. Wheeling and Dealing: An Ethnography of an Upper-Level Drug Dealing and Smuggling Community. New York: Columbia University Press.

Ageton, Suzanne S. 1983. The dynamics of female delinquency, 1976–1980. Criminology 21:555–584.

Amir, Menachem. 1967. Victim precipitated forcible rape. Journal of Criminal Law, Criminology, and Police Science 58:493–502.

Atkinson, Ti-Grace. 1974. Radical Feminism and Love. In Amazon Odyssey. New York: Links Books.

Austin, Roy L. 1982. Women's liberation and increases in minor, major, and occupational offenses. Criminology 20:407–430.

Barry, Kathleen. 1979. Female Sexual Slavery. New York: Avon Books.

Beauvoir, Simone de. 1960. The Second Sex. London: Four Square Books.

Bem, Sandra. 1974. The measurement of psychological androgyny. Journal of Consulting and Clinical Psychology 42:155–162.

Bernstein, Ilene Nagel, Edward Kick, Jan Leung, and Barbara Schulz. 1977. Charge reduction: An intermediary stage in the process of labelling criminal defendants. Social Forces 56:362–384.

Bishop, Cecil. 1931. Women and Crime. London: Chato and Windus Press.

Black, Donald. 1980. On the Manners and Customs of the Police. New York: Academic Press.

Block, Alan. 1977. Aw! Your mother's in the mafia: Women criminals in progressive New York. Contemporary Crises 1:5–22.

Box, Steven. 1983. Power, Crime, and Mystification. London: Tavistock.

Box, Steven and Chris Hale. 1984. Liberation/emancipation, economic marginalization, or less chivalry: The relevance of three theoretical arguments to female crime patterns in England and Wales, 1951–1980. Criminology 22:473–497.

Brittan, Arthur and Mary Maynard. 1984. Sexism, Racism and Oppression. Oxford: Basil Blackwell.

Browne, Angela. 1987. When Battered Women Kill. New York: Free Press.

Brownmiller, Susan. 1975. Against Our Will: Men, Women, and Rape. New York: Simon & Schuster.

Burkhart, Kathryn Watterson. 1973. Women in Prison. Garden City, N.Y.: Doubleday.

Bureau of Justice Statistics. 1987. Special Report: White-Collar Crime. Washington, D.C.: U.S. Department of Justice.

Campbell, Anne. 1984. The Girls in the Gang: A Report from New York City. Oxford: Basil Blackwell.

Carlen, Pat. 1983. Women's Imprisonment: A Study in Social Control. London: Routledge & Kegan Paul.

Chapman, Jane Roberts and Margaret Gates (eds.). 1978. The Victimization of Women. Beverly Hills, Calif.: Sage.

Chesney-Lind, Meda. 1973. Judicial enforcement of the female sex role. Issues in Criminology 8:51–69.

_____. 1980. Rediscovering Lilith: Misogyny and the "new" female criminal. In Curt Taylor Griffiths and Margot Nance (eds.), The Female Offender. Criminology Research Centre. Burnaby, B.C.: Simon Fraser University.

_____. 1986. Women and crime: The female offender. Signs 12:78–96.

Chilton, Roland and Susan K. Datesman. 1987. Gender, race, and crime: An analysis of urban arrest trends, 1960–1980. Gender and Society 1:152–171.

Cloward, Richard A. and Frances Fox Piven. 1979. Hidden protest: The channeling of female innovation and resistance. Signs 4:651–669.

Daly, Kathleen. 1987a. Discrimination in the criminal courts: Family, gender and the problem of equal treatment. Social Forces 66:152–175.

_____. 1987b. Structure and practice of familial-based justice in a criminal court. Law and Society Review 21:267–290.

_____. 1988. Gender and varieties of white-collar crime. Revised version of a paper presented at the annual meeting of the American Society of Criminology, Atlanta.

_____. 1989a. Neither conflict nor labeling nor paternalism will suffice: Intersections of race, ethnicity, gender, and family in criminal court decisions. Crime and Delinquency 35:136–168.

_____. 1989b. Rethinking judicial paternalism: Gender, work-family relations, and sentencing. Gender and Society 3:9–36.

Daly, Kathleen and Meda Chesney-Lind. 1988. Feminism and criminology. Justice Quarterly 5:497–538.

Datesman, Susan K. and Frank R. Scarpitti (eds.). 1980. Women, Crime, and Justice. New York: Oxford University Press.

Davis, Angela. 1981. Women, Race, and Class. New York: Random House.

Dobash, R. Emerson and Russell Dobash. 1979. Violence Against Wives: A Case Against the Patriarchy. New York: Free Press.

Dworkin, Andrea. 1981. Pornography: Men Possessing Women. New York: Perigee Books.

Eaton, Mary. 1986. Justice for Women? Family, Court, and Social Control. Philadelphia: Open University Press.

_____. 1987. The question of bail: Magistrates' responses to applications for bail on behalf of men and women defendants. In Pat Carlen and Anne Worrall (eds.), Gender, Crime and Justice. Philadelphia: Open University Press.

Edwards, Susan M. 1985. Women on Trial: A Study of the Female Suspect, Defendant, and Offender in the Criminal Law and Criminal Justice System. Manchester, N.H.: Manchester University Press.

Eisenstein, Zillah. 1979. Capitalist Patriarchy and the Case for Socialist Feminism. New York: Monthly Review Press.

_____. 1981. The Radical Future of Liberal Feminism. New York: Monthly Review Press.

Elliott, Delbert and Suzanne S. Ageton. 1980. Reconciling race and class differences in self-reported and official estimates of delinquency. American Sociological Review 45:95–110.

Farrington, David and Allison Morris. 1983. Sex, sentencing and reconviction. British Journal of Criminology 23:229–248.

Finkelhor, David. 1979. Sexually Victimized Children. New York: Free Press.

Finley, Nancy J. and Harold G. Grasmick. 1985. Gender roles and social control. Sociological Spectrum 5:317–330.

Firestone, Shulamith. 1970. The Dialectic of Sex: The Case for Feminist Revolution. New York: Bantam.

Freedman, Estelle. 1981. Their Sisters' Keepers: Women's Prison Reform in America, 1830–1930. Ann Arbor: University of Michigan Press.

French, Laurence. 1977. An assessment of the black female prisoner in the South. Signs 3:483–488.

_____. 1978. The incarcerated black female: The case of social double jeopardy. Journal of Black Studies 8:321–335.

Freyerhern, William. 1981. Gender differences in delinquency quantity and quality. In Lee H. Bowker (ed.), Women and Crime in America. New York: Macmillan.

Gilligan, Carol. 1982. In a Different Voice: Psychological Theory and Women's Development. Cambridge, Mass.: Harvard University Press.

Giordano, Peggy, Sandra Kerbel, and Sandra Dudley. 1981. The economics of female criminality: An analysis of police blotters 1890–1975. In Lee H. Bowker (ed.), Women and Crime in America. New York: Macmillian.

Glueck, Sheldon and Eleanor Glueck. 1934. Five Hundred Delinquent Women. New York: Alfred A. Knopf.

Gora, Joann Gennaro. 1982. The New Female Criminal: Empirical Reality or Social Myth? New York: Praeger.

Gordon, Linda. 1988. Heroes of Their Own Lives: The Politics and History of Family Violence. New York: Penguin.

Greer, Germaine. 1970. The Female Eunuch. New York: McGraw-Hill.

Griffin, Susan. 1979. Rape: The Power of Consciousness. San Francisco: Harper & Row.

Haft, Marilyn G. 1980. Women in prison: Discriminary practices and some legal solutions. In Susan Datesman and Frank R. Scarpitti (eds.), Women, Crime, and Justice. New York: Oxford University Press.

Hagan, John, A.R. Gillis, and John Simpson. 1985. The class structure of gender and delinquency: Toward a power control theory of common delinquent behavior. American Journal of Sociology 90:1151–1178.

Hagan, John, John Simpson, and A.R. Gillis. 1979. The sexual stratification of social control: A gender-based perspective on crime and delinquency. British Journal of Sociology 30:25–38.

_____. 1987. Class in the household: A power-control theory of gender and delinquency. American Journal of Sociology 92:788-816.

Hanmer, Jalna. 1981. Violence and the Social Control of Women. Feminist Issues 1:29–46.

Harris, Anthony R. 1977. Sex and theories of deviance: Toward a functional theory of deviant typescripts. American Sociological Review 42:3–16.

Hartman, Heida. 1979. The unhappy marriage of Marxism and feminism: Toward a more progressive union. Capital and Class (Summer):1–13.

Hartz-Karp, Janette. 1981. Women in constraints. In S.K. Mukherjee and Jocelynne A. Scutt (eds.), Women and Crime. Sydney: Australian Institute of Criminology with Allen and Unwin.

Heide, Wilma Scott. 1974. Feminism and the "fallen woman." Criminal Justice and Behavior 1:369–373.

Heidensohn, Frances. 1968. The deviance of women: A critique and an enquiry. British Journal of Sociology 19:160–175.

_____. 1985. Women and Crime. London: Macmillan.

Hill, Gary D. and Elizabeth M. Suval. 1988. Women, race, and crime. A revised version of a paper presented at the annual meeting of the American Society of Criminology, Chicago.

Hindelang, Michael. 1981. Variations in sex-race-age-specific incidence rates of offending. American Sociological Review 46:461–474.

Hooks, Bell. 1987. Feminism: A movement to end sexist oppression. In Anne Phillips (ed.), Feminism and Equality. Oxford: Basil Blackwell.

Jayarate, Toby Epstein. 1983. The value of quantitative methodology for feminist research. In Gloria Bowles and Renate Duelli Klein (eds.), Theories of Women's Studies. Boston: Routledge & Kegan Paul.

Joseph, Gloria I. 1981a. The incompatible menage a trois: Marxism, feminism, and racism. In Lydia Sargent (ed.), Women and Revolution. Boston: South End Press.

_____. 1981b. White promotion, black survival. In Gloria I. Joseph and Jill Lewis (eds.), Common Differences: Conflicts in Black and White Feminist Perspectives. Boston: South End Press.

Joseph, Gloria I. and Jill Lewis (eds.). 1981. Common Differences: Conflicts in Black and White Feminist Perspectives. Boston: South End Press.

Keller, Evelyn Fox. 1982. Feminism and science. In Nannerl O. Keohane, Michele Z. Rosaldo, and Barbara C. Gelpi (eds.), Feminist Theory. Chicago: University of Chicago Press.

Klein, Dorie. 1973. The etiology of female crime: A review of the literature. Issues in Criminology 8:3–29.

_____. 1981. Violence against women: Some considerations regarding its causes and its elimination. Crime and Delinquency 27:64–80.

Kohlberg, Lawrence. 1981. The Philosophy of Moral Development. San Francisco: Harper & Row.

Kruttschnitt, Candace. 1982. Respectable women and the law. The Sociological Quarterly 23:221–234.

_____. 1984. Sex and criminal court dispositions: The unresolved controversy. Journal of Research in Crime and Delinquency 21:213–232.

Kuhn, Thomas. 1970. The Structure of Scientific Revolutions. 2nd ed. Chicago: University of Chicago Press.

Laub, John and M. Joan McDermott. 1985. An analysis of serious crime by young black women. Criminology 23:81–98.

Lewis, Diane. 1981. Black women offenders and criminal justice: Some theoretical considerations. In Marguerite Warren (ed.), Comparing Female and Male Offenders. Beverly Hills, Calif.: Sage.

MacKinnon, Catherine A. 1979. The Sexual Harassment of Working Women. New Haven: Yale University Press.

_____. 1982. Feminism, Marxism, method, and the state: An agenda for theory. In Nannerl O. Keohane, Michele Z. Rosaldo, and Barbara C. Gelpi (eds.), Feminist Theory. Chicago: University of Chicago Press.

Mann, Coramae Richey. 1984. Female Crime and Delinquency. Tuscaloosa: University of Alabama Press.

_____. 1987. Black female homicide in the United States. Paper presented at the Conference on Black Homicide and Public Health, Baltimore.

Martin, Del. 1976. Battered Wives. New York: Pocket Books/Simon & Schuster.

Miles, Maria. 1983. Toward a methodology for feminist research. In Gloria Bowles and Renate Duelli Klein (eds.), Theories of Women's Studies. Boston: Routledge & Kegan Paul.

Miller, Eleanor M. 1985. Street Woman. Philadelphia: Temple University Press.

Millett, Kate. 1971. Sexual Politics. London: Rupert Hart-Davis.

Mitchell, Juliet. 1971. Woman's Estate. New York: Random House.

Moyer, Imogene L. 1985. The Changing Roles of Women in the Criminal Justice System: Offenders, Victims, and Professionals. Prospect Heights, Ill.: Waveland Press.

Moyer, Imogene L. and Garland F. White. 1981. Police processing of female offenders. In Lee H. Bowker (ed.), Women and Crime in America. New York: Macmillan.

Mukherjee, S.K. and R.W. Fitzgerald. 1981. The myth of rising female crime. In S.K. Mukherjee and Jocelynne A. Scutt (eds.), Women and Crime. Sydney: Australian Institute of Criminology with Allen and Unwin.

Mukherjee, S.K. and Jocelynne A. Scutt (eds.). 1981. Women and Crime. Sydney: Australian Institute of Criminology with Allen and Unwin.

Naffine, Ngaire. 1988. Female Crime: The Construction of Women in Criminology. Boston: Allen and Unwin.

Nagel, Ilene H. 1981. Sex differences in the processing of criminal defendants. In A. Morris and L. Gelsthorpe (eds.), Women and Crime. Cambridge: Cambridge Institute of Criminology.

_____. 1983. The legal/extra-legal controversy: Judicial decisions in pretrial release. Law and Society Review 17:481–515.

Nagel, Stuart and Lenore J. Weitzman. 1972. Double standard of American justice. Society 9:18–25, 62–63.

Oakley, Ann. 1981. Subject Women. New York: Pantheon.

Pagelow, Mildred. 1981. Sex roles, power, and woman battering. In Lee H. Bowker (ed.), Women and Crime in America. New York: Macmillan.

Pateman, Carol. 1987. Feminist critiques of the public/private dichotomy. In Anne Phillips (ed.), Feminism and Equality. Oxford: Basil Blackwell.

Phillips, Anne (ed.). 1987. Feminism and Equality. Oxford: Basil Blackwell.

Plenska, Danuta. 1980. Women's criminality in Poland. In Curt Taylor Griffiths and Margot Nance (eds.), The Female Offender. Criminology Research Centre. Burnaby, B.C.: Simon Fraser University.

Rafter, Nicole Hahn. 1985. Partial Justice: Women in State Prisons, 1800–1935. Boston: Northeastern University Press.

Rafter, Nicole Hahn and Elena Natalizaia. 1981. Marxist feminist: Implications for criminal justice. Crime and Delinquency 27:81–98.

Rasche, Christine. 1974. The female offender as an object of criminological research. Criminal Justice and Behavior 1:301–320.

Reinhartz, Shulamit. 1983. Experimental analysis: A contribution to feminist research. In Gloria Bowles and Renate Duelli Klein (eds.), Theories of Women's Studies. Boston: Routledge & Kegan Paul.

Reiss, Albert J., Jr. and Albert P. Biderman. 1980. Data Sources on White-Collar Law-Breaking. National Institute of Justice. Washington, D.C.: U.S. Department of Justice.

Rich, Adrienne. 1980. Compulsory heterosexual and lesbian existence. Signs 5:631–660.

Richards, Pamela and Charles R. Tittle. 1981. Gender and perceived chances of arrest. Social Forces 59:1182–1199.

Riger, Stephanie and Margaret T. Gordon. 1981. The fear of rape: A study in social control. Journal of Social Issues 37:71–92.

Sanday, Peggy Reeves. 1981. The socio-cultural context of rape: A cross-cultural study. The Journal of Social Issues 37:5–27.

Schlossman, Steven and Stephanie Wallach. 1978. The crime of precocious sexuality: Female juvenile delinquency in the progressive era. Harvard Educational Review 48:65–94.

Simpson, Sally S. 1987. Women in elite deviance: A grounded theory. Paper presented at the annual meeting of the American Society of Criminology, Montreal.

_____. 1988. Caste, class, and crime: Violence and the disenfranchised black female. Revised version of a paper presented at the annual meeting of the American Society of Criminology, Chicago.

Simon, Rita. 1975. Women and Crime. Lexington, Mass.: D.C. Heath.

Smart, Carol. 1976. Women, Crime and Criminology: A Feminist Critique. London: Routledge & Kegan Paul.

Smith, Douglas, Christy Visher, and Laura Davidson. 1984. Equity and discretionary justice: The influence of race on police arrest decisions. Journal of Criminal Law and Criminology 75:234–249.

Spelman, Elizabeth V. 1988. Inessential Woman: Problems of Exclusion in Feminist Thought. Boston: Beacon.

Spohn, Cassia, John Gruhl, and Susan Welch. 1982. The effect of race on sentencing: A re-examination of an unsettled question. Law and Society Review 16:71–88.

Stacey, Judith and Barrie Thorne. 1985. The missing feminist revolution in sociology. Social Problems 32:301–316.

Stanko, Elizabeth A. 1985. Intimate Intrusions: Women's Experience of Male Violence. London: Routledge & Kegan Paul.

Steffensmeier, Darrell J. 1978. Crime and the contemporary woman: An analysis of changing levels of female property crime, 1960–75. Social Forces 57:560–584.

_____. 1981. Patterns of female property crime, 1960–1975: A postscript. In Lee H. Bowker (ed.), Women and Crime in America. New York: Macmillan.

_____. 1983. Organization properties and sex-segregation in the underworld: Building a sociological theory of sex differences in crime. Social Forces 61:1010–1043.

Steffensmeier, Darrell J. and Michael J. Cobb. 1981. Sex differences in urban arrest patterns, 1934–79. Social Problems 29:37–50.

Straus, Murray A., Richard J. Gelles, and Suzanne K. Steinmetz. 1980. Behind Closed Doors: Violence in the American Family. Garden City, N.Y.: Anchor/Doubleday.

Tomes, Nancy. 1978. A "torrent of abuse": Crimes of violence between working-class men and women in London, 1840–1875. Journal of Social History 11:328–345.

Tracy, Paul E., Marvin E. Wolfgang, and Robert M. Figlio. In press. Delinquent Careers in Two Birth Cohorts. New York: Plenum Publishing.

Tronto, Joan C. n.d. "Women's morality": Beyond gender difference to a theory of care. Unpublished paper, Hunter College of the City University of New York.

Truth, Sojourner. 1851. Cited in Gloria I. Joseph and Jill Lewis (eds.), Common Differences: Conflicts in Black and White Feminist Perspectives. Boston: South End Press.

Visher, Christy. 1983. Gender, police arrest decisions, and notions of chivalry. Criminology 21:5–28.

Wellman, David. 1977. Portraits of White Racism. New York: Cambridge University Press.

Wilson, James Q. and Richard J. Herrnstein. 1985. Crime and Human Nature. New York: Simon & Schuster.

Wilson, Nanci Koser. 1985. Witches, hookers, and others: Societal response to women criminals and victims. Paper presented at the annual meeting of the American Society of Criminology, San Diego.

Wood, Pamela. 1981. The victim in a forcible rape case: A feminist view. In Lee H. Bowker (ed.), Women and Crime in America. New York: Macmillan.

Young, Vernetta D. 1980. Women, race, and crime. Criminology 18:20–34.

Zietz, Dorothy. 1981. Women Who Embezzle or Defraud: A Study of Convicted Felons. New York: Praeger.

❧ ❧ ❧

Questions

1. What is feminism? How does it differ from other forms of social inquiry?

2. How do feminist theories of crime differ from other criminological theories?

3. How do feminist methods differ from other methodologies?

4. What insights does the feminist perspective give into the criminal justice system?

5. Does the feminist perspective require separate theories of crime, or can it be integrated into existing theories?

Why Americans Fear the Wrong Things

BARRY GLASSNER

Americans fear many things, and often fear the wrong things. One of the more recent moral panics in American society was the fear of school violence, particularly school shootings. The media continually told us that we were in the middle of an epidemic of growing proportion, legislators told school districts that they had to develop emergency response protocols, and parents mobilized to more effectively reach at-risk youth. Underlying this moral panic was little knowledge of the facts: at its peak, slightly more than 50 children were killed in school shootings in a given year while more than 50 million children were enrolled in school. The truth was that a child has better odds of being struck by lightning or killed at the hands of a family member in his own home than being the victim of school violence. So why do we fear school violence more than lightning or domestic violence? In this selection, Barry Glassner explores why Americans fear the wrong things.

Why are so many fears in the air, and so many of them unfounded? Why, as crime rates plunged throughout the 1990s, did two-thirds of Americans believe they were soaring? How did it come about that by mid-decade 62 percent of us described ourselves as "truly desperate" about crime—almost twice as many as in the late 1980s, when crime rates were higher? Why, on a survey in 1997, when the crime rate had already fallen for a half dozen consecutive years, did more than half of us disagree with the statement "This country is finally beginning to make some progress in solving the crime problem"?[1]

In the late 1990s the number of drug users had decreased by half compared to a decade earlier; almost two-thirds of high school seniors had never used any illegal drugs, even marijuana. So why did a majority of adults rank drug abuse as the greatest danger to America's youth? Why did nine out of

"Why Americans Fear the Wrong Things," by Barry Glassner, reprinted from *The Culture of Fear: Why Americans Are Afraid of the Wrong Things*, 1999, Basic Books. Copyright © 1999 by Barry Glassner.

ten believe the drug problem is out of control, and only one in six believe the country was making progress?[2]

Give us a happy ending and we write a new disaster story. In the late 1990s the unemployment rate was below 5 percent for the first time in a quarter century. People who had been pounding the pavement for years could finally get work. Yet pundits warned of imminent economic disaster. They predicted inflation would take off, just as they had a few years earlier— also erroneously—when the unemployment rate dipped below 6 percent.[3]

We compound our worries beyond all reason. Life expectancy in the United States has doubled during the twentieth century. We are better able to cure and control diseases than any other civilization in history. Yet we hear that phenomenal numbers of us are dreadfully ill. In 1996 Bob Garfield, a magazine writer, reviewed articles about serious diseases published over the course of a year in the Washington Post, the New York Times, and USA Today. He learned that, in addition to 59 million Americans with heart disease, 53 million with migraines, 25 million with osteoporosis, 16 million with obesity, and 3 million with cancer, many Americans suffer from more obscure ailments such as temporomandibular joint disorders (10 million) and brain injuries (2 million). Adding up the estimates, Garfield determined that 543 million Americans are seriously sick—a shocking number in a nation of 266 million inhabitants. "Either as a society we are doomed, or someone is seriously double-dipping," he suggested.[4]

Garfield appears to have underestimated one category of patients: for psychiatric ailments his figure was 53 million. Yet when Jim Windolf, an editor of the New York Observer, collated estimates for maladies ranging from borderline personality disorder (10 million) and sex addiction (11 million) to less well-known conditions such as restless leg syndrome (12 million) he came up with a figure of 152 million. "But give the experts a little time," he advised. "With another new quantifiable disorder or two, everybody in the country will be officially nuts."[5]

Indeed, Windolf omitted from his estimates new-fashioned afflictions that have yet to make it into the Diagnostic and Statistical Manual of Mental Disorders of the American Psychiatric Association: ailments such as road rage, which afflicts more than half of Americans, according to a psychologist's testimony before a congressional hearing in 1997.[6]

The scope of our health fears seems limitless. Besides worrying disproportionately about legitimate ailments and prematurely about would-be diseases, we continue to fret over already refuted dangers. Some still worry, for instance, about "flesh-eating bacteria," a bug first rammed into our consciousness in 1994 when the U.S. news media picked up on a screamer headline in a British tabloid, "Killer Bug Ate My Face." The bacteria, depicted as more brutal than anything seen in modern times, was said to be spreading faster than the pack of photographers outside the home of its latest victim. In point of fact, however, we were not "terribly vulnerable" to these "superbugs," nor were they "medicine's worst nightmares," as voices in the media warned.

Group A strep, a cyclical strain that has been around for ages, had been dormant for half a century or more before making a comeback. The British pseudoepidemic had resulted in a total of about a dozen deaths in the previous year. Medical experts roundly rebutted the scares by noting that of 20 to 30 million strep infections each year in the United States fewer than 1 in 1,000 involve serious strep A complications, and only 500 to 1,500 people suffer the flesh-eating syndrome, whose proper name is necrotizing fasciitis. Still the fear persisted. Years after the initial scare, horrifying news stories continued to appear, complete with grotesque pictures of victims. A United Press International story in 1998 typical of the genre told of a child in Texas who died of the "deadly strain" of bacteria that the reporter warned "can spread at a rate of up to one inch per hour."[7]

◎ Roosevelt Was Wrong

We had better learn to doubt our inflated fears before they destroy us. Valid fears have their place; they cue us to danger. False and overdrawn fears only cause hardship. . . .

We all pay one of the costs of panics: huge sums of money go to waste. Hysteria over the ritual abuse of children cost billions of dollars in police investigations, trials, and imprisonments. Men and women went to jail for years "on the basis of some of the most fantastic claims ever presented to an American jury," as Dorothy Rabinowitz of the *Wall Street Journal* demonstrated in a series of investigative articles for which she became a Pulitzer Prize finalist in 1996. Across the nation expensive surveillance programs were implemented to protect children from fiends who reside primarily in the imaginations of adults.[8]

The price tag for our panic about overall crime has grown so monumental that even law-and-order zealots find it hard to defend. The criminal justice system costs Americans close to $100 billion a year, most of which goes to police and prisons. In California we spend more on jails than on higher education. Yet increases in the number of police and prison cells do not correlate consistently with reductions in the number of serious crimes committed. Criminologists who study reductions in homicide rates, for instance, find little difference between cities that substantially expand their police forces and prison capacity and others that do not.[9]

The turnabout in domestic public spending over the past quarter century, from child welfare and antipoverty programs to incarceration, did not even produce reductions in *fear* of crime. Increasing the number of cops and jails arguably has the opposite effect: it suggests that the crime problem is all the more out of control.[10]

Panic-driven public spending generates over the long term a pathology akin to one found in drug addicts. The more money and attention we fritter away on our compulsions, the less we have available for our real needs, which consequently grow larger. While fortunes are being spent to protect children from dangers that few ever encounter, approximately 11 million children lack health insurance, 12 million are malnourished, and rates of illiteracy are increasing.[11]

I do not contend, as did President Roosevelt in 1933, that "the only thing we have to fear is fear itself." My point is that we often fear the wrong things. In the 1990s middle-income and poorer Americans should have worried about unemployment insurance, which covered a smaller share of workers than twenty years earlier. Many of us have had friends or family out of work during economic downturns or as a result of corporate restructuring. Living in a nation with one of the largest income gaps of any industrialized country, where the bottom 40 percent of the population is worse off financially than their counterparts two decades earlier, we might also have worried about income inequality. Or poverty. During the mid- and late 1990s 5 million elderly Americans had no food in their homes, more than 20 million people used emergency food programs each year, and one in five children lived in poverty—more than a quarter million of them homeless. All told, a larger proportion of Americans were poor than three decades earlier.[12]

One of the paradoxes of a culture of fear is that serious problems remain widely ignored even though they give rise to precisely the dangers that the populace most abhors. Poverty, for example, correlates strongly with child abuse, crime, and drug abuse. Income inequality is also associated with adverse outcomes for society as a whole. The larger the gap between rich and poor in a society, the higher its overall death rates from heart disease, cancer, and murder.

❧ Two Easy Explanations

In the following discussion I will try to answer two questions: Why are Americans so fearful lately, and why are our fears so often misplaced? To both questions the same two-word answer is commonly given by scholars and journalists: premillennial tensions. The final years of a millennium and the early years of a new millennium provoke mass anxiety and ill reasoning, the argument goes. So momentous does the calendric change seem, the populace cannot keep its wits about it.

Premillennial tensions probably do help explain some of our collective irrationality. Living in a scientific era, most of us grant the arbitrariness of reckoning time in base-ten rather than, say, base-twelve, and from the birth of Christ rather than from the day Muhammad moved from Mecca. Yet even the least superstitious among us cannot quite manage to think of the year 2000 as ordinary. Social psychologists have long recognized a human urge to convert vague uneasiness into definable concerns, real or imagined. In a classic study thirty years ago Alan Kerckhoff and Kurt Back pointed out that "the belief in a tangible threat makes it possible to explain and justify one's sense of discomfort."[13]

Some historical evidence also supports the hypothesis that people panic at the brink of centuries and millennia. Witness the "panic terror" in Europe around the year 1000 and the witch hunts in Salem in the 1690s. As a complete or dependable explanation, though, the millennium hypothesis fails. Historians emphasize that panics of equal or greater intensity occur in odd years, as demonstrated by anti-Indian hysteria in the mid 1700s and McCarthyism in the 1950s. Scholars point out too that calendars cannot account for why certain fears occupy people at certain times (witches then, killer kids now).[14]

Another popular explanation blames the news media. We have so many fears, many of them off-base, the argument goes, because the media bombard us with sensationalistic stories designed to increase ratings. This explanation, sometimes called the media-effects theory, is less simplistic than the millennium hypothesis and contains sizable kernels of truth. When researchers from Emory University computed the levels of coverage of various health dangers in popular magazines and newspapers they discovered an inverse relationship: much less space was devoted to several of the major causes of death than to some uncommon causes. The leading cause of death, heart disease, received approximately the same amount of coverage as the eleventh-ranked cause of death, homicide. They found a similar inverse relationship in coverage of risk factors associated with serious illness and death. The lowest-ranking risk factor, drug use, received nearly as much attention as the second-ranked risk factor, diet and exercise.[15]

Disproportionate coverage in the news media plainly has effects on readers and viewers. When Esther Madriz, a professor at Hunter College, interviewed women in New York City about their fears of crime they frequently responded with the phrase "I saw it in the news." The interviewees identified the news media as both the source of their fears and the reason they believed those fears were valid. Asked in a national poll why they believe the country has a serious crime problem, 76 percent of people cited stories they had seen in the media. Only 22 percent cited personal experience.[16]

When professors Robert Blendon and John Young of Harvard analyzed forty-seven surveys about drug abuse conducted between 1978 and 1997, they too discovered that the news media, rather than personal experience, provide Americans with their predominant fears. Eight out of ten adults say that drug abuse has never caused problems in their family, and the vast majority report relatively little direct experience with problems related to drug abuse. Widespread concern about drug problems emanates, Blendon and Young determined, from scares in the news media, television in particular.[17]

Television news programs survive on scares. On local newscasts, where producers live by the dictum "if it bleeds, it leads," drug, crime, and disaster stories make up most of the news portion of the broadcasts. Evening newscasts on the major networks are somewhat less bloody, but between 1990 and 1998, when the nation's murder rate declined by 20 percent, the number of murder stories on network newscasts increased 600 percent (*not* counting stories about O.J. Simpson).[18]

After the dinnertime newscasts the networks broadcast newsmagazines, whose guiding principle seems to be that no danger is too small to magnify into a national nightmare. Some of the risks reported by such programs would be merely laughable were they not hyped with so much fanfare: "Don't miss *Dateline* tonight or YOU could be the next victim!" Competing for ratings with drama programs and movies during prime-time evening hours, newsmagazines feature story lines that would make a writer for "Homicide" or "ER" wince.[19]

"It can happen in a flash. Fire breaks out on the operating table. The patient is surrounded by flames," Barbara Walters exclaimed on ABC's "20/20" in 1998. The problem—oxygen from a face mask ignited by a surgical instrument—occurs "more often than you might think," she cautioned in her introduction, even though reporter Arnold Diaz would note later, during the actual report, that out of 27 million surgeries each year the situation arises only about a hundred times. No matter, Diaz effectively nullified the reassuring numbers as soon as they left his mouth. To those who "may say it's too small a risk to worry about" he presented distraught victims: a woman with permanent scars on her face and a man whose son had died.[20]

The gambit is common. Producers of TV newsmagazines routinely let emotional accounts trump objective information. In 1994 medical authorities attempted to cut short the brouhaha over flesh-eating bacteria by publicizing the fact that an American is fifty-five times more likely to be struck by lightning than die of the suddenly celebrated microbe. Yet TV journalists brushed this fact aside with remarks like, "whatever the statistics, it's devastating to the victims" (Catherine Crier on "20/20"), accompanied by stomach-turning videos of disfigured patients.[21]

Sheryl Stolberg, then a medical writer for the *Los Angeles Times,* put her finger on what makes the TV newsmagazines so cavalier: "Killer germs are perfect for prime time," she wrote. "They are invisible, uncontrollable, and, in the case of Group A strep, can invade the body in an unnervingly simple manner, through a cut or scrape." Whereas print journalists only described in words the actions of "billions of bacteria" spreading "like underground fires" throughout a person's body, TV newsmagazines made use of special effects to depict graphically how these "merciless killers" do their damage.[22]

❧ /Morality and /Marketing

To blame the media is to oversimplify the complex role that journalists play as both proponents and doubters of popular fears. It is also to beg the same key issue that the millennium hypothesis evades: why particular anxieties take hold when they do. Why do news organizations and their audiences find themselves drawn to one hazard rather than another?

The short answer to why Americans harbor so many misbegotten fears is that immense power and money await those who tap into our moral insecurities and supply us with symbolic substitutes.

Ɛndnotes

[1]Crime data here and throughout are from reports of the Bureau of Justice Statistics unless otherwise noted. Fear of crime: Esther Madriz, *Nothing Bad Happens to Good Girls* (Berkeley: University of California Press, 1997), ch. 1; Richard Morin,

"As Crime Rate Falls, Fears Persist," *Washington Post* National Edition, 16 June 1997, p. 35; David Whitman, "Believing the Good News," *U.S. News & World Report*, 5 January 1998, pp. 45–46.

[2] Eva Bertram, Morris Blachman et al., *Drug War Politics* (Berkeley: University of California Press, 1996), p. 10; Mike Males, *Scapegoat Generation* (Monroe, ME: Common Courage Press, 1996), ch. 6; Karen Peterson, "Survey: Teen Drug Use Declines," *USA Today*, 19 June 1998, p. A6; Robert Blendon and John Young, "The Public and the War on Illicit Drugs," *Journal of the American Medical Association* 279 (18 March 1998): 827–32. In presenting these statistics and others I am aware of a seeming paradox: I criticize the abuse of statistics by fear-mongering politicians, journalists, and others but hand down precise-sounding numbers myself. Yet to eschew all estimates because some are used inappropriately or do not withstand scrutiny would be as foolhardy as ignoring all medical advice because some doctors are quacks. Readers can be assured I have interrogated the statistics presented here as factual. As notes throughout the book make clear, I have tried to rely on research that appears in peer-reviewed scholarly journals. Where this was not possible or sufficient, I traced numbers back to their sources, investigated the research methodology utilized to produce them, or conducted searches of the popular and scientific literature for critical commentaries and conflicting findings.

[3] Bob Herbert, "Bogeyman Economics," *New York Times*, 4 April 1997, p. A15; Doug Henwood, "Alarming Drop in Unemployment," *Extra*, September 1994, pp. 16–17; Christopher Shea, "Low Inflation and Low Unemployment Spur Economists to Debate 'Natural Rate' Theory," *Chronicle of Higher Education*, 24 October 1997, p. A13.

[4] Bob Garfield, "Maladies by the Millions," *USA Today*, 16 December 1996, p. A15.

[5] Jim Windolf, "A Nation of Nuts," *Wall Street Journal*, 22 October 1997, p. A22.

[6] Andrew Ferguson, "Road Rage," *Time*, 12 January 1998, pp. 64–68; Joe Sharkey, "You're Not Bad, You're Sick. It's in the Book," *New York Times*, 28 September 1997, pp. N1, 5.

[7] Malcolm Dean, "Flesh-eating Bugs Scare," *Lancet* 343 (June 1994): 1418; "Flesh-eating Bacteria," *Science* 264 (17 June 1994): 1665; David Brown, "The Flesh-eating Bug," *Washington Post* National Edition, 19 December 1994, p. 34; Sarah Richardson, "Tabloid Strep," *Discover* (January 1995): 71; Liz Hunt, "What's Bugging Us," *The Independent*, 28 May 1994, p. 25; Lisa Seachrist, "The Once and Future Scourge," *Science News* 148 (7 October 1995): 234–35. Quotes are from Bernard Dixon, "A Rampant Non-epidemic," *British Medical Journal* 308 (11 June 1994): 1576–77; and Michael Lemonick and Leon Jaroff, "The Killers All Around," *Time*, 12 September 1994, pp. 62–69. More recent coverage: "Strep A Involved in Baby's Death," UPI, 27 February 1998; see also, e.g., Steve Carney, "Miracle Mom," *Los Angeles Times*, 4 March 1998, p. A6; KTLA, "News at Ten," 28 March 1998.

[8]Dorothy Rabinowitz, "A Darkness in Massachusetts," *Wall Street Journal,* 30 January 1995, p. A20 (contains quote); "Back in Wenatchee" (unsigned editorial), *Wall Street Journal,* 20 June 1996, p. A18; Dorothy Rabinowitz, "Justice in Massachusetts," *Wall Street Journal,* 13 May 1997, p. A19. See also Nathan and Snedeker, *Satan's Silence;* James Beaver, "The Myth of Repressed Memory," *Journal of Criminal Law and Criminology* 86 (1996): 596–607; Kathryn Lyon, *Witch Hunt* (New York: Avon, 1998); Pam Belluck, "'Memory' Therapy Leads to a Lawsuit and Big Settlement," *New York Times,* 6 November 1997, pp. A1, 10.

[9]Elliott Currie, *Crime and Punishment in America* (New York: Metropolitan, 1998); Tony Pate et al., *Reducing Fear of Crime in Houston and Newark* (Washington, DC: Police Foundation, 1986); Steven Donziger, *The Real War on Crime* (New York: HarperCollins, 1996); Christina Johns, *Power, Ideology and the War on Drugs* (New York: Praeger, 1992); John Irwin et al., "Fanning the Flames of Fear," *Crime and Delinquency* 44 (1998): 32–48.

[10]Steven Donziger, "Fear, Crime and Punishment in the U.S.," *Tikkun* 12 (1996): 24–27, 77.

[11]Peter Budetti, "Health Insurance for Children," *New England Journal of Medicine* 338 (1998): 541–42; Eileen Smith, "Drugs Top Adult Fears for Kids' Well-being," *USA Today,* 9 December 1997, p. D1. Literacy statistic: Adult Literacy Service.

[12]"The State of America's Children," report by the Children's Defense Fund, Washington, DC, March 1998; "Blocks to Their Future," report by the National Law Center on Homelessness and Poverty, Washington, DC, September 1997; reports released in 1998 from the National Center for Children in Poverty, Columbia University, New York; Douglas Massey, "The Age of Extremes," *Demography* 33 (1996): 395–412; Trudy Lieberman, "Hunger in America," *Nation,* 30 March 1998, pp. 11–16; David Lynch, "Rich Poor World," *USA Today,* 20 September 1996, p. B1; Richard Wolf, "Good Economy Hasn't Helped the Poor," *USA Today,* 10 March 1998, p. A3; Robert Reich, "Broken Faith," *Nation,* 16 February 1998, pp. 11–17.

[13]Alan Kerckhoff and Kurt Back, *The June Bug* (New York: Appleton-Century-Crofts, 1968), see esp. pp. 160–61.

[14]Stephen Jay Gould, *Questioning the Millennium* (New York: Crown, 1997); Todd Gitlin, "Millennial Mumbo Jumbo," *Los Angeles Times Book Review,* 27 April 1997, p. 8.

[15]Karen Frost, Erica Frank et al., "Relative Risk in the News Media," *American Journal of Public Health* 87 (1997): 842–45. Media-effects theory: Nancy Signorielli and Michael Morgan, eds., *Cultivation Analysis* (Newbury Park, CA: Sage, 1990); Jennings Bryant and Dolf Zillman, eds., *Media Effects* (Hillsdale, NJ: Erlbaum, 1994); Ronald Jacobs, "Producing the News, Producing the Crisis," *Media, Culture and Society* 18 (1996): 373–97.

[16]Madriz, *Nothing Bad Happens to Good Girls,* see esp. pp. 111–14; David Whitman and Margaret Loftus, "Things Are Getting Better? Who Knew," *U.S. News & World Report,* 16 December 1996, pp. 30–32.

[17]Blendon and Young, "War on Illicit Drugs." See also Ted Chiricos et al., "Crime, News and Fear of Crime," *Social Problems* 44 (1997): 342–57.

[18]Steven Stark, "Local News: The Biggest Scandal on TV," *Washington Monthly* (June 1997): 38–41; Barbara Bliss Osborn, "If It Bleeds, It Leads," *Extra,* September–October 1994, p. 15; Jenkins, *Pedophiles and Priests,* pp. 68–71; "It's Murder," *USA Today,* 20 April 1998, p. D2; Lawrence Grossman, "Does Local TV News Need a National Nanny?" *Columbia Journalism Review* (May 1998): 33.

[19]Regarding fearmongering by newsmagazines, see also Elizabeth Jensen et al., "Consumer Alert," *Brill's Content* (October 1998): 130–47.

[20]ABC "20/20," 16 March 1998.

[21]Thomas Maugh, "Killer Bacteria a Rarity," *Los Angeles Times,* 3 December 1994, p. A29; Ed Siegel, "Roll Over, Ed Murrow," *Boston Globe,* 21 August 1994, p. 14. Crier quote from ABC's "20/20," 24 June 1994.

[22]Sheryl Stolberg, "'Killer Bug' Perfect for Prime Time," *Los Angeles Times,* 15 June 1994, pp. A1, 30–31. Quotes from Brown, "Flesh-eating Bug"; and Michael Lemonick and Leon Jaroff, "The Killers All Around," *Time,* 12 September 1994, pp. 62–69.

◉ ◉ ◉

Questions

1. What are some examples of supporting evidence that Americans fear the wrong things?

2. What are some costs of having misplaced fears?

3. Why does Glassner contend Americans fear the wrong things?

4. Now that the "new millennium" has passed, does the construction of fear seem to have subsided or changed in any way? Explain.

5. Provide two examples of things we are supposed to fear right now in American society. How well do these examples fit the explanation(s) provided by Glassner?

Television Violence: The Power and the Peril

GEORGE GERBNER

Violence on television continues to spark major debate in U.S. society. The television industry now uses a self-imposed rating system; Congress has criticized the motion-picture industry for marketing violent films to children. The timeless question is whether television teaches violence or merely reflects what's already occurring in society. In this selection, George Gerbner first establishes the degree to which violence is portrayed on television. He also assesses changes in these portrayals between 1967 and 1994. Finally, he discusses the "lessons" that TV teaches and speculates about why violent content in television programs continues to grow.

*H*umankind may have had more bloodthirsty eras, but none as filled with *images* of violence as the present. We are awash in a tide of violent representations such as the world has never seen. Images of expertly choreographed brutality drench our homes. There is no escape from the mass-produced mayhem pervading the life space of ever larger areas of the world.

The television overkill has drifted out of democratic reach since it was first reported by the National Association of Educational Broadcasters in 1951. The first Congressional hearings were held by Senator Estes Kefauver's Subcommittee on Juvenile Delinquency in 1954. Through several more rounds of hearings in the 1960s and 1970s, despite the accumulation of critical research results, despite condemnation by government commissions and virtually all medical, law enforcement, parents', educational and other organizations, and in the face of international embarrassment, violence has saturated the airways for the nearly 30 years we have been tracking it in our ongoing Cultural Indicators project[1] (Gerbner, Gross, Morgan, & Signorielli, 1993).

Broadcasters are licensed to serve "the public interest, convenience, and necessity." They are also paid to deliver a receptive audience to their business sponsors. Few industries are as public relations conscious as television. What compels them to endure public humiliation, risk the threat of representative legislation and invite charges of undermining health, security and social order? The answer is not popularity.

The usual rationalization that television violence "gives the audience what it wants" is disingenuous. As the trade knows well, and as we shall see, violence is not highly rated. But there is no free market or box office for television programs through which audiences could express their wants.

Unlike other media use, viewing is a ritual; people watch by the clock and not by the program. Ratings are determined more by the time of the program, the lead-in (previous program) and what else is on at the same time than by their quality or other attractions. Therefore, ratings are important because they set the price the advertiser pays for "buying" viewers available to the set at a certain time, but they have limited use as indicators of popularity. And even to the limited extent that a few violent programs may have a larger share of a certain time slot and can, therefore, extract a higher price for commercials, the incremental profits are hardly worth the social, institutional and political damage they exact. Why would the business establishment subsidize its own undoing?

Therefore, it is clear that something is wrong with the way the problem has been posed and addressed. Either the damage is not what it is commonly assumed to be, or television violence must have some driving force and utility other than popularity, or both. Indeed it is both, and more.

The usual question—"Does television violence incite real-life violence?—is itself a symptom rather than diagnostic tool of the problem. It obscures and, despite its alarming implications and intent, trivializes the issues involved.

Television violence must be understood as a complex scenario and an indicator of social relationships. It has both utility and consequences other than those usually considered in media and public discussion. And it is driven by forces other than free expression and audience demand.

Whatever else it does, violence in drama and news demonstrates power. It portrays victims as well as victimizers. It intimidates more than it incites. It paralyzes more than it triggers action. It defines majority might and minority risk. It shows one's place in the "pecking order" that runs society.

Violence is but the tip of the iceberg of a massive underlying connection to television's role as universal storyteller and an industry dependent on global markets. These relationships have not yet been recognized and integrated into any theory or regulatory practice. Television has been seen as one medium among many rather than as the mainstream of the cultural environment in which most children grow up and learn. Traditional regulatory and public interest conceptions are based on the obsolete assumption that the number of media outlets determines freedom and diversity of content. Today, however, a handful of global conglomerates can own many outlets in all media, deny entry to new and alternative perspectives and homogenize content. The common carrier concept of access and protection applicable to a public utility like the telephone also falls short when the issue is not so much the number of channels and individual access to them but the centralized mass production of stories to grow on.

Let us, then, preview the task of broadening a discourse that has gone on too long in a narrow and shallow groove. Violence on television is an integral part of a system of global marketing. It dominates an increasing share of the world's screens despite its relative lack of popularity in any country. Its consequences go far beyond inciting aggression. The system inhibits the portrayal of diverse dramatic approaches to conflict, depresses independent television production, deprives viewers of more popular choices, victimizes some and emboldens others, heightens general intimidation and invites repressive postures by politicians that exploit the widespread insecurities it itself generates.

The First Amendment to the U.S. Constitution forbade the only censors its authors know—government—from interfering with the freedom of their press. Since then large conglomerates, virtual private governments, have imposed their formulas of overkill on media they own. Therefore, raising the issue of overkill directs attention to the controls that in fact abridge creative freedom, dominate markets and constrain democratic cultural policy.

Behind the problem of television violence is the critical issue of who makes cultural policy on whose behalf in the electronic age. The debate about violence creates an opportunity to move the larger cultural policy issue to center stage, where it has been in other democracies for some time.

The convergence of communication technologies concentrates control over the most widely shared messages and images. Despite all the technocratic fantasies about hundreds of channels, and with antiviolence posturing filling the mass media, it is rare to encounter discussion of the basic issue of who makes cultural policy. In the absence of such discussion, cultural policy is made on private and limited grounds by an invisible corporate directorate whose members are unknown, unelected and accountable only to their clients.

We need to ask the kinds of questions that can place the discussion of television violence as a cultural policy issue in a useful perspective. For example, What creative sources and resources will provide what mix of content moving on the "electronic superhighway" into every home? Who will tell the stories and for what underlying purpose? How can we assure survival of alternative perspectives, regardless of profitability and selling power?

There are no clear answers to these questions because, for one thing, they have not yet been placed on the agenda of public discourse. It will take organization, deliberation and exploration to develop an approach to answering them. What follows, then, is an attempt to draw from our research answers to some questions that can help develop such an approach. We will be asking, What is unique about television and about violence on television? What systems of "casting" and "fate" dominate its representations of life? What conceptions of reality do these systems cultivate? Why does violence play such a prominent, pervasive and persistent role in them? And, finally, how can we as a society deal with the overkill while, at the same time, enhancing rather than further curtailing cultural freedom and diversity.

❧ The New Cultural Environment

Nielsen figures show that, today, an American child is born into a home in which television is on an average of over 7 hours a day. For the first time in human history, most of the stories about people, life and values are told not by parents, schools, churches or others in the community who have something to tell but by a group of distant conglomerates that have something to sell.

Television, the mainstream of the new cultural environment, has brought about a radical change in the way children grow up, learn and live in our society. Television is a relatively nonselectively used ritual; children are its captive audience. Most people watch by the clock and not by the program. The television audience depends on the time of the day and the day of the week more than on the program. Other media require literacy, growing up, going out and selection based on some previously acquired tastes, values and predispositions. Traditional media research assumed such selectivity. But there are no "previously acquired tastes, values and predispositions" with television. Viewing starts in infancy and continues throughout life.

Television helps to shape from the outset the predispositions and selections that govern the use of other media. Unlike other media, television requires little or no attention; its repetitive patterns are absorbed in the course of living. They become part and parcel of the family's style of life, but they neither stem from nor respond to its particular and selective needs and wants. It is television itself that cultivates the tastes, values and predisposition that guide future selection of other media. That is why television has a major impact on what movies, magazines, newspapers and books can be sold best in the new cultural environment.

The roles children grow into are no longer homemade, handcrafted, community inspired. They are products of a complex, integrated and globalized manufacturing and marketing system. Television violence, defined as overt physical action that hurts or kills (or threatens to do so), is an integral part of that system. A study of "The Limits of Selective Viewing" (Sun, 1989) found that, on the whole, prime-time television presents a relatively small set of common themes, and violence pervades most of them.

Now, representations of violence are not necessarily undesirable. There is blood in fairy tales, gore in mythology, murder in Shakespeare. Not all violence is alike. In some contexts, violence can be a legitimate and even necessary cultural expression. Individually crafted, historically inspired, sparingly and selectively used expressions of symbolic violence can indicate the tragic costs of deadly compulsions. However, such a tragic sense of violence has been swamped by "happy violence" produced on the dramatic assembly line. This happy violence is cool, swift, painless and often spectacular, even thrilling, but usually sanitized. It always leads to a happy ending. After all, it is designed to entertain and not to upset; it must deliver the audience to the next commercial in a receptive mood.

The majority of network viewers have little choice of thematic context or cast of character types and virtually no chance of avoiding violence. Nor has the proliferation of channels led to greater diversity of actual viewing (see, for example, Gerbner, 1993; Gerbner et al., 1993; Morgan & Shanahan, 1991). If anything, the dominant dramatic patterns penetrate more deeply into viewer choices through more outlets managed by fewer owners airing programs produced by fewer creative sources.

❧ Message System Analysis

My conclusions are based on the findings of our Cultural Indicators project (CI) that began in 1967. CI is based at the University of Pennsylvania's Annenberg School for Communication. It is a cumulative database and an ongoing research project that relates recurrent features of the world of television to media policy and viewer conceptions of reality. By 1994 its computer archive contained observations on 2,816 programs and 34,882 characters coded according to many thematic, demographic and action categories. The study is directed by this author in collaboration with Michael Morgan at the University of Massachusetts at Amherst and Nancy Signorielli at the University of Delaware.

CI is a three-pronged research effort: "Message system analysis" is the annual monitoring of television program content; "institutional policy analysis" looks at the economic and political bases of media decision making; "cultivation analysis" is an assessment of the long-range consequences of exposure to television's systems of messages.

Message system analysis is the study of the content of television programs. It includes every dramatic (fictional) program in each annual sample. It provides an unusual view of familiar territory. It is not a view of individual programs but an aggregate picture of the world of television, a bird's-eye view of what large communities of viewers absorb over long periods of time.

The role of violence in that world can be seen in our analysis of prime-time network programs and characters. Casting and fate, the demography of that world, are the important building blocks of the storytelling process. They have presented a stable pattern over the almost 30 years of monitoring network television drama and coding every speaking character in each year's sample. Middle-class White male characters dominate in numbers and power. Women play one out of three characters. Young people and the elderly make up one third and one fifth, respectively, of their actual proportions of the population. Most other minorities are even more underrepresented. That cast sets the stage for stories of conflict, violence and the projection of White male prime-of-life power. Most of those who are underrepresented are also those who, when portrayed, suffer the worst fate.

The average viewer of prime-time television drama (serious as well as comedic) sees in a typical week an average of 21 criminals arrayed against an army of 41 public and private law enforcers. There are 14 doctors, 6 nurses, 6 lawyers and 2 judges to handle them. An average of 150 acts of violence and about 15 murders entertain them and their children every week, and that does not count cartoons and the news. Those who watch over 3 hours a day (more than half of all viewers) absorb much more.

About one of three (31%) of all characters and more than half (52%) of major characters are involved in violence either as victims or as victimizers (or both) in any given week. The ratio of violence to victimization defines the price to be paid for committing violence. When one group can commit violence with relative impunity, the price it pays for violence is relatively low. When another group suffers more violence than it commits, the price is high.

In the total cast of prime-time characters, defined as all speaking parts regardless of the importance of the role, the average "risk ratio" (number of victims per 10 violents) is 12. Violence is an effective victimizer—and characterizer. Its distribution is not random; the calculus of risk is not evenly distributed. Women, children, poorer and older people and some minorities pay a higher price for violence than do males in the prime of life. The price paid in victims for every 10 violents is 15 for boys, 16 for girls, 17 for young women, 18.5 for lower class characters and over 20 for elderly characters.

Violence takes on an even more defining role for major characters. It involves more than half of all major characters (58% of men and 41% of women). Most likely to be involved either as perpetrators or victims, or both, are characters portrayed as mentally ill (84%), characters with mental or other disability (70%), young adult males (69%) and Latino/Hispanic Americans (64%). Children, lower class and mentally ill or otherwise disabled characters, pay the highest price—13 to 16 victims for every 10 perpetrators.

Lethal victimization extends the pattern. About 5% of all characters and 10% of major characters are involved in killing (kill or get killed or both). Being Latino/Hispanic or lower class means bad trouble: They are the most likely to kill and be killed. Being poor, old, Hispanic or a woman of color means double trouble, a disproportionate chance of being killed; they pay the highest relative price for taking another's life.

Among major characters, for every 10 "good" (positively valued) men who kill, about 4 are killed. But for every 10 "good" women who kill, 6 are killed, and for every 10 women of color who kill, 17 are killed. Older women characters get involved in violence only to be killed.

We calculated a violence "pecking order" by ranking the risk ratios of the different groups. Women, children, young people, lower class, disabled and Asian Americans are at the bottom of the heap. When it comes to killing, older and Latino/Hispanic characters also pay a higher than average price. In other words, hurting and killing by most majority groups extracts a tooth for a tooth. But minority groups tend to pay a higher price for their show of force. That imbalance of power is, in fact, what makes them minorities even when, as is the case for women, they are a numerical majority.

❧ Cultivation Analysis: The "Lessons" of Television

What are the consequences? These representations are not the sole or necessarily even the main determinants of what people think or do. But they are the most pervasive, inescapable and policy-directed common and stable cultural contributions to what large communities absorb over long periods of time. We use the term *cultivation* to distinguish the long-term cultivation of assumptions about life and values from short-term "effects" that are usually assessed by measuring change as a consequence of exposure to certain messages. With television, one cannot take a measure before exposure and only rarely without exposure. Television tends to cultivate and confirm stable conceptions about life. Cultivation analysis measures these "lessons" as it explores whether those who spend more time with television are more likely than comparable groups of lighter viewers to perceive the real world in ways that reflect the most common and repetitive features of the television world (see Morgan & Signorielli, 1990, for a detailed discussion of the theoretical assumptions and methodological procedures of cultivation analysis).

The systemic patterns in television content that we observe through message system analysis provide the basis for formulating survey questions about people's conceptions of social reality. These questions form the basis of surveys administered to large and representative national samples of respondents. The surveys include questions about fear of crime, trusting other people, walking at night in one's own neighborhood, chances of victimization, inclination to aggression and so on. Respondents in each sample are divided into those who watch the most television, those who watch a moderate amount and those who watch the least. Cultivation is assessed by comparing patterns of responses in the three viewing groups (light, medium and heavy) while controlling for important demographic and other characteristics, such as education, age, income, gender, newspaper reading, neighborhood and so on.

These surveys indicate that long-term regular exposure to violence-laden television tends to make an independent contribution (e.g., in addition to all other factors) to the feeling of living in a mean and gloomy world. The lessons range from aggression to desensitization and to a sense of vulnerability and dependence.

The symbolic overkill takes its toll on all viewers. However, heavier viewers in every subgroup express a greater sense of apprehension than do light viewers in the same groups. They are more likely than comparable groups of light viewers to overestimate their chances of involvement in violence; to believe that their neighborhoods are unsafe; to state that fear of crime is a very serious personal problem and to assume that crime is rising, regardless of the facts of the case. Heavy viewers are also more likely to buy new locks, watchdogs and guns "for protection." It makes no difference what they watch because only light viewers watch more selectively; heavy viewers watch more of everything that is on the air. Our studies show that they cannot escape watching violence (see, for example, Gerbner et al., 1993; Sun, 1989).

Moreover, viewers who see members of their own group underrepresented but overvictimized seem to develop a greater sense of apprehension, mistrust and alienation, what we call the "mean world syndrome." Insecure, angry people may be prone to violence but are even more likely to be dependent on authority and susceptible to deceptively simple, strong, hard-line postures. They may accept and even welcome repressive measures such as more jails, capital punishment, harsher sentences—measures that have never reduced crime but never fail to get votes—if that promises to relieve their anxieties. That is the deeper dilemma of violence-laden television.

● The Structural Basis of Television Violence

Formula-driven violence in entertainment and news is not an expression of freedom, viewer preference or even crime statistics. The frequency of violence in the media seldom, if ever, reflects the actual occurrence of crime in a community. It is, rather, the product of a complex manufacturing and marketing machine.

Mergers, consolidation, conglomeratization and globalization speed the machine. "Studios are clipping productions and consolidating operations, closing off gateways for newcomers," notes the trade paper *Variety* on the front page of its August 2,1993, issue. The number of major studios declines while their share of domestic and global markets rises. Channels proliferate while investment in new talent drops, gateways close and creative sources shrink.

Concentration brings denial of access to new entries and alternative perspectives. It places greater emphasis on dramatic ingredients most suitable for aggressive international promotion. Having fewer buyers for their products forces program producers into deficit financing. That means that most producers cannot break even on the license fees they receive for domestic airings. They are forced into syndication and foreign sales to make a profit. They need a dramatic ingredient that requires no translation, "speaks action" in any language and fits any culture. That ingredient is violence. (Sex is second but, ironically, it runs into more inhibitions and restrictions.)

Syndicators demand *action* (the code word for violence) because it "travels well around the world," said the producer of *Die Hard 2* (which killed 264 compared to 18 in *Die Hard 1*). "Everyone understands an action movie. If I tell a joke, you may not get it but if a bullet goes through the window, we all know how to hit the floor, no matter the language" (quoted in Auletta, 1993). Our analysis shows that violence dominates U.S. exports. We compared 250 U.S. programs exported to 10 countries with 111 programs shown in the United States during the same year. Violence was the main theme of 40% of home-shown and 49% of exported programs. Crime-action series composed 17% of home-shown and 46% of exported programs.

The rationalization for all that is that violence "sells." But what does it sell to whom and at what price? There is no evidence that, other factors being equal, violence per se is giving most viewers, countries and citizens "what they want." The most highly rated programs are usually not violent. The trade paper *Broadcasting & Cable* (Editorial, 1993) editorialized that "the most popular programming is hardly violent as anyone with a passing knowledge of Nielsen ratings will tell you." The editorial added that "Action hours and movies have been the most popular exports for years" (p. 66)— that is, with the exporters, not with audiences. In other words, violence may help sell programs cheaply to broadcasters in many countries despite the dislike of their audiences. But television audiences do not buy programs, and advertisers, who do, pay for reaching the available audience at the least cost.

We compared data from over 100 violent and the same number of nonviolent prime-time programs stored in the CI database. The average Nielsen rating of the violent sample was 11.1; the same for the nonviolent sample was 13.8. The share of viewing households in the violent and nonviolent samples was 18.9 and 22.5, respectively. The amount and consistency of violence in a series further increased the gap. Furthermore, the nonviolent sample was more highly rated than the violent sample for each of the five seasons studied.

However, despite their low average popularity, what violent programs lose on general domestic audiences they more than make up by grabbing the younger viewers that advertisers want to reach and by extending their reach to the global market hungry for a cheap product. Even though, typically, these imports are also less popular abroad than quality shows produced at home, their extremely low cost, compared to local production, makes them attractive to the broadcasters who buy them.

Of course, some violent movies, videos, video games and other spectacles do attract sizable audiences. But those audiences are small compared to the home audience for television. They are the selective retail buyers of what television dispenses wholesale. If only a small proportion of television viewers growing up with the violent overkill become addicted to it, they can make many movies and games spectacularly successful.

❧ Public Response and Action

Most television viewers suffer the violence daily inflicted on them with diminishing tolerance. Organizations of creative workers in media, health professionals, law enforcement agencies and virtually all other media-oriented professional and citizen groups have come out against "gratuitous" television violence. A March 1985 Harris survey showed that 78% disapprove of violence they see on television. A Gallup poll of October 1990 found 79% in favor of "regulating" objectionable content in television. A Times-Mirror national poll in 1993 showed that Americans who said they were "personally bothered" by violence in entertainment shows jumped to 59% from 44% in 1983. Furthermore, 80% said entertainment violence was "harmful" to society, compared with 64% in 1983.

Local broadcasters, legally responsible for what goes on the air, also oppose the overkill and complain about loss of control. *Electronic Media* reported on August 2, 1993, the results of its own survey of 100 general managers across all regions and in all market sizes. Three of four said there is too much needless violence on television; 57% would like to have "more input on program content decisions."

The Hollywood Caucus of Producers, Writers and Directors, speaking for the creative community, said in a statement issued in August 1993:

> We stand today at a point in time when the country's dissatisfaction with the quality of television is at an all-time high, while our own feelings of helplessness and lack of power, in not only choosing material that seeks to enrich, but also in our ability to execute to the best of our ability, is at an all-time low.

Far from reflecting creative freedom, the marketing of formula violence restricts freedom and chills originality. The violence formula is, in fact, a de facto censorship extending the dynamics of domination, intimidation and repression domestically and globally. Much of the typical political and legislative response exploits the anxieties that violence itself generates and offers remedies ranging from labeling and advisories to even more censorship.

There is a liberating alternative. It exists in various forms in most other democratic countries. It is public participation in making decisions about cultural investment and cultural policy. Independent grassroots citizen organization and action can provide the broad support needed for loosening the global marketing noose and the necks of producers, writers, directors, actors and journalists.[2]

More freedom from violent and other inequitable and intimidating formulas, not more censorship, is the effective and acceptable way to increase diversity and reduce the dependence of program producers on the violence formula, and to reduce television violence to its legitimate role and proportion. The role of Congress, if any, is to turn its antitrust and civil rights oversight on the centralized and globalized industrial structures and marketing strategies that impose violence on creative people and foist it on the children and adults of the world. It is high time to develop a vision of the right of children to be born into a reasonable, free, fair, diverse and nonthreatening cultural environment. It is time for citizen involvement in cultural decisions that shape our lives and the lives of our children.

Endnotes

[1] Cutltural indicators is a database and a research project that relates recurrent features of the world of television to viewer conceptions of reality. Its cumulative computer archive contains observations on over 3,000 programs and 35,000 characters coded according to many thematic, demographic and action categories. These form the basis for the content analyses cited in the references. The study is conducted at the University of Pennsylvania's Annenberg School for Communication in collaboration with Michael Morgan at the University of Massachusetts at Amherst and Nancy Signorielli at the University of Delaware. Thanks for research assistance are due to Mariaeleana Bartezaghi, Cynthia Kandra, Robin Kim, Amy Nyman and Nejat Ozyegin.

[2] One such alternative is the Cultural Environment Movement (CEM). CEM is a nonprofit educational corporation, an umbrella coalition of independent media, professional, labor, religious, health-related, women's and minority groups opposed to private corporate as well as government censorship. CEM is working for freedom from stereotyped formulas and for investing in a freer and more diverse cultural environment. It can be reached by writing to Cultural Environment Movement, P.O. Box 31847, Philadelphia, PA 19104.

References

[Editorial]. (1993, September 20). *Broadcasting & Cable*, p. 66.

Auletta, K. (1993, May 17). What won't they do? *The New Yorker*, pp. 45–46.

Gerbner, G. (1993). "Miracles" of communication technology: Powerful audiences, diverse choices and other fairy tales. In J. Wasko (Ed.), *Illuminating the blind spots*. New York: Ablex.

Gerbner, G., Gross, L., Morgan, M., & Signorielli, N. (1993). Growing up with television: The cultivation perspective. In J. Bryant & D. Zillmann (Eds.), *Media effects: Advances in theory and research*. Hillsdale, NJ: Lawrence Erlbaum.

Morgan, M. & Shanahan, J. (1991). Do VCRs change the TV picture?: VCRs and the cultivation process. *American Behavioral Scientist, 35*(2), 122–135.

Morgan, M., & Signorielli, N. (1990). Cultivation analysis: Conceptualization and methodology. In N. Signorielli & M. Morgan (Eds.), *Cultivation analysis: New directions in media effects research* (pp. 13–33). Newbury Park, CA: Sage.

Sun, L. (1989). *Limits of selective viewing: An analysis of "diversity" in dramatic programming.* Unpublished master's thesis, the Annenberg School for Communication, University of Pennsylvania, Philadelphia.

◉ ◉ ◉

Questions

1. In general, what types of portrayals have been consistent over the last 30 years in U.S. television content?

2. How pervasive are violent images on TV? Do any gender or racial/ethnic variations emerge? If so, what are they? What is the "pecking order" for those most and least likely to be portrayed as violent and aggressive on TV? How about the "pecking order" for victimization?

3. What are some long-term consequences of viewing television violence? How do these consequences vary for members of underrepresented groups?

4. What structural features contribute to the continued portrayal of violence on television *and* to its exponential growth over the last several decades?

5. What, if anything, can be done to address the problem of violence on TV? What does Gerbner recommend? Would his proposal be effective? Why or why not?

The Social Organization of Deviants

JOEL BEST, California State University, Fresno

DAVID F. LUCKENBILL, University of Illinois, Chicago Circle

We can loosely categorize the study of deviant behavior into (1) the study of deviance (the behavior itself) and (2) the study of deviants (those who systematically engage in deviant behavior). In this article, Joel Best and David Luckenbill focus on the social organization of deviants. The authors present a typology of organizational structures, ranging from individual beliefs through complex, formal institutions. They also discuss each organizational arrangement in terms of the quality of its resources, the type of deviant behavior that it can sustain, and the social-control strategies associated with it.

*S*thnographic research on particular social scenes provides data for general, grounded theories (Glaser and Strauss, 1967). For the study of deviance, field studies have supplied the basis for the development of general theories of the social psychology of deviance (Goffman, 1963; Lofland, 1969; Matza, 1969). However, while several reports about specific forms of deviance focus on social organization (Einstader, 1969; McIntosh, 1971; Mileski and Black, 1972; Shover, 1977; Zimmerman and Wieder, 1977), there is no satisfactory general theory of the social organization of deviance.

Sociologists of varying perspectives have debated the nature of social organization among juvenile delinquents, professional criminals, organized criminals and white-collar criminals. Others have developed typologies of deviants that include social organizational features (Clinard and Quinney, 1973; Gibbons, 1965, 1977; Miller, 1978). However, these treatments of social organization suffer from several flaws. First, they are often too narrow,

"The Social Organization of Deviants," by Joel Best and David Luckenbill, reprinted from *Social Problems*, vol. 28, no. 1, 1980, pp. 14–31.

focusing on a single type of deviance, such as burglary or, more broadly, crime. Second, they usually are content with describing the organizational forms of different types of deviance. They fail to locate such forms along a dimension of organization or examine the consequences of organizational differences for deviants and social control agents. Third, they typically confuse two different bases for analyzing social organization: a general theory must distinguish between the social organization of *deviants* (the patterns of relationships between deviant actors) and the social organization of *deviance* (the patterns of relationships between the various roles performed in deviant transactions).

In this paper, we present a framework for understanding the social organization of deviants. By examining reports of field research, several forms of social organization are identified and located along a dimension of organizational sophistication. Then some propositions are developed regarding the consequences of organizational variation for deviants and social control agents. Finally, some implications for the study of social organization are considered.

❧ Forms of Deviant Organization

The social organization of deviants refers to the structure or patterns of relationships among deviant actors in the context of deviant pursuits. The social organization of deviants varies along a dimension of sophistication. Organizational sophistication involves the elements of complexity, coordination and purposiveness (cf. Cressey, 1972). Organizations vary in the complexity of their division of labor including the size of membership, degree of stratification, and degree of specialization of organizational roles. Organizations also vary in their coordination among roles including the degree to which rules, agreements, and codes regulating relationships are formalized and enforced. Finally, organizations vary in the purposiveness with which they specify, strive toward, and achieve their objectives. Forms of organization which display high levels of complexity, coordination, and purposiveness are more sophisticated than those forms with lower levels.

Research reports suggest that deviants organize in several identifiable ways along the dimension of sophistication. Beginning with the least sophisticated, we will discuss five forms: loners, colleagues, peers, mobs and formal organizations. These organizational forms can be defined in terms of four variables: 1) whether the deviants associate with one another; 2) whether they participate in deviance together; 3) whether their deviance requires an elaborate division of labor; and 4) whether their organization's activities extend over time and space (see Table 1). *Loners* do not associate with other deviants, participate in shared deviance, have a division of labor, or maintain their deviance over extended time and space. *Colleagues* differ from loners because they associate with fellow deviants. *Peers* not only associate with one another, but also participate in deviance together. In mobs, the shared participation requires an elaborate division of labor. Finally, *formal organizations* involve mutual association and participation, an elaborate division of labor, and deviant undertakings extended over time and space.

The descriptions of these forms of organization must be qualified in two ways. First, the forms are presented as ideal types. There is variation among the types of deviants within each form, as well as between one form and another. The intent is to sketch out the typical features of each form, recognizing that particular types of deviants may not share all of the features of their form to the same degree. Organizational sophistication can be viewed as a continuum, with deviants located between, as well as on, the five points. Describing a number of forms along this continuum inevitably understates the complexities of social life. Second, the descriptions of these forms draw largely from field studies of deviance in the contemporary United States, and attempt to locate the deviants studied along the dimension of organizational sophistication. A particular type of deviant can be organized in various ways in different societies and at different times. The references to specific field studies are intended to place familiar pieces of research within this framework; they are not claims that particular types of deviants invariably organize in a given way.

TABLE 1 *Characteristics of Different Forms of the Social Organization of Deviants*

Variable	Type of Organization				
	Loners	Colleagues	Peers	Mobs	Formal Organizations
Mutual Association	-	+	+	+	+
Mutual Participation	-	-	+	+	+
Division of Labor	-	-	-	+	+
Extended Organization	-	-	-	-	+

ℒoners

Some deviants operate as individuals. These loners do not associate with other deviants for purposes of sociability, the performance of deviant activities, or the exchange of supplies and information. Rather, they must supply themselves with whatever knowledge, skill, equipment and ideology their deviance requires. Loners lack deviant associations, so they cannot receive such crucial forms of feedback as moral support or information about their performance, new opportunities, or changes in social control strategies. They often enter deviance as a defensive response to private troubles (Lofland, 1969). Because their entry does not require contact with other deviants, as long as they can socialize themselves, loners frequently come from segments of the population which are less likely to be involved in the more sophisticated forms of deviance; it is not uncommon for loners to be middle-aged, middle-class or female. Because their deviance often is defensive, and because they lack the support of other deviants, loners' careers typically are short-lived. Examples of loners include murderers (Luckenbill, 1977), rapists (Amir, 1971), embezzlers (Cressey, 1953), check forgers (Lemert, 1967:99–134, Klein and Montague, 1977), physician narcotic addicts (Winick, 1961), compulsive criminals (Cressey, 1962), heterosexual transvestites (Buckner, 1970), amateur shoplifters (Cameron, 1964), some gamblers (Lesieur, 1977), and many computer criminals (Parker, 1976).[1]

𝒞olleagues

Like loners, colleagues perform as individuals. Unlike loners, however, colleagues associate with others involved in the same kind of deviance. Colleagues thus form a simple group which provides important services for members. First, colleagues often socialize newcomers, providing training in deviant skills as well as an ideology which accounts for and justifies their deviance. Association also offers sociability among members with whom one's deviant identity need not be concealed: an actor can take down his or her guard without fear of discovery by agents of social control (Goffman, 1959, 1963). Also, association provides a source of information about ways to obtain deviant equipment, new techniques, new opportunities for engaging in deviance, and strategies for avoiding sanctioning. Colleagues learn and are held to a loose set of norms which direct conduct in both deviant and respectable activities. "Don't inform on a colleague" and "Never cut in on a colleague's score" exemplify such norms. The moral climate established by these expectations increases the stability of colleagues' social scene. At the same time, only some deviant activities and some people are suited for such a loose form of organization. A successful career as a colleague depends ultimately on the individual's performance when operating alone. As a result, newcomers often sample the scene and, when they encounter difficulties, drift away. Only the more successful colleagues maintain extended deviant careers. Some examples of colleagues include most prostitutes (Hirschi, 1962; Bryan, 1965, 1966), pimps (Milner and Milner, 1972), and pool hustlers (Polsky, 1967).

Peers

Like colleagues, peers associate with one another and benefit from services provided by their fellows. Peers are involved in the socialization of novices, considerable sociable interaction, and the maintenance of a loose, unwritten code of conduct to be followed by individuals who wish to remain in the peer group. Unlike colleagues, peers participate in deviant acts together; they are involved in deviant transactions at the same time and in the same place. In some cases, such mutual participation is required by the nature of the deviant activity. This is exemplified in the performance of homosexual acts, or in the "task force raids" where a collection of young men engages in simple acts of violence such as gang fighting or rolling drunks (Cressey, 1972). In other cases, mutual participation is required because peers form a network for supplying one another with essential goods and services, as found in the distribution of illicit drugs. In either event, peers interact basically as equals; there is a minimal division of labor and specialized roles are uncommon. Although individuals pass through these social scenes, peer groups often are quite stable, perhaps because peer groups solve structural problems within society for their members. Two common varieties of deviant peers are young people who have not yet entered integrated adult work roles, and those who frequent a deviant marketplace and depend on their contact with one another for the satisfaction of illicit needs. Examples of peers include hobos (Anderson, 1923), homosexuals (Humphreys, 1970; Mileski and Black, 1972; Warren, 1974), group-oriented gamblers (Lesieur, 1977), swingers (Bartell, 1971), gang delinquents (Shaw, 1930; Matza, 1964; Rosenberg and Silverstein, 1969), motorcycle outlaws (Thompson,

1966), skid row tramps (Wiseman, 1970; Rubington, 1978) and illicit drug users (Blumer, 1967; Carey, 1968; Feldman, 1968; Stoddart, 1974).

/Mobs

Mobs are small groups of professional or career deviants organized to pursue specific, profitable goals.[2] Their deviance requires the coordinated actions of members performing specialized role—a more sophisticated division of labor than that found among peers. Thus, work is divided among confidence artists (the inside man and the outside man), pickpockets (the tool and the stall), or card and dice hustlers (the mechanic and the shootup man; Maurer, 1962, 1964; Prus and Sharper, 1977). Ordinarily, at least one of the roles in the mob is highly skilled, requiring considerable practice and training to perfect. This training (normally via apprenticeship), the need for on-the-job coordination, and the common practice of traveling from city to city as a mob lead to intensive interaction between mobsters. Elaborate technical argots develop, as well as elaborate codes specifying mobsters' obligations to each other.

Mobs have complex links to outsiders. They are organized to accomplish profitable yet safe crimes. McIntosh (1971) describes the historical shift from craft thieving, where mobs develop routine procedures for stealing relatively small sums from individuals, to project thieving, where larger amounts are taken from corporate targets using procedures specifically tailored to the particular crime. In either case, mob operations are planned and staged with an eye toward avoiding arrest. Also, mobs may attempt to neutralize the criminal justice system by bribing social control agents not to make arrests, "fixing" those cases where arrests take place, or making restitution to victims in return for dropped charges. Mobs also have ties to others who purchase stolen goods, provide legal services, and supply information and deviant equipment. Finally, a network of sociable and business contacts ties mobs to one another, enabling strategic information to spread quickly. These arrangements insure that mobs can operate at a consistently profitable level with minimal interference. Consequently, the careers of individual mobsters, as well as those of specific mobs, seem to be more stable than those of deviants organized in less sophisticated ways.[3] Examples of mobs are the groups of professional criminals specializing in confidence games (Sutherland, 1937; Maurer, 1962), picking pockets (Maurer, 1964), shoplifting (Cameron, 1964), armed robbery (Einstader, 1969; Letkemann,

1973), burglary (Shover, 1973) and card and dice hustling (Prus and Sharper, 1977).

Formal Organizations

Formal organizations of deviants differ from mobs in the scope of their actions.[4] Normally they involve more people, but, more importantly, their actions are coordinated to efficiently handle deviant tasks on a routine basis over considerable time and space. While mobsters work as a group in a series of episodic attacks, formal organizations are characterized by delegated responsibility and by routine and steady levels of productivity. In many ways, formal organizations of deviants share the features which characterize such respectable bureaucracies as military organizations, churches and business firms. They have a hierarchal division of labor, including both vertical and horizontal differentiation of positions and roles and established channels for vertical and horizontal communication. A deviant formal organization may contain departments for planning, processing goods, public relations and rule enforcement, with positions for strategists, coordinators, accountants, lawyers, enforcers, and dealers in illicit goods. There may be recruitment policies for filling these diversified positions, and entry into the organization may be marked by a ritual ceremony of passage. Formal organizations usually have binding, but normally unwritten, rules and codes for guiding members in organizational action, and these rules are actively enforced.

Formal organizations of deviants can make large profits by operating efficiently. At the same time, they must protect themselves from harm or destruction. As in less sophisticated forms of organization, loyal members are expected to maintain the group's secrets. In addition, deviant formal organizations attempt to locate power in the office, rather than in an individual charismatic leader. Although charismatic leadership obviously plays a part in some deviant formal organizations, the successful organization is able to continue operations when a leader dies or is arrested. Finally, deviant formal organizations typically invest considerable energy in neutralizing the criminal justice system by corrupting both high and low level officials. The scope and efficiency of their operations, their organizational flexibility, and their ties to agencies of social control make formal organizations of deviants extremely stable. Examples of such deviant formal organizations include very large urban street gangs (Keiser, 1969; Dawley, 1973), smuggling rings (Green, 1969), and organized crime "families" (Cressey, 1969; Ianni, 1972).

❧ The Significance of the Social Organization of Deviants

The identification and description of these different organizational forms permit a comparative analysis. What are the consequences of organizing as loners, colleagues, peers, mobs, or formal organizations? A comparison suggests that the sophistication of a form of deviant social organization has several consequences for both deviants and social control agents. Five propositions can be advanced.

I. The more sophisticated the form of deviant organization, the greater its members' capability for complex deviant operations.

Deviant activities, like conventional activities, vary in their complexity. The complexity of a deviant operation refers to the number of elements required to carry it through; the more component parts to an activity, the more complex it is.[5] Compared to simple activities, complex lines of action demand more careful preparation and execution and take longer to complete. The complexity of a deviant activity depends upon two identifiable types of elements. First, there are the *resources* which the actors must be able to draw upon. Some activities require that the deviant utilize special knowledge, skill, equipment, or social status in order to complete the operation successfully, while simple acts can be carried out without such resources. Second, the *organization of the deviant transaction* affects an activity's complexity.[6] Some deviant acts can be accomplished with a single actor, while others require two or more people. The actors in a transaction can share a common role, as in a skid row bottle gang, or the transaction may demand different roles, such as offender and victim or buyer and seller. Furthermore, the degree to which these roles must be coordinated, ranging from the minimal coordination of juvenile vandals to the precision routines performed by mobs of pickpockets, varies among situations. The more people involved, the more roles they perform; and the more coordination between those roles, the more complex the deviant transaction's organization. The more resources and organization involved in a deviant operation, the more complex the operation is.

In general, deviants in more sophisticated forms of organization commit more complex acts.[7] The deviant acts of loners tend to be simple, requiring little in the way of resources or organization. Although colleagues work apart from one another, they generally share certain resources, such as shared areas. The hustlers' pool hall and the prostitutes' red-light district contain the elements needed to carry out deviant operations, including victims and clients. Peers may interact in situations where they are the only ones present, performing complementary or comparable roles, as when two people engage in homosexual intercourse or a group of motorcycle outlaws makes a "run." Peers also may undertake activities which involved nonmembers, as when members of a delinquent gang rob a passerby. The activities carried out by mobs involve substantially more coordination among the members' roles. In an armed robbery, for instance, one member may be assigned to take the money, while a second provides "cover" and a third waits for the others in the car, ready to drive away on their return. Finally, the activities of formal organizations tend to be particularly complex, requiring substantial resources and elaborate organization. Major off-track betting operations, with staff members at local, district and regional offices who carry out a variety of clerical and supervisory tasks on a daily basis, represent an exceedingly complex form of deviance.

The relationship between sophistication of organization and the complexity of deviant activities is not perfect. Loners can engage in acts of considerable complexity, for example. The computer criminal who single-handedly devises a complicated method of breaking into and stealing from computerized records, the embezzler who carries through an elaborate series of illicit financial manipulations, and the physician who juggles drug records in order to maintain his or her addiction to narcotics are engaged in complex offenses requiring substantial resources. However, these offenses cannot be committed by everyone. These loners draw upon resources which they command through their conventional positions, turning them to deviant uses. The computer criminal typically is an experienced programmer, the embezzler must occupy a position of financial trust, and the physician has been trained in the use of drugs. Possessing these resources makes the loner's deviance possible. Thus, the more concentrated the resources necessary for a deviant operation, the less sophisticated the form of organization required. However, when resources are not concentrated, the more sophisticated forms of organization are necessary to undertake more complex deviant operations.

Sophisticated forms of deviant organization have advantages beyond being able to undertake complex operations by pooling resources distributed among their members. Some deviant activities require a minimal level of organization; for example, homosexual intercourse demands the participation of two parties. In many other cases, it may be possible to carry out a deviant line of action using a relatively unsophisticated form of organization, but the task is considerably easier if a sophisticated form of organization can be employed. This is so because more sophisticated forms of deviant organization enjoy several advantages: they are capable of conducting a larger number of deviant operations; the operations can occur with greater frequency and over a broader range of territory; and, as discussed below, the members are better protected from the actions of social control agents. Of course, sophisticated organizations may engage in relatively simple forms of deviance, but the deviant act is often only one component in a larger organizational context. Taking a particular bet in the policy racket is a simple act, but the racket itself, handling thousands of bets, is complex indeed. Similarly, a murder which terminates a barroom dispute between two casual acquaintances is very different from an execution which is ordered and carried out by members of a formal organization, even though the two acts may appear equally simple. In the latter case, the killing may be intended as a means of maintaining discipline by demonstrating the organization's ability to levy sanctions against wayward members.

II. The more sophisticated the form of deviant organization, the more elaborate the socialization of its members.

Neophyte deviants need to acquire two types of knowledge: 1) they must learn how to perform deviant acts, and how to gain appropriate *skills and techniques;* 2) they must develop a *cognitive perspective,* a distinctive way of making sense of their new, deviant world (cf. Shibutani, 1961: 118–127). Such a perspective includes an ideology which accounts for the deviance, the individual's participation in deviance, and the organizational form, as well as a distinctive language for speaking about these and other matters.

As forms of deviant organization increase in sophistication, socialization becomes more elaborate. Loners do not depend upon other deviants for instruction in deviant skills or for a special cognitive perspective; they learn through their participation in conventional social scenes. Murderers, for instance, learn from their involvement in conventional life how to respond in situations of interpersonal conflict, and they employ culturally wide-spread justifications for killing people (Bohannon, 1960; Wolfgang and Ferracuti, 1967). Embezzlers learn the technique for converting a financial trust in the course of respectable vocational training, adapting justifications such as "borrowing" from conventional business ideology (Cressey, 1953). In contrast, colleagues teach one another a great deal. Although pool hustlers usually know how to shoot pool before they enter hustling, their colleagues provide a rich cognitive perspective, including a sense of "we-ness," some norm behavior, a system for stratifying the hustling world, and an extensive argot (Polsky, 1967).[8] Peers receive similar training or, in some cases, teach one another through a process of emerging norms (Turner, 1964). Juvenile vandals, for example, can devise new offenses through their mutually constructed interpretation of what is appropriate to a particular situation (Wade, 1967). Sometimes, the knowledge peers acquire has largely symbolic functions that affirm the group's solidarity, as when a club of motorcycle outlaws devises a written constitution governing its members (Reynolds, 1967:134–136). In mobs and formal organizations, the cognitive perspective focuses on more practical matters; their codes of conduct spec-ify the responsibilities members have in their dealings with one another, social control agents and others. Greater emphasis is also placed on the acquisition of specialized skills, with an experienced deviant coaching an apprentice, frequently over an extended period of time.

Two circumstances affect the socialization process in different forms of deviant organization. The skills required to perform deviant roles vary, but there is a tendency for more sophisticated forms of organization to incorpo-rate highly skilled roles. Further, the more sophisticated forms of organization often embody cognitive perspectives of such breadth that the deviant must acquire a large body of specialized knowledge. In addition, the socialization process tends to be organized differently in different forms of deviant organization. While loners serve as their own agents of socialization, and colleagues and peers may socialize one another, mobs and formal organ-izations almost always teach newcomers through apprenticeship to an experienced deviant. Second, the socialization process is affected by the newcomer's motivation for entering deviance. Loners, of course, choose deviance on their own. In the more sophisticated forms, newcomers may ask for admission, but they often are recruited by experienced deviants. While peers may recruit widely, as when a delinquent gang tries to enlist all of the neighborhood boys of a given age, mobs and formal organizations recruit selectively, judging the character and commitment of prospective members and sometimes demanding evidence of skill or prior experience. For loners, entry into deviance frequently is a defensive act, intended to ward off some immediate threat. Peers, on the other hand, often are using deviance to experience stimulation; their deviance has an adventurous quality (Lofland, 1969). In contrast, mobs and formal organizations adopt a more professional approach: deviance is instrumental, a calculated means of acquiring economic profits.[9] These differences in the scope of socialization, the way the process is organized, and the neophyte's motivation account for the relationship between sophistication of organization and the elaborateness of socialization.

III. The more sophisticated the form of deviant organization, the more elaborate the services provided its members.

Every social role poses practical problems for its performers. In some cases these problems can be solved by providing the actors with supplies of various sorts. Actors may require certain *equipment* to perform a role. They may also need *information* about their situation in order to coordinate their behavior with the ongoing action and successfully accomplish their part in an operation. One function of deviant social organization is to solve such practical problems by supplying members with needed equipment and information. More sophisticated forms of social organization are capable of providing more of these services.

Deviants differ in their requirements for equipment. Some need little in the way of equipment; a mugger may be able to get by with a piece of pipe. In other cases, deviants make use of specialized items which have few, if any, respectable uses (e.g., heroin or the booster boxes used in shoplifting).[10] Most loners require little equipment. When specialized needs exist, they are met through conventional channels accessible to the deviants, as when a physician narcotic addict obtains illicit drugs from hospital or clinic supplies. Colleagues also supply their own equipment, for the most part, although they may receive some assistance; pool hustlers, for example, provide their own cues, but they may rely on financial backers for funding.

Peers adopt various patterns toward equipment. In some cases, peer groups develop to facilitate the distribution and consumption of deviant goods, such as illicit drugs. In other instances, peers use equipment as a symbol of their deviant status, as when gang members wear special costumes. The equipment used by mobsters is more utilitarian; many of their trades demand specialized tools, for safecracking, shoplifting and so forth. In addition to a craftsman's personal equipment, the mob may require special materials for a specific project. Norms often exist that specify the manner in which these equipment purchases will be financed. In still other instances, some mobsters with expensive pieces of equipment may cooperate with several different mobs who wish to make use of them (such as the "big store" which is centrally located for the use of several confidence mobs). Formal organizations also have extensive equipment requirements. Because their operations extend over considerable time, formal organizations may find it expedient to invest in an elaborate array of fixed equipment. Off-track book-making, for example, may involve the purchase or rental of offices, desks, calculators, computer lines, special telephone lines, office supplies and automobiles. Special staff members may have the responsibility for maintaining this equipment (Bell, 1962: 134). In addition, some formal organizations are involved in producing or distributing deviant equipment for the consumption of other deviants, drug smuggling offers the best example.

Deviants need information in order to determine their courses of action. To operate efficiently, they need to know about new opportunities for deviant action; to operate safely, they need to know about the movements of social control agents. The more sophisticated forms of organization have definite advantages in acquiring and processing information. Loners, of course, depend upon themselves for information; opportunities or threats outside their notice cannot be taken into account. Colleagues and peers can learn more by virtue of their contacts with the deviant "grapevine," and they may have norms regarding a member's responsibility to share relevant information. In mobs, information is sought in more systematic ways. In the course of their careers, mobsters develop perceptual skills, enabling them to "case" possible targets (Letkemann, 1973). In addition, some mobs rely on outsiders for information; spotters may be paid a commission for pointing out opportunities for theft. A formal organization can rely upon its widely distributed membership for information and its contacts with corrupted social control agents.

The degree to which deviants need special supplies varies with the requirements of their operations, the frequency with which they interact with victims or other nondeviants, and their visibility to social control agents. Supplies other than equipment and information may be required in some instances. However, for most supply problems, sophisticated forms of social organization enjoy a comparative advantage.

IV. The more sophisticated the form of deviant organization, the greater its members' involvement in deviance.

Complex deviant operations require planning and coordinated action during the deviant act. Socialization and supply also involve interaction among an organization's members. More sophisticated forms of deviant organization, featuring complex operations and elaborate socialization and supply, are therefore more likely to involve intensive social contact with one's fellow deviants. Furthermore, because deviants face sanctions from social control agents and respectable people, their contacts with other deviants are an important source of social support. The differences in the ability of forms of social organization to provide support for their members have important social psychological consequences for deviants' careers and identities.

The dimensions of deviant careers vary with the form of deviant organization. Longer deviant careers tend to occur in more sophisticated forms of organization. For naive loners, deviance can comprise a single episode, a defensive act to ward off an immediate threat. For systematic loners, an many colleagues and peers, involvement in deviance is limited to one period in their life. Prostitutes grow too old to compete in the sexual marketplace, delinquents move into respectable adult work roles, and so forth. Members of mobs and formal organizations are more likely to have extended careers. Where the roles are not too physically demanding, deviance can continue until the individual is ready to retire from the work force (Inciardi, 1977). Deviant careers also vary in the amount of time they demand while the individual is active; some kinds of deviance take up only a small portion of the person's hours, but other deviant roles are equivalent to full-time, conventional jobs. Although the relationship is not perfect, part-time deviance is associated with less sophisticated forms of deviant organization.[11]

Social organization is also related to the relative prominence of the deviant identity in the individual's self-concept. Individuals may view their deviance as tangential to the major themes in their lives, or as a central focus, an identity around which much of one's life is arranged. The latter pattern is more likely to develop in sophisticated forms of deviant organization, for, as Lofland (1969) points out, several factors associated with deviant social organization facilitate the assumption of deviant identity, including frequenting places populated by deviants, obtaining deviant equipment, and receiving instruction in deviant skills and ideology. These factors also would appear to be associated with the maintenance of deviance as a central identity. Loners seem especially adept at isolating their deviance, viewing it as an exception to the generally conventional pattern their lives take. This is particularly true when the deviance was initially undertaken to defend that conventional life style from some threat. Even when an individual is relatively committed to deviance, normal identities can serve as an important resource. In his discussion of the World War II underground, Aubert (1965) notes that normal identities served to protect its members. In the same way, an established normal status shields the deviant from the suspicion of social control agents and, if the members refrain from revealing their conventional identities to one another, against discovery brought about by deviant associates who invade their respectable lives. Such considerations seem to be most important in middle-class peer groups organized around occasional leisure-time participation in a deviant marketplace, such as homosexuality and swinging.[12] Other deviants, particularly members of mobs and formal organizations, may associate with their fellows away from deviant operations, so that both their work and their sociable interaction take place among deviants. This is also true for peer groups that expand into "communities" and offer a wide range of services to members. Active members of urban gay communities can largely restrict their contacts to other homosexuals (Harry and Devall, 1978; Wolf, 1979). In these cases there is little need to perform conventional roles, aside from their obvious uses as concealment, and the deviant identity is likely to be central for the individual.

The degree to which an individual finds a deviant career and a deviant identity satisfying depends in part, on the form of deviant organization of which he or she is a part. As in any activity, persons continue to engage in deviance only as long as the rewards it offers are greater than the rewards which could be obtained through alternative activities. The relevant rewards vary from one person to the next and from one type of deviance to another; a partial list includes money, physical and emotional satisfaction, valued social contacts and prestige. Because the relative importance of these rewards varies with the individual, it is impossible to measure the differences in rewards between forms of deviant organization. There is some evidence that monetary profits are generally higher in more sophisticated forms of deviant organization. While an occasional loner can steal a very large sum through an embezzlement or a computer crime, most mobs can earn a reasonably steady income, and rackets run by formal organizations consistently bring in high profits. A more revealing measure of satisfaction is career stability; members of more sophisticated forms of deviant organization are more likely to remain in deviance. Loners' careers are short-lived, even when they are involved in systematic deviance. Lemert's (1967) account of the failure of professional forgers to remain at large suggests that the lack of social support is critical. As noted above, persons frequently drift out of their roles as colleagues and peers when other options become more attractive. The long-term careers of members of mobs and formal organizations suggest that these forms are more likely to satisfy the deviant.[13]

V. The more sophisticated the form of deviant organization, the more secure its members' deviant operations.

The social organization of deviants affects the interaction between deviants and social control agents. This relationship is complicated because increased sophistication has consequences which would seem to make social control efforts both easier and more difficult. On the one hand, the more sophisticated the deviant organization, the greater its public visibility and its chances of being subject to social control actions. Because more sophisticated forms of organization have more complex deviant operations, there are more people involved with the organization as members, victims, customers and bystanders. Therefore, there are more people capable of supplying the authorities with information about the identities, operations, and locations of organizational members. On the other hand, more sophisticated forms of organization are more likely to have codes of conduct requiring their members to be loyal to the organization and to maintain its secrets. Further, more sophisticated forms of organization command resources which can be used to protect the organization and its members from social control agents. While highly sophisticated organizations find it more difficult to conceal the fact that deviance is taking place, they often are more successful at shielding their members from severe sanctions. This relationship becomes apparent through a review of the problems members of different organizational forms have in coping with social control.

Loners' operations are relatively insecure, for they must provide their own protection. Many loners depend upon isolating their deviance; the isolated alcoholic drinks at home, and the physician addict uses narcotics in private. Such physical isolation facilitates secrecy of operations and a degree of stability, but the secrecy is shattered easily. Because loners employ limited, conventional channels of information about social control practices they can fall prey to surreptitious methods of social control: sudden spot-checks of narcotic prescriptions may uncover the physician's addiction, and unexpected audits to check computer transactions may foil the computer criminal. Even without surreptitious control practices, ignorance or gaffes can expose loners' secretive operations. In attending to the loner's appearance, behavior or life style, others may observe signs of his or her involvement in deviance. In some cases, loners perform in the presence of respectable persons; others may witness the loner's hallucinatory behavior or be the target of a street robbery. Given knowledge of a loner's involvement in deviance, others can mobilize the appropriate authorities. Such mobilization brings a likelihood of apprehension and legal processing because loners must rely on their personal, often limited, resources to combat social control efforts. A naive loner may have enough social margin to call upon respectable relatives or friends for support (Wiseman, 1970:233), but those with a record of systematic deviance are especially vulnerable, as Bittner's (1967) research on the processing of the lower-class mentally ill demonstrates.

Colleagues' and peers' operations are also insecure. To be sure, colleagues and peers have access through their organizational networks to better information about social control practices. Consequently, they can adjust their operations more effectively to avoid apprehension and legal processing. Colleagues and peers also share codes of conduct which help insure the secrecy of member's identities, activities and locations. Despite such advantages, these deviants encounter conditions rendering their deviant operations insecure. First, colleagues and peers pursue deviant activities which generally are more visible than those undertaken by loners. In some cases, they must make themselves accessible to clients, as found with prostitutes and pool hustlers. In others, they enter public places to contact and trade with other deviants, as when homosexuals exchange sexual services in tearooms, or when drug dealers and buyers do business on streetcorners or in alleys. In still other cases, their resources are so limited that they cannot command private places, as found with skid row tramps and delinquent gangs (Werthman and Piliavin, 1967). Second, while loners operate alone, colleagues and peers associate with others. Hence, the number of people aware of the members' involvement in deviance can be considerably larger, so that individuals may develop a reputation—they may become known for their deviance. Third, colleagues and peers have limited organizational resources with which to manage social control efforts. Even when members feel an obligation to help an arrested comrade, they rarely are able to do more than arrange for bail.

Mobsters' operations are more secure than those of loners, colleagues or peers. Because mobs engage in routine theft, more people are aware of members' identities, activities and locations, including victims, tipsters, fences, fixers, lawyers, and members of other mobs. To offset this visibility, mobs have several features facilitating security. First, mobs organize their operations so as to pose minimal dangers to themselves. In some cases, mobs include roles oriented toward protecting deviant operations from outsiders. For instance, burglars who post a lookout and robbers who have a driver waiting in a running car have anticipated some threatening contingencies. In other cases, the nature of the relationship with the victim offers additional protection; because confidence games call for dishonesty on the part of the mark, fewer victims go to the police. Second, members learn and employ specialized skills to accomplish deviant operations safely. Learning to "case" potential targets and to identify operations which can be managed safely and profitably, and perfecting specialized deviant skills (such as the deft manipulation of the pickpocket), provide insurance for the future. Third, although they possess damaging information about one another, mobsters share a code of conduct which offers some protection for the deviants. These codes warn against revealing the mob's secrets to outsiders and affirm the responsibilities of members toward those deviants who are captured by social control agents. Fourth, the organization supplies resources for managing social control efforts. Where possible, mobs attempt to corrupt social control agents in order to ward off arrests. If members are captured, the mob may have contacts with corrupted agents who can "fix" the case's outcome; the mob may compensate the victim in return for dropping criminal charges, or it may try to influence the testimony of witnesses. Because they are prepared to counter social control agents, mobsters' operations are relatively secure.

Finally, formal organizations are characterized by considerable security. It is possible to trace the histories of some specific formal organizations over several decades; they endured in spite of personnel turnover, succession of leadership, mergers with other organizations, and conflict with other deviant groups and social control agents (Nelli, 1976). Because these organizations touch the lives of so many people, including victims, customers, bystanders, lawyers, politicians, police officers and members of the media, their existence is no secret. Nonetheless, their members enjoy reasonable safety for several reasons. First, a binding code of conduct enjoins members from revealing organizational secrets, and violations of these rules may be punishable by violence. Some organizations even employ members who specialize in enforcing these rules. Second, formal organizations go to considerable lengths to protect members against social control efforts: they may maintain a network of informants who can warn of impending raids; they may employ their own lawyers to defend members who are arrested; and, by systematically corrupting social control agents at all levels of the control hierarchy, formal organizations can insure against aggressive law enforcement. Third, even when arrests occur, organizations can avoid serious damage. The hierarchal division of labor places the lowest ranking members in the positions most vulnerable to arrest. Because organizational leaders rarely commit public violations, law enforcement agencies find it difficult to compile evidence against them. Nor is the arrest of a ranking member enough to cripple an organization; it is easy enough to move another member into the captured deviant's slot in the structure of the organization. The failure of social control agents to destroy several well-known formal organizations reflects some of the advantages of organizational sophistication.

Because forms of deviant organization differ in their vulnerability to social control, control agents must adapt their tactics to fit the form of organization if they hope to apprehend deviants. The structure of the offense has well-established effects on social control: where agents can count on victims to bring cases to their attention, social control tactics can be reactive; but the absence of a complainant forces agencies to adopt proactive tactics. Whether they are pursuing reactive or proactive tactics, control agents must devote more resources to apprehending deviants as the sophistication of the deviant organization increases. Organizational sophistication carries advantages— greater loyalty among members, mechanisms for enforcing such loyalty, better information about control agents' plans and movements, operations designed to minimize risk, and so on—which social control agents must overcome before the deviants can be captured. Thus, in dealing with deviant formal organizations, social control agents must bring extraordinary resources to bear. For instance, in order to protect them from the organization's revenge, members who defect and inform on their fellows may be institutionalized in specially guarded settings or given new identities and set up in legitimate careers in new cities. special task forces of agents may be established and permitted to work independently of the police and other ordinary agents who are thought to have been corrupted. Or, where deviants cannot be prosecuted for their "real" crimes, agents may attempt to compile evidence for ancillary violations, such as income tax evasion. In spite of such control strategies, deviant formal organizations have proven able to withstand attack for decades.

◉ Conclusion

Deviants can be arrayed along a dimension of organizational sophistication. We have focused on five forms of organization: loners, colleagues, peers, mobs and formal organizations. The level of organizational sophistication has important consequences for deviants and social control agents; the complexity of deviant operations, the type of socialization and services provided deviants, the members' involvement in deviance, and the security from social control depend, in part, on the form of deviant organization. The social organization of deviants affects the texture of deviant life; a comparison of field studies reporting on similar types of deviance, such as the various forms of theft, reveals different patterns in the members' routines where organizational differences exist.

The analysis of the social organization of deviants can be extended in two directions. First, the dimension of organizational sophistication can serve as the basis for developing a generalized grounded theory of social organization. Second, the impact of social structure on the social organization of deviants deserves systematic investigation.

The dimension of organizational sophistication developed in this paper could be applied to conventional occupations.[14] For reasons noted below, it is difficult to identify many respectable occupations filled by loners—an unpublished writer, laboring on a manuscript, can serve as one example. In contrast, many respectable careers, including those of doctors, lawyers and other professionals, are organized as relations among colleagues. Ignoring relationships with supervisors, interaction within work groups in factories and farm labor resembles the contacts between deviant peers.[15] The staff in a small store or office works as a mob. And, of course, bureaucracies and other legitimate formal organizations can be easily identified. If an analysis similar to this one—but made among forms of respectable organization— were to compare complexity of operation, patterns of socialization, supply, member involvement, and security from external threats, it could lead to a more general statement about the effects of organizational sophistication on members and relevant audiences (Glaser and Strauss, 1967).

While analogies can be drawn between deviant and respectable forms of organization, the two should be distinguished. They occupy very different positions in the larger social structure. Deviant activities are subject to sanctioning by social control agents, therefore secrecy forms a key theme in the lives of deviants. While conventional workers may want to conceal some details of their work from competitors (who might steal their secrets) and outsiders (who might be shocked by backstage revelations), relatively few respectable occupations require workers to totally conceal their involvement in their careers. Hence the scarcity of respectable loners—virtually every worker is openly linked to the larger social web. Moreover, these ties are affirmed in written documents—licenses, contracts, government regulations, deeds of ownership, company rules and the like. Deviants are far less likely to commit their activities to a written record because they operate outside the larger institutional network. The advantage is the preservation of secrecy, but there are also disadvantages: written records can increase efficiency, particularly in complex organizations of some scope, and links to the institutional order provide respectable organizations with some protections which deviants must do without. Finally, respectable workers are likely to have relationships in which they produce, as well as consume. Some deviants (e.g. robbers), who exploit victims without providing compensating goods or services, can be seen as consistently performing a role as consumer. Workers who produce have stronger ties to the social network; a producer must be visible if someone is to purchase his or her wares. Thus, secrecy is both necessary to the deviant and a consequence of his or her role as an exploiter. In spite of their similarities, deviant and respectable forms of organization are distinguished by their need for secrecy, their use of written records, and their involvement in production.

The structural context within which deviants organize also warrants investigation. Clearly, the social organization of deviants is affected by the larger social structure (cf. Miller, 1978). However, precisely what structural conditions are significant and how they operate to shape deviant organization have been largely ignored in the investigation of deviance.

Studying the conditions under which a particular organizational form develops offers a means of linking the social organization of deviants to the social structure. One method of studying this process is the systematic analysis of historical materials. Although several historical case studies of the invention and vindication of deviant labels and the establishment of social control agencies exist, less has been written about the development or decline of organizational forms (cf. O'Donnell, 1967; McIntosh, 1971; Nelli, 1976; Best, 1977; O'Malley, 1979). A theory linking social structure to deviant organization might focus on structural opportunities, social control and structural supports. Because more sophisticated organizational forms feature routinized and profitable deviance, their development requires sufficient opportunities for deviance. Mobs of professional thieves call for a stable supply of lucrative victims, for example, and formal organizations involved in gambling require a large and stable supply of customers. Changes in structurally constrained opportunities should have consequences for the deviants' organization. Similarly, the organization of social control agencies is consequential. Where control resources are sufficient to allow for effective control within an area, less sophisticated forms of organization may decrease—for they do not have the resources to neutralize control efforts—and more sophisticated forms of organization may increase. Finally, more sophisticated organizational forms are likelier to flourish where there are structural supports. Structural supports include the command of a geographical area (such as the 19th-century urban rookery), the presence of persons who provide services to deviants (such as fences), and the sponsorship of others (such as the peasants who supported the social bandit, or the merchants and government officials who supported the pirate). Structural opportunities, social control, and structural supports constitute important elements in the structural context of the social organization of deviants.

Endnotes

[1]Following Lemert (1967), loners can be subdivided into naïve loners, for whom deviance is an exceptional, one-time experience, and systematic loners, whose deviance forms a repeated pattern. Lemert's analysis of the problems confronting systematic check forgers, who have trouble maintaining a deviant

identity with little social support, suggests that systematic loners may have particularly unstable careers.

[2]The term "mob," as it is used here, is drawn from the glossary in Sutherland: "A group of thieves who work together; same as 'troupe' and 'outfit'" (1937: 239; cf. Maurer, 1962, 1964). A more recent study uses the term "crew" (Prus and Sharper, 1977).

[3]Although the mob is able to accomplish its ends more efficiently, the same tasks are sometimes handled by loners. For example, see Maurer (1964: 166–168) and Prus and Sharper (1977: 22).

[4]Our use of the term "formal organization" is not meant to imply that these organizations have all of the characteristics of an established bureaucracy. Rather, "formal" points to the deliberately designed structure of the organization—a usage consistent with Blau and Scott (1962: 5).

[5]The complexity of a deviant activity must be distinguished from two other types of complexity. First, the definition of organizational sophistication, given above, included the complexity of the division of labor among the deviants in a given organizational form as one criterion of sophistication. Second, the complexity of an activity should not be confused with the complexity of its explanation. A suicide, for example, can be easily accomplished, even though a complex social psychological analysis may be required to explain the act.

[6]This point illustrates the distinction, made earlier, between the social organization of deviance (the pattern of relationships between the roles performed in a deviant transaction) and the social organization of deviants (the pattern of relationships between deviant actors). The former, not the latter, affects an activity's complexity.

[7]In most cases, loners do not possess the resources required for more than one type of complex deviance; physicians, for instance, are unable to commit computer thefts. In contrast, members of more sophisticated forms of organization may be able to manage several types of operations, as when a mob's members shift from picking pockets to shoplifting in order to avoid the police or when an organized crime family is involved in several different rackets simultaneously (Maurer, 1964: 55; Ianni, 1972: 87–106).

[8]Within a given form of organization, some cognitive perspectives may be more elaborate than others. While pool hustlers have a strong oral tradition, founded on the many hours they share together in pool halls, prostitutes have a relatively limited argot. Maurer (1939) argues that this is due to the restricted contact they have with one another during their work.

[9]Here and elsewhere, colleagues represent a partial exception to the pattern. Colleagues resemble members of mobs and formal organizations in that they

adopt an instrumental perspective, view deviance as a career, are socialized through apprenticeship to an experienced deviant, and accept deviance as a central identity. While peers have a more sophisticated form of organization, their mutual participation in deviance is based on their shared involvement in an illicit marketplace or leisure-time activity. In contrast, colleagues usually are committed to deviance as a means of earning a living.

Yet, because colleagues share a relatively unsophisticated form of organization, they labor under restrictions greater than those faced by mobs and formal organizations. Socialization is of limited scope; call girls learn about handling money and difficult clients, but little about sexual skills (Bryan, 1965). The code of conduct governing colleagues is less encompassing and less binding than those for more sophisticated forms, and the deviance of colleagues is usually less profitable. The absence of the advantages associated with organizational sophistication leads colleagues, despite their similarities to mobs and formal organizations, into an unsuitable situation where many individuals drift away from deviance.

[10]Sometimes such equipment is defined as illicit, and its possession constitutes a crime.

[11]Two reasons can be offered to explain this relationship. If a type of deviance is not profitable enough to support the individual, it may be necessary to take other work, as when a pool hustler moonlights (Polsky, 1967). Also, many loners have only a marginal commitment to deviance and choose to allocate most of their time to their respectable roles. This is particularly easy if the form of deviance requires little time for preparation and commission.

[12]Swingers meeting new couples avoid giving names or information which could be used to identify them (Bartell, 1971: 92–95); and Humphreys (1970) emphasizes that many tearoom participants are attracted by the setting's assurance of anonymity.

[13]During their careers, deviants may shift from one organizational form or one type of offense to another. The habitual felons interviewed by Petersilia *et al.* (1978) reported that, while many of their offenses as juveniles involved more than one partner (presumably members of a peer group), they preferred to work alone or with a single partner on the crimes they committed as adults. The most common pattern was for juveniles who specialized in burglaries to turn to robbery when they became adults.

[14]Letkemann (1973), Inciardi (1975) and Miller (1978) have tried to locate some forms of criminal activity within the frameworks developed by sociologists of work and occupations.

[15]Just as many deviant peer groups focus around leisure-time activities, some respectable leisure scenes, such as the tavern and bowling alley, are populated by peers (LeMasters, 1975).

References

Amir, Menachem. 1971. Patterns in forcible Rape. Chicago: University of Chicago Press.

Anderson, Nels. 1923. The Hobo. Chicago: University of Chicago Press.

Aubert, Vilhelm. 1965. The Hidden Society. Totawa, N.J.: Bedminster.

Bartell, Gilbert. 1971. Group Sex. New York: New American.

Bell, Daniel. 1962. The End of Ideology. Revised edition. New York: Collier.

Best, Joel. 1977. "Licensed to steal: Toward a sociology of English piracy, 1550–1750." Paper presented at the Naval History Symposium, Annapolis.

Bittner, Egon. 1967. "Police discretion in apprehending the mentally ill." Social Problems 14: 278–292.

Blau, Peter M., and W. Richard Scott. 1962. Formal Organizations. San Francisco: Chandler.

Blumer, Herbert. 1967. The World of Youthful Drug Use. Berkeley: University of California Press.

Bohannon, Paul. 1960. African Homicide and Suicide. Princeton: Princeton University Press.

Bryan, James H. 1965. "Apprenticeships in prostitution." Social Problems 12: 287–297.

_____. 1966. "Occupational ideologies and individual attitudes of call girls." Social Problems 13: 441–450.

Buckner, H. Taylor. 1970. "The transvestic career path." Psychiatry 33: 381–389.

Cameron, Mary Owen. 1964. The Booster and the Snitch. New York: Free Press.

Carey, James T. 1968. The College Drug Scene. Englewood Cliffs, N.J.: Prentice-Hall.

Clinard, Marshall B. and Richard Quinney. 1973. Criminal Behavior Systems: A Typology. Second edition. New York: Holt, Rinehart and Winston.

Cressey, Donald R. 1953. Other People's Money. New York: Free Press.

_____. 1962. "Role theory, differential association, and compulsive crimes." Pp. 443–467 in Arnold M. Rose (ed.), Human Behavior and Social Processes. Boston: Houghton Mifflin.

_____. 1969. Theft of the Nation. New York: Harper and Row.

_____. 1972. Criminal Organization. New York: Harper and Row.

Dawley, David. 1973. A Nation of Lords. Garden City, N.Y.: Anchor.

Einstader, Werner J. 1969. "The social organization of armed robbery." Social Problems 17: 64–83.

Feldman, Harvey W. 1968. "Ideological supports to becoming and remaining a heroin addict." Journal of Health and Social Behavior 9: 131–139.

Gibbons, Don C. 1965. Changing the Lawbreaker. Englewood Cliffs, N.J.: Prentice-Hall.

_____. 1977. Society, Crime, and Criminal Careers. Third edition. Englewood Cliffs, N.J.: Prentice-Hall.

Glaser, Barney G. and Anselm L. Strauss. 1967. The Discovery of Grounded Theory. Chicago: Aldine.

Goffman, Erving. 1959. The Presentation of Self in Everyday Life. Garden City, N.Y.: Anchor.

_____. 1963. Stigma. Englewood Cliffs, N.J.: Prentice-Hall.

Green, Timothy. 1969. The Smugglers. New York: Walker.

Harry, Joseph and William B. DeVall. 1978. The Social Organization of Gay Males. New York: Praeger.

Hirschi, Travis. 1962. "The professional prostitute." Berkeley Journal of Sociology 7: 33–49.

Humphreys, Laud. 1970. Tearoom Trade. Chicago: Aldine.

Ianni, Francis A. J. 1972. A Family Business. New York: Sage.

Inciardi, James A. 1975. Careers in Crime. Chicago: Rand McNally.

_____. 1977. "In search of the class cannon." Pp. 55–77 in Robert S. Weppner (ed.), Street Ethnography. Beverly Hills, Calif.: Sage.

Keiser, R. Lincoln. 1969. The Vice Lords. New York: Holt, Rinehart and Winston.

Klein, John F. and Arthur Montague. 1977. Check Forgers. Lexington, Mass.: Lexington.

LeMasters, E. E. 1975. Blue Collar Aristocrats. Madison, Wis.: University of Wisconsin Press.

Lemert, Edwin M. 1967. Human Deviance, Social Problems, and Social Control. Englewood Cliffs, N.J.: Prentice-Hall.

Lesieur, Henry R. 1977. The Chase. Garden City, N.Y.: Anchor.

Letkemann, Peter. 1973. Crime as Work. Englewood Cliffs, N.J.: Prentice-Hall.

Lofland, John. 1969. Deviance and Identity. Englewood Cliffs, N.J.: Prentice-Hall.

Luckenbill, David F. 1977. "Criminal homicide as a situated transaction." Social Problems 25: 176–186.

Matza, David. 1964. Delinquency and Drift. New York: Wiley.

_____. 1969. Becoming Deviant. Englewood Cliffs, N.J.: Prentice-Hall.

Maurer, David W. 1939. "Prostitutes and criminal argots." American Journal of Sociology 44: 346–350.

_____. 1962. The Big Con. New York: New American.

_____. 1964. Whiz Mob. New Haven, Conn.: College and University Press.

McIntosh, Mary. 1971. "Changes in the organization of thieving." Pp. 98–133 in Stanley Cohen (ed.), Images of Deviance. Baltimore, Maryland: Penguin.

Mileski, Maureen and Donald J. Black. 1972. "The social organization of homosexuality." Urban Life and Culture 1: 131–166.

Miller, Gale. 1978. Odd Jobs: The World of Deviant Work. Englewood Cliffs, N.J.: Prentice-Hall.

Milner, Christina and Richard Milner. 1972. Black Players. Boston: Little, Brown.

Nelli, Humbert. 1976. The Business of Crime. New York: Oxford University Press.

O'Donnell, John A. 1967. "The rise and decline of a subculture." Social Problems 15: 73–84.

O'Malley, Pat. 1979. "Class conflict, land and social banditry: Bushranging in nineteenth century Australia." Social Problems 26: 271–283.

Parker, Donn B. 1976. Crime by Computer. New York: Scribner's.

Petersilia, Joan, Peter W. Greenwood and Marvin Lavin. 1978. Criminal Careers of Habitual Felons. Santa Monica, Calif.: Rand.

Polsky, Ned. 1967. Hustlers, Beats, and Others. Chicago: Aldine.

Prus, Robert C. and C.R.D. Sharper. 1977. Road Hustler. Lexington, Mass.: Lexington.

Reynolds, Frank. 1967. Freewheelin Frank. New York: Grove.

Rosenberg, Bernard and Harry Silverstein. 1969. Varieties of Delinquent Experience. Waltham, Mass.: Blaisdell.

Rubington, Earl. 1978. "Variations in bottle gang controls." Pp. 383–391 in Earl Rubington and Martin S. Weinberg (eds.), Deviance: The Interactionist Perspective. Third edition. New York: Macmillan.

Shaw, Clifford R. 1930. The Jack Roller. Chicago: University of Chicago Press.

Shibutani, Tamotsu. 1961. Society and Personality. Englewood Cliffs, N.J.: Prentice-Hall.

Shover, Neal. 1977. "The social organization of burglary." Social Problems 20: 499–514.

Stoddart, Kenneth. 1974. "The facts of life about dope." Urban Life and Culture 3: 179–204.

Sutherland, Edwin H. 1937. The Professional Thief. Chicago: University of Chicago Press.

Thompson, Hunter S. 1966. Hell's Angels. New York: Ballantine.

Turner, Ralph H. 1964. "Collective behavior." Pp. 382–425 in Robert E. L. Fans (ed.), Handbook of Modern Sociology. Chicago: Rand McNally.

Wade, Andrew L. 1967. "Social processes in the act of juvenile vandalism." Pp. 94–109 in Marshall B. Clinard and Richard Quinney (eds.), Criminal Behavior Systems: A Typology. New York: Holt, Rinehart and Winston.

Warren, Carol A. B. 1974. Identity and Community in the Gay World. New York: Wiley.

Werthman, Carl and Irving Piliavin. 1967. "Gang members and the police." Pp. 56–98 in David J. Bordua (ed.), The Police. New York: Wiley.

Winick, Charles. 1961. "Physician narcotic addicts." Social Problems 9: 174–186.

Wiseman, Jacqueline P. 1970. Stations of the Lost. Englewood Cliffs, N.J.: Prentice-Hall.

Wolf, Deborah G. 1979. The Lesbian Community. Berkeley: University of California Press.

Wolfgang, Marvin E. and Franco Ferracuti. 1967. The Subculture of Violence. London: Tavistock.

Zimmerman, Don H. and D. Lawrence Wieder. 1977. "You can't help but get stoned." Social Problems 25: 198–207.

❧ ❧ ❧

Questions

1. What types of organizational arrangements do Best and Luckenbill describe? What distinguishes the organizational types at each end of the authors' typology (i.e., loners versus colleagues and mobs versus formal organizations)?

2. How does organizational structure affect the introduction of individuals into deviant behavior? How does it affect the socialization of members?

3. How does organizational structure affect individuals' ability to sustain patterns of deviant behavior over time?

4. How does organizational structure affect the ability of social-control agents to prevent or reduce deviant behavior?

5. According to Best and Luckenbill, what is the "significance" of social organization? Which one aspect of social organization would prove most detrimental for continued deviance if it were eliminated or substantially altered? Why?

The Social Milieu of Dogmen and Dogfights

RHONDA D. EVANS, Texas A&M University

CRAIG J. FORSYTH, University of Southwestern Louisiana

In this selection, Rhonda Evans and Craig Forsyth open a window onto the world of "dogmen"—people who participate in dogfighting for sport or watch it for entertainment. The authors conducted 31 in-depth interviews to describe dogfighting and the social world that surrounds it. This research illustrates the norms that govern this social world, the meaning and value of dogfighting to this subculture's members, and the organization of this form of deviance.

☻ Introduction

The act of baiting animals against one another, for entertainment, has existed throughout history (Ash, 1927; Atyeo, 1971); Foran, 1994; Jones, 1988; Matz, 1984; Semencic, 1984; Scott and Fuller, 1965; Vesey-Fitzgerald, 1948). Bull baiting and bear baiting rose to prominence throughout Europe in the 16th century and maintained their prestige well into the 18th century (Matz, 1984). At this time in history such events were not only tolerated but were also highly acceptable forms of entertainment. Baiting sports were one of the main forms of entertainment at this time, for everyone in society, including royalty. It should be noted that as long as baiting sports enjoyed royal patronage no legal reforms were attempted.

Dogfighting did not rise to prominence in Europe until the 18th century (Atyeo, 1979). It was not coincidental that this event became extremely popular at precisely the time when royalty was beginning to withdraw its support from the baiting sports. It is believed that dogfighting became even more popular at this time due to its lower visibility when compared with the

---

"The Social Milieu of Dogmen and Dogfights," by Rhonda D. Evans and Craig J. Forsyth, reprinted from *Deviant Behavior*, vol. 19, no. 1, 1998, pp. 51–71.

other baiting sports. It could be practiced in relative secrecy unlike bull baiting or bear baiting that were highly visible.

Although the baiting sports had faced opposition throughout their existence, which stemmed largely from their competition with the church and the theater for public audiences, it was not until the upper class completely withdrew its support that they became subject to legislative reform (Matz, 1984). In 1835, the following baiting sports were declared illegal in England: bear baiting, bull baiting, and dogfighting (Atyeo, 1979; Matz, 1984; Semencic, 1984; Vesey-Fitzgerald, 1948). During this period the upper class had shifted its support to cockfighting, which soon became their dominant form of entertainment.

It is believed that dogfighting was transported to the United States by European dog breeders who were looking for a new market for their product and by the Irish immigrants who had also enjoyed a long tradition of baiting sports in their homeland (Atyeo, 1979). There is evidence that baiting sports were being practiced in this country as early as 1726, if not earlier.

The baiting sports faced opposition in the United States, much like they had in Europe. Early laws pertaining to baiting sports varied from state to state and often from county to county within the states. New York passed legislation in 1856, which made dogfighting, cockfighting, and ratting illegal (Matz, 1984).

The most formidable opponent that the baiting sports encountered, in the new world, was Henry Bergh (Matz, 1984). He came onto the scene in 1866 with a version of the Society for the Prevention of Cruelty to Animals and prepared to do battle with the baiting sports. Prior to this time, animal humane laws pertained primarily to horses and cattle and did not specifically include dogs. Bergh's efforts, paradoxically, contributed to the spread of dogfighting rather than to its demise. Bergh's failure to eliminate dogfighting can be contributed in part to upper class patronage of this event, which continued into the 20th century in the United States (Enquist and Leimar, 1990).

The next serious attempt to stop dogfighting did not emerge until 1976 when the federal government passed legislation making it a felony to transport dogs across state lines with the intent to fight them (Atyeo, 1979; Semencic, 1984). This legislation was in part a reaction to efforts by Humane Societies to bring baiting sports to the attention of the general public by use of the media. Despite continued efforts at legislative reform, not to mention the ever increasing social stigma associated with dogfighting, participation continues. Dogfighting is now illegal in all 50 states and a felony in at least 36 states.

❧ The American Pit Bull Terrier

The American Pit Bull Terrier is the exclusive breed employed in pit fights in the United States today. This breed has been selectively bred over centuries to produce a dog, which has an innate ability to fight and overcome his victim. Matz (1984, p. 3) notes the unique characteristics of the American Pit Bull Terrier when engaged in battle.

> The pit bull is unique in its absence of the threat display when fighting. A pit bull almost never bares his teeth and it is rare that he will raise the hair on his back. When fighting he makes little noise, neither growling nor barking. The pit bull does not rear up and snap, but takes hold, shakes and punishes with his hold. He wants to fight, and he fights to damage.

This ability is only found with such virility in this particular breed. The American Pit Bull Terrier (APBT) is specifically bred to fight, just as Border Collies herd sheep and Bloodhounds sniff out game (Foran, 1994).

Arguments have arisen concerning the ethical realities of dog fighting. Some argue that it is cruel to fight dogs; others argue that it is cruel to deprive them the opportunity to display their congenital characteristics within the confines of the sport. Foran (1994, pp. 70–71) described the natural aggression of the breed.

> Although extreme aggression toward conspecifics is almost universally considered to be an unusual and undesirable trait, in the case of the game-bred APBT, it is a sought after attribute, highly prized by breeders engaged in pit fighting. This aggression does not seem to require any of the usual external stimuli, but rather is triggered by some innate mechanism. There is no doubt that environmental factors and positive reinforcement provide a suitable reward system for their antagonistic behavior, but the desire to fight is manifested whether or not these rewards are present. Likewise, punishment has no effect on dulling the desire to fight. Most remarkably, fatal fighting (or willingness to engage in it) is, in this context, considered the norm.

Kavanaugh (1974) stated that the APBT bloodline descends from the Bull Dog and the Rat Terrier. Although the Rat Terrier aided the poor man of the 1800s in helping to control the rat population, bull baiting was the primary occupation of the Bull Dog. Cross breeding the gameness and appearance of these two dogs produced a canine with a fight to the death attitude.

Methodology

This article examines the world of dogfighting, through the use of thick descriptions (Geertz, 1973). The data, for this study, were obtained through field research, using interviews with and observations of people who fight dogs. Our technique was to let the responses speak for themselves, thus presenting the world of dog fighting in full vivid detail and then to offer both summarization and interpretation. This method, which is called interpretative interaction (Denzin, 1978), is concerned with the study and imputation of meaning, motive, emotion, intention, and feeling as life events are experienced and organized by interacting individuals. This method is in stark contrast to thin description, which consists solely of statistical explanation and abstraction. Our purpose was to capture the essence of dogfighting from those who have experienced it.

Interviews were conducted with 31 individuals who fight and breed pit bulls. All of the participants had been involved in dogfighting for several years. Three interviews were conducted with former breeders and fighters of pit bulls who no longer participate in the sport. Interviews ranged from 2 to 4 1/2 hours. These interviews were conducted at the pre-fight meetings, at the fights or at the homes of dogfighters. Several informal interviews were also conducted with spectators and the wives of men who participate in dogfighting. Additional data were obtained from interviews with SPCA officials, veterinarians and local sheriff's officers. Observations took place at 14 formal dogfights. Spectators were represented by all races, ages, and both sexes. In the United States, formal dogfighting is a sport dominated by White men. Although the participation of Black males is on the rise, they make up only a small percentage of the participants within the sport. Women for the most part are there as spectators, but do have an active role in gambling. Women rarely handle dogs. The research took place in several parishes of Louisiana and counties in Mississippi. The authors also examined newspaper accounts of dogfighting.

The goal of this research was to describe the world of the dogfighter so that subsequent researchers will be able recognize its components and proceed with their own research based upon knowledge gained from this study. This is, indeed, the test of validity of qualitative research (Forsyth, 1986).

Both of the authors have relatives who are engaged in dogfighting. Additional respondents were identified through a snowball method. Each respondent was questioned regarding several aspects of dogfighting: the reasons they engage in dogfighting and how they started dogfighting; techniques of breeding and training; the negotiation of a contract; the fight, the setting, and the choice of a setting for the fight; the types of dogs in general and great fighting dogs of the past; changes in dogfighting; and the career of a fighting dog. Additional questions were intended to elicit responses regarding the rationalizations and motivations used by dogmen for their continuance in these illegal activities, and their confrontations with residents, law enforcement and/or humane society officials, or other dogfighters. Respondents interviewed for this research are an available sample, we interviewed all persons who would allow us and who had the time. All questions were intended to be guides for gleaning information, rather than specific responses.

In our interviews with dogmen they continually referred to themselves as a fraternity. McCaghy and Neal (1974) also used the term fraternity in describing the informal association of cockfighters. We will also use the term fraternity in describing dogmen. All the names of dogmen used are pseudonyms.

● Findings

Breeding

Breeding dogs to participate in the sport of dogfighting is the most crucial function within the fraternity of dogmen. It is the facet on which every other element within the sport is based and without it the sport could not exist. Thus, breeders hold the most prestigious positions within the fraternity.

The following responses were from experienced dogmen regarding the importance of breeding and the various techniques employed in breeding.

> You breed meanness to gameness and then you go back twice to your gameness. The dog that stays there and keeps it going regardless of if he's getting whipped is what I'm talking about. Now you got certain bloodlines, if you're a breeder you just don't choose dogs at random. They've got to have a background behind them. Sometimes you have athletes that come

up that are just freaks. Those idiots that don't know anything about breeding they start breeding into them. He's not the one who made that fighting dog it's his daddy and his mama. Hell the people don't know that, they want to breed to that dog because he's a good dog. That's not where it's at. If it's not a line of production of good dogs I don't want him. (INTERVIEW)

I did what's called cold outcrosses and hot outcrosses. . . . Hot outcrosses are the outcrosses that would work and had worked together before. A cold outcross is when you try to introduce something into your line that maybe has never been tried or crossed before. A hot outcross is something that has been proven in the past. You'll always try something new, you know, if you can find good dogs with a good bloodline . . . you're in business. The Pistol/Ms. Spike blood that's what made the dogs, when Carver hit them two dogs that's where he began his production. Then he took that and crossed the Bullyson blood into that. The Pistol and Ms. Spike line was the gamest line there ever was. (INTERVIEW)

It's the bloodline you go by. Just cause a dog won't fight doesn't mean he won't throw good dogs. The genes are still in that dog. (INTERVIEW)

As indicated in these statements of these dogmen breeding is perhaps the most important aspect of dogfighting. Another critical facet of the game is the training of the dog.

Training

When these dogs reach a certain age, anywhere from a year old to 18 months, they are rolled out (briefly put against a proven dog) a few times to test their ability and gameness. If the owner determines that the dog is ready for the pit he then puts out a wager that is open to anyone. The amount of the wager is usually anywhere from a couple hundred dollars to as much as $100,000.

Once the wager is accepted and a contract is drawn up it is time to prepare for the fight. The dogs undergo from 6 weeks to 3 months of rigorous training to prepare for the fight. They must be brought down to their pit weight, which is considered the optimal weight at which a dog can fight. This training seeks to build wind and stamina in the dogs so that they can fight for long periods of time if need be.

Various methods are used in the conditioning of a dog such as a treadmill, flirtpole and sometimes even swimming. The dogs are also fed special lean diets at this time. The following responses were from accomplished dogmen regarding the relevance of training and the sundry of methods utilized.

Rick's all the way from Arizona. He's a good friend of Ron's. As a matter of fact, he's been staying here in Louisiana, at Ron's place, for the past 2 months, so that he could condition Snow for the fight. He had to give her time to adjust to the climate here. There's no way that you call take a dog from Arizona and bring her to Louisiana, where the climate is so humid, and expect her to be able to breath while fighting. She'll kill herself. Well, Rick and Ron both know what they're doing. They've been in the game for at least 30 years. I guess I don't need to tell you who my money is on tonight. L.G. is a good dogman, but I know where my loyalties lie. (INTERVIEW)

It takes a lot of time and money to get these dogs ready for the pit. They don't just throw their dogs into the pit and hope for the best. They go through a lot of trouble to make sure their dogs are in the best condition possible for the fight. They invest in all kinds of equipment to aid in the conditioning of the dogs. They have treadmills, flirtpoles, and turntables that are made just for the dogs. As a matter of fact, there's a man out in Scott, LA that makes dog treadmills, for a living. . . . The object is to make sure that your dog can go the distance in the pit. If your dog is not conditioned property he won't be able to maintain his wind in the pit. Hell, these fights can last anywhere from 30 minutes to 4 or 5 hours. That's why the conditioning is so important. (INTERVIEW)

Around 19 months to 2 years old, if his attitude is right then I will school him out. I'll roll him a few times with different types of dogs to teach him different types of fighting. I'll do that 4 or 5 times. I decide how far to push the next time by what he shows me at each roll. The last time I roll him, I would game check him by putting some time on him and a better dog on him. You let him see the bottom. You make sure he gets some of the worst end of the deal. A lot of people put 2 or 3 dogs on him, one after the other. I find it easier to put him on a jenny or a mill and blow all his air out of him and then put a dog on him for 30 minutes. You see what kind of attitude he has then. When you match a dog he will never have to fight against more than one dog. He only has to whip one dog at a time. (**Interview**)

When you raise puppies you want them to have a good attitude. You do different things in your yard to make them have aggressive attitudes. You want them to be hyped up or pumped up about things. Anywhere from 18 months to 2 years old you roll them out to see what kind of dog they are. People who don't really know a lot about the sport call it sparring. You want to push them a little hard to see if they can take what they can dish out. Then, you would match them. (**Interview**)

As demonstrated in these accounts, experienced dogmen are very cognizant of the significance of proper training. Matches sometimes continue for 4 hours (there is no time limit). Dogs must be trained so they will have the stamina to endure the match. Individuals who place bets also put a lot of weight on the reputation of the dog's trainer.

Negotiating a Contract

When a member of the fraternity has a dog he is ready to fight, he puts out his conditions such as the weight of the dog, sex of the dog, and the amount he wants to bet on the fight. These facts are advertised either in the underground journals or by word of mouth. Once another dogman accepts the conditions and the wager a contract is drawn up.

The process of matching dogs has become a normative process. The owner "puts out a weight," which means they have a dog at a particular weight that they wish to fight.

First thing people do is put a weight out there. They agree upon a weight, like 46 lb. male. They agree on a purse and a forfeit. A forfeit means that if a dog comes in over weight his owner must pay the other owner the agreed upon amount and negotiate a new contract. A match is set at a specific amount of money, let's say three thousand dollars, that is the purse. The forfeit will be set at let's say five hundred dollars. If your dog comes in over weight, you have to pay a $500 forfeit then negotiate a new contract. The first fight was canceled. The man with the dog that was over weight will lay odds. He might agree to pay $3,500 because his dog is over weight, which puts the other dog at a disadvantage. (**Interview**)

One dogman gave us his strategy in setting the amount of the purse.

It's just a hobby. You have to keep it in that area and don't bet a lot of money. A thousand dollar bet is plenty. A person will usually not try to cheat you or to get to you for a thousand dollars. If you bet five thousand dollars that may affect the other guy's lifestyle. He may not be able to pay his bills or eat. He might do something to you or your dog to get your money. If that happens then it becomes just a money deal and that takes the sport out of it. I have a friend who can lose a hundred thousand dollars and go party and have a good time. I would be devastated if I lost that kind of money. I'm a $1000 player and that catches you pretty much in the middle of all the dogfighters. (**Interview**)

Although not as critical to the fight itself as training and breeding, and not as monetarily important as the contract, planning and selecting the location is critical. Because dogfighting is illegal, participants are very secretive about the date and location of the event.

𝒫lanning and 𝒮electing the 𝓛ocation of the 𝓕ight

Dogfights are most commonly staged in secluded rural areas such as barns or fields. There is a national network, consisting of members of the dogfighting fraternity, which facilitates the planning of locations for these events. When a contract is drawn up for a fight the participants decide on a central location. They then contact a dogman in that area to make arrangements to have the fight at a location that he provides. The following are comments about finding a location.

> We like to travel. I would rather go away from home to stage the fight. We meet at a center point somewhere then you come home and nobody hears about it where you live. (**Interview**)

> I try to stay within a 300 to 500 mile radius. I'm a working man so I don't want to go real far. It would take money out of my business if I did that. This is an expensive hobby. It's not a money-making thing for me. It cost me money anytime I match one whether I win or lose. When I have a match I have my mind off my business. I'm thinking about that dog and what I'm going to do with him. What it cost me in my business is far greater than what I would lose in the fight. (INTERVIEW*)

The location of the fight is usually kept secret until the afternoon of the fight with only the two owners and the man providing the location knowing where it will take place. This is done in order to protect themselves against possible raids. When the time arrives for the event to take place everyone is then informed of the location. The people leave the initial location at separate times so as not to attract attention and all meet at the location of the fight.

> When Rick and L.G. agreed to fight their dogs, they called Mike to help them plan a location for the event. They wanted to meet somewhere in

between Florida and Arizona so Mike agreed to have the fight here in North Louisiana. There's a whole network of dogmen who aid one another in finding locations for the fights. They're the only three people who actually know where the fight will be. They keep the location a secret until the night of the fight in order to avoid raids. Once Mike lets everybody know where the fight will take place, we leave his house one vehicle at a time so as not to attract attention. We have to be careful these days with the Humane Society breathing down our necks and pressuring the cops to bust up dogfighting. I don't know why those damned people don't just mind their own business. They act like we're hard core criminals or something. We're not hurting anybody and the dogs love to fight, so what's the harm. (INTERVIEW)

Dogmen realize that keeping this veil over the circumstances of the fight, until immediately before the event, is necessary for the survival of dogfighting. A successful raid can push those marginal dogmen and spectators out of the sport. Dogmen face fines, confiscation of dogs, and in some states prison time. A sport supported by such a small fraternity cannot afford to lose any peers.

The Meeting of Dogmen and Dogs

The Pre-Fight

On the day of the fight the participants and the spectators, usually members of the fraternity, which tends to be almost exclusively male, meet at a dogman's house near the location where the fight will take place. Here they will converse for hours before the fight about such things as the history of champion bloodlines, recent fights that they have attended, breeding and conditioning practices and a vast array of other issues pertaining to their sport. This gathering of the fraternity before the event is a very important element of the dogmen subculture. It is at this time that the social status of the fraternity members is most evident. In these conversations the old timers do most of the talking and the newcomers listen like obedient students eager to learn all that they can. It should be noted that even though dogfighters are seen as deviant by society, they did not have deviant self-concepts.

The following is both a vivid description and summarization of the meeting before a dogfight took place. The fight had been planned for months. The following interview took place during the trip in a car to the pre-fight meeting.

We're almost there now . . . just a little further up the road. Everyone who is anyone, in the dog game, will be at the fight tonight. They've been planning this event for months and people from all over the country will be there. Most of the old timers will be there. Man, they are awesome. They can teach you anything you want to know about the game and the dogs. They know all the champion bloodlines and every champion dog that ever walked on the face of this earth. Well hell, they're the ones that put most of the champion dogs on the ground. Those guys know what the hell they're talking about when it comes to anything having to do with dogfighting. It's important that you listen to them and show them the respect they deserve. If those guys don't accept you, you are not going anywhere in this game. They decide who is going to move in this circle, so don't piss them off. (INTERVIEW)

The following interviews took place at the pre-fight meeting that was held in the home of a dogman.

Dogfighting is just like anything else you've got to start at the bottom and work your way up. If you're lucky, someone who is already established in the game will take you under his wing and teach you everything he knows. Man, I owe everything I know to Ron. He's the one who got me started in the game. Once I was able to convince him that I was serious about the game, he let me buy into his bloodline, brought me with him to some really big fights, and introduced me to all the right people. I would have never been able to gain acceptance without his backing. He's highly respected in the game, for both his bloodline and always bringing good dogs to the pit. That's the way it works here. These people don't like strangers and they are always worried that newcomers might be undercover cops. But, if one of the old timers brings someone to a fight, they know he's all right. Just remember it's all about who you know and what you know. (INTERVIEW)

One of the best things about this sport is the people you will meet. There are people from all walks of life involved in this game and they all have one thing in common, the dogs. Once you become known in the game, you could go anywhere in the U.S. and you will know somebody in that area who is in the game. It's like a huge fraternity. These people will accept you into their homes and offer you food and a place to stay, anytime you're traveling near their homes, just because you're a fellow dogman. (INTERVIEW)

I enjoy the pre-fight gathering almost as much as the fight. Hell, if I have to be honest with myself, I'd say its just as important as the fight. This is where you learn most of the really important stuff, like the history of the bloodlines, and what works and what doesn't in respect to breeding and conditioning. The old timers do most of the talking and we just listen. People will think you're crazy if you go in there talking a lot and you're just a newcomer. That's a privilege that has to be earned and the old timers have more than earned it. Someday we'll be in their position and everybody will listen to what we have to say. We'll be the teachers instead of the Students. I can't wait for the day when people will show me that kind of respect. I want the whole world to be able to say that I was one hell of a dogman and always put good dogs on the ground. After all that's what its all about, respect and loyalty to the sport and your fellow dogmen. (INTERVIEW)

The fight tonight is going to be between Rick's Snow and L.G.'s Black. Snow is a two time champion from the Carver bloodline. When she's in action, its really something to see. Rick was real lucky to get his hands on that dog. I think he paid $25,000 for her. L.G. is from Florida and I believe that Black is from the Corvino bloodline. That's another excellent bloodline. I'm sure the fight will be pretty well matched tonight. Neither one of those guys would bring a dog to the pit unless he was sure that he had a pretty good chance of winning. After all, they each have $20,000 riding on the fight tonight, not to mention all of the time they invested and their reputations. (NTERVIEW)

The fight is going to be at Norman's farm and Norman will be refereeing tonight. They chose Norman to referee because he's known to be very fair and trustworthy. The referee is usually entitled to 10% of the wager. That's a good bit of money on a big fight like this one. They also agreed upon a forfeit fee just in case one of the men get the notion not to show up or to pull some conniving stunt. I don't think Rick or L.G. would do that but they always try to take precautions when a lot of money is riding on the fight. (INTERVIEW)

We'd better head over to Norman's place; we don't want to miss the beginning of the fight. When we get there, park as close as you can to the road and turn your car facing the road. You never know when we might need to make a fast get away. Just remember if the cops ever show up at a fight, always be prepared to leave fast. If they ever catch you, you didn't see or hear anything about dogfighting. Always be loyal to the fraternity and don't ever rat out everybody else. If they catch you they'll try to get a confession out of you. Don't give it to them. (INTERVIEW)

These pre-fight comments reveal the loyalty of dogmen to their sport. Their need for secrecy and loyalty is why the ranks of dogmen are difficult to invade. Although the viewing of these fights were certainly more stirring the pre-fight meetings were more informative. At these meetings one learns about all aspects of the dogmen and their pit bulls.

The Fight

There are two types of dogfights: formal and informal. The informal fight is when two dogs are fought without any contract. There may be only a few people present, it may take place in the streets, is usually engaged in by teenagers and arises spontaneously. Formal fights are defined as organized events in which a contract exist (stating the terms of the fight—amount of the wager, the weight at which the dogs will be fought, the amount of the forfeit and the sex of the dogs). In addition, there is a subculture that maintains it. Our research was only concerned with the formal dog fight. Formal fights were classified as either conventions or private matches.

> There used to be conventions, now its turned into private matches. A convention you might have up to 6 or 7 fights that night. At private matches the most you will have is 2 fights and with the same people . . . at conventions there were up to 300 people. The fights may go on all night into the morning. Law enforcement could catch us at conventions because there are so many people there and you cannot check them all out. In a private match the owner of the place where the fight takes place checks everyone out before they get there. (INTERVIEW)

Prior to the fight the dogs are weighed in and washed to make sure they are free of any noxious substances that could interfere with the dogs ability to fight.

> They're weighing in the dogs now. Snow weighs in at 38 pounds and Black weighs in at 37 pounds. They are very well matched. It's all going to come down to the conditioning and gameness of the dogs. Now they are washing the dogs. They do that to make sure that their opponent didn't put any chemicals on the dogs that could interfere with the fight. If one of the opponents is still suspicious after they wash the dogs, they have the option to taste their opponent's dog. If one of the opponents does try something like putting chemicals on his dog, the ref will rule foul play and the dog will be disqualified. Then that person will have to pay his opponent the forfeit fee. It looks like everything is fair and square here. (INTERVIEW)

The dogfight is a staged event in which two dogs are placed into a pit, much like a boxing ring, and fight until one opponent either quits or dies, at which time the other is declared the winner. There is a referee and two handlers present in the pit with the dogs and many spectators viewing the event. The fight begins when the referee tells the handlers to pit their dogs; at which time the dogs are released and attack one another. Once the fight begins the spectators begin placing bets with one another on which dog will win. The dogs continue fighting until one of them makes a turn, which is defined as turning the head and shoulders away from his or her opponent. Once the referee calls the turn the handlers then handle their dogs when they are out of holds, which means they are not biting each other, and the dog that made the turn must scratch to his opponent. Scratching is defined as crossing the scratch line, which is drawn in the center of the pit, and attacking one's opponent within a specified amount of time, usually 10 to 30 seconds. If a dog fails to scratch, his opponent is declared the winner. If the scratch is successfully completed the fight continues. From this point on the dogs are only handled when they are out of holds and they are required to scratch in turn. At any time in the fight if a dog fails to scratch in turn he is declared the loser.

> It's almost time for the fight to start. We'd better go on into the barn. They're charging $20 per person tonight. That seems like a lot of money but think about the risk that Norman is taking having the fight on his properly. I don't much mind paying. After all, this is the big event that we've been waiting for months to see and it's finally here. It's going to be one hell of a fight. (INTERVIEW)

The owners are bringing the dogs to their corners of the pit. The pit is about 20 feet by 20 feet, and this one is surrounded by 3-feet tall wooden sides. Both of the dogs look eager to fight.

Norman says sternly, "gentlemen pit your dogs." Tile handlers release their dogs and Snow and Black lunge at one another. Snow rears up and overpowers Black, but Black manages to come back with a quick locking of the jaws on Snow's neck. The crowd is cheering wildly and yelling out bets. Once a dog gets a lock on the other, they will hold on with all their might. The dogs flail back and forth and all the while Black maintains her hold. It looks like Black is hung up so Norman motions for the handlers to separate the dogs. They approach the dogs and L.G. pries Black's mouth open with a breaking stick. The dogs are returned to their corners and sponged down with water. Once again Norman calls for the dogs to be pitted. This time Snow must scratch to Black and make contact with her within 10 seconds. Snow races toward Black and is not going to let Black get the best of her.

Snow goes straight for the throat and grabs hold with her razor sharp teeth. Almost immediately, blood flows from Black's throat. Despite a severe injury to the throat Black manages to continue fighting back. They are relentless, each battling the other and neither willing to accept defeat. This fighting continues for an hour. Finally, the dogs are out of holds and Norman gives the okay for them to be handled. He gives the third and final pit call. It is Black's turn to scratch and she is severely wounded. Black manages to crawl across the pit to meet her opponent. Snow attacks Black and she is too weak to fight back. L.G. realizes that this is it for Black and calls the fight. Snow is declared the winner.

Rick collects his money. L.G. then lifts Black from the pit and carries her out back. Her back legs are broken and blood is gushing from her throat. A shot rings out barely heard over the noise in the barn. Black's body is wrapped up and carried by her owner to his vehicle.

Next month it will be Snow and a dog from Mississippi. The owner of the dog from Mississippi was a spectator at the fight; the arrangements for the fight were made immediately after the end of the fight.

> Tonight was a great fight. It's always great when you have two really game dogs, doing what they love to do, and a bunch of us dogmen watching them do it. I can hardly wait until the next fight. (INTERVIEW)

Sometimes the career of a great dog lasts only one fight. This is often the case when the owner is also a breeder.

> To match a dog 3 or 4 times is a lot. In our case if a dog shows all the qualities we are looking for, we will never fight him again. We'll put him at stud after his first fight, which means we'll use him only for breeding. We are probably the only people that do that. (INTERVIEW)

There are four possible ways in which the fight may end: a dog's failure to scratch, the owner calling the fight (this is analogous to the manager of a boxer throwing the towel into the ring that signals that the fighter has quit), the death of one or both dogs, or one of the dogs jumping the pit.

The failure to scratch is described as an opponents failure to cross the scratch line and attack his opponent upon command of the referee and is the most common way in which fights will end. A less common ending is the death of one of the opponents.

> Well I've been in it [dogfighting] for 14 years and I've only seen one dog die in the pit. A fight normally ends when one of the dogs fail to scratch.

> It's very hard to get a game dog. A dead game dog is one that always goes back even if he is beat down. (INTERVIEW)

Although the death of a dog in a fight is rare, it can and does occur in fights between two dogs that are both dead game. Dead game is defined as a dogs willingness to fight until his death. Fights between such opponents will often last for hours at which time they will end in the death of one of the dogs with the other often dying after the fight from the injuries incurred during the fight.

> The match usually ends when a dog fails to scratch. There are very few killers, that's what makes them exceptional dogs. They are the ultimate dog. Moon was the ultimate dog. I don't think there ever was one like him and probably never will be. He's talked about all over the world. He killed every dog he ever fought. He killed himself the last time. If he would have lived I could have sold him for $20,000 easy. (INTERVIEW)

The least common ending is for one of the dogs to jump the pit, which means they literally jump out of the pit in order to escape their opponent. This is very rare because a dogman will not bring a cur dog (coward) to a fight at the risk of facing humiliation. If a dog does jump the pit it will surely result in his death at the hands of his owner.

Within the dogfighting fraternity, the most admirable quality is gameness, that can be described as continued willingness to fight and never stop fighting as long as one is physically and mentally able to continue. The canine opponents employed in these dogfights are expected to show this quality of gameness as long as there is breath left in their bodies. A dog that exhibits this quality in extreme measures is considered to be dead game (some call this a killer dog) and therefore he will be seen as the ultimate canine warrior. So important is this quality that it is the goal of every dogman to own a dog who is dead game.

When dogmen described dogs the emphasis was always on the level of gameness of the dog.

> You have a cur dog, that is a dog who will not fight over an hour. Then you have a pitgame dog, which goes over an hour. A dog who doesn't even fight to 30 minutes is a stone cur dog. Then there's a dead game dog who's exactly that, dead after the fight. (INTERVIEW)

> There aren't many killer dogs, that's why Moon was such a valuable dog. Dogs fight for a sense of threat. When that threat is no longer present most

of them stop, Moon never did. He was just a killer. . . . Moon died during his fourth fight. (INTERVIEW)

A pit game is just an average game dog. He is not near about like dead game. (INTERVIEW)

When asked about curs and what they do with these dogs, the responses varied.

Most of the time I get rid of him. Either I give him to somebody if anybody wants him or I kill him. I can't keep him if he's not useful. I can't afford to . . . you can't turn the dog loose. Sometimes people will try to sell them and get 2 or 3 hundred for them. (INTERVIEW)

I dispose of curs. It's the only thing I can do. These dogs are not going to become pets. (INTERVIEW)

A cur dog is one that quits. If a dog fights for an hour and then quits she is a cur dog. . . . I'm very hard on my dogs. (INTERVIEW)

I will condemn any dog who is capable of standing on his feet and chooses to quit. But it has always aggravated me that if a dog fought for 4 hours and then chose to quit, there will always be people who will say he was a cur dog. It never seemed fair that a 30-minute cur would be compared to a 4-hour cur. (INTERVIEW)

Most people would call any dog who refused to go back across the pit a cur. I used to make a joke out of it when somebody said there was a 2-hour cur I said you could fill my yard up with those 2-hour curs. I'll take any they want to give away. (INTERVIEW)

● Discussion

The sport of fatal fighting (Enquist and Leimar, 1990) in America primarily involves two animals: the fighting cock and the pit bull dog. There is very little literature on dogfighting and little academic interest in the topic. The literature that does exist on fatal fighting is primarily concerned with the fighting cock (Bryant, 1982; Bryant and Capel, 1974, 1975; Forsyth, 1996; Geertz, 1972; Hawley, 1989; McCaghy and Neal, 1974; Ritzer and Walczak, 1986, p. 398; Worden and Darden, 1992). The efforts of law enforcement have taken their toll on the dogmen fraternity. In the past, large meets called conventions took place; now these events have been reduced to private matches.

As deviant transactions (Best and Luckenbill, 1980) increase in complexity, deviants are more likely to be seen as accountable for their behavior. Consequently, efforts of social control agents increase and the range of reactive tactics of deviants expand. These endeavors act to organize deviant transactions. Secrecy about operations and identities of participants construct a central theme of the deviant organization. Dogmen have developed norms that govern conduct between their deviant associates, therefore planning and precautions have assumed law like importance to them. The organization of dogmen, although deviant and secret, resembles respectable transactions. The dogfight has become an ordered, yet deviant activity, by respectable people.

When one views a staged dog fight between pit bulls for the first time, the most macabre aspect of the event is that the only sounds you hear from these dogs are those of crunching bones and cartilage. The dogs rip and tear at each other; their blood, urine and saliva splatter the sides of the pit and clothes of the handlers. This is the American Pit Bull Terrier at work in a role they have been performing for over a century. The emotions of the dogs are conspicuous, but not so striking, even to themselves, are the passions of the owners of the dogs. Whether they hug a winner or in the rare case, destroy a dying loser, whether they walk away from the carcass or lay crying over it, their fondness for these fighters is manifest. Whether it produces admiration or disdain, you will be overwhelmed by the game and the connection between the true dogman and his fighting dog.

The meaning that this sport has for these men can only be gotten from listening to the accounts of dogmen who are willing to share several generations of knowledge and experience. The loyalty and secrecy are important components of sub cultural maintenance. This article has conveyed these sub cultural pieces so that the reader will better understand the complete world of the dogmen. This world is indeed much more than a dogfight. More research is needed into this much-maligned arena of sport. Hopefully this research will serve as a heuristic device for further study on this topic.

◉ Dogfighting: Victimless Crime?

There are two broad research perspectives in the understanding of deviant behavior. Understanding deviance involves studying both those who make the rules and those who break the rules (Becker, 1963; Little, 1995). These two perspectives are both evident if we look at cases of deviance in which there is objective rule breaking but there is not consensus in society, as to the deviance of the act. In other words, there is a law against the behavior but many times when the law is broken the rule breaking is treated as though it were not deviant at all (Little, 1995). Becker (1963) called such behavior secret deviance, meaning that it is so well hidden nobody sees it and if it is seen nobody seems to do anything about it. Closely related to this category of deviance in some respects is the idea of victimless crime. Victimless crimes (Schur, 1965) refer to the willing exchange among adults of goods and services. These goods and services are legally proscribed, but are strongly demanded by the adult public. Homosexuality, illegal gambling, drug misuse, abortion, prostitution, and pornography are examples of victimless crimes. The primary characteristics of so called victimless crimes is a transaction between two participants, both of whom choose to enter into a relationship. Because neither individual in the relationship desire to make a complaint, laws against these exchanges are difficult to enforce. Most activities of this sort go on with little intrusion from law enforcement (Little 1995). Although authors have tended to label several crimes as victimless, they are not all equally deserving of the label. The violation of blue laws may be without victims, but the labeling of other crimes such as prostitution (Yablonsky and Haskell, 1988), pornography (Durham 1980) and abortion (Goode, 1997) as victimless has caused considerable debate. The question in regard to these types of crimes is the following: are there victims and are they disruptive to members of our society (Vito and Holmes, 1994)?

The impediment to these victimless events comes from moral entrepreneurs. The presumption is that they serve the community by protecting its virtue and its members. Dogfighting involves two forms of deviance: gambling and the violation of animal protection laws. Because gambling is widely accepted in the areas where dogfighting takes place (horse racing, casinos, lottery), it is not this aspect that has brought on the concern of moral entrepreneurs. Dogfighting has been labeled as deviant because moral entrepreneurs consider the dog a victim. Dogmen and their supporters see it as a victimless crime. In addition, dogfighting is in conflict with the new environmental sensitivity. Animals have arisen as a highly visible and logical subset of this new environmental awareness/sensitivity and greater respect is accorded them as a somewhat incidental beneficiary in this cultural wave of animal rights (Palmer and Forsyth, 1992). Dogfighting agitates this cultural swell, hence dogmen can expect a persistant storm of moral challenge.

References

Ash, E. C. (1927). *Dogs: Their history and development.* Boston: Houghton Mifflin.

Atyeo, D. (1979). *Blood and guts, violence in sports.* New York: Paddington Press.

Becker, H. S. (1963). *Outsiders.* New York: Free Press.

Best, J., & Luckenbill, D. E. (1980). The social organization of deviants. *Social Problems, 213,* 14–31.

Bryant, C. D. (1982). Cockfighting in sociohistorical context: Some sociological observations on a socially disvalued sport. *The Gamecock, 45,* 65–70,80–85.

Bryant, C. D., & Capel, W. C. (1974). Profiles of the American cocker Parts I–II. *Grit and Steel, 76,* 27–28, 32–32a.

Bryant, C. D., & Capel, W. C. (1975). Profiles of the American cocker Parts III–IV *Grit and Steel, 77,* 27–29, 33d–33f.

Denzin, N. (1978). *The research act.* New York: McGraw-Hill.

Durham, A. (1986). Pornography, social harm, and legal control. *Justice Quarterly, 3,* 95–102.

Enquist, M., & Leimar, O. (1990). The evolution of fatal fighting. *Animal Behavior, 39,* 1–9.

Foran, S. (1994). *The genetic foundation for behavioral varieties in the American pit bull terrier.* Hartford: University of Connecticut.

Forsyth, C. (1986). Sea daddy: An excursus into an endangered social species. *Maritime Policy and Management: The International Journal of Shipping and Port Research, 13,* 53–60.

Forsyth, C. J. (1996). A pecking disorder: Cockfighting in Louisiana. *International Review of Modern Sociology, 26,* 15–25.

Geertz, C. (1972). Deep play: Notes on the Balinese cockfight. *Daedalus, 101,* 1–27.

Geertz, C. (1973). *The interpretation of cultures: Selected essays.* New York: Basic Books.

Goode, E. (1997). *Deviant behavior.* Upper Saddle River, NJ: Prentice-Hall.

Hawley, F. F. (1989). Cockfight in the cotton: A moral crusade in microcosm. *Contemporary Crisis, 13,* 129–144.

Jones, M. (1988). *The dogs of capitalism Book 1: Origins.* Cedar Park, TX: 21st Century Logic.

Kavanaugh, C. (1974). The American pitbull terrier: A brief history of a great breed. *Bloodlines Journal,* (Nov–Dec), 31–35.

Little, C. B. (1995). *Deviance and control.* Itasca, IL: Peacock Publishers.

Matz, K. S. (1984). *The pit bull fact and fable*. Sacramento, CA: De Mortmain Publishing.

McCaghy, C. H., & Neal, A. G. (1974). The fraternity of cockfighters: Ethical embellishments of an illegal sport. *Journal of Popular Culture, 8,* 557–569.

Palmer, C. E., & Forsyth, C. (1992). Animals, attitudes, and anthropormorphic sentiment: The social construction of meat and fur in postindustrial society. *International Review of Modern Sociology, 22,* 29–44.

Ritzer, G., & Walczak, D. (1986). *Working: Conflict and change*. Englewood Cliffs, NJ: Prentice-Hall.

Schur, E. (1965). *Crimes without victims*. Englewood Cliffs, NJ: Prentice-Hall.

Scott, J. P., & Fuller, J. L. (1965). *Genetics and the social behavior of the dog*. Chicago: University of Chicago Press.

Semencic, C. (1984). *The world of fighting dogs*. Neptune City, N.J.: T.F.H. Publications.

Vesey-Fitzgerald, B. (1948). *The book of the dog*. Los Angeles and Toronto: Borden Publishing.

Vito, G. F., & Holmes, R. M. (1994). *Criminology*. Belmont, CA: Wadsworth.

Worden, S., & Darden, D. (1992). Knives and gaffs: Definitions in the deviant world of cockfighting. *Deviant Behavior, 13,* 271–289.

Yablonsky, L., & Hakell, M. (1988). Juvenile delinquency. New York: Harper & Row.

◉ ◉ ◉

Questions

1. Why do "dogmen" refer to themselves as a fraternity?

2. According to Evans and Forsyth, how do dogmen determine the status of individual members of the dogfighting subculture?

3. What norms govern the behavior of dogmen?

4. How would you describe the social organization of dogmen? Do there appear to be leaders? If so, what defines a particular person as a leader?

5. How does the social world of dogfighting compare with the social worlds affiliated with other kinds of animal competition (for example, horseracing or cockfighting)?

Convicted Rapists' Vocabulary of Motive: Excuses and Justifications

DIANA SCULLY AND JOSEPH MAROLLA
Virginia Commonwealth University

In this selection, the authors interview convicted rapists currently serving prison time for their crimes. They find that rapists can be classified into two groups: "admitters" and "deniers." From these two groups, the authors derive a typology of excuses and justifications that rapists use to explain their behavior. According to the authors, the use of excuses and justifications lets rapists think of themselves as non-rapists or ex-rapists.

sychiatry has dominated the literature on rapists since "irresistible impulse" (Glueck, 1925:323) and "disease of the mind" (Glueck, 1925:243) were introduced as the causes of rape. Research has been based on small samples of men, frequently the clinicians' own patient population. Not surprisingly, the medical model has predominated: rape is viewed as an individualistic, idiosyncratic symptom of a disordered personality. That is, rape is assumed to be a psychopathologic problem and individual rapists are assumed to be "sick." However, advocates of this model have been unable to isolate a typical or even predictable pattern of symptoms that are causally linked to rape. Additionally, research has demonstrated that fewer than 5 percent of rapists were psychotic at the time of their rape (Abel *et al.*, 1980).

We view rape as behavior learned socially through interaction with others; convicted rapists have learned the attitudes and actions consistent with sexual aggression against women. Learning also includes the acquisi-

"Convicted Rapists' Vocabulary of Motives: Excuses and Justifications," by Diana Scully and Joseph Marolla, reprinted from *Social Problems*, vol. 31, no. 5, 1984, pp. 530–544.

tion of culturally derived vocabularies of motive, which can be used to diminish responsibility and to negotiate a non-deviant identity.

Sociologists have long noted that people can, and do, commit acts they define as wrong and, having done so, engage various techniques to disavow deviance and present themselves as normal. Through the concept of "vocabulary of motive," Mills (1940:904) was among the first to shed light on this seemingly perplexing contradiction. Wrong-doers attempt to reinterpret their actions through the use of a linguistic device by which norm-breaking conduct is socially interpreted. That is, anticipating the negative consequences of their behavior, wrong-doers attempt to present the act in terms that are both culturally appropriate and acceptable.

Following Mills, a number of sociologists have focused on the types of techniques employed by actors in problematic situations (Hall and Hewitt, 1970; Hewitt and Hall, 1973; Hewitt and Stokes, 1975; Sykes and Matza, 1957). Scott and Lyman (1968) describe excuses and justifications, linguistic "accounts" that explain and remove culpability for an untoward act after it has been committed. *Excuses* admit the act was bad or inappropriate but deny full responsibility, often through appeals to accident, or biological drive, or through scapegoating. In contrast, *justifications* accept responsibility for the act but deny that it was wrong—that is, they show in this situation the act was appropriate. *Accounts* are socially approved vocabularies that neutralize an act or it's consequences and are always a manifestation of an underlying negotiation of identity.

Stokes and Hewitt (1976:837) use the term "aligning actions" to refer to those tactics and techniques used by actors when some feature of a situation is problematic. Stated simply, the concept refers to an actor's attempt, through various means, to bring his or her conduct into alignment with culture. Culture in this sense is conceptualized as a "set of cognitive constraints—objects—to which people must relate as they form lines of conduct" (1976:837), and includes physical constraints, expectations and definitions of others, and personal biography. Carrying out aligning actions implies both awareness of those elements of normative culture that are applicable to the deviant act and, in addition, an actual effort to bring the act into line with this awareness. The result is that deviant behavior is legitimized.

This paper presents an analysis of interviews we conducted with a sample of 114 convicted, incarcerated rapists. We use the concept of accounts (Scott and Lyman, 1968) as a tool to organize and analyze the vocabularies of motive which this group of rapists used to explain themselves and their actions. An analysis of their accounts demonstrates how it was possible for 83 percent (n = 114)[1] of these convicted rapists to view themselves as non-rapists.

When rapists' accounts are examined, a typology emerges that consists of admitters and deniers. Admitters (n = 47) acknowledged that they had forced sexual acts on their victims and defined the behavior as rape. In contrast, deniers[2] either eschewed sexual contact or all association with the victim (n = 35),[3] or admitted to sexual acts but did not define their behavior as rape (n = 32).

The remainder of this paper is divided into two sections. In the first, we discuss the accounts which the rapists used to justify their behavior. In the second, we discuss those accounts which attempted to excuse the rape. By and large, the deniers used justifications while the admitters used excuses. In some cases, both groups relied on the same themes, stereotypes, and images: some admitters, like most deniers, claimed that women enjoyed being raped. Some deniers excused their behavior by referring to alcohol or drug use, although they did so quite differently than admitters. Through these narrative accounts, we explore convicted rapists' own perceptions of their crimes.

◉ Methods and Validity

From September, 1980, through September, 1981, we interviewed 114 male convicted rapists who were incarcerated in seven maximum or medium security prisons in the Commonwealth of Virginia. All of the rapists had been convicted of the rape or attempted rape (n = 8) of an adult woman, although a few had teenage victims as well. Men convicted of incest, statutory rape, or sodomy of a male were omitted from the sample.

Twelve percent of the rapists had been convicted of more than one rape or attempted rape, 39 percent also had convictions for burglary or robbery, 29 percent for abduction, 25 percent for sodomy, and 11 percent for first or second degree murder. Eighty-two percent had a previous criminal history but only 23 percent had records for previous sex offenses. Their sentences for rape and accompanying crimes ranged from 10 years to an accumulation by one man of seven life sentences plus 380 years; 43 percent of the rapists were serving from 10 to 30 years and 22 percent were serving at least one life term. Forty-six percent of the rapists were white and 54 percent were black. Their ranges ranged from 18 to 60 years; 88 percent were between 18 and 35 years. Forty-two percent were either married or cohabitating at the time of their offense. Only 20 percent had a high school education or better, and 85 percent came from working-class backgrounds. Despite the popular belief that rape is due to a personality disorder, only 26 percent of these rapists had any history of emotional problems. When the rapists in this study were compared to a statistical profile of felons in all Virginia prisons, prepared by the Virginia Department of Corrections, rapists who volunteered for this research were disproportionately white, somewhat better educated, and younger than the average inmate.

All participants in this study were volunteers. We sent a letter to every inmate (n = 3500) at each of the seven prisons. The letters introduced us as professors at a local university, described our research as a study of men's attitudes toward sexual behavior and women, outlined our procedures for ensuring confidentiality, and solicited volunteers from all criminal categories. Using one follow-up letter, approximately 25 percent of all inmates, including rapists, indicated their willingness to be interviewed by mailing an information sheet to us at the university. From this pool of volunteers, we constructed a sample of rapists based on age, education, race, severity of current offenses, and previous criminal records. Obviously, the sample was not random and thus may not be representative of all rapists.

Each of the authors—one woman and one man—interviewed half of the rapists. Both authors were able to establish rapport and obtain information. However, the rapists volunteered more about their feelings and emotions to the female author and her interviews lasted longer.

All rapists were given an 89-page interview, which included a general background, psychological, criminal, and sexual history, attitude scales, and 30 pages of open-ended questions intended to explore their perceptions of their crimes, their victims, and theirselves. Because a voice print is an absolute source of identification, we did not use tape recorders. All interviews were hand recorded. With some practice, we found it was possible to record much of the interview verbatim. While hand recording inevitably resulted in some lost data, it did have the advantage of eliciting more confidence and candor in the men.

Interviews with the rapists lasted from three hours to seven hours; the average was about four-and-one-half hours. Most of the rapists were reluctant to end the interview. Once rapport had been established, the men wanted to talk, even though it sometimes meant, for example, missing a meal.

Because of the reputation prison inmates have for 'conning,' validity was a special concern in our research. Although the purpose of the research was to obtain the men's own perceptions of their acts, it was also necessary to establish the extent to which these perceptions deviated from other descriptions of their crimes. To establish validity, we used the same technique others have used in prison research: comparing factual information, including details of the crime, obtained in the interview with pre-sentence reports on file at the prisons (Athens, 1977; Luckenbill, 1977; Queen's Bench Foundation, 1976). Pre-sentence reports, written by a court worker at the time of conviction, usually include general background information, a psychological evaluation, the offender's version of the details of the crime, and the victim's or police's version of the details of the crime. Using these records allowed us to clarify two important issues: first, the amount of change that had occurred in rapists' accounts from pre-sentencing to the time when we interviewed them; and, second, the amount of discrepancy between rapists' accounts, as told to us, and the victims' and/or police versions of the crime, contained in the pre-sentence reports.

The time between pre-sentence reports and our interviews (in effect, the amount of time rapists had spent in prison before we interviewed them) ranged from less than one year to 20 years; the average was three years. Yet despite this time lapse, there were no significant changes in the way rapists explained their crimes, with the exception of 18 men who had denied their crimes at their trials but admitted them to us. There were no cases of men who admitted their crime at their trial but denied them when talking to us.

However, there were major differences between the accounts we heard of the crimes from rapists and the police's and victim's versions. Admitters (including deniers turned admitters) told us essentially the same story as the police and victim versions. However, the admitters subtly understated the force they had used and, though they used words such as *violent* to describe their acts, they also omitted reference to the more brutal aspects of their crime.

In contrast, deniers' interview accounts differed significantly from victim and police versions. According to the pre-sentence reports, 11 of the 32 deniers had been acquainted with their victim. But an additional four deniers told us they had been acquainted with their victims. In the pre-sentence reports, police or victim versions of the crime described seven

TABLE 1 *Comparison of Admitters' and Deniers' Crimes Police/Victim Versions in Pre-Sentence Reports*

Characteristics	Percent Admitters n = 47	Percent Deniers n = 32
White Assailant	57	41
Black Assailant	43	59
Group Rape	23	13
Multiple Rapes	43	34
Assailant a Stranger	72	66
Controversial Situation	06	22
Weapon and/or Injury Present		
(includes victim murdered)	74	69

rapes in which the victim had been hitchhiking or was picked up in a bar; but deniers told us this was true of 20 victims. Weapons were present in 21 of the 32 rapes according to the pre-sentence reports, yet only nine men acknowledged the presence of a weapon and only two of the nine admitted they had used it to threaten or intimidate their victim. Finally, in at least seven of the rapes, the victim had been seriously injured,[4] but only three men admitted injury. In two of the three cases, the victim had been murdered; in these cases the men denied the rape but not the murder. Indeed, deniers constructed accounts for us which, by implicating the victim, made their own conduct appear to have been more appropriate. They never used words such as *violent,* choosing instead to emphasize the sexual component of their behavior.

It should be noted that we investigated the possibility that deniers claimed their behavior was not criminal because, in contrast to admitters, their crimes resembled what research has found the public define as a controversial rape, that is, victim an acquaintance, no injury or weapon, victim picked up hitchhiking or in a bar (Burt, 1980; Burt and Albin, 1981; Williams, 1979). However, as Table 1 indicates, the crimes committed by deniers were only slightly more likely to involve these elements.

This contrast between pre-sentence reports and interviews suggests several significant factors related to interview content validity. First, when asked to explain their behavior, our sample of convicted rapists (except deniers turned admitters) responded with accounts that had changed surprisingly little since their trials. Second, admitters' interview accounts were basically the same as others' versions of their crimes, while deniers systematically put more blame on the victims.

❧ Justifying Rape

Deniers attempted to justify their behavior by presenting the victim in a light that made her appear culpable, regardless of their own actions. Five themes run through attempts to justify their rapes: (1) women as seductresses; (2) women mean "yes" when they say "no"; (3) most women eventually relax and enjoy it; (4) nice girls don't get raped; and (5) guilty of a minor wrongdoing.

1) Women as Seductresses

Men who rape need not search far for cultural language which supports the premise that women provoke or are responsible for rape. In addition to common cultural stereotypes, the fields of psychiatry and criminology (particularly the subfield of victimology) have traditionally provided justifications for rape, often by portraying raped women as the victims of their own seduction (Albin, 1977; Marolla and Scully, 1979). For example, Hollander (1924:130) argues:

> Considering the amount of illicit intercourse, rape of women is very rare indeed. Flirtation and provocative conduct, i.e. tacit (if not actual) consent is generally the prelude to intercourse.

Since women are supposed to be coy about their sexual availability, refusal to comply with a man's sexual demands lacks meaning and rape appears normal. The fact that violence and, often, a weapon are used to accomplish the rape is not considered. As an example, Abrahamsen (1960:61) writes:

> The conscious or unconscious biological or psychological attraction between man and woman does not exist only on the part of the offender toward the woman but, also, on her part toward him, which in many instances may, to some extent, be the impetus for his sexual attack. Often

'a women [sic] unconsciously wishes to be taken by force—consider the theft of the bride in Peer Gynt.

Like Peer Gynt, the deniers we interviewed tried to demonstrate that their victims were willing and, in some cases, enthusiastic participants.. In these accounts, the rape became more dependent upon the victim's behavior than upon their own actions.

Thirty-one percent (n = 10) of the deniers presented an extreme view of the victim. Not only willing, she was the aggressor, a seductress who lured them, unsuspecting, into sexual action. Typical was a denier convicted of his first rape and accompanying crimes of burglary, sodomy, and abduction. According to the pre-sentence reports, he had broken into the victim's house and raped her at knife point. While he admitted to the breaking and entry, which he claimed was for altruistic purposes ("to pay for the prenatal care of a friend's girlfriend"), he also argued that when the victim discovered him, he had tried to leave but she had asked him to stay. Telling him that she cheated on her husband, she had voluntarily removed her clothes and seduced him. She was, according to him, an exemplary sex partner who "enjoyed it very much and asked for oral sex.[5] Can I have it now?" he reported her as saying. He claimed they had spent hours in bed, after which the victim had told him he was good looking and asked to see him again. "Who would believe I'd meet a fellow like this?" he reported her as saying.

In addition to this extreme group, 25 percent (n = 8) of the deniers said the victim was willing and had made some sexual advances. An additional 9 percent (n = 3) said the victim was willing to have sex for money or drugs. In two of these three cases, the victim had been either an acquaintance or picked up, which the rapists said led them to expect sex.

2) Women Mean "Yes" When They Say "No"

Thirty-four percent (n = 11) of the deniers described their victim as unwilling, at least initially, indicating either that she had resisted or that she had said no. Despite this, and even though (according to pre-sentence reports) a weapon had been present in 64 percent (n = 7) of these 11 cases, the rapists justified their behavior by arguing that either the victim had not resisted enough or that her "no" had really meant "yes." For example, one denier who was serving time for a previous rape was subsequently convicted of attempting to rape a prison hospital nurse. He insisted he had actually completed the second rape, and said of his victim: "She semi-struggled but deep down inside I think she felt it was a fantasy come true." The nurse, according to him, had asked a question about his conviction for rape, which he interpreted as teasing. "It was like she was saying, `rape me'." Further, he stated that she had helped him along with oral sex and "from her actions, she was enjoying it." In another case, a 34-year-old man convicted of abducting and raping a 15-year old teenager at knife point as she walked on the beach, claimed it was a pickup. This rapist said women like to be over-powered before sex, but to dominate after it begins.

> A man's body is like a coke bottle, shake it up, put your thumb over the opening and feel the tension. When you take a woman out, woo her, then she says "no, I'm a nice girl," you have to use force. All men do this. She said "no" but it was a societal no, she wanted to be coaxed. All women say "no" when they mean "yes" but its a societal no, so they won't have to feel responsible later.

Claims that the victim didn't resist or, if she did, didn't resist enough, were also used by 24 percent (n = 11) of admitters to explain why, during the incident, they believed the victim was willing and that they were not raping. These rapists didn't redefine their acts until some time after the crime. For example, an admitter who used a bayonet to threaten his victim, an employee of the store he had been robbing, stated:

> At the time I didn't think it was rape. I just asked her nicely and she didn't resist. I never considered prison. I just felt like I had met a friend. It took about five years of reading and going to school to change my mind about whether it was rape. I became familiar with the subtlety of violence. But at the time, I believed that as long as I didn't hurt anyone it wasn't wrong. At the time, I didn't think I would go to prison, I thought I would beat it.

Another typical case involved a gang rape in which the victim was abducted at knife point as she walked home about midnight. According to two of the rapists, both of whom were interviewed, at the time they had thought the victim had willingly accepted a ride from the third rapist (who was not interviewed). They claimed the victim didn't resist and one reported her as saying she would do anything if they would take her home. In this rapist's view, "She acted like she enjoyed it, but maybe she was just acting. She wasn't crying, she was engaging in it." He reported that she had been friendly to the rapist who abducted her and, claiming not to have a home phone, she gave him her office number—a tactic eventually used to catch the three. In retrospect, this young man had decided, "She was scared and just relaxed and enjoyed it to avoid getting hurt." Note, however, that while he had redefined the act as rape, he continued to believe she enjoyed it.

Men who claimed to have been unaware that they were raping viewed sexual aggression as a man's prerogative at the time of the rape. Thus they regarded their act as little more than a minor wrongdoing even though most possessed or used a weapon. As long as the victim survived without major physical injury, from their perspective, a rape had not taken place. Indeed, even U.S. courts have often taken the position that physical injury is a necessary ingredient for a rape conviction.

3) Most Women Eventually Relax and Enjoy It

Many of the rapists expected us to accept the image, drawn from cultural stereotype, that once the rape began, the victim relaxed and enjoyed it.[6] Indeed, 69 percent (n = 22) of deniers justified their behavior by claiming not only that the victim was willing, but also that she enjoyed herself, in some cases to an immense degree. Several men suggested that they had fulfilled their victims' dreams. Additionally, while most admitters used adjectives such as "dirty," "humiliated," and "disgusted," to describe how they thought rape made women feel, 20 percent (n = 9) believed that their victim enjoyed herself. For example, one denier had posed as a salesman to gain entry to his victim's house. But he claimed he had had a previous sexual relationship with the victim, that she agreed to have sex for drugs, and that the opportunity to have sex with him produced "a glow, because she was really into oral stuff and fascinated by the idea of sex with a black man. She felt satisfied, fulfilled, wanted me to stay, but I didn't want her." In another case, a denier who had broken into his victim's house but who insisted the victim was his lover and let him in voluntarily, declared "She felt good, kept kissing me and wanted me to stay the night. She felt proud after sex with me." And another denier, who had hid in his victim's closet and later attacked her while she slept, argued that while she was scared at first, "once we got into it, she was ok." He continued to believe he hadn't committed rape because "she enjoyed it and it was like she consented."

4) Nice Girls Don't Get Raped

The belief that "nice girls don't get raped" affects perception of fault. The victim's reputation, as well as characteristics or behavior which violate normative sex role expectations, are perceived as contributing to the commission of the crime. For example, Nelson and Amir (1975) defined hitchhike rape as a victim-precipitated offense.

In our study, 69 percent (n = 22) of deniers and 22 percent (n = 10) of admitters referred to their victims' sexual reputation, thereby evoking the stereotype that "nice girls don't get raped." They claimed that the victim was known to have been a prostitute, or a "loose" woman, or to have had a lot of affairs, or to have given birth to a child out of wedlock. For example, a denier who claimed he had picked up his victim while she was hitchhiking stated, "To be honest, we [his family] knew she was a damn whore and whether she screwed one or 50 guys didn't matter." According to pre-sentence reports this victim didn't know her attacker and he abducted her at knife point from the street. In another case, a denier who claimed to have known his victim by reputation stated:

> If you wanted drugs or a quick piece of ass, she would do it. In court she said she was a virgin, but I could tell during sex [rape] that she was very experienced.

When other types of discrediting biographical information were added to these sexual slurs, a total of 78 percent (n = 25) of the deniers used the victim's reputation to substantiate their accounts. Most frequently, they referred to the victim's emotional state or drug use. For example, one denier claimed his victim had been known to be loose and, additionally, had turned state's evidence against her husband to put him in prison and save herself from a burglary conviction. Further, he asserted that she had met her current boyfriend, who was himself in and out of prison, in a drug rehabilitation center where they were both clients.

Evoking the stereotype that women provoke rape by the way they dress, a description of the victim as seductively attired appeared in the accounts of 22 percent (n = 7) of deniers and 17 percent (n = 8) of admitters. Typically, these descriptions were used to substantiate their claims about the victim's reputation. Some men went to extremes to paint a tarnished picture of the victim, describing her as dressed in tight black clothes and without a bra; in one case, the victim was portrayed as sexually provocative in dress and carriage. Not only did she wear short skirts, but she was observed to "spread her legs while getting out of cars." Not all of the men attempted to assassinate their victim's reputation with equal vengeance. Numerous times they made subtle and offhand remarks like, "She was a waitress and you know how they are."

The intent of these discrediting statements is clear. Deniers argued that the woman was a "legitimate" victim who got what she deserved. For example, one denier stated that all of his victims had been prostitutes; pre-sentence reports indicated they were not. Several times during his interview, he referred to them as "dirty sluts," and argued "anything I did to them was justified." Deniers also claimed their victim had wrongly accused them and was the type of woman who would perjure herself in court.

5) Only a Minor Wrongdoing

The majority of deniers did not claim to be completely innocent and they also accepted some accountability for their actions. Only 16 percent (n = 5) of deniers argued that they were totally free of blame. Instead, the majority of deniers pleaded guilty to a lesser charge. That is, they obfuscated the rape by pleading guilty to a less serious, more acceptable charge. They accepted being over-sexed, accused of poor judgement or trickery, even some violence, or guilty of adultery or contributing to the delinquency of a minor, charges that are hardly the equivalent of rape.

Typical of this reasoning is a denier who met his victim in a bar when the bartender asked him if he would try to repair her stalled car. After attempting unsuccessfully, he claimed the victim drank with him and later accepted a ride. Out riding, he pulled into a deserted area "to see how my luck would go." When the victim resisted his advances, he beat her and he stated:

> I did something stupid. I pulled a knife on her and I hit her as hard as I would hit a man. But I shouldn't be in prison for what I did. I shouldn't have all this time [sentence] for going to bed with a broad.

This rapist continued to believe that while the knife was wrong, his sexual behavior was justified.

In another case, the denier claimed he picked up his under-age victim at a party and that she voluntarily went with him to a motel. According to pre-sentence reports, the victim had been abducted at knife point from a party. He explained:

> After I paid for a motel, she would have to have sex but I wouldn't use a weapon. I would have explained. I spent money and, if she still said no, I would have forced her. If it had happened that way, it would have been rape to some people but not to my way of thinking. I've done that kind of

thing before. I'm guilty of sex and contributing to the delinquency of a minor, but not rape.

In sum, deniers argued that, while their behavior may not have been completely proper, it should not have been considered rape. To accomplish this, they attempted to discredit and blame the victim while presenting their own actions as justified in the context. Not surprisingly, none of the deniers thought of himself as a rapist. A minority of the admitters attempted to lessen the impact of their crime by claiming the victim enjoyed being raped. But despite this similarity, the nature and tone of admitters' and deniers' accounts were essentially different.

◉ Excusing Rape

In stark contrast to deniers, admitters regarded their behavior as morally wrong and beyond justification. They blamed themselves rather than the victim, although some continued to cling to the belief that the victim had contributed to the crime somewhat, for example, by not resisting enough.

Several of the admitters expressed the view that rape was an act of such moral outrage that it was unforgivable. Several admitters broke into tears at intervals during their interviews. A typical sentiment was,

> I equate rape with someone throwing you up against a wall and tearing your liver and guts out of you. . . . Rape is worse than murder . . . and I'm disgusting.

Another young admitter frequently referred to himself as repulsive and confided:

> I'm in here for rape and in my own mind, its the most disgusting crime, sickening. When people see me and know, I get sick.

Admitters tried to explain their crime in a way that allowed them to retain a semblance of moral integrity. Thus, in contrast to deniers' justifications, admitters used excuses to explain how they were compelled to rape. These excuses appealed to the existence of forces outside of the rapists' control. Through the use of excuses, they attempted to demonstrate that either intent was absent or responsibility was diminished. This allowed them to admit rape while reducing the threat to their identity as a moral person. Excuses also permitted them to view their behavior as idiosyncratic rather than typical and, thus, to believe they were not "really" rapists. Three themes run through these accounts: (1) the use of alcohol and drugs; (2) emotional problems; and (3) nice guy image.

1) The Use of Alcohol and Drugs

A number of studies have noted a high incidence of alcohol and drug consumption by convicted rapists prior to their crime (Groth, 1979; Queen's Bench Foundation, 1976). However, more recent research has tentatively concluded that the connection between substance use and crime is not as direct as previously thought (Ladouceur, 1983). Another facet of alcohol and drug use mentioned in the literature is its utility in disavowing deviance. McCaghy (1968) found that child molesters used alcohol as a technique for neutralizing their deviant identity. Marolla and Scully (1979), in a review of psychiatric literature, demonstrated how alcohol consumption is applied differently as a vocabulary of motive. Rapists can use alcohol both as an excuse for their behavior and to discredit the victim and make her more responsible. We found the former common among admitters and the latter common among deniers.

Alcohol and/or drugs were mentioned in the accounts of 77 percent (n = 30) of admitters and 84 percent (n = 21) of deniers and both groups were equally likely to have acknowledged consuming a substance—admitters, 77 percent (n = 30); deniers, 72 percent (n = 18). However, admitters said they had been affected by the substance; if not the cause of their behavior, it was at least a contributing factor. For example, an admitter who estimated his consumption to have been eight beers and four "hits of acid" reported:

> Straight, I don't have the guts to rape. I could fight a man but not that. To say, "I'm going to do it to a woman," knowing it will scare and hurt her, takes guts or you have to be sick.

Another admitter believed that his alcohol and drug use,

> . . . brought out what was already there but in such intensity it was uncontrollable. Feelings of being dominant, powerful, using someone for my own gratification, all rose to the surface.

In contrast, deniers' justifications required that they not be substantially impaired. To say that they had been drunk or high would cast doubt on their ability to control themself or to remember events as they actually happened. Consistent with this, when we asked if the alcohol and/or drugs had had an effect on their behavior, 69 percent (n = 27) of admitters, but only 40 percent (n = 10) of deniers, said they had been affected.

Table 2 *Rapists' Accounts of Own and Victims' Alcohol and/or Drug (A/D) Use and Effect*

	Admitters n=39 %	Deniers n=25 %
Neither Self nor Victim Used A/D	23	16
Self Used A/D	77	72
Of Self Used, no Victim Use	51	12
Self Affected by A/D	69	40
Of Self Affected, no Victim Use or Affect	54	24
Self A/D Users who were Affected	90	56
Victim Used A/D	26	72
Of Victim Used, no Self Use	0	0
Victim Affected by A/D	15	56
Of Victim Affected, no Self Use or Affect	0	40
Victim A/D Users who were Affected	60	78
Both Self and Victim Used and Affected by A/D	15	16

Even more interesting were references to the victim's alcohol and/or drug use. Since admitters had already relieved themselves of responsibility through claims of being drunk or high, they had nothing to gain from the assertion that the victim had used or been affected by alcohol and/or drugs. On the other hand, it was very much in the interest of deniers to declare that their victim had been intoxicated or high: that fact lessened her credibility and made her more responsible for the act. Reflecting these observations, 72 percent (n = 18) of deniers and 26 percent (n = 10) of admitters maintained that alcohol or drugs had been consumed by the victim. Further, while 56 percent (n = 14) of deniers declared she had been affected by this use, only 15 percent (n = 6) of admitters made a similar claim. Typically, deniers argued that the alcohol and drugs had sexually aroused their victim or rendered her out of control. For example, one denier insisted that his victim had become hysterical from drugs, not from being raped, and it was because of the drugs that she had reported him to the police. In addition, 40 percent (n = 10) of deniers argued that while the victim had been drunk or high, they themselves either hadn't ingested or weren't affected by alcohol and/or drugs. None of the admitters made this claim. In fact, in all of the 15 percent (n = 6) of cases where an admitter said the victim was drunk or high, he also admitted to being similarly affected.

These data strongly suggest that whatever role alcohol and drugs play in sexual and other types of violent crime, rapists have learned the advantage to be gained from using alcohol and drugs as an account. Our sample were aware that their victim would be discredited and their own behavior excused or justified by referring to alcohol and/or drugs.

2) Emotional Problems

Admitters frequently attributed their acts to emotional problems. Forty percent (n = 19) of admitters said they believed an emotional problem had been at the root of their rape behavior, and 33 percent (n = 15) specifically related the problem to an unhappy, unstable childhood or a marital-domestic situation. Still others claimed to have been in a general state of unease. For example, one admitter said that at the time of the rape he had been depressed, feeling he couldn't do anything right, and that something had been missing from his life. But he also added, "being a rapist is not part of my personality." Even admitters who could locate no source for an emotional problem evoked the popular image of rapists as the product of disordered personalities to argue they also must have problems:

> The fact that I'm a rapist makes me different. Rapists aren't all there. They have problems. It was wrong so there must be a reason why I did it. I must have a problem.

Our data do indicate that a precipitating event, involving an upsetting problem of everyday living, appeared in the accounts of 80 percent (n = 38) of admitters and 25 percent (n = 8) of deniers. Of those experiencing a precipitating event, including deniers, 76 percent (n = 35) involved a wife or girlfriend. Over and over, these men described themselves as having been in a rage because of an incident involving a woman with whom they believed they were in love.

Frequently, the upsetting event was related to a rigid and unrealistic double standard for sexual conduct and virtue which they applied to "their" woman but which they didn't expect from men, didn't apply to themselves, and, obviously, didn't honor in other women. To discover that the "pedestal" didn't apply to their wife or girlfriend sent them into a fury. One especially articulate and typical admitter described his feeling as follows. After serving a short prison term for auto theft, he married his "childhood sweetheart" and secured a well-paying job. Between his job and the volunteer work he was doing with an ex-offender group, he was spending long hours away from home, a situation that had bothered his wife. In response to her request, he gave up his volunteer work, though it was clearly meaningful to him. Then, one day, he discovered his wife with her former boyfriend "and my life fell apart." During the next several days, he said his anger had made him withdraw into himself and, after three days of drinking in a motel room, he abducted and raped a stranger. He stated:

> My parents have been married for many years and I had high expectations about marriage. I put my wife on a pedestal. When I walked in on her, I felt like my life had been destroyed, it was such a shock. I was bitter and angry about the fact that I hadn't done anything to my wife for cheating. I didn't want to hurt her [victim], only to scare and degrade her.

It is clear that many admitters, and a minority of deniers, were under stress at the time of their rapes. However, their problems were ordinary—the types of upsetting events that everyone experiences at some point in life. The overwhelming majority of the men were not clinically defined as mentally ill in court-ordered psychiatric examinations prior to their trials. Indeed, our sample is consistent with Abel *et al.* (1980) who found fewer than 5 percent of rapists were psychotic at the time of their offense.

As with alcohol and drug intoxication, a claim of emotional problems works differently depending upon whether the behavior in question is being justified or excused. It would have been counter-productive for deniers to have claimed to have had emotional problems at the time of the rape. Admitters used psychological explanations to portray themselves as having been temporarily "sick" at the time of the rape. Sick people are usually blamed for neither the cause of their illness nor for acts committed while in that state of diminished capacity. Thus, adopting the sick role removed responsibility by excusing the behavior as having been beyond the ability of the individual to control. Since the rapists were not "themselves," the rape was idiosyncratic rather than typical behavior. Admitters asserted a non-deviant identity despite their self-proclaimed disgust with what they had done. Although admitters were willing to assume the sick role, they did not view their problem as a chronic condition, nor did they believe themselves to be insane or permanently impaired. Said one admitter, who believed that he needed psychological counseling: "I have a mental disorder, but I'm not crazy." Instead, admitters viewed their "problem" as mild, transient, and curable. Indeed, part of the appeal of this excuse was that not only did it relieve responsibility, but, as with alcohol and drug addiction, it allowed the rapist to "recover." Thus, at the time of their interviews, only 31 percent (n

= 14) of admitters indicated that "being a rapist" was part of their self-concept. Twenty-eight percent (n = 13) of admitters stated they had never thought of themselves as rapists, 8 percent (n = 4) said they were unsure, and 33 percent (n = 16) asserted they had been a rapist at one time but now were recovered. A multiple "exrapist," who believed his "problem" was due to "something buried in my subconscious" that was triggered when his girlfriend broke up with him, expressed a typical opinion:

> I was a rapist, but not now. I've grown up, had to live with it. I've hit the bottom of the well and it can't get worse. I feel born again to deal with my problems.

3) Nice Guy Image

Admitters attempted to further neutralize their crime and negotiate a non-rapist identity by painting an image of themselves as a "nice guy." Admitters projected the image of someone who had made a serious mistake but, in every other respect, was a decent person. Fifty-seven percent (n = 27) expressed regret and sorrow for their victim indicating that they wished there were a way to apologize for or amend their behavior. For example, a participant in a rape-murder, who insisted his partner did the murder, confided, "I wish there was something I could do besides saying 'I'm sorry, I'm sorry.' I live with it 24 hours a day and, sometimes, I wake up crying in the middle of the night because of it."

Schlenker and Darby (1981) explain the significance of apologies beyond the obvious expression of regret. An apology allows a person to admit guilt while at the same time seeking a pardon by signalling that the event should not be considered a fair representation of what the person is really like. An apology separates the bad self from the good self, and promises more acceptable behavior in the future. When apologizing, an individual is attempting to say: "I have repented and should be forgiven," thus making it appear that no further rehabilitation is required.

The "rice guy" statements of the admitters reflected an attempt to communicate a message consistent with Schlenker's and Darby's analysis of apologies. It was an attempt to convey that rape was not a representation of their "true" self. For example,

> It's different from anything else I've ever done. I feel more guilt about this. It's not consistent with me. When I talk about it, it's like being assaulted myself. I don't know why I did it, but once I started, I got into it. Armed

robbery was a way of life for me, but not rape. I feel like I wasn't being myself.

Admitters also used "nice guy" statements to register their moral opposition to violence and harming women, even though, in some cases, they had seriously injured their victims. Such was the case of an admitter convicted of a gang rape:

> I'm against hurting women. She should have resisted. None of us were the type of person that would use force on a woman. I never positioned myself on a woman unless she showed an interest in me. They would play to me, not me to them. My weakness is to follow. I never would have stopped, let along pick her up without the others. I never would have let anyone beat her. I never bothered women who didn't want sex; never had a problem with sex or getting it. I loved her—like all women.

Finally, a number of admitters attempted to improve their self-image by demonstrating that, while they had raped, it could have been worse if they had not been a "nice guy." For example, one admitter professed to being especially gentle with his victim after she told him she had just had a baby. Others claimed to have given the victim money to get home or make a phone call, or to have made sure the victim's children were not in the room. A multiple rapist, whose pattern was to break in and attack sleeping victims in their homes, stated:

> I never beat any of my victims and I told them I wouldn't hurt them if they cooperated. I'm a professional thief. But I never robbed the women I raped because I felt so bad about what I had already done to them.

Even a young man, who raped his five victims at gun point and then stabbed them to death, attempted to improve his image by stating:

> Physically they enjoyed the sex [rape]. Once they got involved, it would be difficult to resist. I was always gentle and kind until I started to kill them. And the killing was always sudden, so they wouldn't know it was coming.

◉ Summary and Conclusions

Convicted rapists' accounts of their crimes include both excuses and justifications. Those who deny what they did was rape justify their actions; those who admit it was rape attempt to excuse it or themselves. This study does not address why some men admit while others deny, but future research might address this question. This paper does provide insight on how men who are sexually aggressive or violent construct reality, describing the different strategies of admitters and deniers.

Admitters expressed the belief that rape was morally reprehensible. But they explained themselves and their acts by appealing to forces beyond their control, forces which reduced their capacity to act rationally and thus compelled them to rape. Two types of excuses predominated: alcohol/drug intoxication and emotional problems. Admitters used these excuses to negotiate a moral identity for themselves by viewing rape as idiosyncratic rather than typical behavior. This allowed them to reconceptualize themselves as recovered or "exrapists," someone who had made a serious mistake which did not represent their "true" self.

In contrast, deniers' accounts indicate that these men raped because their value system provided no compelling reason not to do so. When sex is viewed as a male entitlement, rape is no longer seen as criminal. However, the deniers had been convicted of rape, and like the admitters, they attempted to negotiate an identity. Through justifications, they constructed a "controversial" rape and attempted to demonstrate how their behavior, even if not quite right, was appropriate in the situation. Their denials, drawn from common cultural rape stereotypes, took two forms, both of which ultimately denied the existence of a victim.

The first form of denial was buttressed by the cultural view of men as sexually masterful and women as coy but seductive. Injury was denied by portraying the victim as willing, even enthusiastic, or as politely resistant at first but eventually yielding to "relax and enjoy it." In these accounts, force appeared merely as a seductive technique. Rape was disclaimed: rather than harm the woman, the rapist had fulfilled her dreams. In the second form of denial, the victim was portrayed as the type of woman who "got what she deserved." Through attacks on the victim's sexual reputation and, to a lesser degree, her emotional state, deniers attempted to demonstrate that since the victim wasn't a "nice girl," they were not rapists. Consistent with both forms of denial was the self-interested use of alcohol and drugs as a justification. Thus, in contrast to admitters, who accentuated their own use as an excuse, deniers emphasized the victim's consumption in an effort to both discredit her and make her appear more responsible for the rape. It is important to remember that deniers did not invent these justifications. Rather, they reflect a belief system which has historically victimized women by promulgating the myth that women both enjoy and are responsible for their own rape.

While admitters and deniers present an essentially contrasting view of men who rape, there were some shared characteristics. Justifications particularly, but also excuses, are buttressed by the cultural view of women as sexual commodities, dehumanized and devoid of autonomy and dignity. In this sense, the sexual objectification of women must be understood as an important factor contributing to an environment that trivializes, neutralizes, and, perhaps, facilitates rape.

Finally, we must comment on the consequences of allowing one perspective to dominate thought on a social problem. Rape, like any complex continuum of behavior, has multiple causes and is influenced by a number of social factors. Yet, dominated by psychiatry and the medical model, the underlying assumption that rapists are "sick" has pervaded research. Although methodologically unsound, conclusions have been based almost exclusively on small clinical populations of rapists—that extreme group of rapists who seek counseling in prison and are the most likely to exhibit psychopathology. From this small, atypical group of men, psychiatric findings have been generalized to all men who rape. Our research, however, based on volunteers from the entire prison population, indicates that some rapists, like deniers, viewed and understood their behavior from a popular cultural perspective. This strongly suggests that cultural perspectives, and not an idiosyncratic illness, motivated their behavior. Indeed, we can argue that the psychiatric perspective has contributed to the vocabulary of motive that rapists use to excuse and justify their behavior (Scully and Marolla, 1984).

Efforts to arrive at a general explanation for rape have been retarded by the narrow focus of the medical model and the preoccupation with clinical populations. The continued reduction of such complex behavior to a singular cause hinders, rather than enhances, our understanding of rape.

Endnotes

[1] These numbers include pretest interviews. When the analysis involves either questions that were not asked in the pretest or that were changed, they are excluded and thus the number changes.

[2] There is, of course, the possibility that some of these men really were innocent of rape. However, while the U.S. criminal justice system is not without flaw, we assume that it is highly unlikely that this many men could have been unjustly convicted of rape, especially since rape is a crime with traditionally low conviction rates. Instead, for purposes of this research, we assume that these men were

guilty as charged and that their attempt to maintain an image of non-rapist springs from some psychologically or sociologically interpretable mechanism.

[3]Because of their outright denial, interviews with this group of rapists did not contain the data being analyzed here and, consequently, they are not included in this paper.

[4]It was sometimes difficult to determine the full extent of victim injury from the pre-sentence reports. Consequently, it is doubtful that this number accurately reflects the degree of injuries sustained by victims.

[5]It is worth noting that a number of deniers specifically mentioned the victim's alleged interest in oral sex. Since our interview questions about sexual history indicated that the rapists themselves found oral sex marginally acceptable, the frequent mention is probably another attempt to discredit the victim. However, since a tape recorder could not be used for the interviews and the importance of these claims didn't emerge until the data was being coded and analyzed, it is possible that it was mentioned even more frequently but not recorded.

[6]Research shows clearly that women do not enjoy rape. Holmstrom and Burgess (1978) asked 93 adult rape victims, "How did it feel sexually?" Not one said they enjoyed it. Further, the trauma of rape is so great that it disrupts sexual functioning (both frequency and satisfaction) for the overwhelming majority of victims, at least during the period immediately following the rape and, in fewer cases, for an extended period of time (Burgess and Holmstrom, 1979; Feldman-Summers *et al.*, 1979). In addition, a number of studies have shown that rape victims experience adverse consequences prompting some to move, change jobs, or drop out of school (Burgess and Holmstrom, 1974; Kilpatrick *et al.*, 1979; Ruch *et al.*, 1980; Shore, 1979).

References

Abel Gene, Judith Becker, and Linda Skinner. 1980. "Aggressive behavior and sex." Psychiatric Clinics of North America 3(2):133–151.

Abrahamsen, David. 1960. The Psychology of Crime. New York: John Wiley.

Albin, Rochelle. 1977. "Psychological studies of rape." Signs 3(2):423–435.

Athens, Lonnie. 1977. "Violent crimes: A symbolic interactionist study." Symbolic Interaction 1(1):56–71.

Burgess, Ann Wolbert, and Lynda Lytle Holmstrom. 1974. Rape: Victims of Crisis. Bowie: Robert J. Brady.

———. 1979. "Rape: Sexual disruption and recovery." American Journal of Orthopsychiatry 49(4):648–657.

Burt, Martha. 1980. "Cultural myths and supports for rape." Journal of Personality and Social Psychology 38(2):217–230.

Burt, Martha, and Rochelle Albin. 1981. "Rape myths, rape definitions, and probability of conviction." Journal of Applied Psychology 11(3):212–230.

Feldman-Summers, Shirley, Patricia E. Gordon, and Jeanette R. Meagher. 1979. "The impact of rape on sexual satisfaction." Journal of Abnormal Psychology 88(1):101–105.

Glueck, Sheldon. 1925. Mental Disorders and the Criminal Law. New York: Little Brown.

Groth, Nicholas A. 1979. Men Who Rape. New York: Plenum Press.

Hall, Peter M., and John P. Hewitt. 1970. "The quasi-theory of communication and the management of dissent." Social Problems 18(1):17–27.

Hewitt, John P., and Peter M. Hall. 1973. "Social problems, problematic situations, and quasi-theories." American Journal of Sociology 38(3):367–374.

Hewitt, John P., and Randall Stokes. 1975. "Disclaimers." American Sociological Review 40(1):1–11.

Hollander, Bernard. 1924. The Psychology of Misconduct, Vice, and Crime. New York: Macmillan.

Holmstrom, Lynda Lytle, and Ann Wolbert Burgess. 1978. "Sexual behavior of assailant and victim during rape." Paper presented at the annual meetings of the American Sociological Association, San Francisco, September 2–8.

Kilpatrick, Dean G., Lois Veronen, and Patricia A. Resnick. 1979. "The aftermath of rape. Recent empirical findings." American Journal of Orthopsychiatry 49(4):658–669.

Ladouceur, Patricia. 1983. "The relative impact of drugs and alcohol on serious felons." Paper presented at the annual meetings of the American Society of Criminology, Denver, November 9–12.

Luckenbill, David. 1977. "Criminal homicide as a situated transaction." Social Problems 25(2):176–187.

McCaghy, Charles. 1968. "Drinking and deviance disavowal: The case of child molesters." Social Problems 16(1):43–49.

Marolla, Joseph, and Diana Scully. 1979. "Rape and psychiatric vocabularies of motive." Pp. 301–318 in Edith S. Gomberg and Violet Franks (eds.), Gender and Disordered Behavior: Sex Differences in Psychopathology. New York: Brunner/Mazel.

Mills, C. Wright. 1940. "Situated actions and vocabularies of motive." American Sociological Review 5(6):904–913.

Nelson, Steve, and Menachem Amir. 1975. "The hitchhike victim of rape: A research report." Pp. 47–65 in Israel Drapkin and Emilio Viano (eds.), Victimology: A New Focus. Lexington, KY: Lexington Books.

Queen's Bench Foundation. 1976. Rape: Prevention and Resistance. San Francisco: Queen's Bench Foundation.

Ruch, Libby O., Susan Meyers Chandler, and Richard A. Harter. 1980. "Life change and rape impact." Journal of Health and Social Behavior 21(3):248–260.

Scott, Marvin, and Stanford Lyman. 1968. "Accounts." American Sociological Review 33(1):46–62.

Schlenker, Barry R., and Bruce W. Darby. 1981. "The use of apologies in social predicaments." Social Psychology Quarterly 44(3):271-278.

Scully, Diana, and Joseph Marolla. 1984. "Rape and psychiatric vocabularies of motive: Alternative perspectives." In Ann Wolbert Burgess (ed.), Handbook on Rape and Sexual Assault. New York: Garland Publishing. Forthcoming.

Shore, Barbara K. 1979. An Examination of Critical Process and Outcome Factors in Rape." Rockville, MD: National Institute of Mental Health.

Stokes, Randall, and John P. Hewitt. 1976. "Aligning actions." American Sociological Review 41(5):837–849.

Sykes, Gresham M., and David Matza. 1957. "Techniques of neutralization." American Sociological Review 22(6):664–670.

Williams, Joyce. 1979. "Sex role stereotypes, women's liberation, and rape: A cross-cultural analysis of attitude." Sociological Symposium 25 (Winter):61–97.

❧ ❧ ❧

Questions

1. What are the distinguishing differences between "admitters" and "deniers"? Are there any similarities between these two groups? If so, what are they?

2. Define *justification*. Define *excuse*. How are the five justifications and three excuses discussed in this article similar? How are they dissimilar?

3. To what degree is there variation in the use of justifications and excuses by admitters and deniers? In other words, do admitters primarily use justifications or excuses for their behavior? What about deniers?

4. To what degree do you think rapists learn justifications through every-day socialization avenues (for example, family, peers, school, media, etc.)? To what degree might rapists learn justifications and excuses while in prison?

5. The authors conclude that their results somewhat refute the "medical explanation" of rape. They base this conclusion on rapists' ability to view and explain their behavior from a popular-culture perspective. Does this conclusion necessarily refute the "sick" or biological view of rape? Might rapists' *behavior* be psychopathological but the *explanations* for their behavior are framed in social terms? Explain your views on this possibility.

Techniques of Neutralization

GRESHAM M. SYKES, Princeton University
DAVID MATZA, Temple University

In this selection, Gresham Sykes and David Matza argue that criminals use various "techniques of neutralization" to rationalize their behavior. These techniques include beliefs that "I didn't mean to do it," "I didn't really hurt anybody," and "everybody does it; why pick on me?" These rationalizations have an important ramification: They let individuals claim allegiance to conventional society's values while at the same excusing their own illegal acts.

In attempting to uncover the roots of juvenile delinquency, the social scientist has long since ceased to search for devils in the mind or stigma of the body. It is now largely agreed that delinquent behavior, like most social behavior, is learned and that it is learned in the process of social interaction.

The classic statement of this position is found in Sutherland's theory of differential association, which asserts that criminal or delinquent behavior involves the learning of (a) techniques of committing crimes and (b) motives, drives, rationalizations, and attitudes favorable to the violation of law.[1] Unfortunately, the specific content of what is learned—as opposed to the process by which it is learned—has received relatively little attention in either theory or research. Perhaps the single strongest school of thought on the nature of this content has centered on the idea of a delinquent subculture. The basic characteristic of the delinquent sub-culture, it is argued, is a system of values that represents an inversion of the values held by respectable, law-abiding society. The world of the delinquent is the world of the law-abiding turned upside down and its norms constitute a countervailing force directed against the conforming social order. Cohen[2] sees the

---

"Techniques of Neutralization," by Gresham M. Sykes and David Matza, reprinted from *American Sociological Review*, vol. 22, no. 6, 1957, pp. 664–670.

process of developing a delinquent sub-culture as a matter of building, maintaining, and reinforcing a code for behavior which exists by opposition, which stands in point by point contradiction to dominant values, particularly those of the middle class. Cohen's portrayal of delinquency is executed with a good deal of sophistication, and he carefully avoids overly simple explanations such as those based on the principle of "follow the leader" or easy generalizations about "emotional disturbances." Furthermore, he does not accept the delinquent sub-culture as something given, but instead systematically examines the function of delinquent values as a viable solution to the lower-class, male child's problems in the area of social status. Yet in spite of its virtues, this image of juvenile delinquency as a form of behavior based on competing or countervailing values and norms appears to suffer from a number of serious defects. It is the nature of these defects and a possible alternative or modified explanation for a large portion of juvenile delinquency with which this paper is concerned.

The difficulties in viewing delinquent behavior as springing from a set of deviant values and norms—as arising, that is to say, from a situation in which the delinquent defines his delinquency as "right"—are both empirical and theoretical. In the first place, if there existed in fact a delinquent subculture such that the delinquent viewed his illegal behavior as morally correct, we could reasonably suppose that he would exhibit no feelings of guilt or shame at detection or confinement. Instead, the major reaction would tend in the direction of indignation or a sense of martyrdom.[3] It is true that some delinquents do react in the latter fashion, although the sense of martyrdom often seems to be based on the fact that others "get away with it" and indignation appears to be directed against the chance events or lack of skill that led to apprehension. More important, however, is the fact that there is a good deal of evidence suggesting that many delinquents *do* experience a sense of guilt or shame, and its outward expression is not to be dismissed as a purely manipulative gesture to appease those in authority. Much of this evidence is, to be sure, of a clinical nature or in the form of impressionistic judgments of those who must deal first hand with the youthful offender. Assigning a weight to such evidence calls for caution, but it cannot be ignored if we are to avoid the gross stereotype of the juvenile delinquent as a hardened gangster in miniature.

In the second place, observers have noted that the juvenile delinquent frequently accords admiration and respect to law-abiding persons. The "really honest" person is often revered, and if the delinquent is sometimes overly keen to detect hypocrisy in those who conform, unquestioned probity is likely to win his approval. A fierce attachment to a humble, pious mother or a forgiving, upright priest (the former, according to many observers, is often encountered in both juvenile delinquents and adult criminals) might be dismissed as rank sentimentality, but at least it is clear that the delinquent does not necessarily regard those who abide by the legal rules as immoral. In a similar vein, it can be noted that the juvenile delinquent may exhibit great resentment if illegal behavior is imputed to "significant others" in his immediate social environment or to heroes in the world of sport and entertainment. In other words, if the delinquent does hold to a set of values and norms that stand in complete opposition to those of respectable society, his norm-holding is of a peculiar sort. While supposedly thoroughly committed to the deviant system of the delinquent sub-culture, he would appear to recognize the moral validity of the dominant normative system in many instances.[4]

In the third place, there is much evidence that juvenile delinquents often draw a sharp line between those who can be victimized and those who cannot. Certain social groups are not to be viewed as "fair game" in the performance of supposedly approved delinquent acts while others warrant a variety of attacks. In general, the potentiality for victimization would seem to be a function of the social distance between the juvenile delinquent and others and thus we find implicit maxims in the world of the delinquent such as "don't steal from friends" or "don't commit vandalism against a church of your own faith."[5] This is all rather obvious, but the implications have not received sufficient attention. The fact that supposedly valued behavior tends to be directed against disvalued social groups hints that the "wrongfulness" of such delinquent behavior is more widely recognized by delinquents than the literature has indicated. When the pool of victims is limited by considerations of kinship, friendship, ethnic group, social class, age, sex, etc., we have reason to suspect that the virtue of delinquency is far from unquestioned.

In the fourth place, it is doubtful if many juvenile delinquents are totally immune from the demands for conformity made by the dominant social order. There is a strong likelihood that the family of the delinquent will agree with respectable society that delinquency is wrong, even though the family may be engaged in a variety of illegal activities. That is, the parental posture conducive to delinquency is not apt to be a positive prodding. Whatever may be the influence of parental example, what might be called the "Fagin" pattern of socialization into delinquency is probably rare. Furthermore, as Redl has indicated, the idea that certain neighborhoods are completely delinquent, offering the child a model for delinquent behavior without reservations, is simply not supported by the data.[6]

The fact that a child is punished by parents, school officials, and agencies of the legal system for his delinquency may, as a number of observers have cynically noted, suggest to the child that he should be more careful not to get caught. There is an equal or greater probability, however, that the child will internalize the demands for conformity. This is not to say that demands for conformity cannot be counteracted. In fact, as we shall see shortly, an understanding of how internal and external demands for conformity are neutralized may be crucial for understanding delinquent behavior. But it is to say that a complete denial of the validity of demands for conformity and the substitution of a new normative system is improbable, in light of the child's or adolescent's dependency on adults and encirclement by adults inherent in his status in the social structure. No matter how deeply enmeshed in patterns of delinquency he may be and no matter how much this involvement may outweigh his associations with the law-abiding, he cannot escape the condemnation of his deviance. Somehow the demands for conformity must be met and answered; they cannot be ignored as part of an alien system of values and norms.

In short, the theoretical viewpoint that sees juvenile delinquency as a form of behavior based on the values and norms of a deviant sub-culture in precisely the same way as law-abiding behavior is based on the values and norms of the larger society is open to serious doubt. The fact that the world of the delinquent is embedded in the larger world of those who conform cannot be overlooked nor can the delinquent be equated with an adult thoroughly socialized into an alternative way of life. Instead, the juvenile delinquent would appear to be at least partially committed to the dominant social order in that he frequently exhibits guilt or shame when he violates its proscriptions, accords approval to certain conforming figures, and distinguishes between appropriate and inappropriate targets for his deviance. It is to an explanation for the apparently paradoxical fact of his delinquency that we now turn.

As Morris Cohen once said, one of the most fascinating problems about human behavior is why men violate the laws in which they believe. This is the problem that confronts us when we attempt to explain why delinquency occurs despite a greater or lesser commitment to the usages of conformity.

A basic clue is offered by the fact that social rules or norms calling for valued behavior seldom if ever take the form of categorical imperatives. Rather, values or norms appear as *qualified* guides for action, limited in their applicability in terms of time, place, persons, and social circumstances. The moral injunction against killing, for example, does not apply to the enemy during combat in time of war, although a captured enemy comes once again under the prohibition. Similarly, the taking and distributing of scarce goods in a time of acute social need is felt by many to be right, although under other circumstances private property is held inviolable. The normative system of a society, then, is marked by what Williams has termed *flexibility;* it does not consist of a body of rules held to be binding under all conditions.[7]

This flexibility is, in fact, an integral part of the criminal law in that measures for "defenses to crimes" are provided in pleas such as nonage, necessity, insanity, drunkenness, compulsion, self-defense, and so on. The individual can avoid moral culpability for his criminal action—and thus avoid the negative sanctions of society—if he can prove that criminal intent was lacking. *It is our argument that much delinquency is based on what is essentially an unrecognized extension of defenses to crimes, in the form of justifications for deviance that are seen as valid by the delinquent but not by the legal system or society at large.*

These justifications are commonly described as rationalizations. They are viewed as following deviant behavior and as protecting the individual from self-blame and the blame of others after the act. But there is also reason to believe that they precede deviant behavior and make deviant behavior possible. It is this possibility that Sutherland mentioned only in passing and that other writers have failed to exploit from the viewpoint of sociological theory. Disapproval flowing from internalized norms and conforming others in the social environment is neutralized, turned back, or deflected in advance. Social controls that serve to check or inhibit deviant motivational patterns are rendered inoperative, and the individual is freed to engage in delinquency without serious damage to his self image. In this sense, the delinquent both has his cake and eats it too, for he remains committed to the dominant normative system and yet so qualifies its imperatives that violations are "acceptable" if not "right." Thus the delinquent represents not a radical opposition to law-abiding society but something more like an apologetic failure, often more sinned against than sinning in his own eyes. We call these justifications of deviant behavior techniques of neutralization; and we believe these techniques make up a crucial component of

Sutherland's "definitions favorable to the violation of law." It is by learning these techniques that the juvenile becomes delinquent, rather than by learning moral imperatives, values or attitudes standing in direct contradiction to those of the dominant society. In analyzing these techniques, we have found it convenient to divide them into five major types.

The Denial of Responsibility. In so far as the delinquent can define himself as lacking responsibility for his deviant actions, the disapproval of self or others is sharply reduced in effectiveness as a restraining influence. As Justice Holmes has said, even a dog distinguishes between being stumbled over and being kicked, and modern society is no less careful to draw a line between injuries that are unintentional, i.e., where responsibility is lacking, and those that are intentional. As a technique of neutralization, however, the denial of responsibility extends much further than the claim that deviant acts are an "accident" or some similar negation of personal accountability. It may also be asserted that delinquent acts are due to forces outside of the individual and beyond his control such as unloving parents, bad companions, or a slum neighborhood. In effect, the delinquent approaches a "billiard ball" conception of himself in which he sees himself as helplessly propelled into new situations. From a psychodynamic viewpoint, this orientation toward one's own actions may represent a profound alienation from self, but it is important to stress the fact that interpretations of responsibility are cultural constructs and not merely idiosyncratic beliefs. The similarity between this mode of justifying illegal behavior assumed by the delinquent and the implications of a "sociological" frame of reference or a "humane" jurisprudence is readily apparent.[8] It is not the validity of this orientation that concerns us here, but its function of deflecting blame attached to violations of social norms and its relative independence of a particular personality structure.[9] By learning to view himself as more acted upon than acting, the delinquent prepares the way for deviance from the dominant normative system without the necessity of a frontal assault on the norms themselves.

The Denial of Injury. A second major technique of neutralization centers on the injury or harm involved in the delinquent act. The criminal law has long made a distinction between crimes which are *mala in se* and *malla prohibita*—that is between acts that are wrong in themselves and acts that are illegal but not immoral—and the delinquent can make the same kind of distinction in evaluating the wrongfulness of his behavior. For the delinquent, however, wrongfulness may turn on the question of whether or not anyone has clearly been hurt by his deviance, and this matter is open to a variety of interpretations. Vandalism, for example, may be defined by the delinquent simply as "mischief"—after all, it may be claimed, the persons whose property has been destroyed can well afford it. Similarly, auto theft may be viewed as "borrowing," and gang fighting may be seen as a private quarrel, an agreed upon duel between two willing parties, and thus of no concern to the community at large. We are not suggesting that this technique of neutralization, labelled the denial of injury, involves an explicit dialectic. Rather, we are arguing that the delinquent frequently, and in a hazy fashion, feels that his behavior does not really cause any great harm despite the fact that it runs counter to law. Just as the link between the individual and his acts may be broken by the denial of responsibility, so may the link between acts and their consequences be broken by the denial of injury. Since society sometimes agrees with the delinquent, e.g., in matters such as truancy, "pranks," and so on, it merely reaffirms the idea that the delinquent's neutralization of social controls by means of qualifying the norms is an extension of common practice rather than a gesture of complete opposition.

The Denial of the Victim. Even if the delinquent accepts the responsibility for his deviant actions and is willing to admit that his deviant actions involve an injury or hurt, the moral indignation of self and others may be neutralized by an insistence that the injury is not wrong in light of the circumstances. The injury, it may be claimed, is not really an injury; rather, it is a form of rightful retaliation or punishment. By a subtle alchemy the delinquent moves himself into the position of an avenger and the victim is transformed into a wrong-doer. Assaults on homosexuals or suspected homosexuals, attacks on members of minority groups who are said to have gotten "out of place," vandalism as revenge on an unfair teacher or school official, thefts from a "crooked" store owner—all may be hurts inflicted on a transgressor, in the eyes of the delinquent. As Orwell has pointed out, the type of criminal admired by the general public has probably changed over the course of years and Raffles no longer serves as a hero;[10] but Robin Hood, and his latter day derivatives such as the tough detective seeking justice outside the law, still capture the popular imagination, and the delinquent may view his acts as part of a similar role.

To deny the existence of the victim, then, by transforming him into a person deserving injury is an extreme form of a phenomenon we have mentioned before, namely, the delinquent's recognition of appropriate and inappropriate targets for his delinquent acts. In addition, however, the existence of the victim may be denied for the delinquent, in a somewhat different sense, by the circumstances of the delinquent act itself. Insofar as the victim is physically absent, unknown, or a vague abstraction (as is often the case in delinquent acts committed against property), the awareness of the victim's existence is weakened. Internalized norms and anticipations of the reactions of others must somehow be activated, if they are to serve as guides for behavior; and it is possible that a diminished awareness of the victim plays an important part in determining whether or not this process is set in motion.

The Condemnation of the Condemners. A fourth technique of neutralization would appear to involve a condemnation of the condemners or, as McCorkle and Korn have phrased it, a rejection of the rejectors.[11] The delinquent shifts the focus of attention from his own deviant acts to the motives and behavior of those who disapprove of his violations. His condemners, he may claim, are hypocrites, deviants in disguise, or impelled by personal spite. This orientation toward the conforming world may be of particular importance when it hardens into a bitter cynicism directed against those assigned the task of enforcing or expressing the norms of the dominant society. Police, it may be said, are corrupt, stupid, and brutal. Teachers always show favoritism and parents always "take it out" on their children. By a slight extension, the rewards of conformity—such as material success—become a matter of pull or luck, thus decreasing still further the stature of those who stand on the side of the law-abiding. The validity of this jaundiced viewpoint is not so important as its function in turning back or deflecting the negative sanctions attached to violations of the norms. The delinquent, in effect, has changed the subject of the conversation in the dialogue between his own deviant impulses and the reactions of others; and by attacking others, the wrongfulness of his own behavior is more easily repressed or lost to view.

The Appeal to Higher Loyalties. Fifth, and last, internal and external social controls may be neutralized by sacrificing the demands of the larger society for the demands of the smaller social groups to which the delinquent belongs such as the sibling pair, the gang, or the friendship clique. It is important to note that the delinquent does not necessarily repudiate the imperatives of the dominant normative system, despite his failure to follow them. Rather, the delinquent may see himself as caught up in a dilemma that must be resolved, unfortunately, at the cost of violating the law. One aspect of this situation has been studied by Stouffer and Toby in their research on the conflict between particularistic and universalistic demands, between the claims of friendship and general social obligations, and their results suggest that "it is possible to classify people according to a predisposition to select one or the other horn of a dilemma in role conflict."[12] For our purposes, however, the most important point is that deviation from certain norms may occur not because the norms are rejected but because other norms, held to be more pressing or involving a higher loyalty, are accorded precedence. Indeed, it is the fact that both sets of norms are believed in that gives meaning to our concepts of dilemma and role conflict.

The conflict between the claims of friendship and the claims of law, or a similar dilemma, has of course long been recognized by the social scientist (and the novelist) as a common human problem. If the juvenile delinquent frequently resolves his dilemma by insisting that he must "always help a buddy" or "never squeal on a friend," even when it throws him into serious difficulties with the dominant social order, his choice remains familiar to the supposedly law-abiding. The delinquent is unusual, perhaps, in the extent to which he is able to see the fact that he acts in behalf of the smaller social groups to which he belongs as a justification for violations of society's norms, but it is a matter of degree rather than of kind.

"I didn't mean it." "I didn't really hurt anybody." "They had it coming to them." "Everybody's picking on me." " I didn't do it for myself." These slogans or their variants, we hypothesize, prepare the juvenile for delinquent acts. These "definitions of the situation" represent tangential or glancing blows at the dominant normative system rather than the creation of an opposing ideology; and they are extensions of patterns of thought prevalent in society rather than something created de novo.

Techniques of neutralization may not be powerful enough to fully shield the individual from the force of his own internalized values and the reactions of conforming others, for as we have pointed out, juvenile delinquents often appear to suffer from feelings of guilt and shame when called into account for their deviant behavior. And some delinquents may be so isolated from the world of conformity that techniques of neutralization need not be called into play. Nonetheless, we would argue that techniques of neutralization are critical in lessening the effectiveness of social controls and that they lie behind a large share of delinquent behavior. Empirical research in this area is scattered and fragmentary at the present time, but the work of Redl,[13] Cressy,[14] and others has supplied a body of significant data that has done much to clarify the theoretical issues and enlarge the fund of supporting evidence. Two lines of investigation seem to be critical at this stage. First, there is need for more knowledge concerning the differential distribution of techniques of neutralization, as operative patterns of thought, by age, sex, social class, ethnic group, etc. On *a priori* grounds it might be assumed that these justifications for deviance will be more readily seized by segments of society for whom a discrepancy between common social ideals and social practice is most apparent. It is also possible however, that the habit of "bending" the dominant normative system—if not "breaking" it—cuts across our cruder social categories and is to be traced primarily to patterns of social interaction within the familial circle. Second, there is need for a greater understanding of the internal structure of techniques of neutralization, as a system of beliefs and attitudes, and its relationship to various types of delinquent behavior. Certain techniques of neutralization would appear to be better adapted to particular deviant acts than to others, as we have suggested, for example, in the case of offenses against property and the denial of the victim. But the issue remains far from clear and stands in need of more information.

In any case, techniques of neutralization appear to offer a promising line of research in enlarging and systematizing the theoretical grasp of juvenile delinquency. As more information is uncovered concerning techniques of neutralization, their origins, and their consequences, both juvenile delinquency in particular, and deviation from normative systems in general may be illuminated.

Endnotes

[1] E. H. Sutherland, *Principles of Criminology,* revised by D. R. Cressey, Chicago: Lippincott, 1955, pp. 77–80.

[2] Albert K. Cohen, *Delinquent Boys,* Glencoe, Ill.: The Free Press, 1955.

[3] This form of reaction among the adherents of a deviant subculture who fully believe in the "rightfulness" of their behavior and who are captured and punished by the agencies of the dominant social order can be illustrated, perhaps, by groups such as Jehovah's Witnesses, early Christian sects, nationalist movements in colonial areas, and conscientious objectors during World Wars I and II.

[4]As Weber has pointed out, a thief may recognize the legitimacy of legal rules without accepting their moral validity. Cf. Max Weber, *The Theory of Social and Economic Organization* (translated by A. M. Henderson and Talcott Parsons), New York: Oxford University Press, 1947, p. 125. We are arguing here, however, that the juvenile delinquent frequently recognizes *both* the legitimacy of the dominant social order and its moral "rightness."

[5]Thrasher's account of the "Itschkies"—a juvenile gang composed of Jewish boys—and the immunity from "rolling" enjoyed by Jewish drunkards is a good illustration. Cf. F. Thrasher, *The Gang,* Chicago: The University of Chicago Press, 1947, p. 315.

[6]Cf. Solomon Kobrin, "The Conflict of Values in Delinquency Areas," *American Sociological Review,* 16 (October, 1951), pp. 653–661.

[7]Cf. Robin Williams, Jr., *American Society,* New York: Knopf, 1951, p. 28.

[8]A number of observers have wryly noted that many delinquents seem to show a surprising awareness of sociological and psychological explanations for their behavior and are quick to point out the causal role of their poor environment.

[9]It is possible, of course, that certain personality structures can accept some techniques of neutralization more readily than others, but this question remains largely unexplored.

[10]George Orwell, *Dickens, Dali, and Others,* New York: Reynal, 1946.

[11]Lloyd W. McCorkle and Richard Korn, "Reassociation Within Walls," *The Annals of the American Academy of Political and Social Science,* 293, (May, 1954), pp. 88–98.

[12]See Samuel A. Stouffer and Jackson Toby, "Role Conflict and Personality," in *Toward a General Theory of Action,* edited by Talcott Parsons and Edward A. Shils, Cambridge: Harvard University Press, 1951, p. 494.

[13]See Fritz Redl and David Wineman, *Children Who Hate,* Glencoe: The Free Press, 1956.

[14]See D. R. Cressey, *Other People's Money,* Glencoe: The Free Press, 1953.

❧ ❧ ❧

Questions

1. What are the five techniques of neutralization? How does each technique excuse individuals from responsibility for their crimes?

2. According to Sykes and Matza, why are "subculture of deviance" theories problematic?

3. Do you think that certain kinds of people use techniques of neutralization more often than other kinds of people do? If so, explain your thinking.

4. Could Sykes and Matza's theory explain gender differences in criminal behavior? If so, how?

Crime and Deviance Over the Life Course

ROBERT J. SAMPSON, University of Illinois, Urbana-Champaign
JOHN H. LAUB, Northeastern University

In this article, Sampson and Laub view social-control theory from a life-course perspective. They hypothesize that antisocial behavior in childhood transmutes into criminal behavior in adulthood. They also suggest that conventional social ties in adulthood, such as employment or a committed partnership, deter criminal behavior. Pathways into crime and turning points away from crime both play central roles in Sampson and Laub's theory.

$\mathcal{S}$ ociological criminology has neglected early childhood characteristics, and consequently has not come to grips with the link between early childhood behaviors and later adult outcomes (Caspi, Bem, and Elder 1989; Farrington 1989; Gottfredson and Hirschi 1990). Although criminal behavior peaks in the teenage years, there is substantial evidence of early delinquency as well as continuation of criminal behavior over the life course. By concentrating on the teenage years, sociological perspectives on crime fail to address the life-span implications of childhood behavior (Wilson and Herrnstein 1985). At the same time, criminologists have not devoted much attention to what Rutter (1988, p. 3) calls "escape from the risk process," limiting our understanding of desistance from crime and the transitions from criminal to noncriminal behavior.

To address these limitations, we develop a theoretical model of age-graded informal social control to account for persistence and desistance in criminal behavior. Our basic thesis is that while continuity in deviant behavior exists, social ties in adulthood—to work, family, and community—explain changes in criminality over the life span. Our model acknowledges the importance of early childhood behaviors while rejecting

"Crime and Deviance Over the Life Course," by Robert J. Sampson and John H. Laub reprinted from *American Sociological Review*, vol. 55, no. 5, 1990, pp. 609–627.

the implication that later adult factors have little relevance (Wilson and Herrnstein 1985). We contend that social interaction with adult institutions of informal social control has important effects on crime and deviance. As such, ours is a "sociogenic" theoretical model of adult crime and deviance. This model is examined using a unique longitudinal data set that follows two samples of delinquent and nondelinquent boys from early adolescence into their thirties.

❧ The Life Course Perspective

The life course has been defined as "pathways through the age differentiated life span," where age differentiation "is manifested in expectations and options that impinge on decision processes and the course of events that give shape to life stages, transitions, and turning points" (Elder 1985, p. 17). Two central concepts underlie the analysis of life course dynamics. A *trajectory* is a pathway or line of development over the life span such as worklife, marriage, parenthood, self-esteem, and criminal behavior. Trajectories refer to long-term patterns of behavior and are marked by a sequence of life events and transitions (Elder 1985, pp. 31–2). *Transitions* are specific life events that are embedded in trajectories and evolve over shorter time spans (e.g., first job or first marriage). Some of them are age-graded and some are not. What is often assumed to be important is the timing and the ordering of significant life events (Hogan 1980).

These two concepts are related: "the interlocking nature of trajectories and transitions, within and across life stages . . . may generate turning points or a change in course" (Elder 1985, p.32). Adaptation to life events is crucial: "The same event or transition followed by different adaptations can lead to different trajectories" (Elder 1985, p. 35). This perspective implies both a strong connection between childhood events and experiences in young adulthood, and that transitions or turning points can modify life trajectories—they can "redirect paths."

Criminology and the Life Course

Criminology has been slow to recognize the importance of the life-course perspective (Hagan and Palloni 1988). Not only are the data needed to explore such relationships sparse (see Blumstein, Cohen, Roth, and Visher 1986), some researchers argue that ordinary life events (e.g., getting married, becoming a parent) have little effect on criminal behavior. Gottfredson and Hirschi argue that crime rates decline with age "whether or not these events occur" and note "that the longitudinal/developmental assumption that such events are important neglects its own evidence on the stability of personal characteristics" (1987, p. 604; see also Hirschi and Gottfredson 1983).

The extent of stability and change in behavior and personality attributes over time is one of the most complex and hotly debated issues in the social sciences (Brim and Kagan 1980; Dannefer 1984). The research literature in criminology contains evidence for both continuity *and* change over the life course. Reviewing over 16 studies on aggressive behavior, Olweus (1979, pp. 854–5) found "substantial" stability: The correlation between early aggressive behavior and later criminality averaged .68 for the studies reviewed. A similar review concluded that a "consensus" in favor of the stability hypothesis had been reached: "Children who initially display high rates of antisocial behavior are more likely to persist in this behavior than children who initially show lower rates of antisocial behavior" (Loeber 1982, p. 1433).

In probably the most influential study, Heusmann, Eron, and Lefkowitz (1984) studied the aggressiveness of 600 subjects, their parents, and their children over a 22-year period. They found that early aggressiveness predicted later antisocial behavior, including criminal behavior, spouse abuse, traffic violations, and self-reported physical aggression and conclude that, whatever its causes, "aggression can be viewed as a persistent trait that . . . possesses substantial cross-situational constancy" (1984, p. 1120). Other work has also demonstrated the effects of early life experiences on adult behavior (McCord 1979; Farrington 1986; Robins 1966, 1978).

At the same time, there is evidence for change over the life course. While studies show that antisocial behavior in children is one of the best predictors of antisocial behavior in adults, "most antisocial children do not become antisocial as adults" (Gove 1985, p. 123). Robins (1978) found identical results in her review of four longitudinal studies. A follow-up of the Cambridge-Somerville Youth study found that "a majority of adult criminals had no history as juvenile delinquents" (McCord 1980, p. 158). Cline (1980) states that although there is "more constancy than change . . . there is sufficient change in all the data to preclude simple conclusions concerning criminal career progressions" (p. 665). He concludes: "There appears to be far more heterogeneity in types and patterns of deviant and criminal behavior than previous work has suggested. There is evidence that many juvenile offenders do not become career offenders" (pp. 669–70).

In the context of personality characteristics, Caspi (1987) found that although the tendency toward explosive behavior in childhood was "re-created across the age-graded life course, especially in problems with subordination (e.g., in education, military, and work settings) and in situations that required negotiating interpersonal conflicts" (e.g., marriage), "invariant action patterns did not emerge across the age-graded life course" (1987, p. 1211). Using a prospective longitudinal design to study the under-class, Long and Vaillant (1984) found both discontinuity and continuity across three generations of subjects:

> For the men in this study, the transmission of their parents' chaotic or dependent life styles was not inevitable or even very likely. If their back-grounds are accepted as having the characteristics of an underclass, then the study refutes the hypothesis that the chances of escape from such a class are minimal. The transmission of disorganization and alienation that seems inevitable when a disadvantaged cohort is studied retrospectively appears to be the exception rather than the norm in a prospective study that locates the successes as well as the failures (p. 344; see also Vaillant 1977).

Some criminological research also suggests that salient life events influence behavior and modify trajectories. A follow-up of 200 Borstal boys found that marriage led to "increasing social stability" (Gibbens 1984, p. 61): Knight, Osborn, and West (1977) discovered that while marriage did not reduce criminality, it reduced some antisocial behavior (e.g., drinking, drug use, etc.). Osborn (1980) examined the effect of leaving London on delinquency and found that subjects who moved had a lower risk of reoffending when compared with a similar group who stayed in London. And there is some evidence that episodes of unemployment lead to higher crime rates (Farrington, Gallagher, Morley, St. Ledger, and West 1986).

● Childhood Behavior and Informal Social Control over the Life Course

Recognizing the importance of both stability and change in the life course, our model focuses on two propositions. First, we contend that childhood antisocial behavior (e.g., juvenile delinquency, conduct disorder, violent temper tantrums) is linked to a wide variety of troublesome adult behaviors including criminality, general deviance, offenses in the military, economic dependency, educational failure, employment instability, and marital discord. These long-term relationships are posited to occur independent of traditional variables such as social class background and race/ethnicity. As Hagan and Palloni (1988) argue (see also Hagan 1989, p. 260), delinquent and criminal events "are linked into life trajectories of broader significance, whether those trajectories are criminal or noncriminal in form" (p. 90). Because most research by criminologists has focused either on the teenage years or adult behavior limited to crime, this hypothesis has not been definitively studied.

Second, we argue that social bonds to adult institutions of informal social control (e.g., family, education, neighborhood, work) influence criminal behavior over the life course despite an individual's delinquent and antisocial background. We seek to identify the transitions embedded in individual trajectories that relate to adult informal social control, and contend that childhood pathways to crime and deviance can be significantly modified over the life course by adult social bonds.

The important institutions of social control vary across the life span: in childhood and adolescence these are the family, school, and peer groups; in the phase of young adulthood they are higher education and/or vocational training, work, and marriage; and in later adulthood, the dominant institutions are work, marriage, parenthood, and investment in the community.

Within this framework, our organizing principle derives from social control theory (Durkheim 1951; Hirschi 1969; Kornhauser 1978): crime and deviance result when an individual's bond to society is weak or broken. We argue that changes that strengthen social bonds to society in adulthood will thus lead to less crime and deviance; changes that weaken social bonds will lead to more crime and deviance. Unlike most life-course research, we emphasize the *quality* or *strength* of social ties more than the occurrence or timing of specific life events. For example, while we agree with Gottfredson and Hirschi (1990, pp. 140–1) that marriage *per se* does not increase social control, a strong attachment to one's spouse and close emotional ties increase the social bond between individuals and, all else equal, should lead to a reduction in criminal behavior. Similarly, employment *per se* does not increase social control. It is employment coupled with job stability, job commitment, and ties to work that should increase social control and, all else equal, lead to a reduction in criminal behavior (see also Crutchfield 1989, p. 495). Therefore, we maintain that it is the *social investment* or social capital (Coleman 1988) in the institutional relationship, whether it be in a family, work, or community setting, that dictates the salience of informal social control at the individual level.

Our model assumes that life-event transitions and adult social bonds can modify quite different childhood trajectories. Whether or not adult development is "uniform and constant" is a controversial issue. Dannefer (1984) sharply critiques existing models of adult development, drawn primarily from biology and psychology, for their "ontogenetic" focus. He argues that ontogenetic models fail to see human development as "socially organized and socially produced, not only by what happens in early life, but also by the effects of social structure, social interaction, and their effects on life chances throughout the life course" (p. 106).

At the same time, sociological models tend to ignore important elements of developmental psychology and biology. Baltes and Nesselroade (1984) criticize models that overemphasize the "intraindividual plasticity (modifiability)" of development and neglect "the first half of life" (p. 842). They go on to acknowledge the importance of "interindividual homogeneity (as reflected in developmental universals)" (1984, p. 845). Our model seeks to integrate these perspectives by bringing the formative period of early childhood back into the picture, and by positing that individuals can change through interaction with key social institutions.[1]

☺ Data

We are currently engaged in a long-term project analyzing data from Sheldon and Eleanor Glueck's *Unraveling Juvenile Delinquency* (1950) and their subsequent follow-up studies (Glueck and Glueck 1968). These data are uniquely suited to our analytical goals due to the sampling design, the extensive measurement of key theoretical concepts, the long-term nature of the follow-up, and the historical context.

The Gluecks' research design began with samples of delinquent and nondelinquent boys born between 1924 and 1935. The *delinquent* sample comprised 500 10- to 17-year-old white males from Boston who, because of their persistent delinquency, were committed to one of two correctional schools in Massachusetts. The *nondelinquent* sample, or what they called a "control-group" (Glueck and Glueck 1950, p. 14), was made up of 500 10-

to 17-year-old white males from the Boston public schools. Nondelinquent status was determined on the basis of official record checks and interviews with parents, teachers, local police, social workers and recreational leaders, as well as the boys themselves. The sampling procedure was designed to maximize differences in delinquency and by all accounts was successful. For example, the average number of convictions in the delinquent sample was 3.5. The nondelinquent boys were different from the Boston youth remanded to reform school, "but compared with national averages the men in this study did *not* represent a particularly law-abiding group" (Long and Vaillant 1984, p. 345). Although clearly not a random selection, the samples appear to be representative of their respective populations at that time.

Boys in the two samples were matched on a case-by-case basis according to age, race/ethnicity, general intelligence, and neighborhood socioeconomic status (for details see Glueck and Glueck 1950, pp. 33–9; Laub and Sampson 1988). These classic variables are widely thought to influence both delinquency and official reaction. Boys in each sample grew up in high-risk environments characterized by poverty, social disorganization, and exposure to delinquency and antisocial conduct (Glueck and Glueck 1950, pp. 30–2).

From 1940 to 1965, the Gluecks' research team collected data on these individuals. They were originally interviewed at an average age of 14, at age 25, and again at age 32. On average, then, the original subjects were followed for 18 years. Data were collected for all three time periods for 438 of the 500 delinquents and 442 of the 500 nondelinquent controls (88 percent). The follow-up success was 92 percent when adjusted for mortality—relatively high by current standards (see e.g., Wolfgang, Thornberry, and Figlio 1987).

During the first wave, a wide range of biological, psychological, and sociological information concerning each boy and his life from birth until adolescence was gathered. The second wave field investigation and interview began as each subject approached his 25th birthday and concerned the period from age 17 to 25 (the juvenile court in Massachusetts had jurisdiction up to the 17th birthday). The third wave interview covered the period from age 25 to 32. The second and third wave interviews concentrated on social factors, including criminal histories. Data are available on life transitions relating to living arrangements, schooling, employment, work habits, marital status, leisure-time activities, companionship, and participation in civic affairs. The data on criminal justice interventions (e.g., all arrests, convictions, and dispositions including actual time served) pertain to the period from first contact to age 32.

The data were gathered through detailed investigations by the Gluecks' research team and included interviews with the subjects and their families, employers, teachers, and neighbors, as well as criminal justice and social welfare officials. The field investigation involved meticulously culling information from the records of public and private agencies that had any involvement with the family. In the first follow-up, an average of 12 sources of information were used for the delinquents and nine for the controls. Not surprisingly, delinquent subjects and their families were more likely to generate contact with various social agencies. In the second follow-up, an average of nine sources of information were used for the delinquents and seven sources for the controls (Glueck and Glueck 1968, p. 47). The basic data represent the comparison, reconciliation, and integration of these independently derived sources of information.

Despite this rich body of longitudinal data, the Gluecks' main analyses were cross-sectional (Glueck and Glueck 1950). Their attention to the follow-up data was sparse and the resulting book (Glueck and Glueck 1968) was a simple descriptive overview of the samples. Fortunately, the Gluecks' coded data and raw interview records were stored in the Harvard Law School Library. A major effort of our project has been devoted to coding and computerizing the full longitudinal data set. The reconstruction and validation of these data involved numerous steps, reported in detail elsewhere (Laub, Sampson, and Kiger 1990; Sampson and Laub, forthcoming).

Measures of Childhood Antisocial Behavior and Adult Crime

We measure antisocial behavior during childhood and adolescence in three ways: (1) official delinquency status as determined by the sampling design of the Glueck study; (2) a composite scale (ranging from 0 to 30) of self, parent, and teacher reports of delinquency and other misconduct that captures both unofficial delinquency as well as incidents known to the police; and (3) temper tantrums—including the extent to which a child engaged in violent and habitual temper tantrums while growing up. The latter measure refers to tantrums that were "the predominant mode of response" by the child to difficult situations growing up (Glueck and Glueck

1950, p. 152). This indicator of childhood tantrums corresponds to one used by Caspi (1987).

Adult crime and deviance was investigated in the follow-up interviews for both groups, including excessive use of alcohol and/or drugs as well as general deviance (e.g., frequent involvement in gambling, illicit sexual behavior, use of prostitutes). The Gluecks' coding scheme indicated the presence of absence of these problem behaviors during each follow-up, and hence our resulting measures are dichotomous.

From the official criminal history, we determined whether the subject had an arrest during each follow-up period. Identical dichotomous variables were constructed for the delinquent and control groups. Because men in the delinquent group committed much more adult crime than the controls . . . reconstructed complete criminal histories of delinquents from the first arrest to age 32 (e.g., date, type of charge or charges, and the sequence of arrests as well as the dates of any incarceration). From this information we created overall measures of crime frequency—the number of arrests divided by the number of days free in the community during the periods from birth to age 17, from ages 17 to 25, and from ages 25 to 32. These measures were then converted to average annual rates for each period (i.e., frequency of arrests per year free). By considering only time free in the community, our measures of crime frequency for the delinquents are more precise than those traditionally used in criminological research.

Since the period of the study included World War II and the Korean War, a majority of the men served in the military (67 percent). At the first follow-up, data were collected on the official military experience of each subject using interviews and records from the appropriate military service, Selective Service, State Adjutant General, Veterans Administration, and Red Cross. Our measure of the subject's criminal/deviant behavior in the military (e.g., AWOL, desertion, theft, etc.) captures illegal conduct that came to the attention of authorities.

Measures of Adult Social Bonds

Our key independent variables are *job stability, commitment,* and *attachment to spouse,* measured at both follow-ups. Information for these measures was collected during the home interview and corroborated whenever possible by record checks.[2] Job stability is measured by a standardized, composite scale of three intercorrelated variables—employment status, stability of most recent employment, and work habits. Employment status measures whether the subject was employed at the time of the interview; employment stability measures length of time employed on present or most recent job (ranging from less than 3 months to 48 months or more); and the work habits variable was based on a three-point scale. Individuals were classified as having poor work habits if they were unreliable in the work setting or if they failed to give any effort to the job; fair work habits were characterized by a generally good job performance except for periodic absences from work or periods of unemployment as chosen by the subject; good work habits were evidenced by reliable performance on the job as noted by the employer as well as instances in which the subject was considered an asset to the organization.[3]

An individual's commitment to occupation-related goals may influence job stability. Our measure of commitment at Time 2 is derived from interviews with the subject and significant others and combines three related variables: work, educational, and economic ambitions (Glueck and Glueck 1968, pp. 124–6). Subjects with low commitment expressed no particular work, educational, or economic aspirations. They had not thought about further schooling or had vague educational ambitions. Subjects with high commitment expressed a strong desire for further schooling (academic, vocational, or professional), and were eager to better themselves and their families (e.g., to become a professional, gain more income, etc.). At Time 3, commitment is a composite scale combining work ambitions and ambitions generally. Work ambition captures efforts to improve occupational status between ages 25–32. These efforts focus on behaviors beyond working hard or joining a union, such as additional on-the-job training or taking courses or civil service exams. The second component of commitment at Time 3 is a measure of the subject's general aspirations.

The third key independent variable in our analysis is attachment to spouse. At Time 2, we use a composite measure derived from interview data describing the general conjugal relationship between the subject and his spouse during the period plus the subject's attitude toward marital responsibility (Glueck and Glueck 1968, pp. 84–8). A weak attachment was indicated by signs of incompatibility such as a brief period of separation, divorce or separation, or desertion. These individuals were also neglectful of marital responsibilities, financial as well as emotional. In contrast, subjects who were strongly attached displayed close, warm feelings toward their wives, or were compatible in a generally constructive relationship. These

TABLE 1 Relationship Between Childhood Antisocial Behavior and Adult Behavioral Outcomes

Adult Behavior	Official Delinquency		Childhood Antisocial Behavior Reported by Self, Parent, Teacher			Temper Tantrums	
	No	Yes	Low (0–3)	Medium (4–13)	High (14–30)	No	Yes
% Charged in military, ages 17–25	20	64	18	35	70	33	62
% Excessive alcohol/drug use, ages 17–25	11	41	7	23	47	22	37
% Excessive alcohol/ drug use, ages 25–32	9	35	6	19	40	19	31
% General deviance, ages 17–25	5	25	5	15	24	11	29
% General deviance, ages 25–32	6	30	5	18	30	14	33
% Arrested, ages 17–25	20	76	15	48	80	41	72
% Arrested, ages 25–32	14	61	10	36	66	32	58
% High school graduate by age 25	34	2	39	13	2	22	3
% Economically dependent, ages 17–25	6	29	5	17	31	14	29
% Economically dependent, ages 25–32	11	39	8	21	44	19	43
% Unstable employment, ages 17–25	5	38	2	20	41	15	41
% Unstable employment, ages 25–32	5	37	3	16	41	15	38
% Divorced/separated, ages 17–25	5	22	5	9	26	12	21
% Divorced/separated, ages 25–32	12	27	10	15	33	16	32

Note: All relationships significant at $p < .05$.

individuals assumed marital responsibilities. At Time 3, attachment to spouse is a composite scale derived from interview data describing the general conjugal relationship during the follow-up period plus a measure of the cohesiveness of the family unit. The measure of conjugal relations at Time 3 is the same as for Time 2. Family cohesiveness assesses the extent to which the family unit was characterized by an integration of interests, cooperativeness, and overall affection for each other. This measure was not available at Time 2.

Taken together, these measures capture the quality of strength of an individual's ties to important institutions of informal social control—family, work, and the community at large. They are also reliable—Cronbach's alpha reliabilities at Time 2 and Time 3 are, respectively, .65 and .78 for job stability, .90 and .91 for marital attachment, and .68 and .70 for commitment. In addition to using multiple indicators of key concepts and composite scales with good reliabilities, we took other steps to ensure the validity of measures. For example, we investigated the longitudinal and construct validity of both individual items and scales. In all cases, the results supported the contention that the job stability, marital attachment, and commitment scales were related both concurrently and predictively in a manner consistent with substantive expectations. Note also that the Glueck data differ from conventional survey research in which measurement error, especially on attitudes and moral beliefs, is often large (see Matsueda 1989). The Gluecks' data integrate multiple sources of information for *individual* items. Moreover, the items used here refer almost exclusively to behavioral outcomes rather than attitudes.

Missing Data

Although the Gluecks' original study involved 1,000 subjects, 12 percent are not in the follow-up interviews either because of death or because they could not be located. Some measures were deemed by the Gluecks to be inapplicable to the 880 subjects who were followed to age 32. For instance, the components of job stability and marital attachment were not assessed for men in institutions (mostly prison) or in the military for a significant portion of a time period. Because we cannot determine the social bonds of long-term prisoners or military personnel, men with inapplicable information on one or more of our key measures were excluded from multivariate analysis. Of the approximately 150 delinquents excluded, the vast majority were institutionalized—less than 40 were excluded because of prolonged military service. For the controls, 50 of the 442 followed to age 32 were deemed inapplicable by the Gluecks; the majority of these exclusions stemmed from military service. Of the cases remaining for analysis, missing data was not a serious problem, averaging about 10 percent for the delinquent group and 5 percent for the control group.[4]

❧ Patterns of Stability and Change

Combining data from the two Glueck samples, we first examine the long-term relationship between childhood delinquency and antisocial behavior and a wide range of later adult behaviors. Table 1 displays the results of cross-tabulations arrayed to reveal the pattern and magnitude of relationships.[5] The pattern is quite remarkable—all relationships are statistically significant,[6] in the predicted direction, and substantively large.

For official delinquency, all seven indicators of adult crime and deviance are much more prevalent among men who were childhood delinquents. For example, 64 percent of official delinquents were charged while in the military compared to only 20 percent of those with no official delinquency in childhood. Although rarely studied in previous research, the military is particularly interesting because it represents a relatively homogeneous yet distinctive social environment in which to explore differences in criminal behavior. The same pattern holds for reports of excessive drinking and general deviance—on average, childhood delinquents were four times more likely than nondelinquents to later abuse alcohol or exhibit deviant behavior. Similarly, arrests in both young and later adulthood are three to four times greater among childhood delinquents.

Results are similar for the other two measures of childhood antisocial behavior, the unofficial (i.e., parent, teacher, self) reports of delinquency and temper tantrums. In all cases, the relationships are monotonic across categories of reported childhood delinquency and in many cases are stronger than those for official delinquency. Boys with high rates of reported delinquency are five times more likely to have been arrested at ages 17–25 than boys with low reported rates of juvenile misbehavior, and almost seven times more likely to be arrested in later adulthood (ages 25–32). Even childhood temper tantrums exhibit a strong relationship with adult criminality, although to a lesser extent than delinquency. Regardless of the measure of childhood delinquent/antisocial behavior there is a powerful relationship with adult misbehavior.

The long-term effects of juvenile delinquency are not limited to adult criminal behavior. Seven adult behaviors spanning economic, educational, employment, and family domains are also strongly related to adolescent delinquency.[7] Antisocial subjects were much less likely to finish high school by age 25. For both delinquency measures, delinquent boys were at least seven times more likely than nondelinquents to have a history of unstable employment as adults. A similar pattern emerges for economic dependence (e.g., welfare) and divorce among those ever married—delinquents were three to five times more likely to be divorced or receive welfare as adults.

In short, childhood delinquent behavior has a significant relationship with a wide range of adult criminal and deviant behaviors, including charges initiated by military personnel, reports of involvement in deviance and excessive drinking, and arrest by the police. The same childhood antisocial behaviors are also predictive of economic, family, educational, and employment problems up to eighteen years later. These results are robust as to measurement of delinquency. Because of the matched design, they cannot be explained in terms of original differences between delinquents and nondelinquents in age, intelligence, socioeconomic status, and race/ethnicity—variables often associated with stratification outcomes. Clearly, the boys in the Gluecks' delinquent and nondelinquent samples exhibited behavioral consistency well into adulthood (Glueck and Glueck 1968).

Adult Social Bonds

In Table 2 we examine how the social factors of *job stability*, *commitment* to educational, work, and economic goals (i.e., aspiration), and *attachment* to spouse among those ever married (all measured for ages 17–25) modify the tendency to persist in deviant and troublesome behaviors over the life span. Because the matched-sample research design maximized differences in delinquency, a within-group analysis controls for original position on delinquency. By definition, the delinquent group sample contains youth who were all delinquent. For them, our goal is to examine the social factors related to subsequent variation in this status. For the control subjects, who were not officially delinquent as juveniles, we also examine whether social bonds in adulthood explain adult crime and deviance.

TABLE 2 *Relationship Between Adult Social Bonds and Adult Crime and Deviance, Controlling for Official Delinquency Status in Childhood*

Adult Crime and Deviance	Delinquent Group			Control Group		
	Job Stability, Ages 17-25					
	Low	Medium	High	Low	Medium	High
% Excessive alcohol, ages 17–25	57	24	15*	32	8	5*
% Excessive alcohol, ages 25–32	53	19	11*	27	6	4*
% General deviance, ages 17–25	31	13	9*	12	4	3*
% General deviance, ages 25–32	47	17	8*	17	7	2*
% Arrested, ages 17–25	91	62	60*	36	17	17*
% Arrested, ages 25–32	74	47	32*	36	11	9*

	Occupational Commitment, Ages 17–25				
	Weak	Strong		Weak	Strong
% Excessive alcohol, ages 17–25	50	21*		21	5*
% Excessive alcohol, ages 25–32	43	16*		15	4*
% General deviance, ages 17–25	29	15*		10	3*
% General deviance, ages 25–32	37	14*		8	5
% Arrested, ages 17–25	82	64*		34	12*
% Arrested, ages 25–32	70	47*		22	10*

	Attachment to Spouse, Ages 17–25				
	Weak	Strong		Weak	Strong
% Excessive alcohol, ages 17–25	53	17*		46	4*
% Excessive alcohol, ages 25–32	47	11*		32	6*
% General deviance, ages 17–25	31	8*		12	4*
% General deviance, ages 25–32	54	16*		36	7*
% Arrested, ages 17–25	87	58*		61	15*
% Arrested, ages 25–32	76	34*		39	12*

* $p < .05$

Job stability in young adulthood has a large inverse relationship with each measure of adult crime and deviance for both the delinquent and nondelinquent samples.[8] Moreover, young-adult job stability has substantial *predictive* power, exhibiting very large negative effects on alcohol use, general deviance, and arrest in the subsequent 25–32 age period. For both samples, subjects with low job stability at ages 17–25 were at least four times more likely to have severe alcohol problems in later adulthood and at least five times more likely to have engaged in deviant behavior compared to those with high job stability. It thus seems unlikely that adult crime itself can account for the patterns observed. Because these relationships obtain within both samples, the results cannot be dismissed on the basis of a "stability" or "self-selection" argument that antisocial children simply replicate their anti-social behavior as adults—that delinquent kids invariably continue their interactional styles in adult spheres of life, and hence have incompatible relations with family, work, and other institutions of social control (Caspi 1987). Rather, it appears that job stability in adulthood significantly modi-fies trajectories of crime and deviance regardless of strong differences in childhood delinquent and antisocial conduct.

Adult commitment to conventional educational and occupational goals results in a similar pattern. Subjects with high aspirations and efforts to advance educationally and occupationally were much less likely to engage in deviant behavior, use alcohol excessively, or be arrested at ages 17–25 and 25–32.

The pattern is consistent for the relationship between attachment to spouse and adult crime among those ever married (approximately 50 percent of each sample). All relationships are in the expected direction, significant, and substantively large. As with job stability and commitment, the influence of attachment to wife at ages 17–25 is salient not only in the concurrent period but in the later 25–32 period as well.

The evidence strongly suggests that informal social controls in young adulthood are significantly and substantially related to adult antisocial behavior, regardless of childhood delinquency. The "ontogenetic" model's emphasis on stability, though partially confirmed in Table 1, is clearly insuf-ficient as an explanatory model for the life course. Social bonds to the adult institutions of work, education, and the family exert a powerful influence on adult crime and deviance.

Models of Adult Crime among Original Delinquents

A major question may be raised concerning these results—do individual differences in crime within the delinquent and control groups confound the results? The most delinquent subjects in the delinquent group may have self-selected themselves into later states of job instability, conflict-ridden marriages, and crime (Caspi 1987). Similarly, despite the absence of an official record, the nondelinquent subjects were not equally nondelinquent.

We address this question through a multivariate strategy that controls for prior delinquency and crime in four ways. First, analyses are conducted separately for the two samples, thereby controlling for official delinquency status. Second, in the delinquent sample we control for the frequency of crimes committed in adolescence using the average number of arrests per year free in the community between birth and age 17. Because this rate adjusts for the opportunity to commit crime (i.e., takes account of incarceration time), it is probably the best overall measure of adolescent criminal "propensity" for the delinquent group (the control group by definition had zero). Third, when analyzing crime at ages 17–25 for both the delinquent and control groups, we control for the extent of reported delinquency. Fourth, when analyzing crime at ages 25–32 for the delinquent group, we control for arrest frequencies per year free at ages 17–25. For the nondelinquent group, we control for a dichotomous indicator of arrest.[9] Therefore, both official and unofficial delinquency are explicitly controlled within the two samples that themselves differ markedly in terms of initial delinquency and adult outcomes.

This research strategy is a strict test of the independent effects of adult social ties on adult crime and deviance. Moreover, this research strategy is directly linked to our theoretical goal as it allows examination of change in crime and delinquency. That is, because prior levels of crime are controlled and the analysis is conducted separately for each group, the resulting multivariate models permit assessment of the independent effects of adult social ties on changes in adult criminality not accounted for by prior "propensities" or labeling effects.[10]

Table 3 presents results for the delinquent group of multivariate analyses of general deviance, excessive drinking, arrest, and crimes per year free in young adulthood. The dichotomous nature of the first three measures violates the assumptions of ordinary least-squares (OLS) regression. For these measures, maximum-likelihood (ML) logistic regression is used, which, unlike log-linear analysis, preserves the interval nature of the majority of our predictor variables (see Aldrich and Nelson 1984). The unstandardized logistic coefficients in Table 3 represent the change in the log-odds of exhibiting antisocial behavior associated with a unit change in the exogenous variable. Because the units of measurement of the independent variables are not consistent, we also present the ML t-ratios of coefficients to standard errors (Aldrich and Nelson 1984, p. 55). For comparative purposes, we present OLS coefficients and t-ratios for the interval-level measure of arrests per year free (logged to reduce skew); beta weights are discussed in the text.[11]

Model 1 displays results for all men in the delinquent group. In assessing the effects of adult social bonds, we control for marital status and income in addition to measures of official and unofficial (reported) juvenile delinquency. Our measure of income for each subject is the weekly gross earnings derived from legitimate occupations (Glueck and Glueck 1968, p. 95). A dummy variable for marital status indicates whether marriage alone is an inhibiting factor in adult crime. The results are rather clear—once other factors are controlled, income and marriage do not have significant effects on adult crime and deviance.

On the other hand, job stability shows consistent effects for all indicators of crime and deviance—all coefficients are at least two times their standard errors. Job stability has the largest effect on the most precise estimate of crime—the number of arrests per year free in the community at ages 17–25 (t-ratio = -4.85). This is particularly important given that two measures of delinquency are controlled and exhibit significant direct effects. More precisely, the number of arrests per year free as a juvenile and the measure of unofficial delinquency yield betas of .23 and .16, respectively, whereas the standardized efect of job stability is -.31.

Model 2 in Table 3 examines the effect of attachment to wife among men who were (or had been) married.[12] The results suggest that it is cohesiveness that is central rather than marriage per se. Marital attachment has significant negative effects on all measures of crime and deviance, net of other factors. Among ever-married men, the influence of job stability declines in magnitude—it has a significant negative effect only on crime frequency. Similar results obtained when we examined arrests in the latter half of the first follow-up (i.e., at ages 22–25). Therefore, the data suggest

TABLE 3 *Coefficients and T-Ratios for Regression of Crime and Deviance in Young Adulthood on Juvenile Delinquency and Young Adult Social Bonds: Delinquent Group*

Independent Variables	Crime and Deviance in Young Adulthood (Ages 17–25)			
	General Deviance	Excessive Drinking	Arrest	Arrests Per Year Free
Model 1 (all men, N = 258)				
Juvenile (age < 17):				
Arrests per	-.05	.60	2.27	.43
year free	(-.07)	(1.08)	(2.63)*	(4.21)*
Unofficial	-.01	.11	.08	.02
delinquency	(-.28)	(3.06)*	(2.16)*	(2.80)*
Young adult (ages 17–25):				
Income	-.19	-.10	-.17	-.03
	(-1.53)	(-.98)	(-1.38)	(-1.42)
Marriage	-.44	-.16	-.61	-.06
	(-1.23)	(-.54)	(-1.77)	(-1.10)
Commitment	-.03	-.12	-.05	-.00
	(-.40)	(-1.90)	(-.64)	(-.10)
Job stability	-.20	-.21	-.24	-.06
	(-2.72)*	(-3.15)*	(-2.44)*	(-4.85)*
"R^2"	.10	.17	.15	.25
Model 2 (ever-married men, N = 160)				
Juvenile age < 17):				
Arrests per	-.72	.86	1.80	.39
year free	(-.65)	(1.16)	(1.84)	(3.51)*
Unofficial	-.03	.12	.07	.01
delinquency	(-.61)	(2.75)*	(1.53)	(1.95)
Young adult (ages 17–25):				
Income	-.03	-.05	-.31	-.02
	(-.16)	(-.34)	(-1.97)	(-1.08)
Commitment	.00	-.09	-.16	-.00
	(.03)	(-1.06)	(-1.38)	(-.13)
Job stability	-.17	-.07	-.12	-.04
	(-1.51)	(-.68)	(-.82)	(-2.63)*
Attachment	-1.36	-1.10	-1.21	-.16
to spouse	(-2.26)*	(-2.42)*	(-2.31)*	(-2.33)*
"R^2"	.12	.18	.18	.27

* $p < .05$

Note: For General Deviance, Excessive Drinking, and Arrest, the table entry is the maximum-likelihood coefficient and t-ratio (coefficient/standard error); for Arrests Per Year Free, the entry is the OLS coefficient and t-ratio.

the importance of both job stability and attachment to wife as factors promoting reductions in crime that are not explained by the original designation as delinquent.

It is possible that crime itself may have influenced observed levels of attachment and job stability. To address this issue, the predictive effects of social bonds were examined. The results mirrored those in Table 3 (analysis not shown). For example, job stability in young adulthood had the largest overall effect on crime frequency at ages 25–32 (t-ratio = -4.63, beta = -.27), controlling for crime frequency in the prior (age 17–25) period. Moreover, marital attachment had significant and consistent negative effects on changes in crime frequency. In fact, for crime frequency at ages 25–32, both job stability and attachment to spouse were significant net of prior crime and other factors.

In Table 4 we explore the independent effects of social bonds in later adulthood (ages 25–32) on antisocial behavior in later adulthood, controlling for prior levels of crime, income, marriage, job stability and commitment. Again, rather than compute change scores, we enter (where feasible) both the prior and concurrent (i.e., Time 2 and Time 3) measures of social bonds, allowing us to estimate their causal effects over time (Plewis 1985, pp. 56–61; Kessler and Greenberg 1981). For all men in the delinquent group (Model 1), the results indicate that controlling for prior levels, job stability in later adulthood has relatively large negative effects for each indicator of crime and deviance. For crime frequency at ages 25–32, both prior and current job stability have significant negative effects. It thus appears that prior levels *and* relative increases in job stability have negative effects on change in adult criminality. Commitment to conventional occupational goals also inhibits general deviance and drinking, but not arrest or crime frequency.

Model 2 in Table 4, confined to ever-married males, suggests that marital attachment at ages 25–32 is a significant and substantively important explanation of crime in later adulthood.[13] Men with close ties to their spouses at ages 25–32 had much lower levels of crime and deviance than men with discordant relations, net of other factors including prior adult crime. The independent effect of marital attachment on crime frequency at ages 25–32 is especially large (t-ratio = -4.45, beta = -.31). The latter compares to a beta of .38 for prior arrest rate at ages 17–25. Moreover, the t-ratios for marital attachment are larger than those for the prior arrest rate in explaining general deviance and excessive drinking. Thus, marital attach-

TABLE 4 *Coefficients and T-Ratios for Regression of Crime and Deviance in Later Adulthood on Young Adult Crime and Social Bonds at Ages 17–25 and Ages 25–32: Delinquent Group*

Independent Variables	Crime and Deviance in Later Adulthood (Ages 25–32)			
	General Deviance	Excessive Drinking	Arrest	Arrests Per Year Free
Model 1 (all men, N = 231)				
Arrest rate,	.06	.78	.86	.14
ages 17–25	(.46)	(3.73)*	(2.95)*	(7.55)*
Income,	.04	.22	.03	.01
ages 17–25	(-.27)	(1.53)	(.27)	(.50)
Married,	.57	-.16	-.18	.08
ages 17–25	(1.47)	(-.40)	(-.51)	(1.76)
Commitment,	.14	-.22	.07	-.01
ages 17–25	(1.66)	(-2.59)*	(.92)	(-.92)
Commitment,	-.47	-.47	-.16	-.02
ages 25–32	(-2.33)*	(-2.44)*	(-1.19)	(-1.23)
Job stability,	-.08	.09	-.11	-.03
ages 17–25	(-.99)	(.97)	(-1.25)	(-2.50)*
Job stability,	-.41	-.39	-.32	-.05
ages 25–32	(-3.33)*	(-3.29)*	(-3.40)*	(-3.89)*
"R^2"	.24	.34	.32	.47
Model 2 (ever-married men, N = 188)				
Arrest rate,	.12	.84	.79	.12
ages 17–25	(.80)	(3.40)*	(2.49)*	(6.61)*
Income,	.04	.32	.10	.02
ages 17–25	(.26)	(1.91)	(.74)	(1.14)
Commitment,	.22	-.21	.15	.00
ages 17–25	(2.12)*	(-1.95)	(1.61)	(.32)
Commitment,	-.43	-.31	-.10	-.01
ages 25–32	(-1.84)	(-1.40)	(-.70)	(-.45)
Job stability,	-.10	.09	-.12	-.03
ages 17–25	(-1.07)	(.82)	(-1.23)	(-2.53)*
Job stability,	-.19	-.18	-.25	-.02
ages 25–32	(-1.27)	(-1.26)	(-2.23)*	(-1.41)
Attachment	-.45	-.48	-.30	-.07
to spouse,	(-3.42)*	(-3.57)*	(-2.54)*	(-4.45)*
ages 25–32				
"R^2"	.32	.40	.33	.51

* $p < .05$

Note: For General Deviance, Excessive Drinking, and Arrest, the table entry is the maximum-likelihood coefficient and t-ratio (coefficient/standard error); for Arrests Per Year Free, the entry is the OLS coefficient and t-ratio.

ment is an important factor in explaining later adult patterns of crime—at least as important as prior levels of crime. Job stability, as in previous models, is reduced in predictive power among ever-married men. The data again suggest a two-part explanation: for the majority of men, job stability is central in explaining adult desistance from crime; however, this effect is reduced among those who were ever married, for whom attachment to wife assumes greater relative importance. Once marital attachmetn and job stability are taken into account, the effect of commitment is relatively weak.

To further validate these findings, all models for delinquent group were replicated using event history analysis. Cox proportional hazards models (Allison 1984, pp. 33–42) were used to examine time-to-failure—the number of days to first arrest in the periods 17–25 and 25–32.[14] The event history results, when compared to results in Table 4 for crime frequency, are very similar. For example, the t-ratios for the direct effects of job stability at ages 17–25 and 25–32 on the log-hazard rate of first arrest after age 25 were -2.08 and -3.06, respectively (Model 1). Similarly, the t-ratio for the effect of marital attachment on the log-hazard rate for ages 25–32 crime was -2.44 (Model 2). These results suggest that the general conclusions are robust to the specific quantitative technique used.

❧ Adult Crime and Deviance among Original Nondelinquents

We turn to an analysis of adult crime and deviance among the men in the control group—a sample that differs dramatically from the one just examined. Table 5 begins with the two-fold model of young adult crime. The results for all men in the control group (Model 1) indicate that variations in reported but unofficial childhood delinquency predict excessive drinking and arrest in young adulthood. Although some of the officially nondelinquent boys committed delinquencies, these unofficial acts were generally minor (e.g., truancy, smoking). Independent of these prior differences in juvenile delinquency, job stability has a significant negative effect on general deviance and excessive drinking but not on arrest. The pattern for commitment to conventoinal goals is more consistent: High commitment in young adulthood reduces involvement in all three antisocial behaviors. As in the delinquent sample, the effects of income and marriage are not significant.

TABLE 5 *Maximum Likelihood Coeficients and T-Ratios for Logistic Regression of Crime and Deviance in Young Adulthood on Unofficial Juvenile Delinquency and Young Adult Social Bonds: Control Group (No Official Juvenile Record)*

	Crime and Deviance in Young Adulthood (Ages 17–25)		
Independent Variables	General Deviance	Excessive Drinking	Arrest
Model 1 (all men, N = 395)			
Juvenile (age < 17):			
Unofficial	.11	.21	.21
delinquency	(1.46)	(3.60)*	(4.45)*
Young adult (ages 17–25):			
Income	.26	-.05	.04
	(1.58)	(-.42)	(.48)
Marriage	-.36	-.56	-.12
	(-.75)	(-1.47)	(-.43)
Commitment	-.27	-.35	-.23
	(-2.65)*	(-3.94)*	(-3.22)*
Job stability	-.27	-.37	-.11
	(-2.30)*	(-3.72)*	(-1.34)
"R^2"	.06	.19	.10
Model 2 (ever-married men, N = 211)			
Juvenile (age < 17):			
Unofficial	.07	.13	.13
delinquency	(.60)	(1.37)	(2.00)*
Young adult (ages 17–25):			
Income	.58	-.24	-.03
	(2.07)*	(-1.19)	(-.20)
Commitment	.19	-.06	-.04
	(.76)	(-.37)	(-.38)
Job stability	-.31	-.31	-.09
	(-1.57)	(-2.03)8	(-.73)
Attachment to	1.36	-2.30	-1.84
spouse	(-1.57)	(-3.99)*	(-3.75)*
"R^2"	.06	.28	.16

* $p < .05$

In Model 2, which is restricted to ever-married men, attachment to spouse has large independent effects on excessive drinking and arrest in oung adulthood. The effects of commitment are eliminated in the married subsample, while job stability has a significant negative effect only on excessive drinking. The model for general deviance is rather weak in explanatory power—the only significant factor is the positive effect of income. Except for this one anomaly, the general pattern is similar to the delinquent group— job instability and weak marital attachment are directly related to adult crime and deviance. These results are also replicated in predictive models (data not shown). For example, job stability at ages 17–25 has large negative effects on deviance, drinking, *and* arrest at ages 25–32 (t-ratios = -3.24, 3.05, and -4.16, respectively).

Table 6 presents models for the control group analogous to those in Table 4 for the delinquent sample. Model 1 for all men displays the results of the logistic regression of the three dichotomous measures of crime at ages 25–32 on prior arrest and prior and contemporaneous measures of adult social bonds. As in the previous models, income and being married tell us almost nothing in terms of later adult crime. By contrast, both commitment to occupation and job stability at ages 25–32 have significant negative effects on crime independent of arrest and social ties at ages 17–25. These data suggest that increased bonds to work and education lead to less crime and deviance in later adulthood.

Among ever-married men (Model 2), job stability at ages 25–32 has a significant negative effect for arrest and excessive drinking. Marital attachment has a significant negative effect only for general deviance.

❧ Comparative Models of Persistence in Adult Crime and Deviance

We now compare the effects of adult social bonds on an overall measure of adult antisocial behavior for the delinquent and control groups. We constructed a scale by summing the indicators of excessive drinking, general deviance, and arrest over the entire 17–32 age span. This scale ranges from 0 to 6, and better reflects an individual's breadth of involvement in crime and deviance during adulthood than previous measures, especially for the control group in which adult crime was relatively rare. The social control variables are determined from the interview at age 25 to reduce the possibility of reciprocal effects from deviancy itself.

TABLE 6 *Maximum Likelihood Coefficients and T-Ratios for Logistic Regression of Crime and Deviance in Later Adulthood on Young Adult Crime and Social Bonds at Ages 17–25 and Ages 25–32: Control Group (No Official Juvenile Record)*

Independent Variables	Crime and Deviance in Later Adulthood (Ages 25–32)		
	General Deviance	Excessive Drinking	Arrest
Model 1 (all men, N = 367)			
Arrest,	.51	2.27	1.12
ages 17–25	(.95)	(4.63)*	(3.312)*
Income,	.05	-.01	.12
ages 17–25	(.24)	(-.04)	(.97)
Married,	.70	.36	.13
ages 17–25	(1.25)	(.74)	(.37)
Commitment,	.08	-.01	.09
ages 17–25	(.58)	(-.04)	(.96)
Commitment,	-.48	-.33	-.28
ages 25–32	(-2.10)*	(-1.79)	(-2.27)*
Job stability,	-.19	-.18	-.20
ages 17–25	(-1.34)	(-1.43)	(-1.98)*
Job stability,	-.33	-.31	-.29
ages 25–32	(-2.21)*	(-2.44)*	(-3.21)*
"R^2"	.14	.30	.26
Model 2 (ever-married men, N = 298)			
Arrest,	.73	2.06	.80
ages 17–25	(1.12)	(3.55)*	(1.82)
Income,	.08	.03	-.11
ages 17–25	(.35)	(.16)	(-.73)
Commitment,	.17	.03	.10
ages 17–25	(.80)	(.05)	(.76)
Commitment,	-.54	-.00	-.25
ages 25–32	(-1.83)	(-.02)	(-1.70)
Job stability,	-.13	-.17	-.17
ages 17–25	(-.69)	(-1.12)	(-1.32)
Job stability,	.13	-.42	-.32
ages 25–32	(.65)	(-2.56)*	(-2.82)*
Attachment to	-.80	-.26	-.09
spouse, ages 25–32	(-3.64)*	(-1.58)	(-.71)
"R2"	.24	.32	.27

* $p < .05$

For purposes of cross-group comparison, unstandardized ordinary least-squares coefficients, beta weights, and the ratios of coefficients to standard errors are displayed in Table 7. The results for all men (Model 1) are consistent across samples—independent of juvenile delinquency, the largest signficant influence on overall adult crime is job stability. The standardized effect of job stability in young adulthood on adult crime is -.37 for delinquents and -28 for nondelinquents. Model 2 based on ever-married men confirms previous analyses—income and commitment are unimportant in the presence of job stability and marital attachment. Job stability has significant and essentially identical negative effects on adult crime (compare unstandardized coefficients). Furthermore, the largest effect on overall adult criminal and deviant behavior for both groups is marital attachment—ever-married men with close ties to their spouses in young adujlthood were much less likely to engage in adult crime and deviance than men with weak ties, net of other factors. The unstandardized coefficients for the two groups are similar and the beta weights are large and identical (-.40).[15]

We also estimated a model that compared persistent offenders with those who desisted completely (analysis not shown). We assigned a 1 to those who were arrested at ages 17–25 *and* 25–32, and a 0 to those with no adult arrests. There were 117 delinquent and 170 non-delinquent "occasional" offenders, i.e., men who had an arrest in one but not both priods. These were eliminated from the analysis to maximize the contrast. Because of the reduced sample size and the insignificant effects of income, marriage, and commitment in preliminary analyses, we estimated reduced models including only the measures of juvenile delinquency (both official and unofficial), marital attachment, and job stability. The maximum-likelihood logistic coefficient for the independent effect of job stability on persistent deviance as an adult was -.41 for the delinquent group and -.54 for the nondelinquent group (t-ratio = -2.01 and-2.85, respectively). The coefficients for marital attachment were -2.28 for delinquents and -2.52 for nondelinquents (t-ratio = -3.18 and -3.64, respectively). Clearly, marital attachment and job stability substantially reduce the log-odds of persistence in crime among men with vastly different delinquent backgrounds.

Although boys in the two samples were matched, within each sample individuals varied on potentially important characteristics. IQ, measured by the Weschler-Bellevue test, was thus entered into the bsic multivariate models, as was a measure of extroversion, a personality trait emphasized by the Gluecks (1950, p. 281).[16] Alternative measures of socioeconomic status

TABLE 7 *OLS Regression of Breadth of Involvement in Crime and Deviance from Age 17 to 32 on Juvenile Delinquency and Social Bonds in Young Adulthood: Delinquent Group and Control Group*

Independent Variables	Crime and Deviance, Ages 17–32					
	Delinquent Group			Control Group		
	b	Beta	t-ratio	b	Beta	t-ratio
Model 1 (all men)						
Juvenile (age < 17):						
Arrests per year free[a]	1.30	.18	3.38*	—	—	—
Unofficial delinquency	.06	.15	2.78*	.12	.25	5.36*
Young adult (ages 17–25):						
Income	-.12	-.10	-1.71	.00	.01	.23
Marriage	-.20	-.06	-.97	-.06	-.02	-.47
Commitment	-.05	-.07	-1.18	-.14	-.18	-3.84*
Job stability	-.27	-.37	-5.89*	-.20	-.28	-5.69*
R^2		.31			.22	
Number of cases		246			376	
Model 2 (ever-married men)						
Juvenile (age < 17):						
Arrests per year free[a]	1.08	.15	2.24*	—	—	—
Unofficial delinquency	.05	.14	2.01*	.04	.08	1.35
Young adult (ages 17–25):						
Income	-.06	-.05	-.69	-.01	-.01	-.20
Commitment	.00	.00	.02	-.01	-.02	-.29
Job stability	-.17	-.21	-2.54*	-.22	-.27	-4.26*
Attachment to spouse	-1.44	-.40	-4.77*	-1.51	-.40	-6.32*
R^2		.39			.35	
Number of cases		150			204	

* $p < .05$

[a] Not included in model specifications for the control group because these men had no arrests prior to sample selection.

(e.g., economic dependency and occupational skill) were also examined. In no case was the substantive picture altered. The effects of IQ were notably inconsistent and weak. For example, in the models in Table 7 the effects of job stability and marital attachment remained unchanged, whereas the effects of IQ on young adult crime were not significant in model 1 or model 2 for delinquents. The models are therefore robust to alternative specifications, especially regarding individual-differences in childhood.[17]

Conclusion

Sociological explanations of crime and delinquency have recently come under strong attack. In probably the most widely cited critique, Wilson and Herrnstein (1985) chastise sociologists for ignoring the fact that crime and delinquency can be traced to early childhood. They argue that high-rate offenders begin deviant behavior very early in their lives, "well before" traditional sociological variables (e.g., labor markets, community, peer groups, marriage) "could play much of a role" (p. 311). We have offered a life-course model that does not deny early childhood differences, but at the same time recognizes that adult life events matter. The basic organizing principle derived from linking the life course perspective with social control theory is that both continuity and change are evident, and that trajectories of crime and deviance are systematically modified by social bonds to adult institutions of informal social control.

This thesis found broad support in a strict test. The delinquent and control groups in the Gluecks' original research design were markedly different in adolescent delinquency, and continued to differ over the life course. In fact, the Gluecks themselves, much like Wilson and Herrnstein (1985), argued that "The Past is Prologue" (1968, p. 168) and that early childhood differences in delinquency that persisted over time undermined sociological explanations of crime (Glueck and Glueck 1968, pp. 170–80). But the Gluecks ignored evidence of changes in criminal behavior within each group, nor did they explore what might account for such changes. Consistent with a model of adult development and informal social control, we have shown that job stability and marital attachment in adulthood are significantly related to changes in adult crime—the stronger the adult ties to work and family, the less crime and deviance among both delinquents and controls. The results were strong, consistent, and robust over a wide variety of measures and analytical techniques. The effects of job stability were independent of prior and concurrent levels of commitment (i.e., aspirations and ambitions), suggesting that labor-market instability rather than weak occupational commitment is a key factor in understanding adult crime and deviance.

Sociologists need not be hostile to research establishing early childhood differences in delinquency and antisocial behavior—influences that may persist well into adulthood. Indeed, the other side of continuity is change, and the latter appears to be systematically structured by adult bonds to social institutions. Our results raise serious questions about perspectives that focus exclusively on childhood and ignore the adult life-course. We hope that future research will explore other dimensions of adult social bonds. Historical changes in adult social roles may also provide insights into current patterns of adult crime. We believe that the historical context of the data can serve as a baseline to identify areas where research findings are consistent across time and, equally important, to identify areas where contemporary research may diverge (see also Elder 1974; Featherman, Hogan, and Sorenson 1984). For example, the men in the Glueck samples grew to young adulthood in a context of expanding economic opportunities after World War II (1947–1965). To what extent does job instability in a period of rapid deindustrialization and increasing secondary labor markets influence adult development (Crutchfield 1989)? Modern data sets can also take advantage of improvements in the measurement of the timing and dura-tion of significant life events, permitting the use of more complex event-history techniques (Featherman and Lerner 1985; Hagan and Palloni 1988).

Finally, early childhood differences should not be ignored as a source of sociological explanation. Just because criminal tendencies emerge early in life does not mean they derive from psychological and/or constitutional differences. Family, school, and neighborhood processes (Laub and Sampson 1988; Sampson and Laub, forthcoming) may provide a sociologi-cal link to a complete life-course explanation of crime.

Endnotes

[1]Our model does not assume that early childhood differences in delinquency and antisocial behavior stem from ontogenetic (i.e., nonsociological) processes. We return to this point later.

[2]Descriptive statistics on key source variables collected during each follow-up period for both delinquent and control groups are found in Glueck and Glueck (1968, pp. 71–130). Further descriptive data on constructed variables are available from the authors upon request.

[3]For job stability and several other measures (e.g., general deviance and drinking) the data at Time 2 refer to the previous five years—age 20 to 25—or to most

recent job rather than the entire age 17–25 span. However, even though the measurement lags do not correspond exactly to causal lags, we believe this is not a major problem because our strategy assumes only that these measures reflect average levels during the periods 17–25 and 25–32 (see also Plewis 1985, p. 60).

[4]To determine whether the exclusion of subjects due to inapplicable or missing data biased our analysis, all multivariate models were replicated using both pairwise deletion and mean substitution of missing data. The results were substantively similar for both the delinquent and control groups and our major conclusions remain.

[5]The total number of cases in Table 1 ranges from a minimum of 482 (ever-married subsample) to 929 (total follow-up sample at Time 2); no percentage is based on fewer than 100 cases.

[6]Tests of statistical significance are technically not appropriate given the research design. We place greater emphasis on the magnitude of relationships (Laub and Sampson 1988, p. 361).

[7]Although crime/deviance is the major outcome of interest, these other domains illustrate the generality of the link between childhood delinquency and troublesome adult behaviors. As with our key independent variables, these measures were derived from home interviews as well as record checks (Glueck and Glueck 1968, pp. 75, 81, 92, 100).

[8]In Table 2, job stability is trichotomized to permit visual display of the pattern and magnitude of the relationships. Because of skew, the attachment and commitment measures are dichotomized. The number of cases ranges from a minimum of 224 for the ever-married subsample at Time 2 to 437 for occupational commitment at Time 2. All of the percentages are based on at least 30 cases.

[9]Data on time served by the control group were not available so we cannot measure frequency rates per time free. However, this seems unlikely to matter since subjects in the control group had relatively few arrests in adulthood—only 20 percent had ever been arrested between 17–25. Because of this infrequent and skewed outcome, we use a dichotomous measure of crime at ages 17–25 as the major control variable in the analyses for crime at ages 25–32.

[10]This strategy follows recent recommendations for analyzing longitudinal data. As Plewis (1985, pp. 59–60) notes, in the equation $y_2 = a + b_1 y_1 + b_2 x_1 + e$, the parameter b_2 measures "the effect of x_1 on a change in y." The idea that change is examined only with the computation of change scores (e.g., $y_2 - y_1$) is simply incorrect; in fact, the latter can have serious disadvantages (see also Kessler and Greenberg 1981). The measures of prior crime and delinquency are considered exogenous because of the long time intervals in the Gluecks's follow-ups and the differing sources of measurement for childhood and adult crime. For exam-

ple, the Time 1 measures refer to behavior in childhood and adolescence (both parent-self-teacher reported and juvenile-justice recorded) whereas the Time 2 measures refer to adult behavior in the late teens and early twenties as recorded in adult interviews and by the adult criminal justice system. This differs from the usual situation in panel data where short (e.g., yearly) lags using identical measurement schemes often induce autocorrelation, leading to biased estimates (see e.g., Matsueda 1989; Plewis 1985, p. 136; Markus 1979). Not surprisingly, then, preliminary two-state least-squares regression of Time 3 crime/deviance, using Time 1 delinquency as an instrumental variable for Time 2 crime/deviance, produced results substantively consistent with this analysis. (Correction for autocorrelation in the age 17–25 analyses is precluded by the lack of plausible instrumental variables.) Because of these results, the long-term nature of the follow-ups, and the theoretically-based model specification that assigns a substantive role to prior crime/delinquency in generating later behavior (see also Allison, forthcoming), we enter Time 1 and Time 2 crime/delinquency as independent variables.

[11]Aldrich and Nelson (1984, pp. 56–9) criticize "pseudo" measures of explained variance in logistic models. However, because ML logistic models are substantively compatible with OLS models, we present the R^2 derived from OLS regression as an overall indicator of explanatory power for all models (denoted in Tables 3–6 as "R^2").

[12]The sub-sample is defined in terms of a variable (marriage that has no effect on crime. See Stoltzenberg and Relles (1990) for a recent discussion of the pitfalls associated with methods commonly used to correct for potential sample selection bias in sociological research. See also endnote 4.

[13]Marital attachment at ages 17–25 was considered in a preliminary estimatoin of model 2 but it had insignificant effects and the sample size was considerably reduced because half of the men had not yet married. Moreover, the prior and concurrent measures of marital attachment were quite highly correlated, suggesting substantial stability in marital cohesiveness among the married men. Therefore, we use attachment to spouse at ages 25–32 as the main indicator to increase sample size and reduce multicollinearity.

[14]If a person was incarcerated on his 17th or 25th birthday, the calculation was from point of release until the first arrest within each age group. Age at release was therefore controlled in these models. Persons not arrested by the end of each follow-up were treated as censored.

[15]The models in Table 7 are fully replicated with the combined crime and deviance scale is restricted to ages 25–32. For example, the standardized effects of young adult job stability and marital attachment on crime/deviance at ages 25–32 are -.22 and -.37, respectively, for the delinquent group (model 2). The correspon-

ding coefficients for the control group are -.31 dan -.26 (all $p < .05$). Reciprocality therefore does not account for the findings in Table 7.

[16]Recall that race and gender do not vary by nature of the research design. In the follow-ups, age is also controlled since the independent and dependent variables refer to the same age epriod (i.e., ages 17–25 and ages 25–32). For example, even though a boy may have entered the study at age 12 and another at 16 (the range was 10–17), the follow-ups were conducted on or near the 25th and 32nd birthdays of both individuals and have the same reference period. Similarly, the requency of juvenile crimes per year free for each boy refers to all offenses from birth to age 17.

[17]We also calculated Variance Inflation Factors (VIF) for all models, defined as the reciprocal of $1 - R^2$ of each independent variable regressed on the vector of remaining independent variables (Fisher and Mson 1981, p. 109). The average VIF was only 1.5 and the largest was 2.5 for job stability at ages 17–25. Moreover, all bivariate correlations were less than .70 and the vast majority were less than .50. Taken together, these results suggest that multicollinearity does not seriously affect the conclusions.

References

Aldrich, John and Forrest Nelson. 1984. Linear Probability, Logit, and Probit Models. Beverly Hills, CA: Sage.

Allison, Paul. 1984. Event History Analysis. Beverly Hills, CA: Sage.

_____. Forthcoming. "Change Scores as Dependent Variables in Regression Analysis." In Sociological Methodology 1990, edited by Clifford Clogg. Oxford: Basil Blackwell Ltd.

Baltes, Paul and John Nesselroade. 1984. "Paradigm Lost and Paradigm Regained: Critique of Dannefer's Portrayal of Life-Span Developmental Psychology." American Sociological Review 49:841–46.

Blumstein, A., J. Cohen, J. Roth, and C. Visher (Eds.). 1986. Criminal Careers and "Career Criminals." Washington, DC: National Academy Press.

Brim, Orville G. and Jerome Kagan. 1980. "Constancy and Change: A View of the Issues." Pp. 125 in Constancy and Change in Human Development, edited by Orville G. Brim and Jerome Kagan. Cambridge: Harvard University Press.

Caspi, Avshalom. 1987. "Personality in the Life Course." Journal of Personality and Social Psychology 53:1203–13.

Caspi, Avshalom, Darryl J. Bem, and Glen J. Elder, Jr. 1989. "Continuities and Consequences of Interactional Styles Across the Life Course." Journal of Personality 57:375–406.

Cline, Hugh F. 1980. "Criminal Behavior over the Life Span." Pp. 641–74 in *Constancy and Change in Human Development*, edited by Orville G. Brim and Jerome Kagan. Cambridge: Harvard University Press.

Coleman, James S. 1988. "Social Capital in the Creation of Human Capital." *American Journal of Sociology* 94:S95–120.

Crutchfield, Robert D. 1989. "Labor Stratification and Violent Crime." *Social Forces* 68:489–512.

Dannefer, Dale. 1984. "Adult Development and Social Theory: A Paradigmatic Reappraisal." *American Sociological Review* 49:100–16.

Durkheim, E. 1951. *Suicide* (translated by J. Spaulding and G. Simpson). New York: Free Press.

Elder, Glen H., Jr. 1974. *Children of the Great Depression*. Chicago: University of Chicago Press.

————. 1985. "Perspectives on the Life Course." Pp. 23–49 in *Life Course Dynamics*, edited by Glen H. Elder, Jr. Ithaca, NY: Cornell Univ. Press.

Farrington, David P. 1986. "Stepping Stones to Adult Criminal Careers." Pp. 359–84 in *Development of Antisocial and Prosocial Behavior*, edited by Dan Olweus, Jack Block, and Marian Radke-Yarrow. New York: Academic Press.

————. 1989. "Later Adult Life Outcomes of Offenders and Nonoffenders." Pp. 220–44 in *Children at Risk: Assessment, Longitudinal Research, and Intervention*, edited by M. Brambring, F. Losel, and H. Skowronek. New York: Walter de Gruyter.

Farrington, David P., Bernard Gallagher, Lynda Morley, Raymond J. St. Ledger, and Donald J. West. 1986. "Unemployment, School Leaving, and Crime." *British Journal of Criminology* 26:335–56.

Featherman, David, Dennis Hogan, and Aage Sorenson. 1984. "Entry in Adulthood: Profiles of Young Men in the 1950s." Pp. 160–203 in *Life-Span Development and Behavior*, edited by Paul Baltes and Orville Brim, Jr. Orlando: Academic Press.

Featherman, David and Richard Lerner. 1985. "Ontogenesis and Sociogenesis: Problematics for Theory and Research About Development and Socialization Across the Lifespan." *American Sociological Review* 50:659–76.

Fisher, Joseph and Robert Mason. 1981. "The Analysis of Multicollinear Data in Criminology." Pp. 99–125 in *Methods by Quantitative Criminology*, edited by James A. Fox. New York: Academic.

Gibbens, T.C.N. 1984. "Borstal Boys After 25 Years." *British Journal of Criminology* 24:49–62.

Glueck, Sheldon and Eleanor Glueck. 1950. *Unraveling Juvenile Delinquency*. New York: Commonwealth Fund.

_____. 1968. *Delinquents and Nondelinquents in Perspective*. Cambridge: Harvard University Press.

Gottfredson, Michael and Travis Hirschi. 1987. "The Methodological Adequacy of Longitudinal Research on Crime." *Criminology* 25:581–614.

_____. 1990. *A General Theory of Crime*. Stanford, CA: Stanford University Press.

Gove, Walter R. 1985. "The Effect of Age and Gender on Deviant Behavior: A Biopsychosocial Perspective." Pp. 115–44 in *Gender and the Life Course,* edited by Alice S. Rossi. New York: Aldine.

Hagan, John. 1989. *Structural Criminology*. New Brunswick, NJ: Rutgers University Press.

Hagan, John and Alberto Palloni. 1988. "Crimes as Social Events in the Life Course: Reconceiving a Criminological Controversy," *Criminology* 26:87–100.

Hirschi, Travis. 1969. *Causes of Delinquency*. Berkeley, CA: University of California Press.

Hirschi, Travis and Michael Gottfredson. 1983. "Age and the Explanation of Crime." *American Journal of Sociology* 89:552–84.

Hogan, Dennis P. 1980. "The Transition to Adulthood as a Career Contingency." *American Sociological Review* 45:261–76.

Huesmann, L. Rowell, Leonard D. Eron, and Monroe M. Lefkowitz. 1984. "Stability of Aggression Over Time and Generations." *Developmental Psychology* 20:1120–34.

Kessler, Ronald and David Greenberg. 1981. *Linear Panel Analysis*. New York: Academic Press.

Knight, B.J., S.G. Osborn, and D. West. 1977. "Early Marriage and Criminal Tendency in Males." *British Journal of Criminology* 17:348–60.

Kornhauser, Ruth. 1978. *Social Sources of Delinquency*. Chicago: University of Chicago Press.

Laub, John H. and Robert J. Sampson. 1988. "Unraveling Families and Delinquency: A Reanalysis of the Gluecks' Data." *Criminology* 26:355–80.

Laub, John H., Robert J. Sampson, and Kenna Kiger. 1990. "Assessing the Potential of Secondary Data Anbalysis: A New Look at the Gluecks' *Unraveling Juvenile Delinquency* Data." Pp. 244–57 in *Measurement Issues in Criminology,* edited by Kimberly Kempf. New York: Springer-Verlag.

Markus, G. 1979. *Analyzing Panel Data*. Beverly Hills, CA: Sage.

Matsueda, Ross. 1989. "The Dynamics of Moral Beliefs and Minor Deviance." *Social Forces* 68:428–57.

_____. 1980. "Patterns of Deviance." Pp. 157–65 in *Human Functioning in Longitudinal Perspective,* edited by S. B. Sells, Rick Crandall, Merrill Roff, John S. Strauss, and William Pollin. Baltimore: Williams and Wilkins.

Loeber, Rolf. 1982. "The Stability of Antisocial Child Behavior: A Review." *Child Development* 53:1431–46.

Long, Jancis V.F. and George E. Vaillant. 1984. "Natural History of Male Psychological Health, XI: Escape from the Underclass." *American Journal of Psychiatry* 141:341–46.

McCord, Joan. 1979. "Some Child-Rearing Antecedents of Criminal Behavior in Adult Men." *Journal of Personality and Social Psychology* 37:1477–86.

Olweus, Daniel. 1979. "Stability of Aggressive Reaction Patterns in Males: A Review." *Psychological Bulletin* 86:852–75.

Osborn, S.G. 1980. "Moving Home, Leaving London, and Delinquent Trends." *British Journal of Criminology* 20:54–61.

Plewis, Ian. 1985. *Analysing Change: Measurement and Explanation Using Longitudinal Data.* New York: Wiley.

Robins, Lee 1966. *Deviant Children Grown Up.* Baltimore: Williams and Wilkins.

_____. 1978. "Sturdy Childhood Predictors of Adult Antisocial Behaviour." *Psychological Medicine* 8:611–22.

Rutter, Michael. 1988. "Longitudinal Data in the Study of Causal Processes: Some Uses and Some Pitfalls." Pp. 1–28 in *Studies of Psychosocial Risk: The Power of Longitudinal Data,* edited by Michael Rutter. Cambridge: Cambridge University Press.

Sampson, Robert J. and John H. Laub. Forthcoming. *Crime and Deviance Over the Life Course.* New York: Springer-Verlag.

Stolzenberg, ross and Daniel Relles. 1990. "Theory Testing in a World of Constrained Research Design: The Significance of Heckman's Censored Sampling Bias Correction for Nonexperimental Research." *Sociological Methods and Research* 18:395–415.

Vaillant, George E. 1977. *Adaptation to Life.* Boston: Little, Brown, and Co.

Wilson, James Q. and Richard Herrnstein. 1985. *Crime and Human Nature.* New York: Simon and Schuster.

Wolfgang, Marvin, Terrence Thornberry, and Robert Figlio. 1987. *From Boy to Man: From Delinquency to Crime.* Chicago: University of Chicago Press.

❂ ❂ ❂

Questions

1. What are "transitions" and "trajectories"?

2. In Sampson and Laub's theory, who commits crime in adulthood?

3. In what ways does this theory emphasize social control? In what ways does it not?

4. How would this theory explain gender differences in criminal behavior—that is, men, on average, commit substantially more crime than women do?

Crime as Social Control

DONALD BLACK
Harvard Law School

Most people think of crime as a violation of society's norms. They also think of social control as an effort to curb crime. In this article, Donald Black maintains that some crimes actually enforce moral norms. As such, they work as informal methods of social control. This blurring of the distinction between crime and its control gives us a richer understanding of both concepts.

*T*here is a sense in which conduct regarded as criminal is often quite the opposite. Far from being an intentional violation of a prohibition, much crime is moralistic and involves the pursuit of justice. It is a mode of conflict management, possibly a form of punishment, even capital punishment. Viewed in relation to law, it is self-help. To the degree that it defines or responds to the conduct of someone else—the victim—as deviant, crime is social control.[1] And to this degree it is possible to predict and explain crime with aspects of the sociological theory of social control, in particular, the theory of self-help.[2] After an overview of help in traditional and modern settings, the following pages briefly examine in turn the so-called struggle between law and self-help, the deterrence of crime, the processing of self-help by legal officials, and, finally, the problem of predicting and explaining self-help itself.

◉ Traditional Self-Help

Much of the conduct described by anthropologists as conflict management, social control, or even law in tribal and other traditional societies is regarded as crime in modern societies. This is especially clear in the case of violent modes of redress such as assassination, feuding, fighting, maiming, and beating, but it also applies to the confiscation and destruction of property and to other forms of deprivation and humiliation. Such actions typically

"Crime as Social Control," by Donald Black, reprinted from *American Sociological Review*, 1983, vol. 48, no. 1, pp. 34–45.

express a grievance by one person or group against another (see Moore, 1972: 67–72). Thus, one anthropologist notes that among the Bena Bena of highland New Guinea, as among most tribes of that region, "rather than being proscribed, violent self-help is prescribed as a method of social control" (Langness, 1972: 182)[3] The same might be said of numerous societies throughout the world. On the other hand, violence is quite rare in many traditional societies, and at least some of it is condemned in all. What follows is not intended as a representative overview, then, since only the more violent societies and modes of self-help are illustrated. First consider homicide.

In one community of Maya Indians in southern Mexico, for example, any individual killed from ambush is automatically labeled "the one who had the guilt." Everyone assumes that the deceased individual provoked his own death through an act of wrongdoing: "Homicide is considered a *reaction* to crime, not a crime in itself" (Nash, 1967: 456). Similarly, it has been observed that in a number of equatorial African societies homicide is rarely predatory—committed for gain—but is nearly always related to a grievance or quarrel of some kind (Bohannan, 1960: 256). The Eskimos of the American Arctic also kill people in response to various offenses, including adultery, insult, and simply being a nuisance (see Hoebel, 1954: 83–88; van den Steenhoven, 1962: Ch. 4); and, to mention still another example, the Ifugao of the Philippines hold that any "self-respecting man" must kill an adulterer discovered *in flagrante delicto* (Barton, [1919] 1969: 66–70). Societies such as these have, in effect, capital punishment administered on a private basis. But unlike penalties imposed by the state, private executions often result in revenge or even a feud, a reciprocal exchange of violence that might last months or years (see, e.g., Otterbein and Otterbein, 1965; Rieder, 1973). Moreover, the person killed in retaliation may not be himself or herself a killer, since in these societies violent conflicts between non-kin are virtually always handled in a framework of collective responsibility—or, more precisely, collective liability—whereby all members of a family or other group are accountable for the conduct of their fellows (see, e.g., Moore, 1972).

Violence of other kinds also expresses a grievance in most instances. Among the Yanomamo of Venezuela and Brazil, for example, women are routinely subjected to corporal punishment by their husbands: "Most reprimands meted out by irate husbands take the form of blows with the hand or with a piece of firewood, but a good many husbands are even more brutal"

(Chagnon, 1977: 82–83). In parts of East Africa, "Husbands often assault their wives, sometimes with a slap, sometimes with a fist, a foot, or a stick" (Edgerton, 1972: 164); and among the Qolla of Peru, a husband may beat his wife "when her behavior warrants it," such as when she is "lazy" or "runs around with other men" (Bolton and Bolton, 1973: 64). Another punishment for women in some societies is rape by a group of men, or "gang rape" (e.g., Llewellyn and Hoebel, 1941: 202–210). Everywhere, however, it appears that most violence is inflicted upon men by other men.

Property destruction may also be a mode of social control. An extreme form is house burning, a practice quite frequent, for example, in parts of East Africa (Edgerton, 1972: 164). Animals, gardens, or other property might be destroyed as well. Among the Cheyenne of the American Plains, a man's horse might be killed (Llewellyn and Hoebel, 1941: 117), and in northern Albania, a dog might be killed (Hasluck, 1954: 76–78). In one case in Lebanon (later punished as a crime), an aggrieved man cut the branches off his adversary's walnut tree (Rothenberger, 1978: 169). Among the Qolla, crops are sometimes damaged as a punishment, such as "when a man methodically uproots his enemy's potato plants before they have produced any tubers" (Bolton, 1973: 234). Netsilik Eskimos may subtly encourage their children to destroy an offender's cache of food, so that what appears to be mischief or vandalism may actually be a carefully orchestrated act of revenge (van den Steenhoven, 1962: 74).

Property may also be confiscated as a form of social control, so that what might at first appear to a modern observer as unprovoked theft or burglary proves in many cases to be a response to the misconduct of the victim. Among the Mbuti Pygmies of Zaire, for instance, a seeming theft may be recognized by all as an "unofficial sanction" against a person who has incurred public disapproval for some reason or another" (Turnbull, 1965: 199). Among the Qolla, the moralistic character of a theft is especially clear "when the object stolen has no value to the thief" (Bolton, 1973: 233). Lastly, it might be noted that where women are regarded as the property of their fathers or husbands, rape may provide a means of retaliation against a man. This seems to have been involved in some of the gang rapes recorded as crimes in fourteenth-century England, for example, where even a widow might be attacked by a group of men as an act of revenge against her deceased husband (Hanawalt, 1979: 109, 153). In some cases, then, rape may be construed as another kind of confiscation.

Modern Self-Help

A great deal of the conduct labeled and processed as crime in modern societies resembles the modes of conflict management—described above—that are found in traditional societies which have little or no law (in the sense of governmental social control—Black, 1972: 1096). Much of this conduct is intended as a punishment or other expression of disapproval, whether applied reflectively or impulsively, with coolness or in the heat of passion. Some is an effort to achieve compensation, or restitution, for a harm that has been done. The response may occur long after the offense, perhaps weeks, months, or even years later; after a series of offenses, each viewed singly as only a minor aggravation but together viewed as intolerable; or as an immediate response to the offense, perhaps during a fight or other conflict, or after an assault, theft, insult, or injury.

As in tribal and other traditional societies, for example, most intentional homicide in modern life is a response to conduct that the killer regards as deviant. In Houston during 1969, for instance, over one-half of the homicides occurred in the course of a "quarrel," and another one-fourth occurred in alleged "self-defense" or were "provoked," whereas only a little over one-tenth occurred in the course of predatory behavior such as burglary or robbery (calculated from Lundsgaarde, 1977: 237; see also Wolfgang, [1958] 1966: Ch. 10). Homicide is often a response to adultery or other matters relating to sex, love, or loyalty, to disputes about domestic matters (financial affairs, drinking, house-keeping) or affronts to honor, to conflicts relating to debts, property, and child custody, and to other questions of right and wrong. Cases mentioned in the Houston study include one in which a young man killed his brother during a heated discussion about the latter's sexual advances toward his younger sisters, another in which a man killed his wife after she "dared" him to do so during an argument about which of several bills they should pay, one where a women killed her husband during a quarrel in which the man struck her daughter (his stepdaughter), one in which a woman killed her 21-year-old son because he had been "fooling around with homosexuals and drugs," and two others in which people died from wounds inflicted during altercations over the parking of an automobile (Lundsgaarde, 1977). Like the killings in traditional societies described by anthropologists, then, most intentional homicide in modern society may be classified as social control, specifically as self-help, even if it is handled by legal officials as crime.[4] From this standpoint, it is apparent that capital punishment is quite common in modern America—in Texas, homicide is one of the ten leading causes of death—though it is nearly always a private rather than a public affair.

Most conduct that a lawyer would label as assault may also be understood as self-help. In the vast majority of cases the people involved know one another, usually quite intimately, and the physical attack arises in the context of a grievance or quarrel (see, e.g., Vera Institute, 1977: 23-42). Commonly the assault is a punishment, such as when a husband beats or otherwise injures his wife because she has not lived up to his expectations. In one case that came to the attention of the police in Boston, for example, a woman complained that her husband had beaten her because supper was not ready when he came home from work (Black, 1980: 161), a state of affairs, incidentally, which might have been the woman's own way of expressing disapproval of her husband (see Baumgartner, 1983: forthcoming). Other standards are enforced violently as well. In one instance that occurred in a major northeastern city and that apparently was not reported to the police, a young woman's brothers attacked and beat her boyfriend "for making her a drug addict," and in another a young man was stabbed for cooperating with the police in a burglary investigation (Merry, 1981: 158, 180–181). In a case in Washington, D.C., that resulted in an arrest, a boy shot his gang leader for taking more than his proper share of the proceeds from a burglary (Allen, 1977: 40–43). Years later, the same individual shot someone who had been terrorizing young women—including the avenger's girlfriend—in his neighborhood. Though he pleaded guilty to "assault with a deadly weapon" and was committed to a reformatory, not surprisingly he described himself as "completely right" and his victim as "completely wrong" (Allen, 1977: 62–66, 69–70).

Indigenous people arrested for violence in colonial societies are likely to have a similar point of view: They may be proud of what they have done and admit it quite openly, even while they are being prosecuted as criminals by the foreign authorities.[5] Those apprehended in Europe for the crime of dueling—also a method of conflict resolution—have typically lacked remorse for the same reasons (see Pitt-Rivers, 1966: 29–31). Thus, when asked by a priest to pray for forgiveness before being hanged for killing a man with a sword, one such offender in France exclaimed, "Do you call one of the cleverest thrusts in Gascony a crime?" (Baldick, 1965: 62). As in duelling, moreover, violence in modern societies is often prescribed by a code of honor. He who shrinks from it is disgraced as a coward (see, e.g., Werthman, 1969; Horowitz and Schwartz, 1974).

Many crimes involving the confiscation or destruction of property also prove to have a normative character when the facts come fully to light. There are, for example, moralistic burglaries, thefts, and robberies. Over one-third of the burglaries in New York City resulting in arrest involve people with a prior relationship (Vera Institute, 1977: 82), and these not infrequently express a grievance the burglar has against his victim. In one such case handled by the Boston police, for instance, a woman who had been informed by a neighbor complained that while she was away "her estranged husband had entered her apartment, wrecked it, loaded all of her clothes into his car, and driven away, presumably headed for his new home several hundred miles away" (Black, 1980: 115). Though the specific nature of this man's grievance was not mentioned, it seems apparent that his actions were punitive to some degree, and surely his estranged wife understood this as well. In a case in New York City, one resulting in two arrests for burglary, two black women barged into the home of an elderly white woman at midnight to confront her because earlier in the day she had remonstrated with their children for throwing rocks at her window (Vera Institute, 1977: 88). A crime may also be committed against a particular individual to express the disapproval of a larger number of people, such as a neighborhood or community, as is illustrated by the report of a former burglar who notes in his autobiography that early in his career he selected his victims partly on moralistic grounds:

> We always tried to get the dude that the neighbors didn't like too much or the guy that was hard on the people who lived in the neighborhood. . . . I like to think that all the places we robbed, that we broke into, was kind of like the bad guys. (Allen, 1977: 39–40)

It should be clear, however, that the victims of moralistic crime may be entirely unaware of why they have been selected, especially when the offender is unknown. Such crimes may therefore be understood as secret social control (compare Becker, 1963: 20).

Another possible mode of self-help is robbery, or theft involving violence. Thus, in New York City, where over one-third of the people arrested for robbery are acquainted with their victims, the crime often arises from a quarrel over money (Vera Institute, 1977: 65-71). In one case, for example, a woman reported that her sister and her sister's boyfriend had taken her purse and $40 after assaulting her and threatening to kill her baby, but she later explained that this had arisen from a misunderstanding: The boyfriend wanted reimbursement for a baby carriage that he had bought for her, whereas she thought it had been a gift (Vera Institute, 1977: 69–70). It seems, in fact, that in many instances robbery is a form of debt collection and an alternative to law. The same applies to embezzlement, though it may also simply express disapproval of the employer who is victimized (see Cressey, 1953: 57–59, 63–66).

Conduct known as vandalism, or malicious destruction of property, proves to be a form of social control in many cases as well. Far from being merely "malicious," "non-utilitarian," or "negativistic," with "no purpose, no rhyme, no reason" (Cohen, 1955: 25–30, including quoted material in note 4), much vandalism in modern society is similar to the moralistic destruction of crops, animals, and other valuables in traditional societies. But whereas, say, a Plains Indian might kill a horse, a modern agent of justice might damage the offender's automobile. Thus, in one American neighborhood where parking spaces on the street are scarce, the residents have evolved their own distribution system, with its own customary rules and enforcement procedures. In the winter, one such rule is that whoever shovels the snow from a parking space is its "owner," and persistent violators may find that their automobile has been spray-painted or otherwise abused (Thomas-Buckle and Buckle, 1982: 84, 86–87). Vandalism may also be reciprocated in a feud-like pattern of mutual destruction: In one case in a northeastern city, a young man found that someone had broken the radio antenna on his automobile, learned from some children who had done it, and thereupon proceeded to slash the tires of the offender's automobile (Merry, 1981: 179).

Business places and dwellings may be damaged to punish their owners or inhabitants. Arson, or burning, has a long history of this kind (see, e.g., Hanawalt, 1979: 90–91). Less severe sanctions, however, are far more frequent. In a case occurring in a suburb of New York City, for example, a young man drove his car across someone's lawn during a quarrel, and in another incident in the same community several young men spray-painted parts of an older man's house in the middle of the night because he had called the police to disperse them when they were sitting in their cars drinking beer and listening to music (Baumgartner, forthcoming). If all of the facts were known, then, it seems likely that much seemingly senseless and random vandalism would prove to be retaliation by young people against adults (see Greenberg, 1977: 202-204). Some may even be done by children on behalf of their parents, in a pattern analogous to that found among the Eskimos mentioned earlier (for a possible example, see Black, 1980: 167–68). If the parents themselves are the offenders, however, other strategies might be followed. Among the Tarahumara Indians of northern Mexico, children with a grievance against their parents often "run away" from home, staying with an uncle or grandparent for a few days before returning (Fried, 1953: 291). Qolla children have a similar custom, locally known as "losing themselves" (Bolton and Bolton, 1973: 15–16). Modern children do this as well, though like vandalism it is commonly regarded as a form of juvenile delinquency.

Finally, it might be noted that the practice of collective liability—whereby all of the people in a social category are held accountable for the conduct of each of their fellows—occurs in modern as well as traditional societies. This is most apparent during a war, revolution, or riot, when anyone might suffer for the deeds of someone else, but during peaceful times too, seemingly random violence may often be understood in the same way. Today a police officer might become the victim of a surprise attack by a stranger, for example, because of the conduct of one or more fellow officers in the past. Seemingly random crime of other kinds may involve collective liability as well. Thus, for instance, a black rapist described his selection of white victims as a process of vengeance against white people in general:

> It delighted me that I was defying and trampling upon the white man's law, upon his system of values, and that I was defiling his women—and this point, I believe, was the most satisfying to me because I was very resentful over the historical fact of how the white man has used the black woman. I felt I was getting revenge. (Cleaver, 1968: 14)

Similarly, a former burglar and robber remarked that he once selected his victims primarily from a relatively affluent neighborhood, but not simply because this provided a chance of greater material gain: "I really disliked them people, 'cause it seemed like they thought they was better 'cause they had more" (Allen, 1977: 32–33). People might be held collectively liable because of their neighborhood, social class, race, or ethnicity. Crime by young people against adult strangers may also have this logic in some cases: All adults might be held liable for the conduct of those known personally, such as police, teachers, and parents.[6] Among young people themselves, particularly in large American cities, rival "gangs" may engage in episodic violence resembling the feud in traditional settings, where each member of a feuding group is liable—to injury or even death—for the conduct of the other members (see, e.g., Yablonsky, 1962). A significant amount of crime in modern society may even resemble what anthropologists describe as "raiding," a kind of predatory behavior often directed at people collectively defined as deserving of revenge (see, e.g., Sweet, 1965; Schneider, 1971: 4). And some might properly be construed as "banditry" since it seems to be a kind of primitive rebellion by those at the bottom of society against their social superiors (see Hobsbawm, 1969). In short, although much crime in modern society directly and unambiguously expresses a grievance by one person against another, this may be only the most visible portion of a much broader phenomenon.

❧ Theoretical Considerations

When a moralistic crime is handled by the police or prosecuted in court, the official definition of the event is drastically different from that of the people involved, particularly from that of the alleged offender. In the case of a husband who shoots his wife's lover, for example, the definition of who is the offender and who is the victim is reversed: The wife's lover is defined as the victim, even though he was shot because of an offense he committed against the woman's husband. Moreover, the lover's offense is precisely the kind for which violent social control—by the husband—is viewed as acceptable and appropriate, if not obligatory, in numerous tribal and other traditional societies. Even in modern society, it might be said that the husband is charged with violating the criminal law because he enforced his rights in what many regard as the customary law of marriage. The victim thus becomes the offender, and vice versa. The state prosecutes the case in its own name, while the original offender against morality (if alive) serves as a witness against the man he has victimized—surely a perverse proceeding from the standpoint of the defendant (compare Christie, 1977). It is also enlightening in this regard to consider criminal cases arising from quarrels and fights, where each party has a grievance against the other. Here the state often imposes the categories of offender and victim upon people who were contesting the proper application of these labels during the altercation in question. Whether there was originally a cross-complaint or not, however, in all of these cases the state defines someone with a grievance as a criminal. The offense lies in how the grievance was pursued. The crime is self-help.

It should be apparent from much of the foregoing that in modern society the state has only theoretically achieved a monopoly over the legitimate use of violence (compare, e.g., Weber, [1919] 1958: 78; Elias, [1939] 1978: 201–202). In reality, violence flourishes (particularly in modern America), and most of it involves ordinary citizens who seemingly view their conduct as a perfectly legitimate exercise of social control. It might therefore be observed that the struggle between law and self-help in the West did not end in the Middle Ages, as legal historians claim (e.g., Pollock and Maitland, [1898] 1968: Vol. 2, 574; Pound, 1921: 139–40; see also Hobhouse, 1906: Ch. 3). It continues.[7] Many people still "take the law into their own hands." They seem to view their grievances as their own business, not that of the police or other officials, and resent the intrusion of law (see Matza, 1964: Ch.5). They seem determined to have justice done, even if this means that they will be defined as criminals.[8] Those who commit murder, for example, often appear to be resigned to their fate at the hands of the authorities; many wait patiently for the police to arrive; some even call to report their own crimes (see generally Lundsgaarde, 1977). In cases of this kind, indeed, the individuals involved might arguably be regarded as martyrs. Not unlike workers who violate a prohibition to strike—knowing they will go to jail— or others who defy the law on grounds of principle, they do what they think is right, and willingly suffer the consequences.

Deterrence and Self-Help

To the degree that people feel morally obligated to commit crimes, it would seem that the capacity of the criminal law to discourage them—its so-called deterrent effect—must be weakened. For example, homicides committed as a form of capital punishment would seem to be more difficult to deter than those committed entirely in pursuit of personal gain (on the deterability of the latter, see Chambliss, 1967). This is not to deny that moralistic homicide can be discouraged to some extent. In fact, one former resident of Harlem has noted that the inhabitants of that unusually violent area appear to debate in their own minds whether or not moralistic homicide is ultimately worth its legal consequences:

> I think everybody was curious about whether or not it was worth it to kill somebody and save your name or your masculinity, defend whatever it was that had been offended—whether it was you or your woman or somebody in your family. (Brown, 1965: 220)

He adds that during his years in Harlem this question loomed especially large whenever anyone was executed in prison (Brown, 1965: 220). That the desirability of killing another person is entertained at all is remarkable, however, particularly when the death penalty is believed to be a possible result (a belief that appears to be largely unfounded—see below). Furthermore, since other crimes of self-help carry fewer risks of a legal nature, they should be even harder to discourage than homicide. In any event, a theory of deterrence surely should recognize that the power of punishment to deter crime partly depends upon whether a given crime is itself a form of social control (for other relevant variables see, e.g., Andenaes, 1966; Chambliss, 1967; Zimring, 1971).

A related question is the extent to which victimizations are deterred by self-help rather than—or in addition to—law. Although many citizens are entirely dependent upon legal officials such as the police to handle criminal offenders, others are prepared to protect themselves and their associates by any means at their disposal, including violence. It is well known among potential predators in one American neighborhood, for example, that a number of the residents would be dangerous to victimize, in some cases because they enjoy the protection of family members who act as their champions (see Merry, 1981: 178–79). Such people are left alone. Entire segments of a community may also be avoided from fear of retaliation. For example, for this reason some thieves and robbers may avoid the poor: "One of the most dangerous things in the world is to steal from poor people. . . . When you steal from the poor, you gamble with your life" (Brown, 1965: 214; see also Allen, 1977; 51–52). Moreover, since the deterrent effect of social control generally increases with its severity (see Zimring, 1971: 83–90, for qualifications), it should be noted that self-help is often more severe than law. Thus, a burglar or robber might be executed by his intended victim, though burglary and robbery are generally not capital crimes in modern codes of law. Accordingly, to the degree that self-help is effectively repressed by the state, crime of other kinds might correspondingly increase. Among the Gusii of Kenya, for instance, rape dramatically increased after the British prohibited traditional violence against strangers—potential rapists—and, when a rape occurred, violence against the offender and possibly his relatives (Le Vine, 1959: 476–77).[9] Perhaps some of the predatory crime in modern society is similarly a result of a decline in self-help.

The Processing of Self-Help

Even while the ancient struggle between law and self-help continues, the response of legal officials to those handling their own grievances by force and violence is not nearly so severe as might be supposed. In fact, crimes of self-help are often handled with comparative leniency. An extreme of this pattern was seen historically, for example, in the generous application of the concept of "self-defense" to justify homicide—otherwise by law a capital offense—in medieval England: In cases in which a killing involved social control, it appears that juries routinely avoided a conviction by fabricating a version of the incident in which the victim had first attacked the defendant, forcing him to resist with violence in order to save his own life (Green, 1976: 428-36). Likewise, in more recent centuries European authorities and juries have generally been reluctant to enforce laws against dueling (see Baldick, 1965: Chs.4–7; Andrew, 1980). Earlier in the present century, the same applied to the handling of so-called lynchings in the American South— executions carried out by a group of private citizens, usually against a black man believed to have victimized a white. Typically no one was arrested, much less prosecuted or punished, though the killers frequently were well known and readily available (see, e.g., Raper, 1933). Today, much violent self-help is still tolerated by American officials and juries. Incidents that a lawyer would normally classify as felonious assault, for example—involving severe bodily injury or the threat thereof—are unlikely to result in arrest if the offender and victim are intimately related (Black, 1980: 180–85; see also Black, 1971: 1097–98). Where an arrest is made, prosecution and conviction are far less likely when the offense entails an element of self-help. Thus, in Houston, people whom the police arrest for homicide are often released without prosecution, and in many cases this seems to be related to the moralistic nature of the killing. In 1969, 40 percent of those arrested for killing a relative (such as a spouse or sibling) were released without prosecution, and the same applied to 37 percent of those arrested for killing a friend or other associate and to 24 percent of those arrested for killing a stranger (Lundsgaarde, 1977: 232). And offenses that do initially result in prosecution are likely to be abandoned or dismissed at a later point in the process when self-help is involved, such as when a burglary or robbery is committed in order to collect an unpaid debt (see, e.g., Vera Institute, 1977: 69–70, 87–88). At every stage, then, crimes of self-help often receive a degree of immunity from law (but see below).

If the capacity of law to deter crimes of self-help is weak in the first place, surely this leniency, insofar as it is known among the population, makes it weaker still. But it might be wondered why so much self-help occurs in a society such as modern America. Why do so many people criminally pursue their own grievances in a society where law is developed to such a high degree? Why, in particular, are they so violent?

The Theory of Self-Help

Several centuries ago, Thomas Hobbes argued that without a sovereign state—without law—a "war of every one against every one" would prevail, and life would be "solitary, poor, nasty, brutish, and short" [1651] 1962: 100). Many stateless societies have since been observed by anthropologists, however, and Hobbes's theory has proven to be somewhat overstated: Life without law does not appear to be nearly as precarious as he believed (see, e.g., Middleton and Tait, [1958] 1970; MacCormack, 1976; Roberts, 1979). Even so, the idea that violence is associated with statelessness still enjoys considerable support. With various refinements and qualifications, an absence of state authority has been used to explain high levels of violence in settings as diverse as the highlands of New Guinea (Koch, 1974: Ch. 7), Lake Titicaca in the Andes (Bolton, 1970: 12–16), and western Sicily (Blok, 1974: 210–12).[10] It has also been used to explain war and other violent self-help in international relations (e.g., Hoffmann, 1968; Koch, 1974: 173–75). A version of the same approach may be relevant to an understanding of self-help in modern society.

Hobbesian theory would lead us to expect more violence and other crimes of self-help in those contemporary settings where law—governmental social control—is least developed, and, indeed, this appears to fit the facts: Crimes of self-help are more likely where law is less available. This is most apparent where legal protection is withheld as a matter of public policy, such as where a contract violates the law. A gambling debt is not legally enforceable, for example, and the same applies to transactions in illicit narcotics, prostitution, stolen goods, and the like. Perhaps for this reason many underworld businesses find it necessary to maintain, in effect, their own police, such as the "strong-arms" of illegal loan operations and the "pimps" who oversee the work of prostitutes (see, e.g., Allen, 1977: 100). Furthermore, it appears that social control within settings of this kind is relatively violent (but see Reuter, 1983).

Law is unavailable, or relatively so, in many other modern settings as well, though not necessarily as a matter of public policy. A teenager with a grievance against an adult, for example, will generally be ignored or even reprimanded by the police (Black, 1980: 152–55).

Lower-status people of all kinds—blacks and other minorities, the poor, the homeless—enjoy less legal protection, especially when they have complaints against their social superiors, but also when conflict erupts among themselves (see Black, 1976: Chs. 2–6). To the police and other authorities the problems of these people seem less serious, their injuries less severe, their honor less important.[11] A fight or quarrel among them may even be viewed as itself a "disturbance of the peace," an offense in its own right, regardless of the issues dividing the parties (see Black and Baumgartner, 1983: forthcoming). People in intimate relationships, too, such as members of the same family or household, find that legal officials are relatively unconcerned about their conflicts, particularly if they occur in private and do not disturb anyone else (see Black, 1976: 40–44, 1980: Ch.5).[12] In all of these settings neglected by law, crimes of self-help are comparatively common. There are, so to speak, stateless locations in a society such as modern America, and in them the Hobbesian theory appears to have some validity.[13]

Before closing, it is possible to specify the relationship between law and self-help more precisely. The likelihood of self-help is not merely a function of the availability of law, and, moreover, crimes of self-help are not always handled leniently by legal officials. Different locations and directions in social space have different patterns. In other words, the relationship between law and self-help depends upon who has a grievance against whom.

Four patterns can be identified: First, law may be relatively unavailable both to those with grievances and to those who are the objects of self-help, as when people of low status and people who are intimate have conflicts with each other (on the distribution of law, see generally Black, 1976). This pattern has been emphasized above. Secondly, law may be relatively unavailable to those with grievances in comparison to those who have offended them. Should the former employ self-help, they may therefore be vulnerable to harsh treatment by legal officials. This is the situation of people with a grievance against a social superior, such as a teenager with a grievance against an adult, and may help to explain why they tend to develop their own techniques of social control, including, for instance, covert retaliation, self-destruction, and flight (see Baumgartner, 1983).

Those with grievances against a social inferior illustrate a third pattern: Law is readily available to them, but not to those against whom they might employ self-help. In this situation, the aggrieved party seemingly has a choice of law or self-help. A man might easily obtain legal help against his teenaged son, for example, but if he simply beats the boy instead—a kind of self help—he is unlikely to be handled with severity by the police or other officials (see Black, 1980: 152–55). The fourth possibility, where law is readily available both to those with grievances and to those who have offended them, is seen where people of high status, and also people who are strangers, have conflicts with each other. Here self-help seems to be relatively infrequent. In sum, law and self-help are unevenly distributed across social space, and each is relevant to the behavior of the other.[14]

● Conclusion

The approach taken in this paper departs radically from traditional criminology (as seen, e.g., in Cohen, 1955; Miller, 1958; Cloward and Ohlin, 1960; Sutherland and Cressey, 1960). Indeed, the approach taken here is, strictly speaking, not criminological at all, since it ignores whatever might be distinctive to crime as such (including, for example, how criminals differ from other people or how their behavior differs from that which is not prohibited). Instead it draws attention to a dimension of many crimes that is usually viewed as a totally different—even opposite—phenomenon, namely, social control. Crime often expresses a grievance. This implies that many crimes belong to the same family as gossip, ridicule, vengeance, punishment, and law itself. It also implies that to a significant degree we may predict and explain crime with a sociological theory of social control, specifically a theory of self-help. Beyond this, it might be worthwhile to contemplate what else crime has in common with conduct of other kinds. As remarked earlier (in note 4), for instance, some crime may be understood as economic behavior, and some as recreation. In other words, for certain theoretical purposes we might usefully ignore the fact that crime is criminal at all.[15] The criminality of crime is defined by law, and therefore falls within the jurisdiction of a completely different theory (see especially Black, 1976).

Endnotes

[1]The concept of social control employed here refers specifically—and exclusively—to any process by which people define or respond to deviant behavior (Black, 1976: 105). This is a broad category that includes such diverse phenomena as a frown or scowl, a scolding or reprimand, an expulsion from an organization, an arrest or lawsuit, a prison sentence, commitment to a mental hospital, a riot, or a military reprisal. But this concept entails no assumptions or implications concerning the impact of social control upon conformity, social order, or anything else, nor does it address the subjective meanings of social control for those who exercise or experience it.

[2]For these purposes, self-help refers to the expression of a grievance by unilateral aggression. It is thus distinguishable from social control through third parties such as police officers or judges and from avoidance behavior such as desertion and divorce. (This conception of self-help derives from work in progress with M. P. Baumgartner.)

[3]Illustrations of traditional self-help are given here in the present tense (known as the "ethnographic present" in anthropology), though many of the practices to be surveyed have changed considerably—if not disappeared altogether—since they were originally observed.

[4]Crimes of self-help may be distinguished from other categories of conduct regarded as criminal, such as certain kinds of economic behavior (e.g., predatory robbery and the selling of illicit goods and services) and recreation (e.g., gambling and underage drinking of alcoholic beverages). This is not to deny that some crime is multidimensional; for instance, an incident might be both moralistic and predatory at the same time, as when someone is killed in a quarrel but then robbed as well.

[5]This reportedly applied, for example, to the Nuer of the Sudan when they lived under British rule:

> I have been told by [a British] officer with wide experience of Africans that Nuer defendants are remarkable in that they very seldom lie in cases brought before Government tribunals. They have no need to, since they are only anxious to justify the damage they have caused by showing that it is retaliation for damage the plaintiff has inflicted earlier. (Evans-Pritchard, 1940: 171–72)

[6]It might be added that sub-populations such as women, old people, and the poor may be particularly vulnerable to vengeance of this kind. Seen in cross-cultural perspective, this is not inconsistent with systems of collective liability. In some tribal societies, for example, retaliation may be taken against those who are physically less dangerous, such as women and children, and against those who are less likely to be revenged, such as social isolates and visitors (e.g., Koch, 1974: 132–54). On the other hand, a "code of honor" may govern revenge and

limit it, for instance, to adult males able to defend themselves (e.g., Hasluck, 1954: Ch. 24).

[7]The struggle, however, was once vastly more rancorous and spectacular, in many cases involving open confrontations between those engaging in self-help—along with their supporters—and the authorities who regarded their conduct as criminal. In medieval England, for example, a prisoner's friends might forcibly seize him from the sheriff, and in some instances armed bands violently challenged the authorities in the courtroom itself (see, e.g., Pike, 1873: 257–58).

[8]It has been suggested that offenders often condemn their victims merely in order to "neutralize" their own feelings of guilt (Sykes and Matza, 1957: 668). By contrast, the argument here is that in many cases condemnations of this kind may be authentic. Some criminals may be telling the truth.

[9]It appears that predatory behavior within tribal and peasant villages is often effectively deterred by the threat of self-help. This was the impression, for example, of an anthropologist who studied the Nuer of the Sudan: "It is the knowledge that a Nuer is brave and will stand up against aggression and enforce his rights by club and spear that ensures respect for person and property" (Evans-Pritchard, 1940: 171). Why people in any society refrain from victimizing their fellows raises difficult questions of motivation, however, and lies beyond the scope of the present discussion.

[10]A cross-cultural survey of 50 societies shows that those with the least "political integration"—which means, *inter alia*, those without a state—are the most likely to have "coercive self-help" as their dominant mode of conflict management (Koch and Sodergren, 1976: 54–55).

[11]It should also be recognized that people in these settings are relatively unlikely to bring their grievances to legal officials in the first place. For instance, it would not occur to most teenagers to call the police about an adult, and the same generally applies when someone has a grievance against an intimate such as a spouse or friend (but see Black, 1980: Ch. 5, especially 124–28). It might even be said that many people choose statelessness as a way of life. This pattern presumably undermines still further the capacity of law to deter crimes of self-help.

[12]To a degree, self-help may function whether by design or not—as a mechanism through which law is mobilized among those who might otherwise be ignored. In at least one tribal society, the Meta of the Cameroon, it appears that violence was consciously employed as a technique of this kind: Village elders were empowered to arbitrate disputes only if the parties became violent, and so it was not uncommon for people to initiate a fight in order to assure a hearing of their case (Dillon, 1980: 664). Children in many societies seem to use the same technique to mobilize adults. In some instances, violence in modern society may

similarly serve as a cry for help from people who are less capable of attracting legal attention without it. Reports of violence occasionally may even be fabricated in order to assure that the police will handle cases that the callers fear—possibly with justification—would otherwise be dismissed as trivial (for a likely example, see Black, 1980: 151). But then, as noted earlier, the police are likely to respond with indifference anyway.

[13]It might be added that the opposite of statelessness can occur as well, with opposite results: The availability of law can be extended to such a degree that it almost entirely displaces self-help. People can become so dependent upon law that they are unwilling to handle their own grievances. It appears, in fact, that this extreme is almost reached by so-called totalitarian societies, such as the Soviet Union under Stalin or Germany under Hitler, where the state insinuates itself throughout the population by actively encouraging citizens to make use of its coercive apparatus however they see fit. Since apparently nearly anyone can have nearly anyone else sent to prison, each person is dangerous to others, and yet vulnerable to them at the same time (see Gross, 1983). The result seems almost what Hobbes called a "war of every one against every one," but within the framework of a state. Under these conditions, self-help tends to wither away.

[14]It should also be understood that other conditions besides the availability of law are relevant to the incidence of self-help in each of its various manifestations. After all, no effort has been made here to develop a comprehensive theory of self-help. The analysis has been intended merely to indicate the relevance of such a theory and to offer a single formulation that it might include. Furthermore, it should be clear that despite the emphasis upon contemporary society in the present discussion, a sociological theory of self-help would ideally apply to all instances of this phenomenon, traditional as well as modern.

[15]This is not to deny that the definition of conduct as criminal may be relevant to its form and frequency. Even so, a given category of crime may share more with particular kinds of non-criminal conduct than with other crime. The use of illicit drugs is seemingly more similar to the legal consumption of alcoholic beverages than to robbery or rape, for example, and extortion is seemingly closer to the practices of many landlords, physicians, and corporations than to vandalism, trespassing, or treason.

References

Allen, John, 1977, Assault with a Deadly Weapon: The Autobiography of a Street Criminal. Edited by Dianne Hall Kelly and Philip Heymann. New York: McGraw-Hill.

Andenaes, Johannes, 1966 "The general preventive effects of punishment." University of Pennsylvania Law Review 114: 949–83.

Andrew, Donna T., 1980 "The code of honour and its critics: the opposition to dueling in England, 1700-1850." Social History 5: 409–34.

Baldick, Robert, 1965 The Duel: A History of Dueling. London: Chapman & Hall.

Barton, Roy Franklin, [1919] 1969 Ifugao Law. Berkeley: University of California Press.

Baumgartner, M. P., 1983 "Social control from below." Forthcoming in Donald Black (ed.), Toward a General Theory of Social Control. New York: Academic Press.

_____. forthcoming The Moral Order of a Suburb. New York: Academic Press.

Becker, Howard S., 1963 Outsiders: Studies in the Sociology of Deviance. New York: Free Press.

Black, Donald, 1971 "The social organization of arrest." Stanford Law Review 23: 1087–1111.

_____. 1972 "The boundaries of legal sociology." Yale Law Journal 81: 1086–1100.

_____. 1976 The Behavior of Law. New York: Academic Press.

_____. 1980 The Manners and Customs of the Police. New York: Academic Press.

Black, Donald and M. P. Baumgartner, 1983 "Toward a theory of the third party." Forthcoming in Keith O. Boyum and Lynn Mather (eds.), Empirical Theories about Courts. New York: Longman.

Blok, Anton, 1974 The Mafia of a Sicilian Village, 1860–1960: A Study of Violent Peasant Entrepreneurs. New York: Harper & Row.

Bohannan, Paul, 1960 "Patterns of murder and suicide." Pp. 230–66 in Paul Bohannan (ed.), African Homicide and Suicide. Princeton: Princeton University Press.

Bolton, Ralph, 1970 "Rates and ramifications of violence: notes on Qolla homicide." Paper presented at the International Congress of Americanists, Lima, Peru, August, 1970.

_____. 1973 "Aggression and hypoglycemia among the Qolla: a study in psychobiological anthropology." Ethnology 12: 227–57.

Bolton, Ralph and Charlene Bolton, 1973 "Domestic quarrels among the Qolla." Paper presented at the annual meeting of the American Anthropological Association, New Orleans, Louisiana, October, 1973. Published in Spanish as Conflictos en la Familia Andina. Cuzco: Centro de Estudios Andinos, 1975.

Brown, Claude, 1965 Manchild in the Promised Land. New York: Macmillan.

Chagnon, Napolean A., 1977 Yanomamo: The Fierce People. Second edition; first edition, 1968. New York: Holt, Rinehart & Winston.

Chambliss, William J., 1967 "Types of deviance and the effectiveness of legal sanctions." Wisconsin Law Review 1967: 703–19.

Christie, Nils, 1977 "Conflicts as property." British Journal of Criminology 17: 1–15.

Cleaver, Eldridge, 1968 Soul on Ice. New York: Dell.

Cloward, Richard A. and Lloyd E. Ohlin, 1960 Delinquency and Opportunity: A Theory of Delinquent Gangs. New York: Free Press.

Cohen, Albert K., 1955 Delinquent Boys: The Culture of the Gang. New York: Free Press.

Cressey, Donald R., 1953 Other People's Money: A Study in the Social Psychology of Embezzlement. Glencoe: Free Press.

Dillon, Richard G., 1980 "Violent conflict in Meta society." American Ethnologist 7: 658–73.

Edgerton, Robert B., 1972 "Violence in East African tribal societies." Pp.159–70 in James F. Short, Jr., and Marvin E. Wolfgang (eds.), Collective Violence. Chicago: Aldine.

Elias, Norbert, [1939] 1978 The Civilizing Process: The Development of Manners. Vol. 1. New York: Urizen Books.

Evans-Pritchard, E. E., 1940 The Nuer: A Description of the Modes of Livelihood and Political Institutes of a Nilotic People London: Oxford University Press.

Fried, Jacob, 1953 "The relation of ideal norms to actual behavior in Tarahumara society." Southwestern Journal of Anthropology 9: 286–95.

Green, Thomas A., 1976 "The jury and the English law of homicide, 1200–1600." Michigan Law Review 74: 413–99.

Greenberg, David F., 1977 "Delinquency and the age structure of society." Contemporary Crises: Crime, Law, Social Policy 1: 189–223.

Gross, Jan T., 1983 "Social control under totalitarianism." Forthcoming in Donald Black (ed.), Toward a General Theory of Social Control. New York: Academic Press.

Hanawalt, Barbara A., 1979 Crime and Conflict in English Communities, 1300–1348. Cambridge: Harvard University Press.

Hasluck, Margaret, 1954 The Unwritten Law in Albania. Cambridge: Cambridge University Press.

Hobbes, Thomas, [1651] 1962 Leviathan: Or the Matter, Form and Power of a Commonwealth Ecclesiastical and Civil. New York: Macmillan.

Hobhouse, L. T., 1906 Morals in Evolution: A Study in Comparative Ethics. New York: Henry Holt.

Hobsbawm, Eric, 1969 Bandits. London: George Weidenfeld & Nicolson.

Hoebel, E. Adamson, 1954 The Law of Primitive Man: A Study in Comparative Legal Dynamics. Cambridge: Harvard University Press.

Hoffmann, Stanley, 1968 International law and the control of force." Pp. 34–66 in Karl Deutsch and Stanley Hoffmann (eds.), The Relevance of International Law. Cambridge: Schenkman.

Horowitz, Ruth and Gary Schwartz, 1974 "Honor, normative ambiguity and gang violence." American Sociological Review 39: 238–51.

Koch, Klaus-Friedrich, 1974 War and Peace in Jalémó: The Management of Conflict in Highland New Guinea. Cambridge: Harvard University Press.

Koch, Klaus-Friedrich and John A. Sodergren (with the collaboration of Susan Campbell), 1976 "Political and psychological correlates of conflict management: a cross-cultural study." Law and Society Review 10: 443–66.

Langness, L. L., 1972 "Violence in the New Guinea highlands." Pp.171–85 in James F. Short, Jr., and Marvin E. Wolfgang (eds.), Collective Violence. Chicago: Aldine.

Le Vine, Robert A., 1969 "Gusii sex offenses: a study in social control." American Anthropologist 61: 965–90.

Llewellyn, Karl N. and E. Adamson Hoebel, 1941 The Cheyenne Way: Conflict and Case Law in Primitive Jurisprudence. Norman: University of Oklahoma Press.

Lundsgaarde, Henry P., 1977 Murder in Space City: A Cultural Analysis of Houston Homicide Patterns. New York: Oxford University Press.

MacCormack, Geoffrey, 1976 "Procedures for the settlement of disputes in 'simple societies.'" The Irish Jurist 11 (new series): 175–88.

Matza, David, 1964 Delinquency and Drift. New York: John Wiley.

Merry, Sally Engle, 1981 Urban Danger: Life in a Neighborhood of Strangers. Philadelphia: Temple University Press.

Middleton, John and David Tait (eds.), [1958] 1970 Tribes without Rulers: Studies in African Segmentary Systems. New York: Humanities Press.

Miller, Walter B., 1958 "Lower class culture as a generating milieu of gang delinquency." Journal of Social Issues 14: 5–19.

Moore, Sally Falk, 1972 "Legal liability and evolutionary interpretation: some aspects of strict liability, self-help and collective responsibility." Pp. 51–107 in Max Gluckman (ed.), The Allocation of Responsibility. Manchester: Manchester University Press.

Nash, June, 1967 "Death as a way of life: the increasing resort to homicide in a Maya Indian community." American Anthropologist 69: 445–70.

Otterbein, Keith F. and Charlotte Swanson Otterbein, 1965 "An eye for an eye, a tooth for a tooth: a cross-cultural study of feuding." American Anthropologist 67: 1470–82.

Pike, Luke Owen, 1873 A History of Crime in England: Illustrating the Changes of the Laws in the Progress of Civilization. Volume 1: From the Roman Invasion to the Accession of Henry VII. London: Smith, Elder.

Pitt-Rivers, Julian, 1966 "Honour and social status." Pp.19–77 in J. G. Peristiany (ed.), Honour and Shame: The Values of Mediterranean Society. Chicago: University of Chicago Press.

Pollock, Frederick and Frederic William Maitland, [1898] 1968 The History of English Law: Before the Time of Edward I, Second edition; first edition, 1895. Cambridge: Cambridge University Press.

Pound, Roscoe, 1921 The Spirit of the Common Law. Boston: Marshall Jones.

Raper, Arthur F, 1933 The Tragedy of Lynching. Chapel Hill: University of North Carolina Press.

Reuter, Peter, 1983 "Social control in illegal markets." Forthcoming in Donald Black (ed.), Toward a General Theory of Social Control. New York: Academic Press.

Rieder, Jonathan, 1983 "The social organization of vengeance." Forthcoming in Donald Black (ed.), Toward a General Theory of Social Control. New York: Academic Press.

Roberts, Simon, 1979 Order and Dispute: An Introduction to Legal Anthropology. New York: Penguin Books.

Rothenberger, John E., 1978 "The social dynamics of dispute settlement in a Sunni Muslim village in Lebanon." Pp. 152-80 in Laura Nader and Harry F. Todd, Jr., (eds.), The Disputing Process—Law in Ten Societies. New York: Columbia University Press.

Schneider, Jane, 1971 "Of vigilance and virgins: honor, shame and access to resources in Mediterranean societies." Ethnology 10: 1–24.

Sutherland, Edwin H. and Donald R. Cressey, 1960 Principles of Criminology. Sixth edition; first edition, 1924. Philadelphia: J. P. Lippincott.

Sweet, Louise E., 1965 "Camel raiding of North Arabian Bedouin: a mechanism of ecological adaptation." American Anthropologist 67: 1132–50.

Sykes, Gresham M. and David Matza, 1957 "Techniques of neutralization: a theory of delinquency." American Sociological Review 22: 664–70.

Thomas-Buckle, Suzann R. and Leonard G. Buckle, 1982 "Doing unto others: disputes and dispute processing in an urban American neighborhood." Pp. 78–90 in Roman Tomasic and Malcolm M. Feeley (eds.), Neighborhood Justice: Assessment of an Emerging Idea. New York: Longman.

Turnbull, Colin M., 1965 Wayward Servants: The Two Worlds of the African Pygmies. Garden City: Natural History Press.

van den Steenhoven, Geert, 1962 Leadership and Law among the Eskimos of the Keewatin District, Northwest Territories. Doctoral dissertation, Faculty of Law, University of Leiden.

Vera Institute of Justice, 1977 Felony Arrests: Their Prosecution and Disposition in New York City's Courts. New York: Vera Institute of Justice.

Weber, Max, [1919] 1958 "Politics as a vocation." Pp. 77–128 in From Max Weber: Essays in Sociology, edited by Hans Gerth and C. Wright Mills. New York: Oxford University Press.

Werthman, Carl, 1969 "Delinquency and moral character." Pp. 613–32 in Donald R. Cressey and David A. Ward (eds.), Delinquency, Crime, and Social Process. New York: Harper & Row.

Wolfgang, Marvin E., [1958] 1966 Patterns in Criminal Homicide. New York: John Wiley.

Yablonsky, Lewis, 1962 The Violent Gang. New York: Macmillan.

Zimbring, Franklin E., 1971 Perspectives on Deterrence. Washington, D.C.: Center for Studies of Crime and Delinquency, National Institute of Mental Health.

❧ ❧ ❧

Questions

1. As used in this article, what is "self-help"?

2. How does self-help keep order in modern U.S. society?

3. How does the U.S. legal system respond to self-help crimes?

4. Cite examples of self-help in your own life.

5. Should self-help crimes be against the law? Why or why not?

Turn-Ons for Money: Interactional Strategies of the Table Dancer

CAROL RAMBO RONAI AND CAROLYN ELLIS

In the past, studies of strippers conceptualized stripping as a deviant behavior. These studies generally focused on accounts of stripping, the impact of culture on stripping, or the ways by which strippers learn strategies and techniques. In this selection, the authors stray from the beaten path. They focus instead on the strategies strippers use to sell "table dances." The authors view this transaction as a dynamic process. They contend that table dancers' strategies mirror negotiation techniques used in mainstream culture and occupations. To gather their data, the authors used in-depth interviews, participant observation, and retrospective and introspective interpretation.

She swayed from side to side above him, her hands on his shoulders, her knee brushing gently against the bulge in his pants. He looked up at the bottom of her breasts, close enough to touch, but subtly forbidden. His breath came in ever shorter gasps.

*T*his is the world of the table dancer—a world where women exchange titillating dances for money. Our study looks at the dynamic processes of interaction that occur in the exchange. Previous studies (Carey et al., 1974; Gonos, 1976; McCaghy and Skipper, 1969, 1972; Salutin, 1971; Skipper and McCaghy, 1970, 1971) have concentrated on "burlesque" or "go-go" dancers, sometimes referring to them more generally as stripteasers. Dancers' interactions with customers were restricted, for the most part, to the stage setting where they danced and received money from customers. Because investigators in these studies occupied positions as

"Turn-Ons for Money: Interactional Strategies of the Table Dancer," by Carol Ronai and Carolyn Ellis, reprinted from *Journal of Contemporary Ethnography*, vol. 18, no. 3, 1989, pp. 271–98.

researchers or researchers as customers, and relied to a large extent on survey and interview techniques, this work led to a static description of this occupation.

Boles and Garbin (1974) have looked at customer-stripper interaction in a setting where strippers sold drinks in addition to performing stage acts. Although they described interaction, they interpreted it in terms of norms, club motif, and customer goals. They found that the conflict between customer's goals and strippers' goals resulted in "counterfeit intimacy" (Foote, 1954), a situation in which an aura of intimacy masked mutually exploitative interactions.

Although counterfeit intimacy is a structural reality in such contexts, this description created another model of behavior that ignored the interactive, dynamic nature of the exchanges and set up in its place stiff caricatures behaving in an unbending, cardboard manner. As actors get caught up in dialogue, they exchange symbols, extract meanings, and modify expectations of what goals they can reasonably expect to reach. Interaction has a tentative quality (Blumer, 1969; Turner, 1962); goals are in a constant state of flux.

The nature of selling and performing table dances that we describe yields more opportunity for interaction between customer and dancer than in previous studies. A table dancer must be a charming and sexy companion, keep the customer interested and turned on, make him feel special, and be a good reader of character and a successful salesperson; at the same time, she must deal with her own negative feelings about the customer or herself, negotiate limits, and then keep him under control to avoid getting fired by management.

Much of the early research literature has described stripping as a deviant occupation. Later, Prus and Irini (1980) looked at stripping as conforming to the norms of a bar subculture. Demystifying this "deviant" activity even further, we show that bargaining strategies in the bar actually mirror "respectable" negotiation in mainstream culture.

We begin by discussing the methods we used to elicit indepth understanding of strategies used by table dancers. After describing the dance club setting, we turn to a description and analysis of particular tactics used on the stage, at the tables between stage acts, and then during the table dances in the pits. Our conclusion analyzes how this exchange reflects buying and selling in service occupations as well as the negotiation of gender relationships in mainstream society.

⊛ Methods

Our study approaches stripping from the point of view of dancers and the dancer as researcher, the people with the most access to the thoughts, feelings, and strategies of exotic dancers. Dancers concentrate on manipulating men as they pursue money in exchange for a turn-on. In order for their strategies to work, they must understand and coordinate them with the games of men.

Our information comes primarily from the experiences of the first author who danced during 1984 and 1985 to pay her way through school. As a "complete-member-researcher" (Adler and Adler, 1987), she conducted opportunistic research (Riemer, 1977), that is, she studied a setting in which she was already a member. She interviewed dancers to find out how and why they began this occupation and kept a journal of events that happened while dancing. Later, she reconstructed, in chronological field notes, a retrospective account of her own dancing history, paying special attention to strategies, emotion work, and identity issues. She used "systematic sociological introspection" (Ellis, forthcoming) to put herself mentally and emotionally back into her experiences and record what she remembered (see Bulmer's, 1982, concept of "retrospective participant observation").

In May 1987, the first author danced in one strip bar for the explicit purpose of gathering data for a master's thesis, chaired by the second author. With approval of bar management, but without the knowledge of other dancers, she acted in the dual capacity of researcher and dancer. This time her primary identity was that of researcher, although as a complete member-researcher she attempted to "become the phenomenon" (Adler and Adler, 1987; Jorgensen, 1989; Mehan and Wood, 1975). When she danced, she took on the identity of a dancer, suffered identity conflicts similar to those she had experienced during earlier dancing, and shared a common set of experiences and feelings with other dancers. She kept field notes of events, which were buttressed by "interactive introspection" (Ellis, 1988), whereas the second author talked her through her experiences, probing at and recording her feelings and thoughts. She conducted informal interviews in the dressing room with dancers and on the floor with customers. Sometimes she revealed her dual role to customers as a strategy to keep them interested in spending more money and to get them to introspect about their own motives for being in the bar.

Because this article is concerned with describing dancers' subtle manipulation strategies that occurred semiprivately, we pulled much of our material from episodes engaged in by the first author, in which process was most easily observed. Because we believe that sociologists should acknowledge the role of their own introspection in their research (Ellis, forthcoming), the first author reveals which of the experiences in the article are hers. Throughout this article, we refer to the first author by her dancer name, Sabrina.

We realize the bias inherent in using introspection primarily from one source. For example, Sabrina, more than most dancers, tended to attract customers interested in mental stimulation as well as physical turn-on. Yet we could not have gained an in-depth understanding of intimate exchange, for example during table dances, in any other way. To understand this bias, we compared Sabrina's strategies and experiences with those of other dancers we observed and other bar participants with whom we talked. Later in 1987, we conducted interviews with four strippers, eight customers, four managers, three bar owners, and a law officer. This article then uses a triangulated method (Denzin, 1978; Webb et al., 1965) to present typical responses from field work and in-depth ones from current and retrospective introspection.

⊛ Setting

An exotic dance club located in the Tampa Bay area of Florida provided the setting for this study. Since liquor was served, full nudity was prohibited by state law. Appearing individually in full costume on stage, each stripper gradually removed her clothing during a dance routine. By the end of the act, the dancer wore pasties that concealed her nipples and panties that covered genitals, pubic hair, and the cheeks of her derriere. Men handed out tips to dancers during performances.

Between acts, dancers strolled around the floor, making themselves available to spend time with customers. They made money if customers bought them drinks. However, the main attraction and source of income in this bar was the table dance. A dancer "sold" dances in a complicated negotiation process through which she convinced the client that he was turned on to her and/or that she was turned on to him. At the same time, she controlled the situation so that she was not caught disobeying "house" rules, many of which corresponded to what county authorities considered illegal.

For example, since "charging" for a table dance was considered soliciting, the dancer, using word games similar to those used by the masseuse studied by Rasmussen and Kuhn (1976), suggested that there was "generally a contribution of $5."

After a dancer successfully sold a dance, she led her customer to one of the two elevated corners of the bar, known generically as the "The Pit," and affectionately nicknamed by customers as "Horny Holler" and "The Passion Pit." Railings and dim lights offered an artificial boundary between this area and the rest of the bar. Clothed in a bralike top and full panties or other revealing costume, the dancer leaned over a seated patron, her legs inside his, and swayed suggestively in rhythm to the music playing in the bar. Theoretically, customers were allowed to touch only the hips, waist, back, and outside of a dancer's legs. Many men tried and some succeeded in doing more. Disobeying rules prohibiting direct sexual stimulation or touching meant more money for dancers, but it also meant risking that management might reprimand them or that a "customer" would turn out to be an undercover officer or a representative looking for infractions on behalf of club management.

❧ Elements Of Strategy

On the Stage

A dancer used symbols that appealed to her audience. At the same time, these symbols distanced her from customers and denoted that the stage was a performance frame (Goffman, 1974; Mullen, 1985). Her appearance, eye contact, manner, and choice of music made up her main expressive equipment.

Having a "centerfold" figure was an obvious asset for dancers. But the best looking woman did not always make the most money. A dancer's presentation of self was also a crucial factor in a customer's decision to tip her. Similar to strippers described by Gonos (1976) and Robboy (1985), women often portrayed exaggerated stereotypes through their clothing style and movement. For instance, a "vamp style" dancer wore suggestive street clothing such as a leather micro-mini skirt, spike-heeled boots, and a halter-style top while strutting around the stage displaying overt sexual mannerisms such as "flushing" (opening her shirt to reveal her pasty-clad breasts). Others had a "gimmick." For example, one woman was an acrobat; another stood on her head while twirling her large breasts. In contrast, a more sensual dancer dressed in sexy bedroom clothing such as a corset and garters or a teddy, and displayed subtle sensual behavior such as slow undulation of the hips.

A dancer chose symbols that drew a certain type of customer to her. Dressing the part of the vamp, for example, reflected an extroverted attitude that attracted customers out to have a good time. Overtly sexual dancers were more likely to perform sexual favors in the bar or meet a man for sex outside the bar. The sensual presentation of self attracted customers who were interested in a "serious," private interaction. Customers interpreted each dancer's symbols as cues to what it might be like to interact with her or, specifically, to have sex with her. For example, Jim, a regular customer, discussed Samantha, a sensual dancer: "She is nothing to look at. God, she's only twenty-six, and we both know she looks like forty. But the way she moves, man! She promises the moon and stars in bed."

Most dancers used eye contact to "feel out" a patron. Managing frequent eye contact while dancing on stage usually meant a tip for the dancer and made a customer feel as if a dancer was specifically interested in him.

A dancer's first close contact with a customer often occurred while accepting a tip. During the exchange, the dancer formed impressions about how the customer was reacting to her, and the customer decided whether he was attracted to the woman. The customer stood at the side of the stage holding currency, which signaled the dancer that he wanted to tip her. The dancer greeted him while accepting the tip in her garter and said "thanks," perhaps giving him a "special" look.

At this point, a dancer might choose from several courses of action, such as "coming on" to a customer, doting on a customer, and using humor. When dancers "came on" to customers, they grinned, wiggled their breasts, spread their legs, struck their buttocks, suggestively sucked their fingers, talked dirty, or French kissed.

Others, such as the sensual dancer, doted on a customer for a few seconds. She caressed his arm, wrapped her arms around his neck, and smiled while he tipped her. If she felt confident of his interest, typical comments she might make were: "I would love a chance to get to know you," or "I look forward to sitting with you," which meant accompanying him to his table after her stage performance.

Humor was an effective and safe tool for generating a good impression while accepting a tip on stage. Customers generally construed a funny statement made by a dancer as friendly and spontaneous. Often it made a nervous client more at ease. Sabrina noted lines she used: "What's a nice guy like you doing in a dump like this?" or "I bet you'd look better up here than I do."

Familiar with the usual "acts" of dancers, such as coming on and showing phony interest, customers were pleased when they thought a woman had "dropped the routine." Often this meant only that she had staged a less frequently displayed one. A dancer had to be careful not to use the same line more than once on the same person, or let a customer overhear it being used on another man. No matter a customer's taste, he wanted a sincere performance.

Dick, a customer who was feeling jilted one evening, commented to Sabrina: "The thing with that chick, Dana, is that she makes a big deal out of you while she is onstage, but if you watch her real close, you notice she looks at everyone who tips her 'that way'." Another customer reported he did not like a dancer in the bar named Tammy because she was insincere: "She frenched me and told me to insert my dollar deeply [in her garter]. Now I ain't stupid. I know a come on like that is a fake."

A dancer's music affected how a customer viewed her. This was reflected in Tim's comment about Jessica: "That girl has a great body, but every time I hear her music [heavy metal] I get the creeps thinking about what she must be like." While most women danced to top-40 music, some used other music to attract a tip from a particular kind of client. Mae, an older dancer in her late thirties, played country music and presented herself as a country woman. Bikers and blue-collar workers were loyal to Mae, expressing sentiments like: "She's the only real woman in the bar."

On the Floor

Offstage, interaction was even more complex. Between stage performances, a dancer circulated among customers and offered her company. Body language, expressions, and general appearance helped define each customer's interest in her and the difficulty of being with him. Once a dancer located an interested customer and introduced herself, or followed up on a contact made while performing on stage, she then had to convince him that he wanted to spend time with her. Ordinarily, her eventual goal was to sell a table dance.

⊛ Choosing a Customer

The ideal customer had a pleasant disposition, was good looking, had time and money to spend, and was sitting at one of the tables on the floor. Most customers did not meet all these criteria. Dancers weighed these features for each customer and also compared them against the circumstances of the evening. Sabrina often asked herself: "What do I want more right now? Money or someone nonthreatening to sit with?" Her answer was different depending upon time of night, how much money she had made already, and how she felt at the moment. Other dancers made the same calculations. For example, three hours before the bar closed one night, Naomi said, "I know this guy I'm sitting with doesn't have a lot of money, but I've made my hundred for the night so I can afford to take it easy." Another time, Vicky said, "God! I know I should be out there hustling instead of drinking with Jim, but I just can't get into it. I guess I'll just get fucked-up and blow it off today." Darcy displayed a more typical attitude, "It's twelve thirty already and I haven't made shit! This guy I'm sitting with better cough it up or I'm taking off." Negotiations with oneself and with the customer were always in process. Throughout the interaction, each participant tried to ascertain what she or he was willing to give and how much could be acquired from the other.

Attractive customers appeared, at first, more appealing. They were pleasant to look at and the dancer could pretend to be on a date while sitting with them. But these men seemed to know they were more desirable than others in the bar and were more likely to bargain with those resources. The end result was that the dancer spent most of the interaction trying to convince the customer to spend money while he tried to persuade her to go out on a date.

When Sabrina was new to the profession, she decided one evening to sit with a good looking, blonde-haired man. She reported the following:

> I started talking to him and eventually led the conversation to the point where I asked, "Would you care for a table dance?"
>
> "Later," he replied.
>
> I continued to make small talk. "Do you come in here often?"
>
> "I stop in once every few months," he responded.

For the next 15 minutes we covered various topics of conversation such as his job and my schooling. Then I asked him again, "Do you want a table dance?"

"Are you going to go to 'le Bistro' with me tomorrow night?"

"I'll think about it," I responded, in hopes of getting a table dance out of him before I turned him down. "Do you want that table dance?"

'Will you go out with me?" he insisted.

"I'm still considering it," I lied.

We volleyed back and forth for 30 minutes. Finally, he told me, "I don't want a dance. I just want to know if you will go out with me."

This customer was aware that Sabrina would not stay with him unless she thought he might want a dance. Both used strategies and gambled time hoping one would give in to the other's goals. Each lost a bet.

Sometimes customers who were old, heavy, unattractive, or otherwise weak in social resources came into the bar. Many women avoided these men, while others, like Sabrina, realized unattractive men were eager for company and tended to treat a dancer better and spend more money than their more attractive competitors would. With the right strategies, dancers could control these men. For example, a dancer might corner a customer into treating her as he would his granddaughter by acting polite and addressing him as "sir." This insinuated that, of course, he would never act inappropriately. Some accepted the role to such an extent that they acted like grandfathers. One man told Scarlet that she was cute, tweaked her cheek, and compared her to his granddaughter.

When scanning the bar and deciding whom to approach first, a dancer tried to find the man who appeared to have the most money. Logically, the better a customer was dressed, the more likely he was to have money. However, he also had a higher probability of already being in the company of another dancer.

Making sure a customer was not spoken for by another dancer was important. It was considered dangerous (one could get into an argument) and rude to sit with another dancer's customer. Some regular customers, for instance, visited the bar to see particular dancers. These customers often turned down another dancer's offer of company by saying they were "waiting for someone." When a dancer entered the bar, she immediately scanned the room, paying particular attention to which women were seated with which customers. If she noticed later that a woman had left a table for a long period of time, she then asked her if it was okay to sit with that customer. This served the dual purpose of following tacit rules (i.e., being polite) and gave the dancer an opportunity to gather information about the customer in question.

Sabrina was warned about a customer in this manner. Upon asking Debbie if she was finished with "the old man in the corner wearing a hat," Debbie replied, "Sure, you can have him. That's 'Merv the perv.' He has lots of money, but he'll want to stick his finger up your asshole for twenty bucks a feel."

A dancer might ignore all other customers to sit with one of her "regulars." When two or more of her regulars were in the bar, she had to juggle them, first sitting with one and then the other. It was difficult to table dance for both of them and still portray "special attachment." Eventually, she had to offer an account (Scott and Lyman, 1968) to one of them. One excuse was to appeal to the principle of fairness: "I really want to be with you, but he came in first and now I have to be with him." Or she might appeal to higher loyalties (Sykes and Matza, 1957), insinuating that the decision was out of her control: "I have to go sit with another customer now. My bosses know I avoid him and they're watching me."

Time in the bar correlated with decreased spending. If a customer had been spending for a while, it was fair to assume that he would run out of money or would soon decide to leave, that is, unless he was intoxicated and freely using a credit card. Dancers in this situation risked having to deal with and control a problematic person who did not remember or pay for the correct number of dances purchased. On the other hand, a dancer might convince a drunk credit card customer to pay for more dances than he actually bought.

A customer's location in the bar indicated his attitude toward female company. In this club, sitting at the bar meant little interest in interacting with dancers. Patrons near the stage wanted to see the show. Being seated at one of the tables in the floor area was conducive to interaction with dancers and to inquiries about table dances.

● At the Tables

Once a customer accepted an offer of company, a dancer sat with him and introduced herself. Her overall goal remained fairly consistent—money with no hassle. Many women also enjoyed the attention they received and got an exhibitionist thrill out of being desired and told how beautiful they were. Others believed the compliments were just part of the game. Some liked the feeling of conquering and being in control. Others felt degraded and out of control.

The customer's manifest goal was impersonal, sexual turn-ons for money; a close examination showed other objectives that shadowboxed with and sometimes transcended this more obvious goal. Although most customers initially focused on the pursuit of sex in or outside the bar, they also came looking for a party, to feel good about themselves, to find a friend or companion, or to develop a relationship. A dancer's strategies varied depending on her personality and her perception of the customer.

Some women said nothing. A customer who wanted passive indifference from an attractive female willing to turn him on liked this approach. Sex, not conversation, was his goal. The dancer did not have to initiate activity nor get to know the customer. Her role was to respond as a sexual nonperson by allowing him to kiss and fondle her body. Verbal interaction potentially endangered the continuance of the exchange.

Most customers wanted a dancer to interact with them. Seduction rhetoric (Rasmussen and Kuhn, 1976) became part of the dancer's sexual foreplay before the table dance as well as a vehicle for the customer to persuade the dancer to see him outside the bar. By talking "dirty" and acting "like a whore"—for example, telling stories about kinky sex in her life outside the bar—a dancer could keep a customer "going," eager to buy the next dance, ready to believe the dancer might have sex with him later.

If a customer wanted a prostitute, he dropped hints such as, "Do you do work on the side?" or "Where does a guy go for a good time around here?" or "Do you date?" Sometimes he propositioned outright: "Will you go to bed with me for a hundred dollars?" The more blatant proposals told the dancer that the customer was not a police officer; all of the requests informed her he had money to spend and opened up the possibility of using strategies to extract it.

One strategy dancers used in this situation was to mislead a customer into thinking she might meet him later if he bought table dances from her now. From the first author:

> Ted bought dances from me two at a time. "After several of these, he asked,
> "Are you going to see me at the Holiday Inn tonight?"

"Why should I?" I responded.

"Because I am new in town and have lots of money."

"I don't go out with strange men," I said.

"Well, why don't you get to know me then," he said. He bought two more dances, then asked, "Do you know me now?" I smiled at him. He continued, "Why don't you meet me after you're done working. What time do you get off?"

In an effort to shift the focus of the conversation, I said suggestively, "When do you get off?"

"I get off on you baby!" He exclaimed. "I'm in room 207. Will you be there?"

To keep him going while not committing myself, I said, "I don't know." We talked a while, and then he asked again. I replied, "I've never turned a trick in my life. I'm not sure I ever will."

"So we won't do it for money," he said. "Come see me tonight." He buys two more dances and we sit down again. I start the conversation first this time to keep him interested yet deter him from bringing up my meeting him. "Tell me, Ted, what is the kinkiest thing you have ever done in bed." This conversation kept us busy for a while, until, sixty dollars later, he asks, "Do I go to the bank machine or not?"

"What do you mean?" I ask.

"If you are going to see me tonight, I need to go to the teller. I'm out of money."

I had a big grin on my face and asked, "Will you be back here after the teller?"

"Probably not," he replied.

"Too bad," I said.

"Would you see me if I bought more dances?" he asked. I was tempted to say maybe, but I thought at this point I was being too obvious.

"Probably not," I said.

He stood to leave. "You show up tonight at room 207 if you want. It was fun."

Similar to the strippers discussed by Prus and Irini (1980), a few women used the bar setting as a place to make contacts for their prostitution careers, while many more had sex occasionally outside the bar to augment their incomes. Before accepting an offer, a woman usually asked other dancers about the customer or spent time getting to know him. Interacting with him then gave her an opportunity to make money table dancing. Most women claimed they had sex "only for the money." A few, such as Sasha, seemed to enjoy sexual contact in and out of the bar. Sasha's enthusiasm—"I'm so horny, I want a cock tonight"—was deemed deviant by the other dancers, who ostracized her—usually avoided her and talked behind her back—for her overt enjoyment.

The customer who wanted a date outside the bar could be handled in a similar manner to the customer looking for a prostitute. Often a dancer conveyed the impression, "if only I knew you were safe" by saying: "You could be Jack-the-Ripper," "You could be a cop," "Its not safe to date everyone you meet in here." Then she suggested interest by saying, "I need a chance to get to know you better." The logical way for a dancer to get to know the customer was for him to spend time and money buying drinks and table dances from her. Lured by the offer of expensive dinners or vacations, and sometimes attracted by a man she liked, most dancers occasionally accepted dates.

If customers were in the bar "to party" (to be entertained) in groups, such as bachelor parties, a dancer wasted no time on interaction. She asked immediately if they wanted a dance. These men interacted mostly with each other, requiring dancers to be lively and entertaining hostesses while treating them like sex objects. Often they commented on her body—her big tits, nice ass, or ugly face—as though she were not there. Party groups purchased dances with the same attitude and frequency as they bought rounds of drinks.

Most men who came to the bar seemed to want to find a friend or companion, or in some other way be treated as a special person. One of Sabrina's customers left the bar twice during an evening to change shirts, just to see if she recognized him when he returned. The best ploy in this situation was for the dancer to put on an honest front, altercasting (Weinstein and Deutschberger, 1963) her customer into the role of being special and "different" from other men.

Most successful dancers were able to hold conversations with these men. Asking his name, where he lived, occupation, and what he did with his spare time provided initial interaction. Finding common ground helped conversation run smoothly. Asking questions at a leisurely pace, making comments, and showing interest both verbally and nonverbally afforded a semblance of credibility to the conversational process. This dialogue helped the dancer to "check out" (Rasmussen and Kuhn, 1976) the customer to make sure he was not a police officer, determine how much money he had to spend and which of her interactional strategies might make him willing to part with it. Giving the customer an opportunity to talk about himself and to demonstrate whatever expertise he had made him feel good about himself. A customer pleased with his presentation of self was more apt to spend money. Sabrina told this story:

> In the field, I had a regular customer, Ray, who was a systems' analyst. I was shopping for a computer at the time, so I enlisted Ray's assistance. Ray had an opportunity to show off his expertise, and feel like he was helping. He turned-on to the contrast of seeing me as intellectual and a sex object.

The best way for a dancer to convince a customer that she found him appealing and unique was to find a likable characteristic about the customer and continually tell him how impressed she was with him and with that trait. For example, some men liked to be praised for their appearance, success, intelligence, sexual desirability, trustworthiness, or sensitivity. The dancer had to convey to him directly that she preferred his company to others in the bar, or indirectly through such statements as "You're not as vulgar as the rest of these guys in here"; "You're more intelligent than most men I meet in here"; "You're not just another one of these assholes," or "I appreciate your spending time with me. When I'm sitting with you I'm safe from those animals out there." The message was that because of his special-ness, she could be "straight" with him, be who she really was, instead of putting on one of her usual acts.

This tactic worked best with customers the dancer liked and enjoyed talking to; otherwise, it was difficult to muster up and maintain the sincer-ity necessary for a believable performance. When this strategy worked, the dancer had close to total control of the interaction. Then the customer tried hard to meet the dancer's expectations, spending money and treating her like a date or friend to avoid disappointing her. If he stopped spending money, the dancer might say, and sometimes mean, "I'll see you later. Don't get angry with me. I know you understand that I have to make money, although I would rather spend time with you. If I don't find anything, I'll come back and visit." Sometimes the customer responded by spending more money to keep the dancer around. If not, he was forced to "understand" her leaving because he and the dancer had an honest relationship and she had been "straight" with him about the nature of her job. This strategy was an effective way to cultivate regular customers.

Sometimes a dancer did not have anything in common with a customer. Over time, most dancers worked up routine questions to keep conversation flowing. Sabrina frequently used lines such as: "What do you look for in a woman?" "Why do you visit strip bars?" "What is your opinion of that dancer over there?" I try," she said, "to get the customer to share something personal with me. I like for him to feel like there is something more solid than a salesperson-customer relationship."

Some regular customers acted as if they were involved in a long-term, serious relationship with a dancer. They bought her expensive gifts such as diamonds, minks, cars, and flowers. These customers seemed to forget the businesslike nature of the bar setting.

Dancers in these interactions appeared involved with the customers. However, most did not take the relationship outside the bar, since this would have cut off a source of income. But they tried to convince the men of their desire to leave the bar scene and be saved by them, even though it was impossible now. Sabrina, for example, had many offers from men who wanted to rescue her from the bar. She developed a routine to solicit this desire from men—it usually meant more money for her in the bar—but that allowed her to reject their proposals without causing anger. She explained:

> I presented myself as attractive and intelligent, but helpless, trapped by circumstances. When they asked me to leave the bar, I told them I had to work to pay for school. When they suggested setting me up in a place of my own, I told them I was independent and wanted to do it on my own. This put them off, but kept them interested and earned their respect.

Mae, a dancer mentioned earlier, seemed to have a knack for cultivating these types of relations. Sabrina describes a discussion with Mae while sharing a ride home.

> Mae had been given a mink coat that night by a customer and she had given it back to him.

> Always intimidated by this woman, I took a moment to get up some nerve and finally asked, "Why did you give back the mink?" "I couldn't hock it for very much, and I won't use it here in Florida. I'd rather get money," she stated.

> "How are you going to get money?" I asked.

"I'll get more money from him by being the type of person who gives this stuff back than if I keep it. I have lots of customers who give me nicer stuff than that mink."

She spoke to the driver, "Hey, do you remember that necklace Tom gave me?"

The driver replied, "It's true, Mae can really get them going. That necklace was a grand, easy."

"Did you keep the necklace?" I asked.

"Hell yes!" she responded.

Mae had a routine that could "really get them going." But she and other dancers, usually the older ones, who used this technique often, took some aspect of the relationship seriously. They saw these men as "options" or possibilities for a life change. On the other hand, they felt this was too good to be true, or were unsure about making the change because of other factors in their lives, such as a husband or children. Keeping the interaction going, yet not allowing it to take place outside the bar, meant they were able to have romance, feel appreciated, and, to some extent, have a relationship while they continued making money in their occupations. However, the occasional relationship that did work out in the bar kept everyone hoping. Sabrina, for example, met her husband there.

☺ Closing the Sale

A dancer rapidly closed a sale on a table dance to a man who wanted sexual favors in the bar. But since these men often violated rules regarding touching and sexual stimulation, some dancers did not feel that they were worth the trouble. For example, one night Annette came into the dressing room and announced, "I just left this old geezer who wanted me to rub him off with my knee. I'm not into it. If someone else wants to, go for it."

The same problems existed after a quick sale to men in the bar for a party. In this situation, a dancer had to concentrate on not acting offended long enough to perform table dances and collect her money. For some dancers, the money was not worth the degradation. As a result, they avoided the bachelor parties.

The customer who wanted to be treated as special took more time. Questioning allowed time for the dancer to convince him that he wanted a table dance from her. It was important that she not appear pushy, yet she needed to determine quickly whether she could make money from this person. Would he buy table dances? Did he want to spend time getting to know a dancer or go directly to a dance? Answers to such questions guided the dancer in constructing her behavior toward the customer.

If a customer purchased a drink for a dancer, she then knew that he was interested enough to spend some time with her. Some customers, however, bought drinks for dancers but refused to purchase table dances, claiming table dances got them "worked up for nothing." If a customer acknowledged that right away, a dancer then had to make a decision about staying or leaving based on the availability of other moneymaking opportunities in the bar. If the action in the club was slow, she might stay with him since she made $1 on every drink he bought for her. Regular customers were always good for a drink: "I'll go sit with Jim today," said Sharon. "At least I know he'll buy me a drink if nothing else." Often a dancer gave the waitress a secret signal indicating that no liquor should be put in her glass. The waitress brought the drink in a special glass, placed a dollar under the dancer's napkin and the drink on top of it.

Most women closed on a dance after the first drink had arrived and it was apparent that the customer liked her. If the customer said no, most dancers left fairly quickly. But in rare cases a customer paid $50–100 for a dancer to sit with him for a while. This guaranteed the dancer money without trouble and bought the customer companionship. Customers who saw themselves in an involved relationship with a dancer generally rejected table dances in favor of company. When these customers bought dances they treated the dancer gently, barely touching her for fear of offending her.

Even when a dancer was not paid for her company, it was not always a good idea for her to leave immediately when a man refused a table dance. As a rare and novel routine, staying made the dancer appear sincere in her interest and less concerned about making money. Sabrina occasionally used this approach:

> "Why are you still sitting here?" the customer asked immediately after he had turned me down for a table dance.
>
> "I'm finishing my drink," I replied.
>
> "Then you are leaving?" he asked.
>
> "Oh, sir, I had no idea you wanted me to go. You must be waiting for someone. Forgive me for being so rude," I said tongue in cheek. I stood to leave.

"Hold it, hold it. Sit back down. I don't necessarily want you to leave. The girls always leave after you say no to a dance. You must be new here. You really should leave when customers say no. You won't make any money this way."

During this exchange he was clutching my arm. He loosened his grip. "Wouldn't that be rude to just up and walk off?" I asked incredulously.

He stares at me a minute, and then smiles. "Lady," he says. "You are a card. I want a table dance." He bought four.

Jn the Þits

Once a customer agreed to a table dance, another set of complex exchanges took place. Although interaction varied with the particular dancer and customer, common routines offered promise of what was to come. Leading the customer to the pit, one acrobatic dancer followed a routine of bending from the waist and peering at her customer from between straight legs. Ascending the stairs to the pit, she performed various kicks and other gestures to demonstrate her flexibility. Another dancer sashayed gracefully in an elegant and poised, yet seductive, manner. Sabrina's style was to talk in a sexy way as she walked: "See that corner. That's my corner. I love to take my men there."

Once in the pit, a woman sat close to the man. Often she put her hand on his leg, draped an arm on his shoulder, or swung a leg over his lap. Some girls necked with their customers, French kissing with a frenzied passion. Other dancers allowed kisses only on the cheek.

If a customer tried to French kiss when a dancer did not want it, she had several "routines" to control him. Leveling a questioning look at the customer and then backing away from him was enough to stop most men. When a client voiced dissatisfaction over the limitation—"What did you do that for?" or "What's your problem? Why are you so cold?"—it usually indicated an aggressive and potentially problematic customer. Sabrina's response to this was, "Imagine if I kissed every guy in the bar like that before I kissed you. Would that be a turn-on for you?" Most customers backed off then with comments such as, "You're absolutely right. I never thought of that before." By their continuous attempts, however, it was apparent that some were being insincere, assuming, like the dancer, that if they moved more slowly, they would get more of what they wanted. But sometimes the restriction reflected positively on the customer's impression of the dancer.

One customer stated to Sabrina after she used this routine: "You have a lot of respect for yourself. I like that."

While some women danced immediately, many waited one or two songs before actually starting a table dance. Sabrina noted that she rarely danced on the first available song because it gave off the impression that she was just interested in making money quickly. She preferred to sit with a customer for a while, talk, drink, and get to know him better. This created a sexual or intimate atmosphere and convinced him that she liked spending time with him. Often this cultivated customers who were likely to buy a greater number of dances, and return to visit her later.

At the beginning of a new song, a dancer might say: "Would you like that table dance now?" or "Let's go for it, baby," depending on the type of interaction in which they were involved. Sexually oriented behavior on the part of the customer called for aggressive behavior from the dancer; less sexually overt actions required more subtle requests.

⊚ Table Dances

Strategy became important during a table dance; close quarters meant a dancer's presentation could be difficult to maintain and a customer hard to control. Normally, a dancer attempted to maintain eye contact with a patron, operating on the premise that it demonstrated interest and that if he had his eyes on her, he wouldn't have his hands on her as much. Sabrina hypothesized that a customer confronting a dancer's eyes was forced to acknowledge her "personhood," and that he then was less likely to violate it. Another impression given off (Goffman, 1959) by the dancer's body language was that the intimate exchange demonstrated by this eye contact might be impinged upon by the customer's groping at her body. Sometimes eye contact was difficult if a customer caused the dancer to laugh or feel disgusted (for example, if he was ugly or panting). In this situation, a dancer could turn away from him and make an impersonal shaking of her derriere part of her dance.

Sexual activity was illegal during table dances, but it sometimes occurred. Customers and dancers acknowledged that "hand jobs," oral sex, and intercourse happened, although infrequently. Once a customer requested that Sabrina wear a long skirt during a table dance so that intercourse could take place unobserved.

More common were body-to-penis friction and masturbation. The most frequent form consisted of the customer sliding down to the end of his seat, spreading his legs, and pulling the dancer in close to him where she could then use her knees discreetly to rub his genitals while she danced. Customers sometimes wore shorts without underwear to allow their genitals to hang out the side, or they unzipped their pants to bare their genitals, or masturbated themselves by hand while watching the dancer.

If a customer insisted on violating rules—putting his fingers inside the dancer's briefs or touching her breasts—a dancer might dance much faster than normal, or sway quickly side to side, to escape the wandering hands. If he was insistent, a dancer might grab his wrists teasingly, but firmly, and say, "No, no," addressing him as if he were a misbehaving child.

These attempts to control the customer could not be too aggressive at the outset, or the customer would be turned off. A subtle game was being played: The customer attempted to get the dancer to go as far as she would, and bend the rules, without antagonizing her so much that she stopped dancing; the dancer attempted to keep him in line, but in such a way that he still wanted to buy dances from her. A particularly good strategy at this point was for the dancer to make it look as if she was interested in what he wanted to do, but, because of management, was unable to oblige him: "Look, this would be fine, but I'm going to get in trouble with management. They're going to catch us if you keep acting like this." This disclaimer (Hewitt and Stokes, 1975) shifted the focus of the patron's annoyance to management and away from her and reasserted the idea that this was a respectable occupation with rules (see Hong et al., 1975).

If a man continued to act inappropriately, the dancer most likely lost her money and the negotiation process broke down. If the customer did not pay after the dance, the dancer had no recourse. Her only power was her seductiveness or ability to persuade the customer subtly that he "owed" it to her. Fights between customers and dancers started occasionally because a man did not want to pay a woman who "didn't give him a good dance." Management quickly squelched these and fired or fined dancers who were involved.

Most dances, however, were successful. After one of these, a dancer might give the customer a reward for "being good." Sabrina reported that she kissed the customer, closed mouthed, on the cheek or on the corner of his mouth. By gently resting her fingers on his chin, tilting up his head, and delivering a kiss, she left the impression, "I'm involved with you. I like you."

After a table dance had been completed, the next goal was to keep the interaction going so that the customer would buy more dances. If a customer continued to hold onto a dancer after the song ended, it usually signaled that he wanted her to dance through the next song. If he let her go, a dancer might look inquisitively at the customer and ask, "Is that all for now? Do you want to continue?" or "Will you want a dance later?" The questions asked depended on the dancer's impression of how involved the customer was with the dance. At the least, she encouraged him to look her up the next time he returned to the bar.

❧ Exchange from the Bottom Up

Interaction in strip bars reflects negotiation in "respectable" society. What is being exchanged—economic resources for sexual titillation, ego gratification, and submission—is viewed in our society as honorable (Lasch, 1977; Lipman-Blumen, 1984; Safilios-Rothschild, 1977). The strategies dancers use to sell their product are similar to those used by sellers in reputable service occupations (Bigus, 1972; Browne, 1973; Davis, 1959; Henslin, 1968; Prus, 1987; Katovich and Diamond, 1986). Unlike many deviant sales (Luckenbill, 1984), dancers and customers normally are protected by a structured, bureaucratic setting with formal rules.

Interaction in a strip club represents negotiation in a buyer's market: sexual turn-on is available for the asking. Although men show some interest in being customers simply by walking through the door, they must be persuaded to "buy" from a certain dancer. To establish control, women use facilitating (Prus, 1987) or cultivating techniques (Bigus, 1972), much like those used by service workers trying to sell a product directly to a client. To acquire customers, a dancer must develop mutual trust. The most important weapon in the arsenal of interaction is to present oneself as sincere: be warm and imply realness, appear spontaneous, give out insider information to show loyalty, accentuate honesty, demonstrate that one is different from others in similar positions, or tell hard-luck stories. At the same time, a dancer must attempt to determine the trustworthiness of her customer: Will he pay for the dance, and will he hassle her later?

Once trust is established, the dancer must promote repeat patronage and customer loyalty (Prus, 1987). This is done by calling on the norm of reciprocity (Gouldner, 1960). The expectation is that the customer will repay friendship, special attention, and favors with money. Thus a hard sell often is not as productive as other more indirect techniques, such as taking personal interest in customers (Prus, 1987), nurturing pseudo friendships, or effecting obligation (Bigus, 1972). Much like any business relationship, the seller must gauge time spent in an encounter to pay-off potential.

Interaction in the bar also reflects power dynamics in mainstream society. As a subordinate group, women in general have responded to men's macromanipulation of societal institutions by using micromanipulation—interpersonal behaviors and practices—to influence the power balance (Lipman-Blumen, 1984). Women in the bar play a game that they know well; in some form, they have been forced to play it for years. They are accustomed to anticipating male behavior, pleasing and charming men, appearing to be what they want, and following their rules. At the same time, dancers are skilled at manipulating to get their own needs met. The bar is a haven for them; they are old hands.

Women who dance for a living have fewer resources or opportunities to manipulate the macrostructure than do most women. Many come from broken homes where fathers often were absent. They frequently had distant relations with parents and left home at an early age. They had sexual experience earlier than other females had. Financial crisis often served as the impetus for starting this occupation. Few have sufficient training or education to make as much money in other occupations (Carey et al., 1974; Skipper and McCaghy, 1971).

Although dancers often have few resources, they are used to taking care of themselves. The occupation of stripping demands that they be tough. It provides them with a context of control. Being the purveyors and gatekeepers of sexuality has always provided powerful control for women (Safilios-Rothschild, 1977); it served this function even more for those women who make sexual turn-on into an occupation.

In male-female relationships, sex is "shrouded in romantic mystique" (Salutin, 1971). It has been okay for women to exchange sex for financial security (Salutin, 1971), as long as they confined the exchange to the context of love and marriage (Safilios-Rothschild, 1977). On this level, the activity in the bar is deviant. There this shroud is removed, revealing the rawness of the exchange, the unequal distribution of macropower, and the often cold, calculating nature of the microstrategies. There, sexuality is carried out in public between people who are often strangers. The dancers use sex as a direct currency of exchange: turn-ons for money. They are not likely to have illusions of love. For them, this is a job. When they are tempted to redefine the situation, their histories with men or the realities of their lives remind them otherwise.

For some dancers then, there is a feeling that they have won the ultimate game in American society, which continues to judge the value of women by their attractiveness and seductiveness (Chernin, 1982). Dancers get validation, attention, and money for displaying these characteristics and argue that they are doing nothing more than most women do, not as much as some.

Yet, this world is not a haven for women. If they could make the same money and have the same freedom in another occupation, most dancers would pursue an alternative to table dancing, but they cannot (Prus and Irini, 1980; Robboy, 1985). Most also have internalized "honorable" exchange, and, without the shroud of romance, outright trading of their bodies sometimes breaks through as degrading (Prus and Irini, 1980; Salutin, 1971; Skipper and McCaghy, 1971). They suffer identity problems as they take on the negative attitudes of mainstream society toward their occupation (Rambo [Ronai], 1987; Skipper and McCaghy, 1970; 1971). Many are disillusioned with males to the point that they characterize their audience as degenerates (McCaghy and Skipper, 1969), yet these same degenerates decide their take-home pay.

The negotiation process we have described then is a case study of exchange between those differentially empowered. As in other occupations in which a person's job requires emotion management, stripping has high emotional costs (Hochschild, 1983). Stripping, as a service occupation, pays well, but costs dearly.

References

Adler, P. A. and P. Adler (1987) Membership Roles in Field Research. Newbury Park, CA: Sage.

Bigus, O. (1972) "The milkman and his customer: a cultivated relationship." Urban Life and Culture 1: 131-165.

Blumer, H. (1969) Symbolic Interactionism: Perspective and Method. Englewood Cliffs, NJ: Prentice-Hall.

Boles, J. and A. P. Garbin (1974) "The strip club and customer-stripper patterns of interaction." Sociology and Social Research 58: 136-144.

Browne, J. (1973) The Used-Car Game: A Sociology of the Bargain. Lexington, MA: Lexington Books.

Bulmer, M. (1982) "When is disguise justified? alternatives to covert participant observations." Qualitative Sociology 5: 251-264.

Carey, S. H., R. A. Peterson, and L. K. Sharpe (1974) "A study of recruitment and socialization in two deviant female occupations." Soc. Symposium 11: 11 -24.

Chernin, K. (1982) The Obsession: Reflections on the Tyranny of Slenderness. New York: Harper Collo9phon.

Davis, F. (1959) "The cab driver and his fare: facets of a fleeting relationship." Amer. J. of Sociology 65:158-165.

Denzin, N. K. (1978) The Research Act. New York: McGraw-Hill.

Ellis, C. (1988) "Keeping emotions in the sociology of emotions." University of South Florida. (unpublished)

Ellis, C. (forthcoming) "Sociological introspection and emotional experience." Symbolic Interaction 13.

Foote, N. N. (1954) "Sex as play." Social Problems 1: 159-163.

Goffman, E. (1959) The Presentation of Self in Everyday Life. Garden City, NY: Doubleday.

Goffman, E. (1974) Frame Analysis: An Essay on the Organization of Experience. Cambridge, MA: Harvard Univ. Press.

Gonos, G. (1976) "Go-Go dancing: a comparative frame analysis." Urban Life 9: 189-219.

Gouldner, A. (1960) "The norm of reciprocity." Amer. Soc. Rev. 25:161-178.

Henslin, J. (1968) "Trust and the cab driver," pp. 138-155 in M. Truzzi (ed.) Sociology and Everyday Life. Englewood Cliffs, NJ: Prentice-Hall.

Hewitt, J. and R. Stokes (1975) "Disclaimers." Amer. Soc. Rev. 40: 1-11.

Hochschild, A. (1983) The Managed Heart: Commercialization of Human Feeling. Berkeley: Univ. of California Press.

Hong. L K., W. Darrough and R. Duff (1975) "The sensuous rip-off: consumer fraud turns blue." Urban Life and Culture 3: 464-470

Jorgensen, D. L. (1989) Participant Observation. Newbury Park, CA: Sage.

Katovich, M. A. and R. L. Diamond (1986) "Selling time: situated transactions in a noninstitutional environment." Soc. Q. 27: 253-271.

Lasch, C. (1977) Haven in a Heartless World. New York: Basic Books.

Lipman-blumen, J. (1984) Gender Roles and Power. Englewood Cliffs, NJ: Prentice-Hall.

Luckenbill, D. F. (1984) "Dynamics of the deviant sale." Deviant Behavior 5:337-353.

McCaghy, C. H. and J. K. Skipper (1969) "Lesbian behavior as an adaptation to the occupation of stripping." Social Problems 17: 262-270.

McCAGHY , C. H. and J. K. Skipper (1972) "Stripping: anatomy of a deviant life style," pp. 362-373 in S. D. Feldman and G. W. Thielbar (eds.) Life Styles: Diversity in American Society. Boston: Little, Brown.

Mehan, H. and H. Wood (1975) The Reality of Ethnomethodology. New York: John Wiley.

Mullen, K. (1985) "The impure performance frame of the public house entertainer." Urban Life 14:181-203.

Prus, R. (1987) "Developing loyalty: fostering purchasing relationships in the marketplace." Urban Life 15: 331-366.

Prus, R. and S. Irini (1980) "Hookers, Rounders, and Desk Clerks: The Social Organization of the Hotel Community." Salem, WI: Sheffield.

Rambo [Ronai], C. (1987) "Negotiation strategies and emotion work of the stripper." University of South Florida. (unpublished)

Rasmussen, P. and L. KUHN (1976) "The new masseuse: play for pay." Urban Life 5: 271-292.

Riemer, J. W. (1977) "Varieties of opportunistic research." Urban Life 5: 467-477.

Robboy, H. (1985) "Emotional labor and sexual exploitation in an occupational role." Presented at the annual meetings of the Mid South Sociological Society, Little Rock, AK.

Safilios-Rothschild, C. (1977) "Love, Sex, and Sex Roles." Englewood Cliffs, NJ: Prentice-Hall.

Salutin, M. (1971) "Stripper morality." Transaction 8: 12-22.

Scott, M. B. and S. M. Lyman (1968) "Accounts." Amer. Soc. Rev. 33:46-62.

Skipper, J. K. and C. H. McCaghy (1970) "Stripteasers: the anatomy and career contingencies of a deviant occupation." Social Problems 17: 391-405.

Skipper, J. K. and C. H. McCaghy (1971) "Stripteasing: a sex oriented occupation," pp. 275-296 in J. Hensfin (ed.) The Sociology of Sex. New York: Appleton Century Crofts.

Sykes, G. and D. Matza (1957) "Techniques of neutralization: a theory of delinquency." Amer. Soc. Rev. 22: 664-670.

Turner, R. (1962) "Role-taking: process versus conformity," pp. 20-40 in A. M. Rose (ed.) Human Behavior and Social Process. Boston: Houghton Mifflin.

Webb, E. J., D. T. Campbell, R. D. Schwarts. and L. Sechrest (1965) Unobtrusive Measures. Chicago: Rand McNally.

Weinstein, Eugene A., and Paul Deutschberger (1963) "Some dimensions of after-casting." Sociometry 26: 454-466.

◉ ◉ ◉

Questions

1. How do table dancers persuade prospective clients to buy table dances?

2. How do table dancers' negotiation strategies compare with negotiation strategies used in "mainstream" transactions?

3. How do the strategies used "at the table," "closing the sell," and "in the pit" compare with one another? Is any stage of the negotiation process more important than the others? Explain your response.

4. How do table dancers' strategies for controlling clients compare with those used by women in mainstream society to negotiate gender relations?

5. Who has more power, the table dancer or the male client? Why?

6. The authors argue that table dancers' strategies and techniques resemble those used in other economic and power exchanges in mainstream society. Do you find their argument convincing? Why or why not?

The Culture of the Corporation and Illegal Behavior

MARSHALL B. CLINARD AND PETER C. YEAGER

Why do some corporations commit deviant and illegal acts? Does the responsibility for such behavior rest solely on senior executives, or do cultural norms and expectations for employees also play a role? In this selection, Marshall Clinard and Peter Yeager examine how corporations and entire industries establish cultural norms and expectations for their employees. According to the authors, these norms and expectations make executives feel pressured into committing deviant, unethical, and illegal behavior.

$\bullet \quad \bullet \quad \bullet$

Although the ethical behavior of a firm is influenced by the economic and political climate, it is also a product of cultural norms operating within a given corporation or even an industry that may be conducive to law violation. In a sense, one may speak of internal cultural factors and external economic factors, which may not be independent but tend to interact to produce violations. For example, Sutherland (1949), although he stressed unethical and illegal cultural factors (differential association), found that "position in the economic structure has great significance in the variations among the corporations as to the number of violations" (p. 259). He argued that differential association with corporate criminal and unethical norms is crucial, yet he also stressed that violations may result when firms face similar economic conditions in an industry. The living code of a corporation "is an ever-shifting pattern of guidelines set by the necessities of the market, the conditions and traditions of the industry, the goals of the corporation, the aspirations of management, and the nature of the executives themselves" (Goodman, 1963, p. 82).

The cultural environment within which the modern American corporation operates may actually encourage or discourage criminal or deviant behavior. Some corporations appear to be more legally ethical in their business operations. In research conducted . . . it was found that approximately 40 percent of the largest U.S. manufacturing corporations were not charged with a law violation by any of the 25 federal agencies during 1975 and 1976 (p. 113). Some of the *Fortune* 500, such as the Digital Equipment Corporation, have a reputation for high ethical standards. (*Wall Street Journal,* October 24, 1977). Many corporations, for example, appear not to have made illegal political contributions to the Nixon campaign or to have been charged with violations connected with foreign payments (p. 171). On the other hand, some corporations have been charged with numerous violations of various types (p. 116).

Corporate norms of doing business may conflict with one or several ethical and legal norms. The interplay among corporate norms of unethical behavior, societal norms, and law violations may run throughout a given corporation and be present in much of the decisionmaking (Clark and Hollinger, 1977). Businessmen are subject to contradictory expectations—a universalistic one (as citizen) and a particularistic one (as businessman)—with the obligation to the firm generally guiding behavior. A corporation that emphasizes profits above business ethics and ignores corporate responsibility to the community, the consumer, or society is likely to have difficulty complying with legal norms. The policies of some corporations can encourage the "criminal tendencies" of particular executives. For example, the persons involved in the electrical price-fixing case of the 1960s found illegal activity "an established way of life" when they began their jobs (Geis, 1973, p. 109).

In this connection, it has been suggested that we should begin our studies of why corporations break the law by learning more about why different corporations, like different political administrations, appear to become permeated with their own particular attitudes and stands in relation to law obedience and good citizenship generally (Stone, 1975, p. 237). Stone has referred to the "culture of a corporation," which is an entire constellation of attitudes and forces, some of which contribute to illegal behavior. Those factors contributing to illegal behavior include

> a desire for profits, expansion, power; desire for security (at corporate as well as individual levels); the fear of failure (particularly in connection with shortcomings in corporate innovativeness); group loyalty identification

(particularly in connection with citizenship violations and the various failures to "come forward" with internal information); feelings of omniscience (in connection with adequate testing); organizational diffusion of responsibility (in connection with the buffering of public criticism); corporate ethnocentrism (in connection with limits in concern for the public's wants and desires). (Stone 1975, p. 236)

In a follow-up of Baumhart's mid-1950s survey of corporate ethics, Brenner and Molander (1977) found that superiors continued to be ranked as the primary influence in unethical decisionmaking. About half of those surveyed in the 1977 study thought that their superiors frequently did not wish to know how results were obtained as long as they achieved the desired outcome: "Respondents frequently complained of superiors' pressure to support incorrect viewpoints, sign false documents, overlook superiors' wrongdoing, and do business with superiors' friends" (p. 60).

Under conditions such as these the use of sanctions to accomplish compliance with law is but one of the various forces operating within a corporation encouraging or opposing violations of law. The success of law enforcement

ultimately depends upon its consistency with and reinforcement from other vectors—the organization's rules for advancement and reward, its customs, conventions, and morals. If the law is too much at odds with these other forces, its threats will make the employees more careful to cover their tracks before it makes them alter their institutionally supportive behavior. (Stone, 1975, p. 67)

Woodmansee, writing in 1975, illustrated what happens when corporate codes of conduct clash with legal norms.

General Electric has been charged with price fixing and other monopoly practices not only for its light bulbs, but for turbines, generators, transformers, motors, relays, radio tubes, heavy metals, and lightning arresters. At least 67 suits have been brought against General Electric by the Antitrust Division of the Justice Department since 1911, and 180 antitrust suits were brought against General Electric by private companies in the early 1960s alone. General Electric's many trips to court hardly seem to have "reformed" the company; in 1962, after 50 years experience with General Electric, even the Justice Department was moved to comment on "General Electric's proclivity for frequent and persistent involvement in antitrust violations." And there have been new suits in the years since 1962. (p. 52)

Lawbreaking can become a normative pattern within a corporation, with or without pressure for profits or from the economic environment. In confidential interviews with a number of board chairmen and chief executive officers of very large corporations, a consensus emerged that the top management, particularly the chief executive officer, sets ethical tone. The president and chief executive officer of a large manufacturing corporation noted that "by example and holding a tight rein a chief executive . . . can set the level of ethical or unethical practices in his organization. This influence can spread throughout the organization." As another high executive pointed out, price fixing or kickbacks must be "congenial to the climate of the corporation." Still another board chairman said, "Some corporations, like those in politics, tolerate corruption."

⊚ Diffusion of Illegal Behavior Within Industries

Corporate wrongdoing sometimes reflects the normative structure of a particular industry. That is, criminal behavior by the corporation and its executives often is the result of the diffusion of illegal practices and policies within the industry (Sutherland, 1949, p. 263). Frequently it is not the corporate organization itself that must be examined but the corporation's place in the industry (Riedel, 1968, p. 94).

In a recent reanalysis of some old data on restraint of trade collected by Sutherland during the 1930s and 1940s for his study of corporate crime, Cressey (1976) found that generally corporations in the same industry have similar rates of recidivism. "For example, neither of the two mail-order houses included in Sutherland's study were repeaters of the restraint of trade offense—Sears Roebuck had no adverse decisions against it, and Montgomery Ward had only one. But all three motion-picture companies had high recidivism rates—Paramount and Warner Brothers each had 21, and Loew's had 22. Two dairy companies, Borden and National Dairy Products, had middle-range rates of 7 and 8" (pp. 216–217). A study of price fixing reported that this offense is more likely to occur when the companies deal with a homogeneous product line (Hay and Kelley, 1974). Relying on his studies of corporate crime in the Federal German Republic, Tiedemann (1974, 1976) concluded that much of this activity is a response to competition in certain industries. For example, 50 percent of all scrap imports in the European Coal and Steel Community were found to be faked: one-third of the subsidized scrap metal was nonexistent. In 1978 almost all Mercedes establishments in Germany, as well as their clients, were charged with having changed the contract dates on motor cars and trucks so that they could get the high subsidies paid by the German government in 1976 in an effort to stimulate the national economy (*Frankfurter Allgemeine Zeitung,* November 17, 1978).

The atmosphere thus becomes one in which participants, as in the Equity Funding case, learn the necessary values, motives, rationalizations, and techniques favorable to particular kinds of crimes. A corporation may socialize its members to normative systems conducive to criminality. The head of the Enforcement Division of the SEC has said: "Our largest corporations have trained some of our brightest young people to be dishonest" (*New York Times Magazine,* September 25, 1976, p. 58). Diffusion of industry practices was evident in the electrical price fixing conspiracy of the 1960s in the manner in which the corporation representatives arranged meetings far from the home offices of the corporation, used code names in meetings of representatives of the corporations, sent mail in plain envelopes rather than business envelopes, used public telephones to avoid wiretaps, and falsified accounts to conceal their meeting places. (Herling, 1962). Although large aircraft manufacturers commonly made foreign payoffs, particularly in Japan, Lockheed is generally believed to have set the pace. As the chairman of the board testified before a Senate subcommittee, "If you are going to win it is necessary." Still, officials of the Northrop Corporation, "which, like Lockheed, made similar payments through a special subsidiary company established in Switzerland to handle the financing," told the subcommittee, Senator Church said, that "*they learned how to do that from Lockheed*" (Shaplen, 1978, p. 54).

The role of industry ethics in law violations is shown in a widespread price conspiracy that resulted in the indictment of 23 carton manufacturing corporations and 50 of their executives in 1976 (United States of America, Plaintiff, v. Alton Box Board Company, et. al., Defendants, Criminal Action No. 76, CR 199, U.S. District Court, Northern District of Illinois, Eastern Division. All references and quotes are from court documents). Included were International Paper Company, Container Corporation of America, Packaging Corporation of America, Weyerhauser, Diamond International Corporation, and Alton Box. American industry and consumers depend enormously on goods packaged in folding cartons, and in terms of corporate annual sales (over $1 billion), number of defendants, duration of the conspiracy (1960 to 1974), and number of transactions involved, this case represents one of the most flagrant violations of the Sherman Antitrust Act in the law's 86-year history. In the indictment the conspirators were charged with the following crimes:

1. Disclosing to other members of the conspiracy the price being charged or to be charged for a particular folding carton to the buyer of that folding carton, with the understanding that the other members of the conspiracy would submit a noncompetitive bid, or no bid, on that folding carton to that buyer.

2. Agreeing with other members of the conspiracy who were supplying the same folding carton to a buyer on the price to be charged to that buyer.

3. Agreeing with other members of the conspiracy on increases in list prices of certain folding cartons.

Shortly after being indicted, all but one of the corporate executives pleaded guilty; later some tried to change their pleas to *nolo contendere*, an effort that was vigorously opposed by the government. According to the government statement,

These defendants were not engaged in a short-term violation based on sudden market pressures; price-fixing was their way of doing business. The participants demonstrated a knowing, blatant disregard for antitrust laws. One grand jury witness testified that during a six-year period he personally engaged in thousands of price-fixing transactions with competitors which were illegal.[1] This illegal conduct was carried on in all parts of the country by all management levels in the billion-dollar folding-carton industry. The thousands upon thousands of exchanges of prices with competitors, the dozens upon dozens of meetings with competitors were done with a single purpose and design—to eliminate price competition in this industry. (Government's Statement of Reasons and Authorities in Opposition to Defendants' Motions to Plead *Nolo Contendere, United States v. Alton Box Board Company*, Criminal Action No. 76 CR 199 [May 7, 1976] at 10–11)

One executive of a large corporation stated: "The meetings and exchange of price information were well known to the senior management and in the industry as a whole." Another stated: "Meetings of competitors were a way of life in the folding carton industry."

Community standards can also encourage wrongdoing in an industry. Some businessmen may be able to justify illicit behavior if they see it as conforming to community norms (Chibnall and Saunders, 1977). Discussing the variations in obedience to laws by a group of manufacturing companies within the shoe industry, Lane (1953) concluded that "the [community's] attitude toward the law, government, and the morality of illegality" (p. 160) is highly influential. Even though the companies he studied were in the same industry and were subject to the same laws, variation in law disobedience was great. In Haverhill, Massachusetts, 7 percent of the companies were in violation, while in Auburn, Maine, 44 percent were. Lane concluded that such differences might be explained by the home community's attitudes about the importance of law and government and its tolerance of illegal behavior.

❧ The Executive in the Corporation: The Making of a Corporate Criminal

In their well-known analysis of large-scale organization, March and Simon (1958) developed a theory to explain how employees can be induced to make decisions that are correct from the standpoint of an organization such as a corporation. Basically, they claimed that the organization's elite controls the premises of decisionmaking for subordinates by setting priorities and regulating the flow of communication; thus, top officials manipulate subordinates' assessments of situations in a system of unobtrusive control (cf. Perrow, 1972, pp. 152–157).

In his discussion of the nature of corporations, Drucker (1972, p. 40) affirmed that a natural tendency exists in every large-scale organization to discourage initiative and encourage conformity. A primary means of fostering conformity in corporations is through the training of persons who are likely to hold positions of responsibility. Studies have been made in detail of how corporations lead new managers through an initiation period designed to weaken their ties with external groups, including their own families, and encourage a feeling of dependence on and attachment to the corporation (Madden, 1977; Margolis, 1979). Outside connections are reduced, and a club mentality is bred through overwork, frequent transfers, which inhibit attachment to local communities, and provisions for recreational and educational needs during leisure time. Co-workers and higher-ups become "significant others" in the individual's work and social life. "Briefly, this all suggests that organization members can be socialized to accept the goal structure of the organization" (Meier, 1975, p. 10). After interviews with corporate executives, Margolis (1979) concluded that executive transfers to other communities play a key role in the psychological initiation of managers. By last-minute assignments and out-of-town work the priority of the corporation is established. Not surprisingly, recruiters of top executives claim that corporations tend to hire "our kind of person" in terms of managerial style and family commitments, which might interfere with corporate responsibilities, "physical appearance, and personal habits" (*Wall Street Journal,* September 19, 1979). In an advertisement in the *Wall Street Journal* (September 20, 1979), the president of Solfan Corporation bluntly noted: "The job of personnel director at our company is not for everyone. I know because this year I have already had two men in this position. It wasn't for them. If your family or your 'lifestyle' or your kid's boy scout experience is more important to you than your job, then this isn't for you."

Ability to socialize employees so thoroughly into the corporate world insures one of the main characteristics of bureaucratic organizations described by Max Weber: "The very nature of a bureaucracy, as Weber so well demonstrated, is to make the *individual dispensable*" (Stone, 1975, p. 65). In this sense, the corporation is constructed not of persons but of roles and positions that it has created and defined and therefore over which it has control. This permits individual movement into and out of the corporation without a disruption of activity; the only function of persons is to carry out the activities that belong to those positions they hold (Coleman, 1978, p. 26).

The end product in many cases is what has been called a "functionary" in other contexts, "a new kind of man who in his role of serving the organization is morally unbounded. . . . His ethic is the ethic of the good soldier: take the order, do the job" (Howton, 1969, pp. 5–6). Given the outcomes desired at the higher levels, generally the employee neither questions these ends nor his use of the most efficient or quickest means of achieving them. In his examination of the electrical price-fixing conspiracy, Cook (1966) discussed at length the mentality of the organizational man that encouraged illegal behavior throughout the entire industry: "They were men who surrendered their own individualities to the corporate gods they served. Though they knew that their acts were illegal, not to say unethical, though the shady maneuvering at times affronted their sense of decency, not one found it possible to pronounce an unequivocal 'no'" (p. 38). Similarly, in a case involving the side effects of an anticholesterol drug HE/14 several pharmaceutical corporation executives were convicted of lying about animal studies testing the drug's effects: "No one involved expressed any strong repugnance or even opposition to selling the unsafe drug. Rather they all seemed to drift into the activity without thinking a great deal about it" (Carey, 1978, p. 384).

In his study of the electrical industry price-fixing conspiracy, Geis (1967) discussed a theme common to many studies of individuals involved in corporate crime. That is, the individual has been trained in the illegal behavior as a part of his occupational role. Schrager and Short (1978) believe that individual personality becomes unimportant; criminal behavior stemmed more from the roles they were expected to fulfill than from individual pathology (p. 410).

Some of the testimony in the folding carton price conspiracy specifically indicated how an individual executive learns to use price fixing as an accepted business practice in the industry. One corporate executive said: "Each was introduced to price-fixing practices by his superiors as he came to that point in his career when he had price-fixing responsibility." Another testified as follows:

Q.: Mr. DeFazia, how were you informed that discussing prices was part of your job?

A.: I don't think I was ever really told it was part of my job. I think it was just something I sort of worked right into. That was Mr. Cox's responsibility back in those years. I was young, I was still a green kid, I just picked it right up from working along with him.

Q.: Mr. Cox provided guidance to you? Kind of discussed?

A.: No. We worked in the same office. I guess you just pick it up. I don't know how you would want to say it, just like learning your ABC's, you hear it repeated so often that it's just part of your daily activity.

Lockheed's special review committee established to investigate foreign and domestic illegal payments and practices reported to the SEC in 1976 that senior corporate management was responsible for this strategy. Accountants as well as other employees, however, were aware of the devious methods used in securing, recording, and transferring money to foreign sources for bribes: "Employees learned not to question deviations from standard operating procedures and practices. Moreover, the Committee was told by several witnesses that employees who questioned foreign marketing practices damaged their claims for career advancement." A similar committee for the 3M Company reported to the SEC in 1976: "We felt that employees should have asked more questions and should have challenged their supervisors more, but realistically, the internal control systems did not provide a means or an atmosphere for challenges to executives at the level of president, chairman of the board, and chief executive officer" (p. 31). And yet another review committee, this time of J. Ray McDermott and Co., in a 1977 report to the SEC, stated that the corporation (extracts)

> has retained the atmosphere of a privately held company. Employees from senior management on down have taken the position that "the boss's word is law." The critical issue, even in questionable payments, was whether the boss was aware and approved the transaction. . . . Employees who balked at orders from the boss were likely to be fired (p. 6).

Pressures often exist at all levels of the corporation to promote attitudes and behaviors conducive to corporate goals regardless of means. At the lower and middle levels, the corporate actors are encouraged to develop a short-term perspective that "leads them to believe the future is now," thereby producing an overemphasis on corporate objectives and short-run advantages (Madden, 1977, p. 60). Some characterize this process in terms of a great moral struggle between the individual and the "massed corporate hierarchy"—"a man can be crushed and beaten and forced into actions against which his ethical sense rebels" by a hierarchy "supreme in its power and a law unto itself" (Cook, 1966, p. 72). It is far more likely, however, that this process is subtle, and the individual, in the course of his work, gradually comes to identify with the main goals and ideology of the corporation: "If operative goals take on qualities of normative requirements for organizational behavior, and if these norms conflict with those of the legal order, then corporate crime may be indigenous to organizational processes" (Meier, 1975, p. 10).

It would be a mistake to imagine a scenario in which the corporation's directors or highest officers generate these pressures for the lower levels without being affected themselves. Like other social organizations, corporations have inherent socialization pressures that are passed on through the generations. Corporate executives assume roles into which they are duly socialized by the structure and nature of work and the status system, as are lower level employees. Socialization is therefore structural and cultural.

Executives are subject, in fact, to the same kinds of indoctrination into the corporate mind as are employees at lower levels—through their associations with others who play similar roles, through their training and education, and through their isolation from potentially countervailing influences (Henning, 1973, p. 158). Drucker (1972) noted that executives' contacts outside business tend to be restricted to persons of similar background if not those who work for the same organization. And the very insistence upon loyalty and the restriction of competing interests characteristic of the army is typical of corporations: "Hence executive life not only breeds a parochialism of the imagination comparable to the 'military mind' but places a considerable premium on it" (p. 81).

One does not have to picture a corporation composed of automatons marching to the same beat in order to understand how individuals as corporate actors could participate in activities that they might never consider outside the corporate environment.[2] Motivations besides the ones discussed here range from altruistic loyalty to the corporate good to outright self-interest. Many involved in illegal corporate activities regard their acquiescence and active participation as necessary in order to keep their jobs, although they may have no illusions about the illegal and immoral nature of their behavior. A former high-ranking General Motors executive, John Z. DeLorean, contended, for example, that the company knew about the safety problems of the Corvair before production began but failed to take remedial action: "Claims DeLorean: 'Charlie Chayne, vice president of engineering, along with his staff, took a very strong stand against the Corvair as an unsafe car long before it went on sale in 1959. He was not listened to but instead told in effect: "You're not a member of the team. Shut up, or go looking for another job"'" (*Time,* November 19, 1979, p. 85). The decisionmakers were "not immoral men," said DeLorean, but he claimed that they were operating in a business atmosphere in which all was reduced to costs, atmosphere in which approval was given to a product that the individuals acting alone would not have considered approving (Wright, 1979).

*E*xecutives' *R*ationalizations

A variety of justifications are available to those executives who are confronted with doubt or guilt about illegal or unethical behavior; these justifications allow them to neutralize the negative connotations of their behavior. In an examination of a famous case of business corruption and bribery in England, Chibnall and Saunders (1977) pointed out that an individual can fully understand the illegal nature of his actions but can justify them by citing the pervasiveness of such practices in the business world. There is considerable evidence that business executives believe that unethical practices are common. A *Harvard Business Review* survey found that four out of five executives maintained that at least some generally accepted practices in their industries were unethical, and when asked whether they thought that other executives would violate a code of ethics if they knew they would not be caught, four out of seven replied affirmatively (Baumhart, 1961). Studies made in 1976 by Uniroyal and a University of Georgia professor found that 70 percent of Uniroyal managers and 64 percent of a random sample of corporate managers perceived company pressure on personal ethics. "Most managers believed that their peers would not refuse orders to market off-standard and possibly dangerous products (although an even larger majority insisted they would personally reject such orders), and a majority thought young managers automatically go along with superiors to show loyalty" (Madden, 1977, p. 66). Confidential interviews with top officials, usually chief executive officers, of 57 of the largest U.S. corporations in 1975 indicated that they felt unethical behavior was widespread in industry and, for the most part, had to be accepted as part of daily business (Silk and Vogel, 1976). Business results and the survival of the corporation inevitably came before personal ethics: "If we wait until all businessmen are ethical before we start our sales job, we will never get started" (p. 228). Moreover, there was great reluctance to criticize other businessmen for illegal actions. Finally, the behavior was legitimized through the good intentions of the actors and through its consequences; that is, no one was actually harmed, the firm benefited, and customer needs were served.

The issue of morals and corporate conduct became a topic of discussion in 1979 when it was reported that a Harvard Business School professor, in his business decisionmaking course, trained students to misrepresent their positions in negotiations and other business dealings (*Wall Street Journal,* January 15, 1979). Students found that hiding certain facts, bluffing, and even outright lying got them a better deal and, in part, a better grade. The course was designed to teach budding businessmen to negotiate in the "real world," in which "lying"—or "strategic misrepresentation"—is resorted to in some cases. As the article in the *Wall Street Journal* commented, "It's a safe bet that in the course students will eventually get to practice what they learn." (According to surveys by the school, 14 percent of its alumni are presidents or chief executive officers of their firms, and 19 percent of the top three officers of all *Fortune* 500 companies are Harvard Business School graduates.)

● *C*orporate *D*efenses for *L*aw *V*iolations

The diverse defenses continually offered by corporations, their executives and counsel, business organizations, and trade and other journals, particularly the editorials in the prestigious *Wall Street Journal*, to explain corporate violations of law serve to justify illegal activity in a society that professes law obedience to be one of its highest ideals. In so rationalizing their behavior, however, corporations follow a general tendency in our society to obey laws selectively, that is, according to one's situational needs as determined by such factors as social class and occupation. Many businessmen, for example, firmly believe, and act accordingly, that the laws regulating securities and banking procedures, trade, labor arrangements, and environmental pollution are not as formally binding on individual decisionmakers as are burglary and robbery laws.

To a certain degree corporate executives are insulated from persons who might disagree with their beliefs (Sutherland, 1949, p. 247). As we have seen, they tend to associate almost exclusively with persons who are pro-business, politically conservative, and generally opposed to government regulation. Many of the beliefs held within the corporate world about laws and government are nourished in a climate in which there is a lack of consensus about the values society is trying to advance. On the one hand, people do not want to deplete natural resources too rapidly or to pollute the air, land, and water, but on the other, they want abundant consumer goods at the lowest possible prices. The question also arises as to how much future generations must be considered in planning the use of our natural resources: "Problems of this sort exist everywhere we look. Consider a drug that can benefit 99 percent of people who suffer from a disease but seriously injures 1 percent. Should it be banned from the market?" (Stone, 1975, p. 97).

Some maintain that laws affecting corporations often fail because the public does not regard the behavior to be regulated as "morally reprehensible" (Kadish, 1963, p. 436). Moreover, numerous beliefs of the corporate world help to neutralize government efforts to deter or to prevent violations and thus reduce the effectiveness of legal sanctions applied to corporations and their executives. It would of course be unfair to presume that everyone in top corporate management accepts these beliefs without question, but some were widely expressed by top executives of the largest corporations in confidential interviews done by Silk and Vogel (1976). From various sources the following beliefs have been identified as most significant;[3] in general, however, they lack validity or they are greatly exaggerated.

1. *All legal measures proposed constitute government interference with the free enterprise system.* Since we have had 200 years of prosperity under a capitalist system, the argument goes, we should not interfere with the system. This argument obviously disregards consumer protection, the protection of the environment, and the protection of free competition afforded by antitrust laws. In this connection one might mention Ralph Nader's often-quoted reply as a witness during a congressional hearing. When a senator insisted that Nader's criticism of the auto industry failed to recognize the industry's contribution to American society, he responded, "Do you give credit to a burglar because he doesn't burglarize 99 percent of the time?" (Geis, 1973, p. 183).

2. *Government regulations are unjustified because the additional costs of regulations and bureaucratic procedures cut heavily into profits.* This represents an effort to condemn the condemners by expressing contempt for government interference and law enforcement staffs. Compliance with federal regulations such as those of the Environmental Protection Agency (EPA), the Consumer Product Safety Commission (CPSC), and the Occupational Safety and Health Administration (OSHA) has been estimated to cost nearly $103 billion. (*Wall Street Journal,* December 1, 1978). As a result, it has been estimated, business must invest $10 billion in new capital spending each year merely to meet these regulations. According to Dow Chemical, compliance with federal regulations cost the company $147 million in 1975 and, a year later, $186 million, an increase of 27 percent. Dow reported that costs of federal regulations for 1976 constituted 50 percent of after-tax profits and 6 percent of sales. Many corporate cost estimates for compliance have been challenged as highly exaggerated. The National Association of Automobile Dealers publicly stated in 1979 that adoption of the proposed FTC rule requiring inspection and stricter disclosure of the condition of used cars would raise prices by hundreds of dollars. Yet research conducted under the

auspices of the Center for Public Representation for the congressional hearings indicated that a similar Wisconsin law increased the prices of automobiles by no more than $15, even adjusting for inflation (private conversations with Professor Gerald Thain, University of Wisconsin Law School). In fact, the differences between what corporations report as excessive regulatory costs to government agencies such as the EPA and the less glowing story, or none at all, that they report to their shareholders and the SEC became a subject of congressional interest and of Ralph Nader's Public Citizen group in 1980 (*Wall Street Journal,* May 6, 1980). According to the *Wall Street Journal* article, officials of the EPA and OSHA planned "to take a closer look at SEC filings so that they can assess more critically the cost estimates filed with their agency."

3. *Regulation is faulty because most government regulations are incomprehensible and too complex.* In addition, according to this argument, regulations are so numerous that no corporation could be well informed on all of them; for example, the steel industry is controlled by some 5,600 regulations involving 27 different federal agencies (Madden, 1977, p. 52). Even though they have existed for nearly a century,

> antitrust laws are seen as inconsistent, hypocritical, poorly defined, and rarely enforced. Although the interpretation of these laws is constantly evolving, many businessmen who violate the law are aware that they are taking a risk when they engage in certain actions. They test the limits of the law and try to keep "just inside an imaginary boundary thought to separate the condoned from the condemned." Price-fixing is a clear violation of the law which is regularly prosecuted by the Department of Justice's Antitrust Division, but even businessmen who are charged with this crime often claim that the law is excessively vague. (Conklin, 1977, p. 92)

Most regulations must be written in detail, however, in order to cover as many contingencies as possible; otherwise, they could not be enforced and they would not hold up in the courts. In any event, large corporations generally employ adequate legal counsel to interpret government regulations.

4. *Regulation is unnecessary because the matters being regulated are unimportant.* OSHA regulations have been a favorite subject for such attacks in recent years. The chairman of United States Steel, in an address on February 7, 1977, spoke about OSHA regulations that had just gone into effect.

These new requirements run from the ridiculous to the extreme. For example, the performance standard says that no employee can be exposed to more than 0.15 milligrams of particulates per cubic meter of air during an eight-hour period. And that 0.15 milligrams is roughly equivalent to an ounce of material dispersed in an air space twenty feet high and three football fields long. Other requirements call for collecting air samples at every coke battery—perhaps a minimum of 600 samples a month at our Clairton Works and 14,000 a year across our entire company . . . providing annual and semi-annual physical examinations for coke oven employees . . . supplying work clothes and laundering them every week . . . making employees take a shower before they go home . . . forbidding them from eating or using tobacco on the job . . . and like mothers of old, requiring them to wash their hands and faces before they eat their lunch. (Madden, 1977, pp. 52–53)

Although it is true that some rules may be overzealous, as also happens within a corporation itself, it is unreasonable to include in this category the vast majority of laws that regulate trusts, advertising, environmental pollution, taxes, and other important areas of corporate behavior. Syndicated economic columnist Sylvia Porter wrote in 1979, for example, that corporations in virtually all sectors of the economy are "fiercely defending" arrangements that keep prices high and restrain trade. She cited the following activities.

Prescription drug companies are in a last-ditch fight to preserve state laws that prevent pharmacists from selling lower-priced generic drugs instead of more expensive brand-name equivalents. The Federal Trade Commission along with the Department of Health, Education and Welfare are drawing up a model state law to encourage feasible drug substitution. Potential consumer savings: an estimated $70 million a year.

Industries ranging from blue jeans manufacturers to makers of footwear and audio components have been charged with fixing retail prices through a variety of means. The FTC, for instance, recently sued and obtained a consent order against Levi Strauss. The day the agency sued, Levi's were selling for $15–$17. Today, in many areas of the U.S., they sell for $10–$14. (*Wisconsin State Journal*, February 4, 1979)

5. *There is little deliberate intent in corporate violations: many of them are errors of omission rather than commission, and many are mistakes.* There is some truth to this claim but ample evidence has also been cited of highly concealed

conspiracies in many antitrust cases and clear intent to violate in domestic and foreign illegal payments, as is the case with many other corporate violations.

6. *Other concerns in the same line of business are violating the law, and if the government cannot prevent this situation there is no reason why competing corporations should not also benefit from illegal behavior.* Obviously, the government lacks the resources to prosecute all violators; it must be selective. The general belief among businessmen that the "other fellow" is regularly violating the law with relative impunity does constitute a major support to those who do violate. A 1961 Harvard Business Review survey found that this belief was extraordinarily widespread (Baumhart, 1961).

7. *Although it is true, as in price-fixing cases, for example, that some corporate violations involve millions of dollars, the damage is so diffused among a large number of consumers that individually there is little loss.* In this sense corporate violations are not like ordinary crimes, but price fixing is theft regardless of what it is called. C. Wright Mills (1956) once wrote that "it is better, so the image runs, to take one dime from each of ten million people at the point of a corporation than $100,000 from each of ten banks at the point of a gun" (p. 95); Mills added that it is also safer. Geis (1973, p. 183) explained that although corporate crime is serious, it is less infuriating as well as less frightening to be victimized a little bit at a time over a long period than to be victimized all at once.

8. *If there is no increase in corporate profits a violation is not wrong.* According to this view, some corporate violations do not necessarily result in an increase in profit; in fact, some simply are efforts to prevent profit loss. The plumbing industry price-fixing conspirators used this argument as a defense. This defense views violations in terms of a corporation's right to exercise selective obedience to law. Actually, many violations do result in increased profits, and violations are often for this purpose.

9. *Corporations are actually owned by the average citizen so that the claims that big business can dominate American society and violate the law with impunity are false.* It is a fact that stock ownership of most corporations is widely dispersed. In 1970, for example, some 31 million persons owned some stock: the ownership of stocks, however, and therefore of corporations, is

heavily concentrated in a small group of institutions such as banks, insurance companies, and universities, and individuals. A few large corporations are principally owned by families like the DuPonts, Mellons, Rockefellers, Fords, Dukes, and Firestones. Moreover, as has been previously indicated, control of corporate activities remains largely in the hands of management, not stockholders.

10. *Violations are caused by economic necessity: they aim to protect the value of stock, to insure an adequate return for stockholders, and to protect the job security of employees by insuring the financial stability of the corporation.* This argument again represents the belief that laws can be selectively obeyed with impunity.

Sometimes indicted corporations will submit multiple defenses for their actions. In the folding carton price conspiracy, numerous arguments were presented to the court by various corporations for the reduction of their penalties. Among them were: (1) abysmal losses were jeopardizing the folding carton industry generally, and some corporations particularly; (2) a given corporation does not play a serious economic part in total industry sales; (3) some corporations had no record of antitrust cases brought against them; (4) corporate management had changed since the violations had occurred; and (5) a new antitrust compliance program was in effect and determined efforts were being made to follow it. But, as the government contended, "Neither ruinous competition, competitive evils, nor good intentions or motives of the parties constitute any legal excuse for such agreement. . . . Profitability is irrelevant to the determination of guilt or innocence in a price-fixing case."

We have seen how both the internal and external environments of the corporation often facilitate the use of illegal behavior. The culture of the corporation is also likely to furnish a set of facilitating beliefs or rationale—either in defense of deviant acts or as charges against the propriety of government regulation. Clearly, however, the corporate record does not warrant placing the onus for illegal and unethical behavior on the laws. In view of the tremendous potential for harm carried by these massive, complex organizations, special measures of social control are necessary. . . .

Endnotes

[1]Illegal telephone calls between corporate executives were frequent. As one conspirator put it concerning price increases of cartons sold to the frozen food industry, "If there was a need for an increase he would call the others, see if [the] . . .

percentage increase that he proposed was acceptable to them and if it was, then all the companies would move in the general area of the same percentage."

[2]"Some may even find covert activity exciting, as noted in the case of Equity Funding. In this environment of fun, excitement, and do-as-you're-told corporate loyalty, the law's threats are simply no guarantee that people are going to comply. Indeed, what is worse, I have a strong suspicion—shared by others who have represented corporate clients in their tangled affairs—that being on the edge of the law can even lend a tingle of 007 intrigue to the life of middle-level corporate operatives" (Stone, 1975, p. 69).

[3]Some of these beliefs are from Silk and Vogel and some are from business journal editorials and statements of business executives; others were expressed in interviews with government enforcement officials questioned about the explanations given by corporate counsels and others for a corporation's law violations. Irving Kristol (1978), an influential contributor to the *Wall Street Journal*, offered several of these defenses of corporate behavior, although, in fairness, he at times somewhat tempered them.

References

Baumhart, Raymond C. (1961). "How Ethical Are Businessmen?" *Harvard Business Review* 39 (July–August):5–176.

Brenner, S. N., and E. A. Molander (1977). "Is the Ethics of Business Changing?" *Harvard Business Review* 55(January–February):59–70.

Carey, James T. (1978). *Introduction to Criminology.* Englewood Cliffs: Prentice-Hall.

Chibnall, S., and P. Saunders (1977). "Worlds Apart: Notes on the Social Reality of Corruption." *British Journal of Sociology* 28(June):138–153.

Clark, John P., and Richard Hollinger (1977). "On the Feasibility of Empirical Studies of White-Collar Crime," in Robert F. Meier (ed.), *Theory in Criminology: Contemporary Views.* Beverly Hills: Sage.

Conklin, John E. (1977). *Illegal but Not Criminal: Business Crime in America.* Englewood Cliffs: Prentice-Hall.

Cook, Fred J. (1966). *The Corrupted Land: The Social Morality of Modern America.* New York: Macmillan.

Cressey, Donald R. (1976). "Restraint of Trade, Recidivism, and Delinquent Neighborhoods." In James F. Short, Jr. (ed.), *Delinquency, Crime, and Society.* Chicago: University of Chicago Press.

Drucker, Peter F. (1972). *Concept of the Corporation.* Revised edition. New York: Mentor.

Geis, Gilbert (1967). "White Collar Crime: The Heavy Electrical Equipment Antitrust Cases of 1961." In Marshall B. Clinard and Richard Quinney (eds.), *Criminal Behavior Systems: A Typology*. New York: Holt, Rinehart & Winston.

_____. (1973). " Deterring Corporate Crime." In Ralph Nader and Mark J. Green (eds.), *Corporate Power in America*. New York: Grossman.

Goodman, Walter (1963). *All Honorable Men: Corruption and Compromise in American Life*. Boston: Little, Brown.

Hay, George, and Daniel Kelley (1974). "An Empirical Survey of Price-fixing Conspiracies." *Journal of Law and Economics* 17(April):13–39.

Henning, Joel F. (1973). "Corporate Social Responsibility: Shell Game for the Seventies?" In Ralph Nader and Mark J. Green (eds.), *Corporate Power in America*. New York: Grossman.

Herling, John (1962). *The Great Price Conspiracy: The Story of the Antitrust Violations in the Electrical Industry*. Washington, D.C.: Luce.

Howton, F. W. (1%9). *Functionaries*. Chicago: Quadrangle.

Kadish, Sanford H. (1963). "Some Observations on the Use of Criminal Sanctions in Enforcing Economic Regulations." *University of Chicago Law Review* 30(Spring):423–449.

Lane, Robert E. (1953). "Why Businessmen Violate the Law." *Journal of Criminal Law, Criminology, and Police Science* 44(July):151–165. Reprinted in Gilbert Geis and Robert F. Meier (eds.), *White-collar Crime: Offenses in Business, Politics, and the Professions*. Revised edition. New York: Free Press.

Madden, Carl (1977). "Forces which Influence Ethical Behavior." In Clarence Walton (ed.), *The Ethics of Corporate Conduct*. Englewood Cliffs: Prentice-Hall.

March, J., and H. Simon (1958). *Organizations*. New York: Wiley.

Margolis, D. R. (1979). *The Managers: Corporate Life in America*. New York: Morrow.

Meier, Robert F. (1975). "Corporate Crime as Organizational Behavior." Address presented at the American Society of Criminology meeting, November.

Mills, C. Wright (1956). *The Power Elite*. New York: Oxford University Press.

Perrow, Charles (1972). *Complex Organizations: A Critical Essay*. Chicago: Scott, Foresman.

Riedel, Marc (1968). "Corporate Crime and Interfirm Organization: A Study of Penalized Sherman Act Violations." *Graduate Sociology Club Journal* 8:74–97.

Schrager, Laura S., and James R. Short, Jr. (1978). "Toward a Sociology of Organizational Crime." *Social Problems* 25(No. 4):407–419.

Shaplen, Robert (1978). "Annals of Crime: The Lockheed Incident." *New Yorker* (January 23):48–74, (January 30):78–91.

Silk, L. Howard, and David Vogel (1976). *Ethics and Profits: The Crisis of Confidence in American Business.* New York: Simon and Schuster.

Stone, Christopher (1975). *Where the Law Ends: The Social Control of Corporate Behavior.* New York: Harper & Row.

Sutherland, Edwin H. (1949). *White Collar Crime.* New York: Holt.

Tiedemann, Klaus (1974). *Subventions: Kriminalität in der Bundesrepublik.* Reinbek bei Hamburg: Rowohlt.

Woodmansee, John (1975). *The World of a Giant Corporation: A Report from the GE Project.* Seattle: North Country.

Wright, J. Patrick (1979). *On a Clear Day You Can See G.M.* Detroit: Wright Enterprises.

⊛ ⊛ ⊛

Questions

1. What are some examples of internal cultural factors? What are some examples of external economic factors? How are these factors related?

2. Explain the relationship between cultural norms of corporations and various ethical and legal actions that corporations and executives take.

3. How does a corporation ensure that its members learn the necessary values, norms, rationalizations, and techniques to ensure that employees make the corporation's well-being a priority?

4. How do executives justify their actions, especially unethical or illegal ones?

5. Of the various beliefs regarding the defensibility of corporate crime, which seems most valid to you? Which of these beliefs strike you as primarily myth?

6. Corporate criminal rationalizations would also apply to what other forms of deviant or criminal behavior?

7. After reading this article, what changes do you think would have to occur to reduce the incidence of corporate crime?